I0289113

Edward B. Cowell, Robert Chalmers

The Jataka

stories of the Buddha's former births - Vol. 2

Edward B. Cowell, Robert Chalmers

The Jataka
stories of the Buddha's former births - Vol. 2

ISBN/EAN: 9783337246907

Printed in Europe, USA, Canada, Australia, Japan

Cover: Foto ©Lupo / pixelio.de

More available books at **www.hansebooks.com**

THE JATAKA

OR

STORIES OF THE BUDDHA'S FORMER BIRTHS.

TRANSLATED FROM THE PĀLI BY VARIOUS HANDS

UNDER THE EDITORSHIP OF

PROFESSOR E. B. COWELL.

VOL. II.

TRANSLATED BY

W. H. D. ROUSE, M.A.,

SOMETIME FELLOW OF CHRIST'S COLLEGE, CAMBRIDGE.

CAMBRIDGE:
AT THE UNIVERSITY PRESS.
1895

Cambridge:

PRINTED BY J. AND C. F. CLAY,

AT THE UNIVERSITY PRESS.

PREFACE.

In a book like this, where a translation is made for the first time from a language little known, mistakes there needs must be. For any such I ask the indulgence of scholars; and assure them that no trouble has been spared to get accuracy. A word or phrase dismissed in a footnote as obscure or inexplicable has often cost hours of research before it has been given up.

Although it has not been possible to reproduce the rhythm of the verses, yet I hope something of the same effect has been given by keeping in each story to one metre where the Pāli has but one, and changing where it changes; and a pretty consistent rule has been observed, of giving long lines for long and short for short, two short lines being held equivalent to one long. But in different stories the same metre has often been differently translated for convenience.

For parallels I have looked through all the Pāli books as far as they are printed; but I have not had time to read them carefully, and many must have escaped me. The notes must then not be considered as exhaustive. Other illustrations have been noted where I have come across them, and I hope that students of folk-tales may be interested in one unpublished variant which I have been able to give (page 110).

It remains to acknowledge my indebtedness to those friends who have helped me. The members of our "Guild" who are resident at Cambridge have been so kind as to revise the proofs; and to them I owe very many corrections and improvements. Mr R. Chalmers lent me a MS. translation of a few of the 'Stories of the Past,' for which I thank him. But my chief thanks are due to my Master, Professor Cowell; who, for many years past, has with unfailing patience and kindliness helped me in my Oriental studies. I feel that what I know of these things has been his gift to me almost entirely; and I hope he may consider this book not all unworthy of his teaching.

By the kind permission of the Secretary of State for India, an illustration of one of the stories from the Bhārhut Stūpa is given in this volume as in the first. The story is No. 267: the words beneath the picture are *Nāga Jātaka.*

W. H. D. ROUSE.

CHRIST'S COLLEGE, CAMBRIDGE,
July 30, 1895.

MANIBVS

GVILLELMI ROBERTSON SMITH

SVMMO DESIDERIO

D. D. D.

CONTENTS.

PAGE

151. RĀJOVĀDA-JĀTAKA 1

Two kings, both wise and good, meet in a narrow way, and a dispute arises who is to give place. Both are of the same age and power. Their drivers sing each his master's praises. One is good to the good, and bad to the bad; the other repays evil with good. The first acknowledges his superior, and gives place.

152. SIGĀLA-JĀTAKA 4

The Bodhisatta is a young lion, one of seven brothers; a Jackal proposes love to his sister. Six of the brothers set out to kill the jackal, but seeing him as he lies in a crystal grotto, imagine him to be in the sky, leap up and kill themselves. The Bodhisatta roars, and the jackal dies of fear.

153. SŪKARA-JĀTAKA 7

A boar challenges a lion to fight; and then in fear wallows amid filth until he smells so foul that the lion will not come near him, but owns himself vanquished rather than fight with him.

154. URAGA-JĀTAKA 9

A Garuḷa chases a serpent, which taking the form of a jewel, fixes himself upon an ascetic's garment, and by this means wins safety.

155. GAGGA-JĀTAKA 11

How a goblin had power over all people who did not wish each other well at a sneeze, and how he was foiled.

156. ALĪNA-CITTA-JĀTAKA 13

An elephant runs a thorn into its foot; it is tended by some carpenters, and serves them out of gratitude. His young one takes his place afterwards, and is bought by the king for a large sum. How on the king's death, it routs a hostile host, and saves the kingdom for the king's infant son.

PAGE

157. GUṆA-JĀTAKA 17

A jackal rescues a lion, who out of gratitude makes him a friend. The lioness is jealous of the she-jackal; then the whole matter is explained, and maxims given in praise of friendship.

158. SUHANU-JĀTAKA 21

Two savage horses, that maltreat all other of their kind, strike up a sudden friendship with each other, thus illustrating the proverb, 'Birds of a feather.'

159. MORA-JĀTAKA 23

How a peacock kept itself safe by reciting spells; how its mind was disturbed by hearing the female's note, and it was caught; how the king desired to eat it, but the peacock discoursed such good divinity that he was stayed; and finally the bird was set free again to return to the mountains.

160. VINĪLAKA-JĀTAKA 26

A bird, the offspring of a goose with a crow, is being carried by his father's two other sons to see him, but is arrogant and compares them to horses that serve him; so he is sent back again.

161. INDASAMĀNAGOTTA-JĀTAKA 28

How a man kept a fat elephant, which turned against him and trampled him to death.

162. SANTHAVA-JĀTAKA 29

How a man had his house burnt by reason of the great offerings which he made to his sacred fire.

163. SUSĪMA-JĀTAKA 31

How a lad whose hereditary right it was to manage a festival, journeyed 2000 leagues in a day, learnt the ceremonial, and returned in time to conduct the ceremony.

164. GIJJHA-JĀTAKA 34

About a merchant who succoured some vultures, and they in return stole cloths and other things and brought to him; how one was caught, and the king learnt the story, and all the goods were restored.

165. NAKULA-JĀTAKA 36

How a mungoose and a snake were friends, and distrusted each other nevertheless; and how they were made at one.

166. UPASĀḶHA-JĀTAKA 37

How a certain man was particular in choice of burying-grounds, and how he was shown that there is no spot free of taint from some dead body.

PAGE

167. SAMIDDHI-JĀTAKA 39

How a nymph tempted the saint to love, and he resisted, since no man knows the time of death.

168. SAKUṆAGGHI-JĀTAKA 40

How a quail beat a falcon by fighting on his own ground.

169. ARAKA-JĀTAKA 42

How the Buddha forsook the world, and discoursed on charity.

170. KAKAṆṬAKA-JĀTAKA 43

(See *Mahā-ummagga*.)

171. KALYĀṆA-DHAMMA-JĀTAKA 44

How a certain man became a recluse all because of a lucky greeting.

172. DADDARA-JĀTAKA 45

How a jackal amongst lions betrayed himself by his tongue.

173. MAKKAṬA-JĀTAKA 47

How a monkey disguised himself as an ascetic, and was found out.

174. DŪBHIYA-MAKKAṬA-JĀTAKA 48

How the Bodhisatta drew water for a monkey, and all he got for his pains was a grimace and an insult.

175. ĀDICCUPAṬṬHĀNA-JĀTAKA 50

How a rascally monkey made havoc in the settlement, and the people took him for a holy being.

176. KALĀYA-MUṬṬHI-JĀTAKA 51

How a monkey threw away a handful of peas to find one.

177. TIṆḌUKA-JĀTAKA 53

How a troop of monkeys entered a village by night, and were surrounded by the villagers; and the device by which they were saved.

178. KACCHAPA-JĀTAKA 55

How a tortoise came to grief because he loved his home too much.

179. SATADHAMMA-JĀTAKA 57

How a proud young brahmin ate the leavings of a low-caste man, and then felt ashamed of himself.

180. DUDDADA-JĀTAKA . . 59

Where faith is, no gift is small.

PAGE

181. ASADISA-JĀTAKA 60
Of a clever archer, and his feats.

182. SAṀGĀMĀVACARA-JĀTAKA 63
How a noble elephant obeyed the word of command.

183. VĀLODAKA-JĀTAKA 65
He that is noble keeps a steady brain even though he drain most potent liquor dry.

184. GIRIDANTA-JĀTAKA . . . 67
Evil communications corrupt good manners.

185. ANABHIRATI-JĀTAKA 68
On serenity of mind.

186. DADHI-VĀHANA-JĀTAKA . . 69
The Magic Razor-axe, Milk-bowl, and Drum.

187. CATUMAṬṬA-JĀTAKA . . . 73
How a jackal was reproved for intruding.

188. SĪHAKOṬṬHUKA-JĀTAKA 75
How a mongrel cub among lions was betrayed by its voice.

189. SĪHACAMMA-JĀTAKA . 76
The ass in the lion's skin.

190. SĪLĀNISAṀSA-JĀTAKA 77
How a virtuous barber saved another man by his merit.

191. RUHAKA-JĀTAKA 79
How a wicked wife fooled her husband, and sent him prancing down the street in horse-trappings.

192. SIRI-KĀḶAKAṆṆI-JĀTAKA 80
(See *Mahā-ummagga.*)

193. CULLA-PADUMA-JĀTAKA 81
Of a wicked wife, who tried to murder her husband, and finally with her paramour was brought for trial before her husband, then become king.

194. MAṆICORA-JĀTAKA 85
Of the plot devised by a king to take the wife of another man; and how Sakka caused him to change bodies with his victim, and so to be executed himself.

195. PABBATŪPATTHARA-JĀTAKA 88
How the Bodhisatta advised a king to condone an intrigue.

196. VALĀHASSA-JĀTAKA 89
How some shipwrecked mariners escaped from a city of goblins by aid of a flying horse.

PAGE

197. MITTĀMITTA-JĀTAKA . 91

How to tell friend from foe.

198. RĀDHA-JĀTAKA 92

How a parrot told tales of his mistress, and had his neck wrung.

199. GAHAPATI-JĀTAKA 94

How a wife tried to trick her husband, and was found out.

200. SĀDHUSĪLA-JĀTAKA 96

How a father chose a husband for his daughters.

201. BANDHANĀGĀRA-JĀTAKA . 97

The real fetters are those of desire.

202. KEḶI-SĪLA-JĀTAKA . . . 98

How Sakka rebuked an irreverent king.

203. KHANDHA-VATTA-JĀTAKA . 100

How to win the goodwill of snakes.

204. VĪRAKA-JĀTAKA 103

How a crow tried to steal meat, and was plucked.

205. GAṄGEYYA-JĀTAKA 104

How two fish disputed which should be the more beautiful, and a tortoise answered that he was more beautiful than either.

206. KURUṄGA-MIGA-JĀTAKA 106

How a woodpecker and a tortoise rescued their friend the antelope from a trap.

207. ASSAKA-JĀTAKA 108

How a king was cured of love for his dead wife by a revelation of her present condition.

208. SUṀSUMĀRA-JĀTAKA 110

How a crocodile wanted the heart of a monkey, and how the monkey pretended that it was hanging on a fig-tree.

209. KAKKARA-JĀTAKA 112

How a fowler tried to stalk a bird by covering himself with branches.

210. KANDAGALAKA-JĀTAKA 113

How a woodpecker struck a tree too hard for it, and perished.

211. SOMADATTA-JĀTAKA 115

How a foolish man gave when he meant to crave.

PAGE

212. UCCHIṬṬHA-BHATTA-JĀTAKA 117

How a husband found out his wife's intrigue by the state of the rice.

213. BHARU-JĀTAKA 118

How the king of Bharu made two bands of hermits to quarrel.

214. PUṆṆA-NADĪ-JĀTAKA 121

How a king sent a riddling message to his former preceptor.

215. KACCHAPA-JĀTAKA 123

How a tortoise was conveyed through the air, biting with his teeth upon a stick; and how he answered to a taunt, and fell.

216. MACCHA-JĀTAKA 125

How a fish being captured lamented for loss of his wife, and was set at liberty.

217. SEGGU-JĀTAKA 126

How a pious greengrocer tested his daughter's virtue.

218. KŪṬA-VĀṆIJA-JĀTAKA 127

How a man deposited ploughshares with a friend, and the friend protested that they had been eaten by rats; and of the clever device by which the man's guilt was brought home to him.

219. GARAHITA-JĀTAKA 129

How a monkey had been a captive of men, and escaped, and his censure upon mankind.

220. DHAMMADDHAJA-JĀTAKA 131

How impossible tasks were set to a good man, who did them all by aid of Sakka.

221. KĀSĀVA-JĀTAKA 138

How a man disguised himself in holy robes, and killed elephants; and how he was put to shame.

222. CŪLA-NANDIYA-JĀTAKA 140

How two monkeys sacrificed their lives to save their mother, and what befel the hunter.

223. PUṬA-BHATTA-JĀTAKA . . 142

How a harsh husband was rebuked.

224. KUMBHĪLA-JĀTAKA 145

225. KHANTI-VAṆṆANA-JĀTAKA 145

How two sinners were made to amend their ways.

PAGE

226. KOSIYA-JĀTAKA 146

How an owl came to grief through sallying forth untimely.

227. GŪTHA-PĀṆA-JĀTAKA 147

How an intoxicated beetle challenged an elephant, and was ignominiously destroyed.

228. KĀMANĪTA-JĀTAKA . . 149

How a king was cured of greed.

229. PALĀYI-JĀTAKA 151

How a king was frightened away by the mere sight of a city gate.

230. DUTIYA-PALĀYI-JĀTAKA 153

How a hostile king was frightened away by the sight of the Bodhisatta, and the hearing of his threats.

231. UPĀHANA-JĀTAKA . . . 154

How a pupil tried to outdo his teacher, and was worsted.

232. VĪṆĀ-THŪṆA-JĀTAKA 156

How a girl thought a humpback was a right royal man, and how she was undeceived.

233. VIKAṆṆAKA-JĀTAKA 157

How some fish came to feed at the sound of a drum; and how a malevolent crocodile was speared.

234. ASITĀBHU-JĀTAKA 158

How a man, enamoured of a sprite, lost his wife by this lust.

235. VACCHA-NAKHA-JĀTAKA 160

How a Brother was tempted to return to the world, and the evil of a worldly life shown forth.

236. BAKA-JĀTAKA 161

How a crane shammed sleep, in order to catch fish; and how he was exposed.

237. SĀKETA-JĀTAKA 162

(As No. 68.)

238. EKAPADA-JĀTAKA 163

Of a precocious boy who asked a philosophical question; and the answer to the same.

239. HARITA-MĀTA-JĀTAKA 164

A water-snake that fell into a fish-trap, and how the fish all fell upon him; with a moral.

PAGE

240. MAHĀ-PIṄGALA-JĀTAKA 165

How the porter mourned when his tyrannical master died, lest he should prove too much for the King of Death, and should be sent back to earth again.

241. SABBA-DĀṬHA-JĀTAKA 168

How a jackal learnt the spell 'Of subduing the world,' and by it collected a great army of wild beasts; and how he was discomfited.

242. SUNAKHA-JĀTAKA 170

How a dog gnawed through his leash, and escaped from servitude.

243. GUTTILA-JĀTAKA 172

How a great musician played by aid of Sakka to the delight of all that heard.

244. VĪTICCHA-JĀTAKA 178

How a certain man tried to catch the Master with phrases.

245. MŪLA-PARIYĀYA-JĀTAKA 180

How the Master discomfited some would-be clever youths.

246. TELOVĀDA-JĀTAKA 182

That there is no harm in eating meat, but only in taking life.

247. PĀDAÑJALI-JĀTAKA 183

How a fool was found out.

248. KIṀSUKOPAMA-JĀTAKA 184

How four lads saw a tree, and each described it differently.

249. SĀLAKA-JĀTAKA 186

How soft words failed to bring down a monkey from a tree.

250. KAPI-JĀTAKA 187

How a monkey disguised himself as an ascetic, and was found out.

251. SAṀKAPPA-JĀTAKA 189

How an ascetic was tempted by lust, and how he was saved.

252. TILA-MUṬṬHI-JĀTAKA 193

How a teacher chastised a pupil, and the pupil meditated revenge, but was appeased.

253. MAṆI-KAṆṬHA-JĀTAKA 197

How a serpent and an ascetic were friends, and how the ascetic got rid of the serpent.

PAGE

254. KUṆḌAKA-KUCCHI-SINDHAVA-JĀTAKA 199

Of a high-bred foal; how he knew his own worth, and what he could do for a marvel.

255. SUKA-JĀTAKA 203

Of a parrot that used to bring food oversea for his parents, and how he ate too much, and was drowned.

256. JARUDAPĀNA-JĀTAKA 205

How some men won a treasure by digging, and by digging too much lost it again.

257. GĀMAṆI-CAṆḌA-JĀTAKA 207

How a prince's wisdom was tried. Also how a man was haled to the king's tribunal for injuries done unwittingly, and the judgements of the king thereupon; and of certain problems propounded to him by those he met. [Several stories in one.]

258. MANDHĀTU-JĀTAKA 216

How a king could not win contentment, not though he ruled as King of Heaven.

259. TIRĪṬA-VACCHA-JĀTAKA 218

How a king's life was saved, and the gratitude which he showed to his deliverer.

260. DŪTA-JĀTAKA . 221

How a man got a meal by calling himself 'Belly's Messenger.'

261. PADUMA-JĀTAKA 222

How some boys tried to wheedle a noseless gardener that he might give them a bunch of lotus.

262. MUDU-PĀṆI-JĀTAKA 224

Love will find a way; and the nature of womankind.

263. CULLA-PALOBHANA-JĀTAKA . . 227

How the Bodhisatta is tempted by a woman, and succumbs.

264. MAHĀ-PANĀDA-JĀTAKA . 229

(Incomplete: as No. 489.)

265. KHURAPPA-JĀTAKA . . . 231

How one brave man saved a caravan from robbers.

266. VĀTAGGA-SINDHAVA-JĀTAKA . . . 233

How a she-ass fell in love with a fine horse, and by coquetry lost him.

PAGE

267. KAKKAṬA-JĀTAKA 235

How an elephant, by aid of his faithful mate, destroyed an immense crab.

268. ĀRĀMA-DŪSA-JĀTAKA 237

How some monkeys were left to water a garden, and how they pulled up the trees to proportion the water to the length of the roots.

269. SUJĀTA-JĀTAKA 239

How the shrew was tamed by observation of a cuckoo and a jay.

270. ULŪKA-JĀTAKA 242

How the owl was proposed as king of the birds, but because of his sour looks, not taken.

271. UDAPĀNA-DŪSAKA-JĀTAKA 243

The vile nature of jackals.

272. VYAGGHA-JĀTAKA 244

How a sprite drove away from its wood a lion and tiger, and how men came and cut the trees down.

273. KACCHAPA-JĀTAKA 246

How a monkey insulted a tortoise, and how he was punished.

274. LOLA-JĀTAKA 248

How a crow lost his life through greed.

275. RUCIRA-JĀTAKA 250

(As No. 274.)

276. KURU-DHAMMA-JĀTAKA 251

How there was a drought, and by observance of virtue the rain was made to come.

277. ROMAKA-JĀTAKA 260

How a sham ascetic tried to kill a bird, and failed.

278. MAHISA-JĀTAKA 262

Of a wicked monkey, that was killed for his vileness; and of the patience of the Bodhisatta.

279. SATAPATTA-JĀTAKA 264

How a man did not know his friend from his enemy; and how the Bodhisatta was a robber.

280. PUṬA-DŪSAKA-JĀTAKA 266

Of a monkey who thought to please a gardener by destroying the pottles which he made.

PAGE

281. ABBHANTARA-JĀTAKA . . 267

How a queen longed for a 'middle mango'; and how a pet parrot procured one.

282. SEYYA-JĀTAKA 273

How a marauding monarch was conquered by kindness.

283. VAḌḌHAKI-SŪKARA-JĀTAKA 275

How a boar drilled an army of boars to conquer a tiger; and how a sham ascetic was done to death.

284. SIRI-JĀTAKA 279

How luck came of eating the flesh of certain birds.

285. MAṆI-SŪKARA-JĀTAKA 283

How some boars tried to sully crystal by rubbing it, and only made it shine the more.

286. SĀLŪKA-JĀTAKA . . . 285

How an ox envied the fatted pig.

287. LĀBHA-GARAHA-JĀTAKA 287

Of the evil of a worldly life.

288. MACCH-UDDĀNA-JĀTAKA 288

How a parcel of money was lost in the river, and restored by the river-spirit in the belly of a fish.

289. NĀNA-CCHANDA-JĀTAKA 290

How a king fell into the hands of thieves, and a brahmin saw it; and what were the boons he asked.

290. SĪLA-VĪMAṀSA-JĀTAKA 292

How a man tried his own reputation for virtue.

291. BHADRA-GHAṬA-JĀTAKA . . 293

The Wishing-Bowl, with a moral ending.

292. SUPATTA-JĀTAKA 295

How a queen of the crows desired some meat, and a brave crow got it for her.

293. KĀYA-VICCHINDA-JĀTAKA 297

Of a sick man who on his recovery became religious, to his own great advantage.

294. JAMBU-KHĀDAKA-JĀTAKA . 299

The Fox and the Crow, with a difference.

PAGE

295. ANTA-JĀTAKA . . 300

Similar to the last, but *vice versa*.

296. SAMUDDA-JĀTAKA 301

Of a crow that feared the sea might be drunk dry.

297. KĀMA-VILĀPA-JĀTAKA . . 302

How desire is stronger than pain.

298. UDUMBARA-JĀTAKA . . 303

Old birds cannot be caught with chaff.

299. KOMĀYA-PUTTA-JĀTAKA . . . 305

Upon the reformation of a mischievous monkey.

300. VAKA-JĀTAKA . . . 306

How a wolf kept a holy day service.

ADDITIONS AND CORRECTIONS.

Page 10, *note*. The Garuḷa is often represented as a Winged Man in art. See Fergusson, *Tree and Serpent Worship*, pl. xxvi. 1, xxviii. 1, &c. Examples are numerous; e.g. British Museum, 2nd N. Gallery, 'Brahmanism,' side case, sect. 5 (little bronzes); a large steatite image, *ibid.*; Berlin, Mus. f. Völkerkunde, Indian Section, Case 45, I. c. 448, praying Garuḷa from Siam, with wings and bird feet. Often the Garuḷa is a bird of peculiar shape. One or two of each are figured in Grünwedel, *Buddhistische Kunst in Indien*, pp. 47—50.

„ 53. With this story compare *Tibetan Tales*, p. 348.

„ 60, *note*, *before* 'on the Sanchi Tope' *insert* 'possibly.' (The archer is not shooting at the mango tree; and other things are present not referred to in the story. I took this reference at second hand, before I was able to see the plate myself.)

„ 80, *note*, 216, *note*, *read:* Tibetan.

„ 92, *No.* 198, *insert title:* Rādha-jātaka.

„ 129, *note* 1, *read:* Tunisische.

„ 158, *title*, *read:* Asitābhu *for* -ū-.

„ 207, *note*, *add:* Compare *Tibetan Tales*, p. 29, *Ādarśamukha*, and pref. p. xli.

„ 220, *line* 6 *infra*, *for* Perfections *read* Faculties.

„ 235, *title*, *read:* Kakkaṭa- *for* -ā-.

No. 151[1].

RĀJOVĀDA-JĀTAKA.

[1] "*Rough to the rough,*" *etc.*—This story the Master told whilst he was living in Jetavana, to explain how a king was taught a lesson.

This will be set forth in the Tesakuṇa Birth[2].

It is said that one day the king of Kosala had just passed sentence in a very difficult case involving moral wrong[3]. After his meal, with hands not yet dry, he proceeded in his splendid chariot to visit the Master; and the king saluted him, his feet beautiful like the open lotus flower, and sat down aside.

Then the Master addressed him in these words. "Why, my lord king, what brings you here at this time of day?" "Sir," said he, "I missed my time because I was sitting on a difficult case, involving moral wrong; now I have finished it, and eaten, and here I am, with my hands hardly dry, to wait upon you." "My lord king," replied the Master, "to judge a cause with justice and impartiality is the right thing; that is the way to heaven. Now when you first have the advice of a being all-wise like me, it is no wonder if you should judge your case fairly and justly; but the wonder is when kings have only had the advice of scholars who are not all-wise, and yet have decided fairly and justly, avoiding the Four Ways of Wickedness, and observing the Ten Royal Virtues, and after ruling justly have gone to swell the hosts of heaven." Then, at the king's request, he told a story of the olden time.

---

[2] Once upon a time, when Brahmadatta was king of Benares, the Bodhisatta was conceived by his Queen Consort; and the ceremonies proper to her state having been duly done[4], she was afterwards safely

[1] Fausbøll, *Ten J.*, pp. 1 and 57; Rhys Davids, *Buddhist Birth Stories*, p. xxii. A similar contest of two minstrels occurs in the *Kalevala* (Crawford's translation, i. p. 30). The young drives fiercely into the old, who says—'Thou shouldst give me all the highway, for I am the older.' 'What matters that?' says the other; 'let the least wise give place.' There they stand and each sings his legends by way of deciding the matter.

[2] No. 521.

[3] Reading, with Childers (*Dict.* p. 613), *agatigataṁ*.

[4] Lit. "protection to the embryo;" doubtless some magical rite.

delivered. On his name-day, the name they gave him was Prince Brahmadatta.

In course of time, he grew up, and at sixteen years went to Takkasilā[1] for his education; where he mastered all branches of learning, and on his father's death he became king in his stead, and ruled with uprightness and all rectitude, administering justice with no regard had to his own will or whim. And as he ruled thus justly, his ministers on their part were also just; thus, while all things were justly done, there was none who brought a false suit into court. Presently all the bustle of suitors ceased within the precincts of the palace; all day long the ministers might sit on the bench, and go away without seeing a single suitor. The courts were deserted.

Then the Bodhisatta thought to himself, "Because of my just government not one suitor comes to try issue in court; the old hubbub is quiet; the courts of law are deserted. Now I must search whether I have any fault in me; which if I find, I will eschew it, and live a good life hereafter." From that time he tried continually to find some one who would tell him of a fault; but of all who were about him at court he could not find one such; nothing could he hear but good of himself. "Perhaps," thought he, "they are all so much afraid of me that they say no ill of me but only good," and so he went about to try those who were outside his walls. But with these it was just the same. Then he made inquisition of the citizens at large, and outside the city questioned those who belonged to the suburbs at the four city gates. Still there was none who had any fault to find; nothing but praises could he hear. Lastly, with intent to try the country side, he entrusted all government to his ministers, and mounted in his carriage, and taking only the driver with him, left the city in disguise. All the country he traversed, even to the frontier; [3] but not a faultfinder could he light upon; all he could hear was only his own praises. So back he turned from the marches, and set his face homewards again by the highroad.

Now it fortuned that at this very time Mallika, the king of Kosala, had done the very same thing. He too was a just king, and he had been searching for his faults; but amongst those about him there was none who had any fault to find; and hearing nothing but praise, he had been making enquiry throughout all the country, and had but then arrived at that same spot.

These two met, in a place where the carriage-road was deeply sunk between two banks, and there was no room for one carriage to pass another.

[1] The great University town of India; it was in the Punjab (Τάξιλα).

"Get your carriage out of the way!" said king Mallika's driver to the driver of the king of Benares.

"No, no, driver," said he, "out of the way with yours! Know that in this carriage sits the great monarch Brahmadatta, lord of the kingdom of Benares!"

"Not so, driver!" replied the other, "in this carriage sits the great king Mallika, lord of the realm of Kosala! It is for you to make way, and to give place to the carriage of our king!"

"Why, here's a king too," thought the driver of the king of Benares. "What in the world is to be done?" Then a thought struck him; he would enquire what should be the age of the two kings, so that the younger should give way to the elder. And he made enquiry of the other driver how old his king was; but he learnt that both were of the same age. Thereupon he asked the extent of this king's power, wealth, and glory, and all points touching his caste and clan and his family; discovering that both of them had a country three hundred leagues long, and that they were alike in power, wealth, glory, and the nature of their family and lineage. Then he bethought him that place might be given to the better man; so he requested that the other driver should describe his master's virtues. The man replied by the first verse of poetry following, in which he set forth his monarch's faults as though they were so many virtues:—

"Rough to the rough, king Mallika the mild with mildness sways,
Masters the good by goodness, and the bad with badness pays.
Give place, give place, O driver! such are this monarch's ways!"

[4] "Oh," said the man of the king of Benares, "is that all you have to say about your king's virtues?" "Yes," said the other.—"If these are his virtues, what must his vices be!" "Vices be it, then," quoth he, "if you will; but let us hear what your king's virtues may be like!" "Listen then," rejoined the first, and repeated the second verse:—

"He conquers wrath by mildness, the bad with goodness sways,
By gifts the miser vanquishes and lies with truth repays.
Give place, give place, O driver! such are this monarch's ways[1]!"

At these words both king Mallika and his driver descended from their carriage, and loosed the horses, and moved it out of the way, to give place to the king of Benares. Then the king of Benares gave good admonition to king Mallika, saying, "Thus and thus [5] must you do;" after which he returned to Benares, and there gave alms and did good all his life, till at the last he went to swell the hosts of heaven. And king Mallika took the lesson to heart; and after traversing the length and breadth of the

[1] *Dhammapada*, verse 223.

land, and lighting upon none who had any fault to find, returned to his own city; where he gave alms all his life and did good, till at the end he too went to swell the hosts of heaven.

When the Master had ended this discourse, which he began for the purpose of giving a lesson to the king of Kosala, he identified the Birth: "Moggallāna was then the driver of king Mallika, Ānanda was the king, Sāriputta was the driver of the king of Benares, but I myself was the king."

No. 152.

SIGĀLA-JĀTAKA.

"*Who rashly undertakes,*" *etc.*—This story the Master told while staying in his gabled chamber, about a barber who lived at Vesāli.

This man, as we are told, used to do shaving and hairdressing and cross-plaiting for the royal household, kings and queens, princes and princesses, indeed he did all of that kind that had to be done. He was a true believer, sheltered in the Three Refuges[1], resolved to keep the Five Precepts; and from time to time he would listen to the Master's discoursing.

One day he set out to do his work in the palace, taking his son with him. The young fellow, seeing a Licchavi girl drest up fine and grand, like a nymph, fell in love for desire of her. He said to his father, as they left the palace in company, "There is a girl—if I get her, I shall live; but if I don't, there's nothing but death for me." He would not touch a morsel of food, but lay down hugging the bedstead. His father found him and said, "Why, son, don't set your mind on forbidden fruit. You are a nobody—a barber's son; this Licchavi girl is a highborn lady. You're no match for her. I'll find you somebody else; a girl of your own place and station." But the lad would not listen to him. Then came mother, brother, and sister, aunt and uncle, all his kinsfolk, and all his friends and companions, trying to pacify him; but pacify him they could not. So he pined and pined away, and lay there until he died.

Then the father performed his obsequies, and did what is usual to do for the spirits of the dead. [6] By and by, when the first edge of grief had worn off, he thought he would wait upon the Master. Taking a large present of flowers, scents, and perfumes, he repaired to Mahāvana, and did reverence to the Master, saluted him, and sat down on one side. "Why have you kept out of sight all this time, layman?" the Master asked. Then the man told him what had happened. Said the Master, "Ah, layman, 'tis not the first time he has perished by setting his heart on what he must not have; this is only what he has done before." Then at the layman's request, he told a story of the olden time.

---

[1] Buddha, the Law, and the Order of Brethren.

Once upon a time, while Brahmadatta was king of Benares, the Bodhisatta came into the world as a young Lion in the region of Himalaya. Of the same family there were some younger brothers, and one sister; and all of them lived in a Golden Cave.

Now hard by this cave was a Cave of Crystal on a silver hill, where a Jackal lived. By and by the Lions lost their parents by the stroke of death. Then they used to leave the Lioness, their sister, behind in the cave, while they ranged for food; which when they obtained, they would bring it back for her to eat.

Now the Jackal had caught sight of this Lioness, and fell in love with her; but while the old Lion and Lioness lived, he could win no access. Now, when the seven brothers went to seek food, out he came from his Crystal Cave, and made all haste to the Golden Cave; where, taking his stand before the young Lioness, he addressed her slily with these seductive and tempting words:

"O Lioness, I am a fourfoot creature, and so are you. Therefore do you be my mate, and I will be your husband! We will live together in friendship and amity, and you shall love me always!"

Now on hearing this the Lioness thought to herself, "This Jackal here is mean amongst beasts, vile, and like a man of low caste: but I am esteemed to be one of royal issue. That he to me should so speak is unseemly and evil. How can I live after hearing such things said? I will hold my breath until I shall die."—Then, bethinking her awhile, "Nay," quoth she, "to die so would not be comely. My brothers will soon be home again; I will [7] tell them first, and then I will put an end to myself."

The Jackal, finding that no answer came, felt sure she cared nothing for him; so back he went to his Crystal Cave, and lay down in much misery.

Now one of the young Lions, having killed a buffalo, or an elephant, or what not, himself ate some of it, and brought back a share for his sister, which he gave her, inviting her to eat. "No, brother," says she, "not a bite will I eat; for I must die!" "Why must that be?" he asked. And she told him what had happened. "Where is this Jackal now?" he asked. She saw him lying in the Crystal Cave, and thinking he was up in the sky[1], she said, "Why, brother, cannot you see him there on Silver Mountain, lying up in the sky?" The young Lion, unaware that the Jackal lay in a Crystal Cave, and deeming that he was truly in the sky, made a spring, as lions do, to kill him, and struck against the crystal: which burst his heart asunder, and falling to the foot of the mountain, he perished straightway.

[1] *i.e.* because of the transparency.

Then came in another, to whom the Lioness told the same tale. This Lion did even as the first, and fell dead by the mountain foot.

When six of the brother Lions had perished in this way, last of all entered the Bodhisatta. When she had told her story, he enquired where was the Jackal now? "There he is," said she, "up in the sky, above Silver Mountain!" The Bodhisatta thought—"Jackals lying in the sky? nonsense. I know what it is: he is lying in a Crystal Cave." So he repaired to the mountain's foot, and there he saw his six brothers lying dead. "I see how it is," thought he; "these were all foolish, and lacked the fulness of wisdom; not knowing that this is the Crystal Cave, they beat their hearts out against it, and were killed. This is what comes of acting in rashness without due reflection;" and he repeated the first stanza:—

"Who rashly undertakes an enterprise,
Not counting all the issue may arise,
Like one who burns his mouth in eating food
Falls victim to the plans he did devise."

[8] After repeating these lines, the Lion continued: "My brothers wanted to kill this Jackal, but knew not how to lay their plans cleverly; so they leapt up too quickly at him, and so came by their death. This I will not do; but I will make the Jackal burst his own heart as he lies there in the Crystal Cave." So he espied out the path whereby the Jackal used to go up and down, and turning that way he roared thrice the lions' roar, that earth and heaven together were all one great roaring! The Jackal lying in the Crystal Cave was frightened and astounded, so that his heart burst; and he perished on the spot incontinently.

The Master continued, "Thus did this Jackal perish on hearing the Lion roar." And becoming perfectly enlightened, he repeated the second stanza:—

On Daddara the Lion gave a roar,
And made Mount Daddara resound again.
Hard by a Jackal lived; he feared full sore
To hear the sound, and burst his heart in twain.

---

[9] Thus did our Lion do this Jackal to death. Then he laid his brothers together in one grave, and told the sister they were dead, and comforted her; and he lived the rest of his days in the Golden Cave, until he passed away to the place which his merits had earned for him.

When the Master had ended this discourse, he revealed the Truths, and identified the Birth:—at the conclusion of the Truths, the layman was established in the Fruit of the First Path:—"The barber's son of to-day was then the Jackal; the Licchavi girl was the young Lioness; the six younger Lions are now six Elders; and I myself am the eldest Lion."

No. 153.

SŪKARA-JĀTAKA[1].

"*You are a fourfoot,*" *etc.*—This is a story told by the Master while at Jetavana, about a certain Elder well stricken in years.

Once, we are told, there happened to be a night service, and the Master had preached standing upon a slab of the jewelled staircase at the door of his scented cell. After delivering the discourse of the Blessed, he retired into his scented chamber; and the Captain of the Faith, saluting his Master, went back to his own cell again. Mahāmoggallāna too retired to his cell, and after a moment's rest returned to ask the Elder Sāriputta a question. As he asked and asked each question, the Captain of the Faith made it all clear, as though he were making the moon rise in the sky. There were present the four classes of disciples[2], who sat and heard it all. Then a thought came into the mind of one aged Elder. "Suppose," he thought, "I can puzzle Sāriputta before all this crowd, by asking him some question? They will all think, What a clever fellow! and I shall gain great credit and repute." So he rose up in the crowd, and stepping near to the Elder, stood on one side, and said, "Friend Sāriputta, I too have a question for you; will you let me speak? Give me a decision in discrimination or in undiscrimination, in refutation or in acceptation, in distinction or in counter-distinction[3]." The Elder looked at him. "This old man," thought he, "stands within the sphere of desire still; he is empty, and knows nothing." He said not a single word to him for very shame; laying his fan down, he rose from his seat, [10] and returned to his cell. And Elder Moggallāna likewise returned to his cell. The bystanders jumped up, crying, "Seize this wicked old fellow, who wouldn't let us hear the sweet words of the sermon!" and they mobbed him. Off he ran, and fell through a hole in the corner of a cesspool just outside the monastery; when he got up he was all over filth. When the people saw him, they felt sorry for it, and went away to the Master. He asked, "Why have you come at this unseasonable hour, laymen?" They told him what had happened. "Laymen," said he, "this is not the only time this old man has been puffed up, and not knowing his own power, pitted himself against the strong, only to be covered all over with filth. Long, long ago he knew not his powers, pitted himself against the strong, and was covered with filth as he is covered now." Then, at their request, he told them a story of the olden time.

---

[1] Fausbøll, *Ten Jātakas*, pp. 12, 63, 94 (he compares Nos. 278 and 484); R. Morris in *Contemp. Rev.* 1881, vol. 39, p. 737.

[2] Monks, nuns, laymen and lay sisters.

[3] These words appear to be nonsense.

Once upon a time, when Brahmadatta was king of Benares, the Bodhisatta was a Lion who dwelt in a mountain cave in the Himalayas. Hard by were a multitude of Boars, living by a lakeside; and beside the same lake lived a company of anchorites in huts made of leaves and the branches of trees.

One day it so happened that the Lion had brought down a buffalo or elephant or some such game; and, after eating what he listed, he went down to drink at this lake. Just as he came out, a sturdy Boar happened to be feeding by the side of the water. "He'll make a meal for me some other day," thought the Lion. But fearing that if the Boar saw him, he might never come there again, the Lion as he came up out of the water slunk away to the side. This the Boar saw; and at once the thought came into his mind,—"This is because he has seen me, and is afraid! He dare not come nigh me, and off he runs for fear! This day shall see a fight between me and a lion!" So he raised his head, and made challenge against the Lion in the first stanza:

"You are a fourfoot—so am I: thus, friend, we're both alike, you see;
Turn, Lion, turn; are you afraid? Why do you run away from me?"

[11] The Lion gave ear. "Friend Boar," he said, "to-day there will be no fight between you and me. But this day week let us fight it out in this very spot." And with these words, he departed.

The Boar was highly delighted in thinking how he was to fight a lion; and he told all his kith and kin about it. But the tale only terrified them. "You will be the bane of us all," they said, "and yourself to boot. You know not what you can do, or you would not be so eager to do battle with a lion. When the Lion comes, he'll be the death of you and all of us as well; do not be so violent!" These words made the Boar fear on his part. "What am I to do, then?" he asked. Then the other Boars advised him to roll about in the anchorites' dunghill for the next seven days, and let the muck dry on his body; then on the seventh day he should moisten himself with dewdrops, and be first at the trysting place; he must find how the wind should lie, and get to the windward; and the Lion, being a cleanly creature, would spare his life when he had a whiff of him.

So accordingly he did; and on the day appointed, there he was. No sooner had the Lion scented him, and smelt the filth, says he, "Friend Boar, a pretty trick this! Were you not all besmeared with filth, I should have had your life this very day. But as it is, bite you I cannot, nor so much as touch you with my foot. Therefore I spare your life." And then he repeated the second stanza:

"O dirty Boar, your hide is foul, the stench is horrible to me;
If you would fight I yield me quite, and own you have the victory."

Then the Lion turned away, and procured his day's food; and anon, after a drink at the lake, he went back again to his cave on the mountain. And the Boar told his kindred how he had beaten the Lion! [12] But they were terrified for fear the Lion should come again another day and be the death of them all. So they ran away and betook them to some other place.

When the Master had ended this discourse, he identified the Birth: "The Boar of those days is now the ancient Elder, and I myself was the Lion."

No. 154.

URAGA-JĀTAKA.

"*Concealed within a stone*," *etc.*—This story the Master told at Jetavana, about a soldiers' quarrel.

Tradition tells how two soldiers, in the service of the king of Kosala, of high rank, and great persons at court, no sooner caught sight of one another than they used to fall at ill words. Neither king, nor friends, nor kinsfolk could make them agree.

It happened one day that early in the morning the Master, looking around to see which of his friends were ripe for Release, perceived that these two were ready to enter upon the First Path. Next day he went all alone seeking alms in Sāvatthi, and stopt before the door of one of them, who came out and took the Master's bowl; then led him within, and offered him a seat. The Master sat, and then enlarged on the profit of cultivating Lovingkindness. When he saw the man's mind was ready, he declared the Truths. This done, the other was established in the Fruit of the First Path. Seeing this, the Master persuaded him to take the Bowl; then rising he proceeded to the house of the other. Out came the other, and after salutation given, begged the Master to enter, and gave him a seat. He also took the Master's bowl, and entered along with him. To him the Master lauded the Eleven Blessings of Lovingkindness; and perceiving that his heart was ready, declared the Truths. And this done, he too became established in the Fruit of the First Path.

Thus they were both converted; they confessed their faults one to the other, and asked forgiveness; peaceful and harmonious, they were at one together. That very same day they ate together in the presence of the Blessed One.

His meal over, the Master returned to the monastery. They both returned with him, bearing a rich present of flowers, scents and perfumes, of ghee, honey, and sugar. The Master, having preached of duty [13] before the Brotherhood, and uttered a Buddha's admonition, retired to his scented chamber.

Next morning, the Brethren talked the matter over in the Hall of Truth. "Friend," one would say to another, "our Master subdues the unsubdued.

Why, here are these two grand persons, who have been quarrelling all this time, and could not be reconciled by the king himself, or friends and kinsfolk: and the Master has humbled them in a single day!" The Master came in. "What are you talking about," asked he, "as you sit here together?" They told him. Said he, "Brethren, this is not the first time that I have reconciled these two; in bygone ages I reconciled the same two persons." And he told a story of the olden time.

Once on a time, while Brahmadatta was king of Benares, a great multitude gathered together in Benares to keep festival. Crowds of men and of gods, of serpents, and garuḷas[1], came together to see the meeting.

It so happened that in one spot a Serpent and a Garuḷa were watching the goings-on together. The Serpent, not noticing that this was a Garula beside him, laid a hand on his shoulder. And when the Garuḷa turned and looked round to see whose hand had been laid upon his shoulder, he saw the Serpent. The Serpent looked too, and saw that this was a Garuḷa; and frightened to death, he flew off over the surface of a river. The Garuḷa gave chase, to catch him.

Now the Bodhisatta was a recluse, and lived in a leaf-hut on the river bank. At that time he was trying to keep off the sun's heat by putting on a wet cloth and doffing his garment of bark; and he was bathing in the river. "I will make this recluse," thought the Serpent, "the means of saving my life." Putting off his own proper shape, and assuming the form of a fine jewel, he fixed himself upon the bark garment. The Garuḷa in full pursuit saw where he had gone; but for very reverence he would not touch the garment; so he thus addressed the Bodhisatta:

"Sir, I am hungry. Look at your bark garment:—in it there is a serpent which I desire to eat." And to make the matter clear, he repeated the first stanza:

[14] "Concealed within a stone this wretched snake
Has taken harbourage for safety's sake.
And yet, in reverence of your holiness,
Though I am hungry, yet I will not take."

Standing where he was in the water, the Bodhisatta said the second stanza in praise of the Garuḷa king:

"Live long, preserved by Brahma, though pursued,
And may you never lack for heavenly food.
Do not, in reverence of my holiness,
Do not devour him, though in hungry mood."

In these words the Bodhisatta expressed his approval, standing there in the water. Then he came out, and put on his bark garment, and took

[1] A mythical bird, which we see is able to assume human form. Morris (*J. P. T. S.*, 1893, p. 26) concludes that the *supaṇṇa*, here translated *Garuḷa*, was a "winged man."

both creatures with him to his hermitage; where he rehearsed the blessings of Lovingkindness until they were both at one. Thenceforward they lived together happily in peace and harmony.

When the Master had ended this discourse, he identified the Birth, saying, "In those days, the two great personages were the Serpent and the Garuḷa, and I myself was the recluse."

No. 155.

GAGGA-JĀTAKA[1].

[15] "*Gagga, live an hundred years,*" *etc.*—This story the Master told when he was staying in the monastery made by King Pasenadi in front of Jetavana; it was about a sneeze which he gave.

One day, we are told, as the Master sat discoursing with four persons round him, he sneezed. "Long life to the Blessed One, long life to the Buddha!" the Brothers all cried aloud, and made a great to-do.

The noise interrupted the discourse. Then the Master said to the Brethren: "Why, Brothers, if one cry 'Long life!' on hearing a sneeze, does a man live or die any the more for that?" They answered, "No, no, Sir." He went on, "You should not cry 'Long life' for a sneeze, Brethren. Whosoever does so is guilty of sin."

It is said that at that time, when the Brethren sneezed, people used to call out, "Long life to you, Sir!" But the Brethren had their scruples, and made no answer. Everybody was annoyed, and asked, "Pray, why is it that the priests about Buddha the Sakya prince make no answer, when they sneeze, and somebody or other wishes them long life?"

All this was told to the Blessed One. He said: "Brethren, common folk are superstitious. When you sneeze, and they say, 'Long life to you, Sir!' I permit you to answer, 'The same to you'." Then the Brethren asked him—"Sir, when did people begin to answer 'Long life' by 'The same to you'?" Said the Master, "That was long, long ago;" and he told them a tale of the olden time.

Once upon a time, when Brahmadatta was king of Benares, the Bodhisatta came into the world as a brahmin's son of the kingdom of Kāsi; and his father was a lawyer by calling. When the lad was sixteen years old or so, his father gave a fine jewel into his charge, and they both

[1] The introductory story is repeated in the Cullavagga, v. 33 (iii. 153 of Rhys Davids' translation of Vinaya Texts in the *S. B. E.*).

travelled through town after town, village after village, until they came to Benares. There the man had a meal cooked in the gatekeeper's house; and as he could find nowhere to put up, he asked where there was lodging to be had for wayfarers who came too late? The people told him that there was a building outside the city, but that it was haunted; but however he might lodge there if he liked. Says the lad to his father, "Have no fear of any goblin, father! I will subdue him, and bring him to your feet." [16] So he persuaded his father, and they went to the place together. The father lay down upon a bench, and his son sat beside him, chafing his feet.

Now the Goblin that haunted the place had received it for twelve years' service of Vessavana[1], on these terms: that if any man who entered it should sneeze, and when long life was wished him, should answer, "Long life to you!" or "The same to you!"—all except these the Goblin had a right to eat. The Goblin lived upon the central rafter of the hut[2].

He determined to make the father of the Bodhisatta sneeze. Accordingly, by his magic power he raised a cloud of fine dust, which entered the man's nostrils; and as he lay on the bench, he sneezed. The son did not cry "Long life!" and down came the Goblin from his perch, ready to devour his victim. But the Bodhisatta saw him descend, and then these thoughts passed through his mind. "Doubtless it is he who made my father sneeze. This must be a Goblin that eats all who do not say 'Long life to you'." And addressing his father, he repeated the first verse as follows:

"Gagga, live an hundred years,—aye, and twenty more, I pray!
May no goblin eat you up; live an hundred years, I say!"

The Goblin thought, "This one I cannot eat, because he said 'Long life to you.' But I shall eat his father;" and he came close to the father. But the man divined the truth of the matter—"This must be a Goblin," thought he, "who eats all who do not reply, 'Long life to you, too!'" and so addressing his son, he repeated the second verse:

"You too live an hundred years,—aye, and twenty more, I pray;
Poison be the goblins' food; live an hundred years, I say!"

[17] The Goblin hearing these words, turned away, thinking "Neither of these is for me to eat." But the Bodhisatta put a question to him: "Come, Goblin, how is it you eat the people who enter this building?"

"I earned the right for twelve years' service of Vessavana."

"What, are you allowed to eat everybody?"

[1] A monster with white skin, three legs, and eight teeth, guardian of jewels and the precious metals, and a kind of Indian Pluto.

[2] See Eggeling, Çatap.-Brāhm. vol. 2, p. 3, *S. B. E.*, for the construction of the hut.

"All except those who say 'The same to you' when another wishes them long life."

"Goblin," said the lad, "you have done some wickedness in former lives, which has caused you to be born now fierce, and cruel, and a bane to others. If you do the same kind of thing now, you will pass from darkness to darkness. Therefore from this time forth abstain from such things as taking life." With these words he humbled the Goblin, scared him with fear of hell, established him in the Five Precepts, and made him as obedient as an errand-boy.

Next day, when the people came and saw the Goblin, and learnt how that the Bodhisatta had subdued him, they went and told the king: "My lord, some man has subdued the Goblin, and made him as obedient as an errand-boy!" So the king sent for him, and raised him to be Commander-in-Chief; while he heaped honours upon the father. Having made the Goblin a tax-gatherer, and established him in the Bodhisatta's precepts, after giving alms and doing good he departed to swell the hosts of heaven.

When the Master had ended this story, which he told to explain when the custom first arose of answering 'Long life' by 'The same to you,' he identified the Birth: "In those days, Ānanda was the king, Kassapa the father, and I myself was the lad his son."

No. 156.

ALĪNACITTA-JĀTAKA.

"*Prince Winheart once upon a time,*" *etc.*—This story the Master told at Jetavana, about a fainthearted Brother. The circumstances will be set forth in the Saṁvara Birth in the eleventh Book[1]. When the Master asked this Brother if he really were fainthearted, as was said, he replied, [18] "Yes, Blessed One." To which the Master said, "What, Brother! in former days did you not gain supremacy over the kingdom of Benares, twelve leagues either way, and give it to a baby boy, like a lump of flesh and nothing more, and all this just by perseverance! And now that you have embraced this great salvation, are you to lose heart and faint?" And he told a story of olden days.

---

[1] No. 462.

Once upon a time, when Brahmadatta was king of Benares, there was a village of carpenters not far from the city, in which five hundred carpenters lived. They would go up the river in a vessel, and enter the forest, where they would shape beams and planks for housebuilding, and put together the framework of one-storey or two-storey houses, numbering all the pieces from the mainpost onwards; these then they brought down to the river bank, and put them all aboard; then rowing down stream again, they would build houses to order as it was required of them; after which, when they received their wage, they went back again for more materials for the building, and in this way they made their livelihood.

Once it befel that in a place where they were at work in shaping timbers, a certain Elephant trod upon a splinter of acacia wood, which pierced his foot, and caused it to swell up and fester, and he was in great pain. In his agony, he caught the sound of these carpenters cutting wood. "There are some carpenters will cure me," thought he; and limping on three feet, he presented himself before them, and lay down close by. The carpenters, noticing his swollen foot, went up and looked; there was the splinter sticking in it. With a sharp tool they made incision about the splinter, and tying a string to it, pulled it right out. Then they lanced the gathering, and washed it with warm water, and doctored it properly; and in a very short time the wound was healed.

Grateful for this cure, the Elephant thought: "My life has been saved by the help of these carpenters; now I must make myself useful to them." So ever after that, [19] he used to pull up trees for them, or when they were chopping he would roll up the logs; or bring them their adzes and any tools they might want, holding everything in his trunk like grim death. And the carpenters, when it was time to feed him, used to bring him each a portion of food, so that he had five hundred portions in all.

Now this Elephant had a young one, white all over, a magnificent high-bred creature. The Elephant reflected that he was now old, and he had better bring his young one to serve the carpenters, and himself be left free to go. So without a word to the carpenters he went off into the wood, and brought his son to them, saying, "This young Elephant is a son of mine. You saved my life, and I give him to you as a fee for your leechcraft; from henceforward he shall work for you." So he explained to the young Elephant that it was his duty to do the work which he had been used to do himself, and then went away into the forest, leaving him with the carpenters. So after that time the young Elephant did all their work, faithfully and obediently; and they fed him, as they had fed the other, with five hundred portions for a meal.

His work once done, the Elephant would go play about in the

river, and then return again. The carpenters' children used to pull him by the trunk, and play all sorts of pranks with him in water and out. Now noble creatures, be they elephants, horses, or men, never dung or stale in the water[1]. So this Elephant did nothing of the kind when he was in the water, but waited until he came out upon the bank.

One day, rain had fallen up river; and by the flood a half-dry cake of his dung was carried into the river. This floated down to the Benares landing place, where it stuck fast in a bush. Just then the king's elephant keepers had brought down five hundred elephants to give them a bath. But the creatures scented this soil of a noble animal, and not one would enter the water; up went their tails, and off they all ran. The keepers told this to the elephant trainers; who replied, "There must be something in the water, then." So orders were given to cleanse the water; [20] and there in the bushes this lump was seen. "That's what the matter is!" cried the men. So they brought a jar, and filled it with water; next powdering the stuff into it, they sprinkled the water over the elephants, whose bodies then became sweet. At once they went down into the river and bathed.

When the trainers made their report to the king, they advised him to secure the Elephant for his own use and profit.

The king accordingly embarked upon a raft, and rowed up stream until he arrived at the place where the carpenters had settled. The young Elephant, hearing the sound of drums as he was playing in the water, came out and presented himself before the carpenters, who one and all came forth to do honour to the king's coming, and said to him, "Sire, if woodwork is wanted, what need to come here? Why not send and have it brought to you?"

"No, no, good friends," the king answered, "'tis not for wood that I come, but for this elephant here."

"He is yours, Sire!"—But the Elephant refused to budge.

"What do you want me to do, gossip Elephant?" asked the king.

"Order the carpenters to be paid for what they have spent on me, Sire."

"Willingly, friend." And the king ordered an hundred thousand pieces of money to be laid by his tail, and trunk, and by each of his four feet. But this was not enough for the Elephant; go he would not. So to each of the carpenters was given a pair of cloths, and to each of their wives robes to dress in, nor did he omit to give enough whereby his playmates the children should be brought up; then with a last look upon the carpenters, and the women, and the children, he departed in company with the king.

[1] Compare Hesiod, *Op.* 753: *μηδέ ποτ' ἐν προχοῇ ποταμῶν ἄλαδε προρεόντων, μηδ' ἐπὶ κρηνάων οὐρεῖν.* Hdt. i. 138 (the Persians) *ἐς ποταμὸν δὲ οὔτε ἐνουρέουσι....*

To his capital city the king brought him; and city and stable were decked out with all magnificence. He led the Elephant round the city in solemn procession, and thence into his stable, which was fitted up with splendour and pomp. There he solemnly sprinkled the Elephant, and appointed him for his own riding; like a comrade he treated him, and gave him the half of his kingdom, [21] taking as much care of him as he did of himself. After the coming of this Elephant, the king won supremacy over all India.

In course of time the Bodhisatta was conceived by the Queen Consort; and when her time was near come to be delivered, the king died. Now if the Elephant learnt news of the king's death, he was sure to break his heart; so he was waited upon as before, and not a word said. But the next neighbour, the king of Kosala, heard of the king's death. "Surely the land is at my mercy," thought he; and marched with a mighty host to the city, and beleaguered it. Straight the gates were closed, and a message was sent to the king of Kosala:—"Our Queen is near the time of her delivery; and the astrologers have declared that in seven days she shall bear a son. If she bears a son, we will not yield the kingdom, but on the seventh day we will give you battle. For so long we pray you wait!" And to this the king agreed.

In seven days the Queen bore a son. On his name-day they called him Prince Winheart, because, said they, he was born to win the hearts of the people.

On the very same day that he was born, the townsfolk began to do battle with the king of Kosala. But as they had no leader, little by little the army gave way, great though it was. The courtiers told this news to the Queen, adding, "Since our army loses ground in this way, we fear defeat. But the state Elephant, our king's bosom friend, has never been told that the king is dead, and a son born to him, and that the king of Kosala is here to give us battle. Shall we tell him?"

"Yes, do so," said the Queen. So she dressed up her son, and laid him in a fine linen cloth; after which she with all the court came down from the palace and entered the Elephant's stable. There she laid the babe at the Elephant's feet, [22] saying, "Master, your comrade is dead, but we feared to tell it you lest you might break your heart. This is your comrade's son; the king of Kosala has run a leaguer about the city, and is making war upon your son; the army is losing ground; either kill your son yourself, or else win the kingdom back for him!"

At once the Elephant stroked the child with his trunk, and lifted him upon his own head; then making moan and lamentation he took him down and laid him in his mother's arms, and with the words—"I will master the king of Kosala!" he went forth hastily.

Then the courtiers put his armour and caparison upon him, and unlocked the city gate, and escorted him thither. The Elephant emerging trumpeted, and frightened all the host so that they ran away, and broke up the camp; then seizing the king of Kosala by his topknot, he carried him to the young prince, at whose feet he let him fall. Some rose to kill him, but them the Elephant stayed; and he let the captive king go with this advice: "Be careful for the future, and be not presumptuous by reason that our Prince is young."

After that, the power over all India fell into the Bodhisatta's own hand, and not a foe was able to rise up against him. The Bodhisatta was consecrated at the age of seven years, as King Winheart; just was his reign, and when he came to life's end he went to swell the hosts of heaven.

When the Master had ended this discourse, having become perfectly enlightened, he repeated this couple of verses:—

"Prince Winheart took king Kosala, ill pleased with all he had;
By capturing the greedy king, he made his people glad."

"So any brother, strong in will, who to the Refuge flies,
Who cherishes all good, and goes the way Nirvana lies,
By slow degrees will bring about destruction of all ties."

[23] And so the Master, bringing his teaching to a climax in the eternal Nirvana, went on to declare the Truths, and then identified the Birth: after the Truths, this backsliding Brother was established in sainthood:—"She who now is Mahāmāyā was then the mother; this backslider was the Elephant who took the kingdom and handed it over to the child; Sāriputta was the father Elephant, and I myself was the young Prince."

No. 157.

GUṆA-JĀTAKA.

"*The strong will always have their way,*" *etc.*—This was told by the Master whilst at Jetavana, how Elder Ānanda received a present of a thousand robes.

The Elder had been preaching to the ladies of the king of Kosala's palace as described above in the Mahāsāra Birth[1].

As he preached there in the manner described, [24] a thousand robes, worth each a thousand pieces of money, were brought to the king. Of these the king

[1] No. 92. Compare *Cullavagga*, xi. 1. 13 ff. (trans. in *S. B. E.*, iii. p. 382).

gave five hundred to as many of his queens. The ladies put these aside, and made them a present to our Elder, and then the next day in their old ones went to the palace where the king took breakfast. The king remarked, "I gave you dresses worth a thousand pieces each. Why are you not wearing them?" "My lord," said they, "we have given them to the Elder." "Has Elder Ānanda got them all?" he asked. They said, yes, he had. "The Supreme Buddha," said he, "allows only three robes. Ānanda is doing a little trade in cloth, I suppose!" He was angry with the Elder; and after breakfast, visited him in his cell, and after greeting, sat down, with these words:—

"Pray, Sir, do my ladies learn or listen to your preaching?"

"Yes, Sire; they learn what they ought, and what they ought to hear, they hear."

"Oh, indeed. Do they only listen, or do they make you presents of upper-garments or under-garments?"

"To-day, Sire, they have given me five hundred robes worth a thousand pieces each."

"And you accepted them, Sir?"

"Yes, Sire, I did."

"Why, Sir, didn't the Master make some rule about three robes?"

"True, Sire, for every Brother three robes is the rule, speaking of what he uses for himself. But no one is forbidden to accept what is offered; and that is why I took them—to give them to Brothers whose robes are worn out."

"But when these Brothers get them from you, what do they do with their old ones?"

"Make them into a cloke."

"And what about the old cloke?"

"That they turn into a shirt."

"And the old shirt—?"

"That serves for a coverlet."

"The old coverlet?"—"Becomes a mat." [25] "The old mat?"—"A towel." "And what about the old towel?"

"Sire, it is not permitted to waste the gifts of the faithful; so they chop up the old towel into bits, and mix the bits with clay, which they use for mortar in building their houses."

"A gift, Sir, ought not to be destroyed, not even a towel."

"Well, Sir king, we destroy no gifts, but all are used somehow."

This conversation pleased the king so much, that he sent for the other five hundred dresses which remained, and gave them to the Elder. Then, after receiving his thanks, he greeted the Elder in solemn state, and went his way.

The Elder gave the first five hundred robes to Brothers whose robes were worn out. But the number of his fellow priests was just five hundred. One of these, a young Brother, was very useful to the Elder; sweeping out his cell, serving him with food and drink, giving him toothbrush and water for cleansing his mouth, looking after the privies, living rooms, and sleeping rooms, and doing all that was needed for hand, foot, or back. To him, as his by right for all his great service, the Elder gave all the five hundred robes which he had received afterwards. The young Brother in his turn distributed them among his fellow-students. These all cut them up, dyed them yellow as a kaṇikāra[1] flower; then drest therein they waited upon the Master, greeted him, and sat down on one side. "Sir," they asked, "is it possible for a holy disciple who has entered on the First Path to be a respecter of persons in his gifts?" "No, Brothers, it is not possible for holy disciples to be respecters of persons in their gifts." "Sir, our spiritual Teacher, the Treasurer of the Faith, gave five hundred robes, each worth a thousand pieces, to a young Brother; and he has divided them amongst us." "Brothers, in giving these Ānanda was no respecter of persons. [26] That young fellow was a very useful servant; so he made the present to his own attendant for service' sake, for goodness'

[1] Pterospermum acerifolium.

sake, and by right, thinking that one good turn deserves another, and with a wish to do what gratitude demands. In former days, as now, wise men acted on the principle that one good turn deserves another." And then, at their request, he told them a story of the olden time.

Once upon a time, while Brahmadatta was king of Benares, the Bodhisatta was a Lion living in a cave on the hills. One day he came out from his lair and looked towards the mountain foot. Now all round the foot of that mountain stretched a great piece of water. Upon some ground that rose out of this was a quantity of soft green grass, growing on the thick mud, and over this mud ran rabbits and deer and such light creatures, eating of the grass. On that day, as usual, there was a deer eating grass upon it.

"I'll have that deer!" thought the Lion; and with a lion's leap he sprang from the hillside towards it. But the deer, frightened to death, scampered away belling. The Lion could not stop his onset; down on the mud he fell, and sank in, so that he could not get out; and there he remained seven days, his feet fixed like four posts, with not a morsel to eat.

Then a Jackal, hunting for food, chanced to see him; and set off running in high terror. But the Lion called out to him—"I say, Jackal, don't run—here am I, caught fast in the mud. Please save me!" Up came the Jackal. "I could pull you out," says he, "but I much fear that once out you might eat me." "Fear nothing, I won't eat you," says the Lion. "On the contrary, I'll do you great service; only get me out somehow."

The Jackal, accepting this promise, worked away the mud around his four feet, and the holes wherein his four feet were fixed he dug further towards the water; [27] then the water ran in, and made the mud soft. Then he got underneath the Lion, saying—"Now, Sir, one great effort," making a loud noise and striking the Lion's belly with his head. The Lion strained every nerve, and scrambled out of the mud; he stood on dry land. After a moment's rest, he plunged in the lake, and washed and scoured the mud from him. Then he killed a buffalo, and with his fangs tore up its flesh, of which he proffered some to the Jackal, saying, "Eat, comrade!" and himself after the Jackal had done did eat too. After this, the Jackal took a piece in his mouth. "What's that for?" the Lion asked. "For your humble servant my mate, who awaits me at home." "All right," says the Lion, taking a bit for his own mate. "Come, comrade," says he again, "let us stay awhile on the mountain top, and then go to the lady's house." So there they went, and the Lion fed the she-jackal; and after they were both satisfied, said he, "Now I am going to take care of you." So he conducted them to the place where he dwelt, and settled them in a cave near to the entrance of his own.

Ever after that, he and the Jackal used to go a-hunting together, leaving their mates behind; all kinds of creatures they would kill, and eat to their hearts' content, and then bring back some for the two others. And as time went on, the she-Jackal and the Lioness had each two cubs, and they all lived happily together.

One day, a sudden thought struck the Lioness. "My Lion seems very fond of the Jackal and his mate and young ones. What if there be something wrong between them! That must be the cause why he is so fond of them, I suppose. Well, I will plague her and frighten her, and get her away from this place."

So when the Lion and the Jackal were away on the hunt, she plagued and terrified the Jackal's mate, asking her why she stayed there, [28] why she did not run away? And her cubs frightened the young Jackals after the same fashion. The she-Jackal told her mate what had been said. "It is clear," said she, "that the Lion must have dropt a hint about us. We have been here a long time; and now he will be the death of us. Let us go back to the place where we lived before!"

On hearing this, the Jackal approached the Lion, with these words. "Master, we have been here a long time. Those who stay too long outstay their welcome. While we are away, your Lioness scolds and terrifies my mate, by asking why she stays, and telling her to begone; your young ones do the same to mine. If any one does not like a neighbour, he should just bid him go, and send him about his business; what is the use of all this plaguing?" So saying, he repeated the first stanza:

"The strong will always have their way; it is their nature so to do;
Your mate roars loud; and now I say I fear what once I trusted to."

[29] The Lion listened; then turning to his Lioness, "Wife," said he, "you remember how once I was out hunting for a week, and then brought back this Jackal and his mate with me?" "Yes, I remember." "Well, do you know why I stayed away all that week?" "No, Sir." "My wife, in trying to catch a deer, I made a mistake, and stuck fast in the mud; there I stayed—for I could not get out—a whole week without food. My life was saved by this Jackal. This my friend saved my life! A friend in need is a friend indeed, be he great or small. Never again must you put a slight upon my comrade, or his wife, or his family." And then the Lion repeated the second stanza:

"A friend who plays a friendly part, however small and weak he be,
He is my kinsman and my flesh and blood, a friend and comrade he;
Despise him not, my sharp-fanged mate! this Jackal saved my life for me."

The Lioness, when she heard this tale, made her peace with the Jackal's mate, and ever after lived at amity with her and her young ones. And the young of the two pairs played together in their early days, and when the parents died, [30] they did not break the bond of friendship, but lived happily together as the old ones had lived before them. Indeed, the friendship remained unbroken through seven generations.

When the Master had ended this discourse, he declared the Truths and identified the Birth:—(at the end of the Truths some entered on the First Path, some on the Second, some on the Third, and some the Fourth:)—"Ānanda was the Jackal in those days, and the Lion was I myself."

No. 158.

SUHANU-JĀTAKA.

"*Birds of a feather*," *etc.*—This story the Master told whilst at Jetavana, about two hot-tempered Brothers.

It happened that there were two Brothers, passionate, cruel, and violent, one living at Jetavana and one in the country. Once the country Brother came to Jetavana on some errand or other. The novices and young Brothers knew the passionate nature of this man, so they led him to the cell of the other, all agog to see them quarrel. No sooner did they spy one another, those two hot-tempered men, than they ran into each other's arms, stroking and caressing hands, and feet, and back!

The Brothers talked about it in the Hall of Truth. "Friend, these passionate Brothers are cross, cruel, angry to every body else, but with each other they are the best of friends, cordial and sympathetic!" The Master came in, asking what they sat there talking about? They told him. Said he, "This, Brothers, is not the only time that these men, who are cross, cruel, and angry to all else, have shown themselves cordial, and friendly, and sympathetic to each other. It happened just so in olden days"; and so saying, he told an old-world tale.

Once upon a time when Brahmadatta was king of Benares, the Bodhisatta was his do-all, a courtier who advised him on things temporal and things spiritual. Now this king was of a somewhat covetous nature; [31] and he had a brute of a horse, named Mahāsoṇa, or Big Chestnut.

Some horse-dealers from the north country brought down five hundred horses; and word was sent to the king that these horses had arrived. Now heretofore the Bodhisatta had always asked the dealers to fix their own price, and then paid it in full. But now the king, being displeased with him, summoned another of his court, to whom he said,

"Friend, make the men name their price; then let loose Big Chestnut so that he goes amongst them; make him bite them, and when they are weak and wounded get the men to reduce their price."

"Certainly," said the man; and so he did.

The dealers in great dudgeon told the Bodhisatta what this horse had done.

"Have you not such another brute in your own city?" asked the Bodhisatta. Yes, they said, there was one named Suhanu, Strongjaw, and a fierce and savage brute he was. "Bring him with you the next time you come," the Bodhisatta said; and this they promised to do.

So the next time they came this brute came with them. The king, on hearing how the horse-dealers had arrived, opened his window to look at the horses, and caused Chestnut to be let loose. Then as the dealers saw Chestnut coming, they let Strongjaw loose. No sooner had the two met, than they stood still licking each other all over!

The king asked the Bodhisatta how it was. "Friend," said he, "when these two rogue horses come across others, they are fierce, wild, and savage, they bite them, and make them ill. But with each other—there they stand, licking one another all over the body! What's the reason of this?" "The reason is," said the Bodhisatta, "that they are not dissimilar, but like in nature and character." And he repeated this couple of verses:

"Birds of a feather flock together: Chestnut and Strongjaw both agree:
In scope and aim both are the same—there is no difference I can see."

[32] "Both savage are, and vicious both; both always bite their tether;
So sin with sin, and vice with vice, must e'en agree together."

Then the Bodhisatta went on to warn the king against excessive covetise, and the spoiling of other men's goods; and fixing the value, he made him pay the proper price. The dealers received the due value, and went away well satisfied; and the king, abiding by the Bodhisatta's admonition, at last passed away to fare according to his deeds.

When the Master had ended this discourse, he identified the Birth: "The bad Brothers were then these two horses, Ānanda was the king, and I was the wise counsellor."

No. 159.

MORA-JĀTAKA.

[33] "*There he rises, king all-seeing,*" *etc.* This story the Master told at Jetavana about a backsliding Brother. This Brother was led by some others before the Master, who asked, "Is it true, Brother, as I hear, that you have backslidden?" "Yes, Sir." "What have you seen that should make you do so?" "A woman drest up in magnificent attire." Then said the Master, "What wonder that womankind should trouble the wits of a man like you! Even wise men, who for seven hundred years have done no sin, on hearing a woman's voice have transgressed in a moment; even the holy become impure; even they who have attained the highest honour have thus come to disgrace—how much more the unholy!" and he told a story of the olden time.

Once upon a time, when Brahmadatta was king of Benares, the Bodhisatta came into this world as a Peacock. The egg which contained him had a shell as yellow as a kaṇikāra bud; and when he broke the shell, he became a Golden Peacock, fair and lovely, with beautiful red lines under his wings. To preserve his life, he traversed three ranges of hills, and in the fourth he settled, on a plateau of a golden hill in Daṇḍaka. When day dawned, as he sat upon the hill, watching the sun rise, he composed a Brahma spell to preserve himself safe in his own feeding-ground, the charm beginning "There he rises":—

"There he rises, king all-seeing,
Making all things bright with his golden light.
Thee I worship, glorious being,
Making all things bright with thy golden light,
Keep me safe, I pray,
Through the coming day."

[34] Worshipping the sun on this wise by the verse here recited, he repeats another in worship of the Buddhas who have passed away, and all their virtues:

"All saints, the righteous, wise in holy lore,
These do I honour, and their aid implore:
All honour to the wise, to wisdom honour be,
To freedom, and to all that freedom has made free."

Uttering this charm to keep himself from harm, the Peacock went a-feeding[1].

[1] This line of the text is metrical in the Pali.

[35] So after flying about all day, he came back at even and sat on the hilltop to see the sun go down; then as he meditated, he uttered another spell to preserve himself and keep off evil, the one beginning "There he sets":—

"There he sets, the king all-seeing,
He that makes all bright with his golden light.
Thee I worship, glorious being,
Making all things bright with thy golden light.
Through the night, as through the day,
Keep me safe, I pray.

"All saints, the righteous, wise in holy lore,
These do I honour and their aid implore:
All honour to the wise, to wisdom honour be,
To freedom, and to all that freedom has made free."

Uttering this charm to keep himself from harm, the Peacock fell a-sleeping[1].

[36] Now there was a savage who lived in a certain village of wild huntsmen, near Benares. Wandering about among the Himalaya hills he noticed the Bodhisatta perched upon the golden hill of Daṇḍaka, and told it to his son.

It so befel that on a day one of the wives of the king of Benares, Khemā by name, saw in a dream a golden peacock holding a religious discourse. This she told to the king, saying that she longed to hear the discourse of the golden peacock. The king asked his courtiers about it; and the courtiers said, "The Brahmins will be sure to know." The Brahmins said: "Yes, there are golden peacocks." When asked, where? they replied, "The hunters will be sure to know." The king called the hunters together and asked them. Then this hunter answered, "O lord king, there is a golden hill in Daṇḍaka; and there a golden peacock lives." "Then bring it here—kill it not, but just take it alive."

The hunter set snares in the peacock's feeding-ground. But even when the peacock stepped upon it, the snare would not close. This the hunter tried for seven years, but catch him he could not; and there he died. And Queen Khemā too died without obtaining her wish.

The king was wroth because his Queen had died for the sake of a peacock. He caused an inscription to be made upon a golden plate to this effect: "Among the Himalaya mountains is a golden hill in Daṇḍaka. There lives a golden peacock; and whoso eats of its flesh becomes ever young and immortal." This he enclosed in a casket.

After his death, the next king read this inscription: and thought he, "I will become ever young and immortal;" so he sent another

[1] This line of the text is metrical in the Pali.

hunter. Like the first, this hunter failed to capture the peacock, and died in the quest. In the same way the kingdom was ruled by six successive kings.

Then a seventh arose, who also sent forth a hunter. The hunter observed that when the Golden Peacock came into the snare, it did not shut to, [37] and also that he recited a charm before setting out in search of food. Off he went to the marches, and caught a peahen, which he trained to dance when he clapped his hands, and at snap of finger to utter her cry. Then, taking her along with him, he set the snare, fixing its uprights in the ground, early in the morning, before the peacock had recited his charm. Then he made the peahen utter a cry. This unwonted sound—the female's note—woke desire in the peacock's breast; leaving his charm unsaid, he came towards her; and was caught in the net. Then the hunter took hold of him and conveyed him to the king of Benares.

The king was delighted at the peacock's beauty; and ordered a seat to be placed for him. Sitting on the proffered seat, the Bodhisatta asked, "Why did you have me caught, O king?"

"Because they say all that eat of you become immortal and have eternal youth. So I wish to gain youth eternal and immortality by eating of you," said the king.

"So be it—granted that all who eat of me become immortal and have eternal youth. But that means that I must die!"

"Of course it does," said the king.

"Well—and if I die, how can my flesh give immortality to those that eat of it?"

"Your colour is golden; therefore (so it is said) those who eat your flesh become young and live so for ever[1]."

"Sir," replied the bird, "there is a very good reason for my golden colour. Long ago, I held imperial sway over the whole world, reigning in this very city; I kept the Five Commandments, and made all people of the world keep the same. For that I was born again after death in the World of the Thirty-Three Archangels; there I lived out my life, but in my next birth I became a peacock in consequence of some sin; however, golden I became because I had aforetime kept the Commandments."

"What? Incredible! You an imperial ruler, who kept the Commandments! born gold-coloured as the fruit of them! A proof, prithee!"

[1] Perhaps because they are supposed to live as long as gold lasts. On the same principle, pieces of jade are placed in the coffin of the Chinese, to preserve the soul of the dead. Groot, in a work on Chinese religions, quotes a Chinese writer of the 4th century, who says: "He who swallows gold will exist as long as gold; he who swallows jade will exist as long as jade;" and recommends it for the living (cp. Groot, *Religious Systems of China*, i. pp. 271, 273).

[38] "I have one, Sire."

"What is it?"

"Well, Sire, when I was monarch, I used to pass through mid-air seated in a jewelled car, which now lies buried in the earth beneath the waters of the royal lake. Dig it up from beneath the lake, and that shall be my proof."

The king approved the plan; he caused the lake to be drained, and dug out the chariot, and believed the Bodhisatta. Then the Bodhisatta addressed him thus:

"Sire, except Nirvana, which is everlasting, all things else, being composite in their nature, are unsubstantial, transient, and subject to living and death." Discoursing on this theme he established the king in keeping of the Commandments. Peace filled the king's heart; he bestowed his kingdom upon the Bodhisatta, and showed him the highest respect. The Bodhisatta returned the gift; and after a few days' sojourn, he rose up in the air, and flew back to the golden hill of Daṇḍaka, with a parting word of advice—"O king, be careful!" And the king on his part clave to the Bodhisatta's advice; and after giving alms and doing good, passed away to fare according to his deeds.

This discourse ended, the Master declared the Truths, and identified the Birth:—now after the Truths the backsliding Brother became a Saint:—"Ānanda was the king of those days, and I myself was the Golden Peacock."

No. 160.

VINĪLAKA-JĀTAKA.

"*As yonder king goes galloping*," *etc.*—This story the Master told during a sojourn in Veḷuvana, how Devadatta imitated the Buddha.

The two chief Disciples[1] went to visit Gayāsīsa[2], where Devadatta imitated the Buddha, and fell; the Elders then both returned, after delivering a discourse, taking with them their own pupils. On arriving at Veḷuvana, the Master asked them what Devadatta had done when he saw them? [39] "Sir," they said, "he

[1] Sāriputta and Moggallāna. See *Cullavagga*, vii. 4 (trans. in *Vinaya Texts*, iii. 256 ff.).

[2] A mountain near Gayā in Behar. It is now called Brahmayoni (see Rājendralāla Mitra, *Buddha Gayā*, p. 23).

imitated the Buddha, and was utterly destroyed." The Master answered, "It is not only now, Sāriputta, that Devadatta came to dire destruction by mimicking me; it was just the same before." Then at the Elder's request, he told an old-world tale.

Once upon a time, when Videha was reigning at Mithilā in the realm of Videha, the Bodhisatta became a son of his Queen Consort. He grew up in due course, and was educated at Takkasilā; and on his father's decease he inherited his kingdom.

At that time a certain king of the Golden Geese paired with a Crow at the feeding-grounds, and to them was born a son. He was like neither mother nor father. All dingy blue-black he was, and accordingly they gave him Dingy to his name. The Goose-king often visited his offspring; and he had besides two other sons, geese like himself. These remarked that he often used to go to the regions where mankind do frequent, and asked him what should be the reason. "My sons," said he, "I have a mate there, a Crow, and she has given me a son, whose name is Dingy. He it is I go to visit." "Where do they live?" they asked. "On a palm-top near Mithilā in the kingdom of Videha," describing the spot. "Father," said they, "where men are, there is fear and peril. You ought not to go there; let us go and fetch him to you."

So they took a stick, and perched Dingy upon it; then catching the ends in their beaks, they flew over the city of Mithilā.

At that moment King Videha chanced to be sitting in a magnificent carriage drawn by a team of four milk-white thoroughbreds, as he made a triumphal circuit of the city. Dingy saw him, and thought he—"What is the difference between King Videha and me? He is riding in state around his capital in a chariot drawn by four white horses; and I am carried in a vehicle drawn by a pair of Geese." So as he passed through the air he repeated the first stanza:

[40] "As yonder king goes galloping with his milk-white four-in-hand,
Dingy has these, his pair of Geese, to bear him over the land!"

These words made the Geese angry. Their first thought was "Let us drop him here, and leave him!" But then again they bethought them—"What will our father say!" So for fear of rebuke, they brought the creature to their father, and recounted all that he had done. The father grew angry when he heard it: "What!" said he, "are you my sons' superior, that you make yourself master over them, and treat them like horses in a carriage? You don't know your measure. This is no place for you; get you back to your mother!" And with this censure he repeated the second stanza:

"Dingy, my dear, there's danger here; this is no place for you;
By village gates your mother waits—there you must hasten too."

With this censure, he bade his sons convey the bird to the dunghill outside the city of Mithilā; and so they did.

This lesson ended, the Master identified the Birth: "Devadatta in those days was Dingy, the two Elders were the two young Geese, Ānanda was the father Goose, and I was king Videha myself."

No. 161.

INDASAMĀNAGOTTA-JĀTAKA.

[41] "*Friendship with evil,*" *etc.*—This is a story told by the Master while at Jetavana, about a headstrong person; and the circumstances will be found in the Vulture Birth[1], of the Ninth Book. The Master said to this Brother—"In olden days, as now, you were trampled to death by a mad elephant because you were so headstrong and careless of wise men's advice." And he told the old story.

Once upon a time, while Brahmadatta was king of Benares, the Bodhisatta was born of a brahmin family. On growing up he left his worldly home and took to the religious life, and in time became the leader of a company of five hundred anchorites, who all lived together in the region of Himalaya.

Amongst these anchorites was a headstrong and unteachable person named Indasamānagotta. He had a pet elephant. The Bodhisatta sent for him when he found this out, and asked if he really did keep a young elephant? Yes, the man said, he had an elephant which had lost its dam. "Well," the Bodhisatta said, "when elephants grow up they kill even those who foster them; so you had better not keep it any longer." "But I can't live without him, my Teacher!" was the reply. "Oh, well," said the Bodhisatta, "you'll live to repent it."

Howbeit he still reared the creature, and by and bye it grew to an immense size.

It happened once that the anchorites had all gone far afield to gather roots and fruits in the forest, and they were absent for several days. At the first breath of the south wind this elephant fell in a frenzy.

[1] Gijjha-jātaka, No. 427.

"Destruction to this hut!" thought he, "I'll smash the water-jar! I'll overturn the stone bench! I'll tear up the pallet! I'll kill the hermit, and then off I'll go!" So he sped into the jungle, and waited watching for their return.

The master came first, [42] laden with food for his pet. As soon as he saw him, he hastened up, thinking all was well[1]. Out rushed the elephant from the thicket, and seizing him in his trunk, dashed him to the ground, then with a blow on the head crushed the life out of him; and madly trumpeting, he scampered into the forest.

The other anchorites brought this news to the Bodhisatta. Said he, "We should have no dealings with the bad;" and then he repeated these two verses:—

"Friendship with evil let the good eschew,
The good, who know what duty bids them do:
They will work mischief, be it soon or late,
Even as the elephant his master slew."

"But if a kindred spirit thou shalt see,
In virtue, wisdom, learning like to thee,
Choose such an one to be thy own true friend;
Good friends and blessing go in company."

[43] In this way the Bodhisatta showed his band of anchorites that it is well to be docile and not obstinate. Then he performed Indasamānagotta's obsequies, and cultivating the Excellences, came at last into Brahma's heaven.

After concluding this discourse, the Master identified the Birth: "This unruly fellow was then Indasamānagotta, and I was myself the teacher of the anchorite band."

No. 162.

SANTHAVA-JĀTAKA.

"*Nothing is worse*," *etc.*—This story the Master told while dwelling at Jetavana, about feeding the sacred fire. The circumstances are the same as those of the Naṅguṭṭha Birth related above[2]. The Brethren, on seeing those who kept up this fire, said to the Blessed One, "Sir, here are topknot ascetics practising all sorts of false asceticism. What's the good of it?" "There is no

[1] Or, "with his usual greeting, or signal."
[2] No. 144.

good in it," said the Master. "It has happened before that even wise men have imagined some good in feeding the sacred fire, but after doing this for a long time, have found out that there is no good in it, and have quenched it with water, and beat it down, beat it down with sticks, never giving it so much as a look afterwards." Then he told them a story.

Once upon a time, when Brahmadatta was king of Benares, the Bodhisatta was born in a brahmin family. When he was about sixteen years old, his father and mother took his birth-fire[1] and spoke to him thus: "Son, will you take your birth-fire into the woods, and worship the fire there; or will you learn the Three Vedas, settle down as a married man, and live in the world?" Said he, "No worldly life for me: I will worship my fire in the woodland, and go on the way to heaven." So taking his birth-fire, he bade farewell to his parents, and entered the forest, where he lived in a hut made of branches and leaves and did worship to the fire.

One day he had been invited to some place where he received a present of rice and ghee. "This rice," thought he, "I will offer to Great Brahma." [44] So he took home the rice, and made the fire blaze. Then with the words, "With this rice I feed the sacred flame," he cast it upon the fire. Scarce had this rice dropt upon it, all full of fat as it was—when a fierce flame leapt up which set his hermitage alight. Then the brahmin hurried away in terror, and sat down some distance off. "There should be no dealings with the wicked," said he; "and so this fire has burnt the hut which I made with so much trouble!" And he repeated the first stanza:—

"Nothing is worse than evil company;
I fed my fire with plenteous rice and ghee;
And lo! the hut which gave me such ado
To build it up, my fire has burnt for me."

"I've done with you now, false friend!" he added; and he poured water upon the fire, and beat it out with sticks, and then buried himself in the mountains. There he came upon a black hind licking the faces of a lion, a tiger, and a panther. This put it into his mind how there was nothing better than good friends; and therewith he repeated the second stanza:—

"Nothing is better than good company;
Kind offices of friendship here I see;
[45] Behold the lion, tiger, and the pard—
The black hind licks the faces of all three."

[1] Cp. vol. i. no. 61, and 144, *init.*; a sacred fire was also kindled at a wedding, to be used for sacrifice and constantly kept up (Manu, 3. 67). So too now, the Agni-hotṛi in Kumaon begins fire-worship from the date of his marriage. The sacred fire of the marriage altar is carried in a copper vessel to his fire-pit. It is always kept alight, and from it must be kindled his funeral pyre (*North Indian Notes and Queries*, iii. 284).

With these reflections the Bodhisatta plunged into the depths of the mountains, and there he embraced the true religious life, cultivating the Faculties and the Attainments, until at his life's end he passed into Brahma's heaven.

After delivering this discourse, the Master identified the Birth: "In those days I was the ascetic of the story."

No. 163.

SUSĪMA-JĀTAKA.

"*Five score black elephants,*" *etc.*—This story the Master told at Jetavana, about arbitrary giving of alms.

We hear that at Sāvatthi, a family used sometimes to give alms to the Buddha and his friends, sometimes they used to give to the heretics, or else the givers would form themselves into companies, or again the people of one street would club together, or the whole of the inhabitants would collect voluntary offerings, and present them.

On this occasion all the inhabitants had made such a collection of all necessaries; but counsels were divided, some demanding that this be given to the heretics, some speaking for those who followed the Buddha. Each party stuck to their point, the disciples of the heretics voting for the heretics, and the disciples of Buddha for Buddha's company. Then it was proposed to divide upon the question, and accordingly they divided; those who were for the Buddha were in the majority.

So their plan was followed, and the disciples of the heretics could not prevent the gifts being offered to the Buddha and his followers.

The citizens gave invitation to the Buddha's company; for seven days they set rich offerings before them, and on the seventh gave over all the articles they had collected. The Master returned thanks, [46] after which he instructed a host of people in the fruition of the Paths. Next he returned to Jetavana; and when his followers had done their duties, he delivered a Buddha's discourse standing before his scented chamber, into which he then retired.

At evening time the Brethren talked the matter over together in the Hall of Truth: "Friend, how the heretics' disciples tried to prevent this from coming to the saints! Yet they couldn't do it; all the collection of articles was laid before the saints' own feet. Ah, how great is the Buddha's power!" "What is this you are talking about now together?" asked the Master, coming in. They told him. "Brethren," said he, "this is not the first time that the disciples of the heretics have tried to thwart an offering which should have been made to me. They did the same before; but always these articles have been finally laid at my feet." So saying, he told them a tale of long ago.

Once upon a time there lived in Benares a king Susīma; and the Bodhisatta was the son of his chaplain's lady. When he was sixteen years old, his father died. The father while he lived was Master of the Ceremonies in the king's elephant festivals. He alone had right to all the trappings and appointments of the elephants which came into the place of festival. By this means he gained as much as ten millions at each festival.

At the time of our story the season for an elephant festival came round. And the Brahmins all flocked to the king, with these words: "O great king! the season for an elephant festival has come, and a festival should be made. But this your chaplain's son is very young; he knows neither the three Vedas nor the lore of elephants[1]. Shall we conduct the ceremony?" To this the king consented.

Off went the Brahmins delighted. "Aha," said they, "we have barred this lad from performing the festival. We shall do it ourselves, and keep the gains!"

But the Bodhisatta's mother heard that in four days there was to be an elephant festival. [47] "For seven generations," thought she, "we have managed the elephant festivals from father to son. The old custom will pass from us, and our wealth will all melt away!" She wept and wailed. "Why are you weeping?" asked her son. She told him. Said he—"Well, mother, shall I conduct the festival?" "What, you, sonny? You don't know the three Vedas or the elephant lore; how can you do it?" "When are they going to have the festival, mother?" "Four days from now, my son." "Where can I find teachers who know the three Vedas by heart, and all the elephant lore?" "Just such a famous teacher, my son, lives in Takkasilā, in the realm of Gandhāra, two thousand leagues away." "Mother," says he, "our hereditary right we shall not lose. One day will take me to Takkasilā; one night will be enough to teach me the three Vedas and the elephant lore; on the morrow I will journey home; and on the fourth day I will manage the elephant festival. Weep no more!" With these words he comforted his mother.

Early next morning he broke his fast, and set out all alone for Takkasilā, which he reached in a single day. Then seeking out the teacher, he greeted him and sat on one side.

"Where have you come from?" the teacher asked.

"From Benares, Teacher."

"To what end?"

"To learn from you the three Vedas and the elephant lore."

"Certainly, my son, you shall learn it."

[1] An elephant trainer's manual, the *hastisūtram* or *hastiçikṣā*, cf. Mallinātha, Raghuv. vi. 27.

"But, Sir," said our Bodhisatta, "my case is urgent." Then he recounted the whole matter, adding, "In a single day I have traversed a journey of two thousand leagues. Give me your time for this one night only. Three days from now there is to be an Elephant festival; I will learn the whole after one lesson."

The Teacher consented. Then the lad washed his master's feet, and laid before him a fee of a thousand pieces of money; [48] he sat down on one side, and learnt his lesson by heart; as day broke, even as the day broke, he finished the three Vedas and the Elephant Lore. "Is there any more, Sir?" asked he. "No, my son, you have it all." "Sir," he went on, "in this book such a verse comes in too late, such another has gone astray in the reading. This is the way to teach your pupils for the future," and then he corrected his teacher's knowledge for him.

After an early meal he took his leave, and in a single day he was back again in Benares, and greeting his mother. "Have you learnt your lesson, my boy?" said she. He answered, yes; and she was delighted to hear it.

Next day, the festival of the elephants was prepared. A hundred elephants were set in array, with golden trappings, golden flags, all covered with a network of fine gold; and all the palace courtyard was decked out. There stood the Brahmins, in all their fine gala dress, thinking to themselves, "Now we shall do the ceremony, we shall do it!" Presently came the king, in all his splendour, and with him the ornaments and other things that were used.

The Bodhisatta, apparelled like a prince, at the head of his suite, approached the king with these words.

"Is it really true, O great king, that you are going to rob me of my right? Are you going to give other brahmins the managing of this ceremony? Have you said that you mean to give them the various ornaments and vessels that are used?" and he repeated the first stanza as follows:

"Five score black elephants, with tusks all white
Are thine, in gold caparison bedight.
'To thee, and thee I give them'—dost thou say,
Remembering my old ancestral right?"

[49] King Susīma, thus addressed, then repeated the second stanza:—

"Five score black elephants, with tusks all white,
Are mine, in gold caparison bedight.
'To thee, and thee I give them'—so I say,
My lad, remembering thine ancestral right."

Then a thought struck the Bodhisatta; and he said, "Sire, if you do remember my ancient right and your ancient custom, why do you neglect me and make others the masters of your festival?" "Why, I was told that you did not know the three Vedas or the Elephant Lore, and that is why I have caused the festival to be managed by others." "Very well, Sire. If there is one amongst all these brahmins who can recite a portion of the Vedas or the Elephant Lore against me, let him stand forward! Not in all India is there one save me who knows the three Vedas and the Elephant Lore for the ordering of an Elephant festival!" [50] Proud as a lion's roar rang out the answer! Not a brahmin durst rise and contend with him. So the Bodhisatta kept his ancestral right, and conducted the ceremony; and laden with riches, he returned to his own home.

When the Master had ended this discourse, he declared the Truths, and identified the Birth:—some entered on the First Path, some on the Second, some the Third, and some the Fourth:—"Mahāmāyā was at that time my mother, king Suddhodana was my father, Ānanda was king Susīma, Sāriputta the famous Teacher and I myself was the young Brahmin."

No. 164.

GIJJHA-JĀTAKA.

"*A vulture sees a corpse,*" etc.—This story the Master told about a Brother who had his mother to support. The circumstances will be related under the Sāma Birth[1]. The Master asked him whether he, a Brother, was really supporting persons who were still living in the world. This the Brother admitted. "How are they related to you?" the Master went on. "They are my parents, Sir." "Excellent, excellent," the Master said; and bade the Brethren not be angry with this Brother. "Wise men of old," said he, "have done service even to those who were not of kin to them; but this man's task has been to support his own parents." So saying, he told them this story of bygone days.

Once upon a time, when Brahmadatta was king of Benares, the Bodhisatta came to life as a young Vulture on the Vulture Hill, and had his mother and father to nourish.

[1] No. 532 in Westergaard's Copenhagen Catalogue (*Cat. Or. MSS. Bibl. Haun.*); not yet printed.

Once there came a great wind and rain. The Vultures could not hold their own against it; half frozen, they flew to Benares, and there near the wall and near the ditch they sat, shivering with the cold.

A merchant of Benares was issuing from the city on his way to bathe, when he spied these miserable Vultures. He got them together in a dry place, made a fire, sent and brought them some cowflesh from the cattle's burning-place, and put some one to look after them.

When the storm fell, [51] our Vultures were all right and flew off at once among the mountains. Without delay they met, and thus took counsel together. "A Benares merchant has done us a good turn; and one good turn deserves another, as the saying is[1]: so after this when any of us finds a garment or an ornament it must be dropt in that merchant's courtyard." So thenceforward if they ever noticed people drying their clothes or finery in the sun, watching for an unwary moment, they snatched them quickly, as hawks swoop on a bit of meat, and dropt them in the merchant's yard. But he, whenever he observed that they were bringing him anything, used to cause it to be laid aside.

They told the king how vultures were plundering the city. "Just catch me one vulture," says the king, "and I will make them bring it all back." So snares and gins were set everywhere; our dutiful Vulture was caught. They seized him with intent to bring him to the king. The Merchant aforesaid, on the way to wait upon his majesty, saw these people walking along with the Vulture. He went in their company, for fear they might hurt the Vulture.

They gave the Vulture to the king, who examined him.

"You rob our city, and carry off clothes and all sorts of things," he began.—"Yes, Sire."—"Whom have they been given to?"—"A merchant of Benares."—"Why?"—"Because he saved our lives, and they say one good turn deserves another; that is why we gave them to him."

"Vultures, they say," quoth the king, "can spy a corpse an hundred leagues away; and can't you see a trap set ready for you?" And with these words he repeated the first stanza:

"A vulture sees a corpse that lies one hundred leagues away:
When thou alightst upon a trap dost thou not see it, pray?"

[52] The Vulture listened, then replied by repeating the second stanza:

"When life is coming to an end, and death's hour draws anigh,
Though you may come close up to it, nor trap nor snare you spy."

After this response of the Vulture, the king turned to our Merchant. "Have all these things really been brought to you, then, by the Vultures?"

[1] This seems to be another form of the "Grateful Beasts" incident which so often occurs in folk-tales.

"Yes, my lord." "Where are they?" "My lord, they are all put away; each shall receive his own again:—only let this Vulture go!" He had his way; the Vulture was set at liberty, and the Merchant returned all the property to its owners.

This lesson ended, the Master declared the Truths, and identified the Birth:—at the conclusion of the Truths the dutiful Brother was established in the fruition of the First Path:—"Ānanda was the king of those days; Sāriputta was the Merchant; and I myself was the Vulture that supported his parents."

No. 165.

NAKULA-JĀTAKA.

"*Creature, your egg-born enemy,*" *etc.*—This story the Master told during a sojourn at Jetavana, about two officers who had a quarrel. The circumstances have been given above in the Uraga Birth[1]. Here, as before, the Master said, "This is not the first time, Brethren, these two nobles have been reconciled by me; in former times I reconciled them too." Then he told an old story.

Once on a time, when Brahmadatta was king of Benares, the Bodhisatta was born in a certain village as one of a brahmin family. When he came of age, [53] he was educated at Takkasilā; then, renouncing the world he became a recluse, cultivated the Faculties and the Attainments, and dwelt in the region of Himalaya, living upon wild roots and fruits which he picked up in his goings to and fro.

At the end of his cloistered walk lived a Mongoose in an ant-heap; and not far off, a Snake lived in a hollow tree. These two, Snake and Mongoose, were perpetually quarrelling. The Bodhisatta preached to them the misery of quarrels and the blessing of peace, and reconciled the two together, saying, "You ought to cease your quarrelling and live together at one."

When the Serpent was abroad, the Mongoose at the end of the walk lay with his head out of the hole in his ant-hill, and his mouth open, and

[1] Above, No. 154.

thus fell asleep, heavily drawing his breath in and out. The Bodhisatta saw him sleeping there, and asking him, "Why, what are you afraid of?" repeated the first stanza:

"Creature[1], your egg-born enemy a faithful friend is made:
Why sleep you there with teeth all bare? of what are you afraid?"

"Father," said the Mongoose, "never despise a former enemy, but always suspect him": and he repeated the second stanza:

"Never despise an enemy nor ever trust a friend:
A fear that springs from unfeared things uproots and makes an end."

[54] "Fear not," replied the Bodhisatta. "I have persuaded the Snake to do you no harm; distrust him no more." With this advice, he proceeded to cultivate the Four Excellences, and set his face toward Brahma's heaven. And the others too passed away to fare hereafter according to their deeds.

Then this lesson ended, the Master identified the Birth: "The two noblemen were at that time Snake and Mongoose, and I was myself the ascetic."

No. 166.

UPASĀḶHA-JĀTAKA.

"*Fourteen thousand Upasāḷhas,*" *etc.*—This story the Master told whilst at Jetavana, about a brahmin named Upasāḷha, who was fastidious in the matter of cemeteries.

This man, we learn, was rich and wealthy; but, though he lived over against the monastery, he showed no kindness to the Buddhas, being given to heresy. But he had a son, wise and intelligent. When he was growing old, the man said to his son, "Don't let my body be burnt in a cemetery where any outcast can be burnt, but find some uncontaminated place to burn me in." "Father," said the young fellow, "I know no cemetery fit to burn your body in. Good my father, take the lead and yourself point out the place where I shall have you burnt." So the brahmin consenting led his son out of the city to the top of Vulture Peak, and then said he, "Here, my son, no outcast is ever burnt; here I would have you burn me." Then he began to descend the hill in his son's company.

On that day, in the evening, the Master was looking around to see which of his friends was ripe for Release, and perceived that this father and son were

[1] Lit. 'O viviparous one.'

ready to enter upon the First Path. So he took their road, and came to the hill-foot, like a hunter waiting for his quarry; there he sat till they should come down from the top. Down they came, and noticed the Master. He gave them greeting, and asked, "Where are you bound, brahmins?" The young man told him their errand. "Come along, then," said the Master, "show me the place your father pointed out." So he and they two together climbed up the mountain. "Which place?" he asked. "Sir," said the lad, "the space between these three hills is the one he showed me." [55] The Master said, "This is not the first time, my lad, that your father has been nice in the matter of cemeteries; he was the same before. Nor is it now only that he has pointed you out this place for his burning; long ago he pointed out the very same place." And at his request the Master told them a tale of long ago.

Once upon a time, in this very city of Rājagaha, lived this same brahmin Upasāḷhaka[1], and he had the very same son. At that period the Bodhisatta had been born in a brahmin family of Magadha land; and when his education was finished, he embraced a religious life, cultivated the Faculties and the Attainments, and lived a long time in the region of Himalaya, plunged in mystic exaltation.

Once he left his hermitage on Vulture Peak to go buy salt and seasoning. While he was away, this brahmin spoke in just the same way to his son, as now. The lad begged him to point out a proper place, and he came and pointed out this very place. As he was descending, with his son, he observed the Bodhisatta, and approached him, and the Bodhisatta put the same question as I did just now, and received the son's answer. "Ah," said he, "we'll see whether this place which your father has shown you is contaminated or not," and made them go with him up the hill again. "The space between these three hills," said the lad, "is pure." "My lad," the Bodhisatta replied, "there is no end to the people who have been burned in this very spot. Your own father, born a brahmin, as now, in Rājagaha, and bearing the very same name of Upasālhaka, has been burnt on this hill in fourteen thousand births. On the whole earth there's not a spot to be found where a corpse has not been burnt, which has not been a cemetery, which has not been covered with skulls." This he discerned by the faculty of knowing all previous lives: and then he repeated these two stanzas:—[56]

"Fourteen thousand Upasāḷhas have been burnt upon this spot,
Nor is there the wide world over any place where death is not.

"Where is kindness, truth, and justice, temperance and self-control,
There no death can find an entrance; thither hies each saintly soul."

[1] This added suffix makes no practical difference in the word: it is often put on to adjectives and substantives without affecting their meaning. But sometimes it has a diminutive force.

When the Bodhisatta had thus discoursed to father and son, he cultivated the Four Excellences and went his way to Brahma's heaven.

When this discourse was ended, the Master declared the Truths and identified the Birth:—at the conclusion of the Truths father and son were established in the Fruit of the First Path:—"The father and son were the same then as they are now, and the ascetic was I myself."

No. 167.

SAMIDDHI-JĀTAKA.

"*Begging Brother, do you know,*" *etc.*—This story was told by the Master whilst he was staying in Tapoda Park near Rājagaha, about Elder Samiddhi, or Goodluck.

Once Father Goodluck had been wrestling in the spirit all night long. At sunrise he bathed; then he stood with his under garment on, holding the other in his hand, as he dried his body, all yellow as gold. Like a golden statue of exquisite workmanship he was, the perfection of beauty; [57] and that is why he was called Goodluck.

A daughter of the gods, seeing the Elder's surpassing beauty, fell in love with him, and addressed him thus. "You are young, Brother, and fresh, a mere stripling, with black hair, bless you! you have youth, you are lovely and pleasant to the eyes. Why should a man like you turn religious without a little enjoyment? Take your pleasure first, and then you shall become religious and do what the hermits do!" He replied, "Nymph, at some time or other I must die, and the time of my death I know not; that time is hid from me. Therefore in the freshness of my youth I will follow the solitary life, and make an end of pain."

Finding she received no encouragement, the goddess at once vanished. The Elder went and told his Master about it. Then the Master said, "Not now alone, Goodluck, are you tempted by a nymph. In olden days, as now, nymphs tempted ascetics." And then at his request the Master told an old-world tale.

Once upon a time, when Brahmadatta was king in Benares, the Bodhisatta became a brahmin's son in a village of Kāsi. Coming of years, he attained perfection in all his studies, and embraced the religious life; and he lived in Himalaya, hard by a natural lake, cultivating the Faculties and the Attainments.

All night long he had wrestled in the spirit; and at sunrise he bathed him, and with one bark garment on and the other in his hand, he stood, letting the water dry off his body. At the moment a daughter of the gods observed his perfect beauty, and fell in love with him. Tempting him, she repeated this first stanza:—

"Begging brother, do you know
What of joy the world can show?
Now's the time—there is no other:
Pleasure first, then—begging brother!"

[58] The Bodhisatta listened to the nymph's address, and then replied, declaring his set purpose, by repeating the second stanza:—

"The time is hid—I cannot know
When is the time that I must go:
Now is the time: there is no other:
So I am now a begging brother[1]."

When the nymph heard the Bodhisatta's words, she vanished at once.

After this discourse the Master identified the Birth: "The nymph is the same in both stories, and the hermit at that time was I myself."

No. 168.

SAKUṆAGGHI-JĀTAKA.

"*A Quail was in his feeding-ground,*" *etc.*—This story the Master told at Jetavana, about his meaning in the Bird Preaching[2].

One day the Master called the Brethren, saying, "When you seek alms, Brethren, keep each to your own district." And repeating that sutta from the Mahāvagga which suited the occasion, [59] he added, "But wait a moment: aforetime others even in the form of animals refused to keep to their own

[1] The commentator, in explaining this passage, adds another couplet:

"Life, sickness, death, the putting off the flesh,
Re-birth—these five are hidden in this world."

[2] I have not been able to trace this *Sakuṇovāda-sutta.* Perhaps it refers to a speech of the Buddha as a bird; cp. *Kukkurovādo* i. p. 178 (Pali).

districts, and by poaching on other people's preserves, they fell into the way of their enemies, and then by their own intelligence and resource got free from the hands of their enemies." With these words he related an old story.

Once upon a time, when Brahmadatta was king in Benares, the Bodhisatta came into the world as a young Quail. He got his food in hopping about over the clods left after ploughing.

One day he thought he would leave his feeding ground and try another; so off he flew to the edge of a forest. As he picked up his food there, a Falcon spied him, and attacking him fiercely, he caught him fast.

Held prisoner by this Falcon, our Quail made his moan: "Ah! how very unlucky I am! how little sense I have! I'm poaching on some one else's preserves! O that I had kept to my own place, where my fathers were before me! then this Falcon would have been no match for me, I mean if he had come to fight!"

"Why, Quailie," says the Falcon, "what's your own ground, where your fathers fed before you?"

"A ploughed field all covered with clods!"

At this the Falcon, relaxing his strength, let go. "Off with you, Quail! You won't escape me, even there!"

The Quail flew back and perched on an immense clod, and there he stood, calling—"Come along now, Falcon!"

Straining every nerve, poising both wings, down swooped the Falcon fiercely upon our Quail. "Here he comes with a vengeance!" thought the Quail; and as soon as he saw him in full career, just turned over and let him strike full against the clod of earth. The Falcon could not stop himself, and struck his breast against the earth; this broke his heart, and he fell dead with his eyes starting out of his head.

---

[60] When this tale had been told, the Master added, "Thus you see, Brethren, how even animals fall into their enemies' hands by leaving their proper place; but when they keep to it, they conquer their enemies. Therefore do you take care not to leave your own place and intrude upon another's. O Brethren, when people leave their own station Māra[1] finds a door, Māra gets a foothold. What is foreign ground, Brethren, and what is the wrong place for a Brother? I mean the Five Pleasures of Sense. What are these five? The Lust of the Eye... [and so on].[2] This, Brethren, is the wrong place for a Brother." Then growing perfectly enlightened he repeated the first stanza:—

> "A Quail was in his feeding ground, when, swooping from on high,
> A Falcon came; but so it fell he came to death thereby."

---

[1] Māra is Death, and is used by Buddha for the Evil One.

[2] The passage is corrupt. We must read 'cakkhu-*ādi-viññeyā*.'

When he had thus perished, out came the Quail, exclaiming, "I have seen the back of my enemy!" and perching upon his enemy's breast, he gave voice to his exultation in the words of the second stanza:—

"Now I rejoice at my success: a clever plan I found
To rid me of my enemy by keeping my own ground."

This discourse at an end, the Master declared the Truths and identified the Birth:—At the conclusion of the Truths many Brethren were established in the Paths or their Fruition:—"Devadatta was the Falcon of those days, and the Quail was I myself."

No. 169.

ARAKA-JĀTAKA.

"*The heart that boundless pity feels,*" *etc.*—This story the Master told at Jetavana, about the Scripture on Lovingkindness.

On one occasion the Master thus addressed the Brotherhood: "Brethren, charity practised with all devotion of thought, [61] meditated upon, increased, made a vehicle of progress, made your one object, practised, well begun, may be expected to produce Eleven Blessings[1]. What are these eleven? Happy he sleeps and happy he awakes; he sees no bad dreams; men love him; spirits guard him; fire, poison, and sword come not near him; quickly he becomes absorbed in mind; his look grows calm; he dies undismayed; without need of further wisdom he goes to Brahma's heaven. Charity, Brethren, practised with renunciation of one's wishes"—and so forth—"may be expected to produce these Eleven Blessings. Praising the Charity which holds these Eleven Blessings, Brethren, a Brother ought to show kindness to all creatures, whether expressly commanded or not, he should be a friend to the friendly, aye a friend to the unfriendly, and a friend to the indifferent: thus to all without distinction, whether expressly bidden or not, he should show Charity: he should show sympathy with joy and sorrow and practise equanimity; he should do his work by means of the Four Excellences. By so doing he will go to Brahma's heaven even without Path or Fruit. Wise men of old by cultivating charity for seven years, have dwelt in Brahma's heaven seven ages, each with its one period to wax and one to wane[2]." And he told them a story of the past.

---

[1] The Eleven Blessings are discussed in the *Questions of Milinda*, iv. 4. 16 (trans. in the *S. B. E.*, i. p. 279).

[2] See Childers, *Dict.* p. 185 *b*. The belief still lives. Two gentlemen who visited the Chief of Chinese Lamaism and the High Priest of Buddhism in Pekin, in 1890, talked with them over the decline of Buddhism in this age. Both admitted it, the

Once upon a time, in a former age, the Bodhisatta was born in a brahmin's family. When he grew up, he forsook his lusts and embraced the religious life, and attained the Four Excellences. His name was Araka, and he became a Teacher, and lived in Himalaya region, with a large body of followers. Admonishing his band of sages, he said, "A recluse must show Charity, sympathetic must he be both in joy and sorrow, and full of equanimity; for this thought of charity attained by resolve prepares him for Brahma's heaven." And explaining the blessing of charity, he repeated these verses:—

"The heart that boundless pity feels for all things that have birth,
In heaven above, in realms below, and on this middle earth,

"Filled full of pity infinite, infinite charity,
In such a heart nought narrow or confined can ever be."

[62] Thus did the Bodhisatta discourse to his pupils on the practice of charity and its blessings. And without a moment's interruption of his mystic trance, he was born in the heaven of Brahma, and for seven ages, each with his time to wax and wane, he came no more to this world.

After finishing this discourse, the Master identified the Birth: "The band of sages of that time are now the Buddha's followers; and I myself am he that was the Teacher Araka."

No. 170.

KAKAṆṬAKA-JĀTAKA.

[63] This Kakaṇṭaka Birth will be given below in the Mahā-Ummagga Birth[1].

Buddhist attributing it to want of government support, while the Lama thought it was because this is a waning period in religion; but as the waxing follows the waning he looked forward to a revival. (*Baptist Missionary Herald*, 1890.)

[1] No. 538 in Westergaard's Catalogue.

No. 171.

KALYĀṆA-DHAMMA-JĀTAKA[1].

"*O king, when people hail us,*" *etc.*—This story the Master told in Jetavana, about a deaf mother-in-law.

It is said that there was a squire in Sāvatthi, one of the faith, a true believer, who had fled to the Three Refuges, endowed with the Five Virtues. One day he set out to listen to the Master at Jetavana, bearing plenteous ghee and condiments of all sorts, flowers, perfumes, etc. At the same time, his wife's mother started to visit her daughter, and brought a present of solid food and gruel. She was a little hard of hearing.

After dinner—one feels a little drowsy after a meal—she said, by way of keeping herself awake—"Well, and does your husband live happily with you? do you agree together?" "Why, mother, what a thing to ask! you could hardly find a holy hermit who is so good and virtuous as he!" The good woman did not quite take in what her daughter said, but she caught the word—"Hermit" and cries she—"O dear, why has your husband turned hermit!" and a great to-do she made. Everybody who lived in that house heard it, and cried, "News—the squire has turned hermit!" People heard the noise, and a crowd gathered at the door to find out what it was. "The squire who lives here has turned hermit!" was all they heard.

Our Squire listened to the Buddha's sermon, then left the monastery to return to the city. Midway a man met him, who cried—"Why, master, they do say you've turned hermit, and all your family and servants are crying at home!" [64] Then these thoughts passed through his mind. "People say I have turned hermit when I have done nothing of the kind. A lucky speech must not be neglected; this day a hermit I must be." Then and there he turned right round, and went back to the Master. "You paid your visit to the Buddha," the Master said, "and went away. What brings you back here again?" The man told him about it, adding, "A lucky speech, Sir, must not be neglected. So here I am, and I wish to become a hermit." Then he received the lesser and the greater orders, and lived a good life; and very soon he attained to sainthood.

The story got known amongst the community. One day they were discussing it all together in the Hall of Truth, on this fashion: "I say, friend, Squire So-and-so took orders because he said 'a lucky speech must never be neglected,' and now he has attained to sainthood!" The Master came in and wanted to know what it was they were talking about. They told him. Said he, "Brethren, wise men in days long past also entered the Brotherhood because they said that a lucky speech must never be neglected;" and then he told them a story of olden days.

Once upon a time, when Brahmadatta was king of Benares, the Bodhisatta came into the world as a rich merchant's son; and when he grew up and his father died he took his father's place.

Once he had gone to pay his respects to the king: and his mother-in-law came on a visit to her daughter. She was a little hard of hearing, and all happened just as it has happened now. The husband was on

[1] No. 20 in Jātaka-Mālā: *Çreṣṭhi-jātaka.*

his way back from paying his respects to the king, when he was met by a man, who said, "They say you have turned hermit, and there's such a hullabaloo in your house!" The Bodhisatta, thinking that lucky words must never be neglected, turned right round and went back to the king. The king asked what brought him back again. "My lord," said he, "all my people are bewailing me, as I am told, because I have turned hermit, when I have done nothing of the kind. But lucky words must not be neglected, and a hermit I will be. I crave your permission to become a hermit!" And he explained the circumstances by the following verses: [65]

"O king, when people hail us by the name
Of holy, we must make our acts the same:
We must not waver nor fall short of it;
We must take up the yoke for very shame.

"O king, this name has been bestowed on me:
To-day they cry how holy I must be:
Therefore I would a hermit live and die;
I have no taste for joy and revelry."

Thus did the Bodhisatta ask the king's leave to embrace the religious life. Then he went away to the Himalayas, and becoming an ascetic he cultivated the Faculties and the Attainments and at last came to Brahma's heaven.

The Master, having ended this discourse, identified the Birth: "Ānanda was king in those days, and I myself was the rich Benares merchant."

No. 172.

DADDARA-JĀTAKA[1].

"*Who is it with a mighty cry, etc.*"—This is a story which the Master told at Jetavana about one Kokālika. At this time we hear that there were a number of very learned Brethren in the district of Manosilā, who spoke out like young lions, loud enough to bring down the heavenly Ganges[2], [66] while reciting passages of scripture before the Community. As they recited their texts, Kokālika (not knowing what an empty fool he showed himself) thought he would like to do the same. So he went about among the Brethren, not however taking the Name upon him, but saying, "They don't ask me to recite a piece of scripture. If

[1] Fausbøll, *Five Jātakas*, p. 45 (not translated); below, Nos. 188 and 189.
[2] The Milky Way. See the *Introd. Story* to No. 1, above.

they were to ask me, I would do it." All the Community got to know of it; and they thought they would try him. "Friend Kokālika," said they, "give the Community a recital of some scriptures to-day." To this he agreed, not knowing his folly; that day he would recite before the Community.

He first partook of gruel made to his liking, ate some food, and had some of his favourite soup. At sundown the gong sounded for sermon time; all the community gathered together. The 'yellow robe' which he put on was blue as a bluebell; his outer robe was pure white. Thus clad, he entered the meeting, greeted the Elders, stepped up to a Preaching Seat under a grand jewelled pavilion, holding an elegantly carved fan, and sat down, ready to begin his recitation. But just at that moment beads of sweat began to start out all over him, and he felt ashamed. The first verse of the first stanza he repeated; but what came next he could not think. So rising from the seat in confusion, he passed out through the meeting, and sought his own cell. Some one else, a real scholar, recited the Scripture. After that all the Brethren knew how empty he was.

One day the Brethren fell a talking of it in the Hall of Truth: "Friend, it was not easy to see formerly how empty Kokālika is; but now he has given tongue of his own accord, and shown it." The Master entered, and asked what they were discussing together. They told him. He said—"Brethren, this is not the first time Kokālika has betrayed himself by his voice; the very same thing happened before;" and then he told them an old-world tale.

Once upon a time, when Brahmadatta was reigning in Benares, the Bodhisatta was born as a young Lion, [67] and was the king of many lions. With a suite of lions he dwelt in Silver Cave. Near by was a Jackal, living in another cave.

One day, after a shower of rain, all the Lions were together at the entrance of their leader's cave, roaring loudly and gambolling about as lions use. As they were thus roaring and playing, the Jackal too lifted up his voice. "Here's this Jackal, giving tongue along with us!" said the Lions; they felt ashamed, and were silent. When they all fell silent, the Bodhisatta's cub asked him this question. "Father, all these Lions that were roaring and playing about have fallen silent for very shame on hearing yon creature. What creature is it that betrays itself thus by its voice?" and he repeated the first stanza:

"Who is it with a mighty cry makes Daddara resound?
Who is it, Lord of Beasts? and why has he no welcome found?"

At his son's words the old Lion repeated the second stanza:

"The Jackal, of all beasts most vile, 'tis he that makes that sound:
The Lions loathe his baseness, while they sit in silence round."

"Brethren," the Master added, "'tis not the first time Kokālika has betrayed himself by his voice; it was just the same before;" and bringing his discourse to an end, he identified the Birth: "At that time Kokālika was the Jackal, Rāhula was the young lion, and I was myself the Lion king."

No. 173.

MAKKAṬA-JĀTAKA.

[68] "*Father, see! a poor old fellow,*" *etc.*—This story the Master told whilst staying in Jetavana, about a rogue.—The circumstances will be explained in the Uddāla Birth[1], Book XIV. Here too the Master said, "Brethren, not this once only has the fellow turned out a rogue; in days of yore, when he was a monkey, he played tricks for the sake of a fire." And he told a tale of days long gone by.

Once upon a time, when Brahmadatta was reigning in Benares, the Bodhisatta was born in a brahmin family in a village of Kāsi. When he came of years, he received his education at Takkasilā, and settled down in life.

His lady in time bore him a son; and when the child could just run to and fro, she died. The husband performed her obsequies, and then, said he, "What is home to me now? I and my son will live the life of hermits." Leaving his friends and kindred in tears, he took the lad to the Himalaya, became a religious anchorite, and lived on the fruits and roots which the forest yielded.

On a day during the rainy season, when there had been a downpour, he kindled some sticks, and lay down on a pallet, warming himself at the fire. And his son sat beside him chafing his feet.

Now a wild Monkey, miserable with cold, spied the fire in the leaf-hut of our hermit. "Now," thought he, "suppose I go in: they'll cry out Monkey! Monkey! and beat me back: I shan't get a chance of warming myself.—I have it!" he cried. "I'll get an ascetic's dress, and get inside by a trick!" So he put on the bark dress of a dead ascetic, lifted his basket and crooked stick, and took his stand by the hut door, where he crouched down beside a palm tree. The lad saw him, and cried to his father (not knowing he was a monkey) "Here's an old hermit, sure enough, miserably cold, come to warm himself at the fire." [69] Then he addressed his father in the words of the first stanza, begging him to let the poor fellow in to warm himself:

"Father, see! a poor old fellow huddled by a palmtree there!
Here we have a hut to live in; let us give the man a share."

[1] No. 487.

When the Bodhisatta heard this, up he got and went to the door. But when he saw the creature was only a monkey, he said, "My son, men have no such face as that; 'tis a monkey, and he must not be asked in here." Then he repeated the second stanza:

"He would but defile our dwelling if he came inside the door;
Such a face—'tis easy telling—no good brahmin ever bore."

The Bodhisatta seized a brand, crying—"What do you want there?"—threw it at him, and drove him away. Mr Monkey dropt his bark garments, sprang up a tree, and buried himself in the forest.

Then the Bodhisatta cultivated the Four Excellences until he came unto Brahma's heaven.

When the Master had ended this discourse, he identified the Birth: "This tricky Brother was the Monkey of those days; Rāhula[1] was the hermit's son, and I myself was the hermit."

No. 174.

DŪBHIYA-MAKKAṬA-JĀTAKA.

[70] "*Plenty of water,*" *etc.*—This story the Master told in his sojourn at Veluvana, about Devadatta. One day it happened that the Brethren were talking in the Hall of Truth about Devadatta's ingratitude and treachery to his friends, when the Master broke in, "Not this once only, Brethren, has Devadatta been ungrateful and treacherous to his own friends. He was just the same before." Then he told them an old story.

Once upon a time, when Brahmadatta was king of Benares, the Bodhisatta was born into a brahmin family in a certain Kāsi village, and when he grew of age, married and settled down. Now in those days there was a certain deep well by the highway in Kāsi-land, which had no way

[1] Gotama Buddha's son.

down to it. The people who passed by that way, to win merit, used to draw water by a long rope and a bucket, and fill a trough for the animals; thus they gave the animals water to drink. All around lay a mighty forest, wherein troops of monkeys dwelt.

It happened by a chance that for two or three days the supply of water ceased which wayfarers used to draw; and the creatures could get nothing to drink. A Monkey, tormented with thirst, walked up and down by the well looking for water.

Now the Bodhisatta came that way on some errand, drew water for himself, drank it, and washed his hands; then he noticed our Monkey. Seeing how thirsty he was, the traveller drew water from the well and filled the trough for him. Then he sat down under a tree, to see what the creature would do.

The Monkey drank, sat down near, and pulled a monkey-grimace, to frighten the Bodhisatta. "Ah, you bad monkey!" said he, at this—"when you were thirsty and miserable, [71] I gave you plenty of water; and now you make monkey-faces at me. Well, well, help a rascal and you waste your pains." And he repeated the first stanza:

"Plenty of water did I give to you
When you were chafing hot and thirsty too:
Now full of mischief you sit chattering,—
With wicked people best have nought to do."

Then this spite-friend monkey replied, "I suppose you think that's all I can do. Now I'll drop something on your head before I go." Then, repeating the second stanza, he went on—

"A well-conducted monkey who did ever hear or see!
I leave my droppings on your head; for such our manners be."

As soon as he heard this the Bodhisatta got up to go. But at the very instant this Monkey from the branch where he sat dropt it like a festoon upon his head; and then made off into the forest shrieking. The Bodhisatta washed, and went his way.

---

[72] When the Master had ended this discourse, after saying "It is not only now that Devadatta is so, but in former days also he would not acknowledge a kindness which I showed him," he identified the Birth: "Devadatta was the Monkey then, and the brahmin was I myself."

No. 175.

ĀDICCUPAṬṬHĀNA-JĀTAKA.

"*There is no tribe,*" *etc.*—This is a story told by the Master in Jetavana, about a rogue.

Once upon a time, when Brahmadatta was reigning in Benares, the Bodhisatta was born in a brahmin family of Kāsi. Coming of years, he went to Takkasilā, and there completed his education. Then he embraced the religious life, cultivated the Faculties and the Attainments, and becoming the preceptor of a large band of pupils he spent his life in Himalaya.

There for a long time he abode; until once having to buy salt and seasoning, he came down from the highlands to a border village, where he stayed in a leaf-hut. When they were absent seeking alms, a mischievous monkey used to enter the hermitage, and turn everything upside down, spill the water out of the jars, smash the jugs, and finish by making a mess in the cell where the fire was.

The rains over, the anchorites thought of returning, and took leave of the villagers; "for now," they thought, "the flowers and fruit are ripening on the mountains." "To-morrow," was the answer, "we will come to your dwelling with our alms; you shall eat before you go." So next day they brought thither plenty of food, solid and liquid. The monkey thought to himself, "I'll trick these people and cajole them into giving me some food too." So he put on the air of a holy man seeking alms, [73] and close by the anchorites he stood, worshipping the sun. When the people saw him, they thought, "Holy are they who live with the holy," and repeated the first stanza:

"There is no tribe of animals but hath its virtuous one:
See how this wretched monkey here stands worshipping the sun!"

After this fashion the people praised our monkey's virtues. But the Bodhisatta, observing it, replied, "You don't know the ways of a mischievous monkey, or you would not praise one who little deserves praise;" adding the second stanza:

"You praise this creature's character because you know him not;
He has defiled the sacred fire, and broke each waterpot."

When the people heard what a rascally monkey it was, seizing sticks and clods they pelted him, and gave their alms to the Brethren. The sages returned to Himalaya; and without once interrupting their mystic ecstasy they came at last to Brahma's heaven.

At the end of this discourse, the Master identified the Birth: "This hypocrite was in those days the Monkey; the Buddha's followers were the company of sages; and their leader was I myself."

No. 176.

KALĀYA-MUṬṬHI-JĀTAKA.

[74] "*A foolish monkey*," *etc.*—This story the Master told at Jetavana, about a king of Kosala.

One rainy season, disaffection broke out on his borders. The troops stationed there, after two or three battles in which they failed to conquer their adversaries, sent a message to the king. Spite of the season, spite of the rains he took the field, and encamped before Jetavana Park. Then he began to ponder. "'Tis a bad season for an expedition; every crevice and hollow is full of water; the road is heavy: I'll go visit the Master. He will be sure to ask 'whither away'; then I'll tell him. It is not only in things of the future life that our Master protects me, but he protects in the things which we now see. So if my going is not to prosper, he will say 'It is a bad time to go, Sire'; but if I am to prosper, he will say nothing." So into the Park he came, and after greeting the Master sat down on one side.

"Whence come you, O King," asked the Master, "at this unseasonable hour?" "Sir," he replied, "I am on my way to quell a border rising; and I come first to bid you farewell." To this the Master said, "So it happened before, that mighty monarchs, before setting out for war, have listened to the word of the wise, and turned back from an unseasonable expedition." Then, at the king's request, he told an old story.

Once upon a time, when Brahmadatta was reigning in Benares, he had a Councillor who was his right-hand man and gave him advice in things spiritual and temporal. There was a rising on the frontier, and the troops there stationed sent the king a letter. The king started, rainy season though it was, and formed a camp in his park. The Bodhisatta stood before the king. At that moment the people had steamed some peas for the horses, and poured them out into a trough. One of the monkeys that lived in the park jumped down from a tree, filled his mouth and hands with the peas, then up again, and sitting down in the tree he began to eat. As he ate, one pea fell from his hand upon the ground. Down dropped at once all the peas from his hands and mouth, [75] and down from the tree he came, to hunt for the lost pea. But that pea he could not find; so he climbed up his tree again, and sat still, very glum, looking like some one who had lost a thousand in some lawsuit.

The king observed how the monkey had done, and pointed it out to the Bodhisatta. "Friend, what do you think of that?" he asked. To which the Bodhisatta made answer: "King, this is what fools of little wit are wont to do; they spend a pound to win a penny;" and he went on to repeat the first stanza:

"A foolish monkey, living in the trees,
O king, when both his hands were full of peas,
Has thrown them all away to look for one:
There is no wisdom, Sire, in such as these."

Then the Bodhisatta approached the king, and addressing him again, repeated the second stanza:

"Such are we, O mighty monarch, such all those that greedy be;
Losing much to gain a little, like the monkey and the pea."

[76] On hearing this address the king turned and went straight back to Benares. And the outlaws hearing that the king had set forth from his capital to make mincemeat of his enemies, hurried away from the borders.

At the time when this story was told, the outlaws ran away in just the same fashion. The king, after listening to the Master's utterances, rose and took his leave, and went back to Sāvatthi.

The Master, after this discourse was at an end, identified the Birth: "In those days Ānanda was the king, and the wise councillor was I myself."

No. 177.

TIṆḌUKA-JĀTAKA.

"*All around us see them stand,*" *etc.*—This is a story told by the Master whilst at Jetavana, about perfect knowledge. As in the Mahābodhi Birth[1], and the Ummagga Birth[2], on hearing his own knowledge praised, he remarked, "Not this once only is the Buddha wise, but wise he was before and fertile in all resource;" and told the following old story.

Once upon a time, when Brahmadatta was king in Benares, the Bodhisatta was born as a Monkey, and with a troop of eighty thousand monkeys he lived in Himalaya. Not far off was a village, sometimes inhabited and sometimes empty. And in the midst of this village was a tiṇḍuka[3] tree, with sweet fruit, covered with twigs and branches. When the place was empty, all the monkeys used to go thither and eat the fruit.

Once, in the fruit time, the village was full of people, a bamboo palisade set about it, and the gates guarded. And this tree [77] stood with all its boughs bending beneath the weight of the fruit. The monkeys began to wonder: "There's such and such a village, where we used to get fruit to eat. I wonder has that tree fruit upon it or no; are the people there or no?" At last they sent a scout monkey to spy. He found that there was fruit on the tree, and the village was crammed with people. When the monkeys heard that there was fruit on the tree, they determined to get that sweet fruit to eat; and waxing bold, a crowd of them went and told their chief. The chief asked was the village full or empty; full, they said. "Then you must not go," said he, "because men are very deceitful." "But, Sire, we'll go at midnight, when everybody is fast asleep, and then eat!" So this great company obtained leave of their chief, and came down from the mountains, and waited on a great rock hard by until the people retired to rest; in the middle watch, when people were asleep, they climbed the tree and began eating of the fruit.

A man had to get up in the night for some necessary purpose; he went out into the village, and there he saw the monkeys. At once he gave the alarm; out the people came, armed with bow and quiver, or holding any

[1] No. 528.
[2] No. 538 (*Westergaard*).
[3] Diospyros Embryopteris (*Childers*).

sort of weapon that came to hand, sticks, or lumps of earth, and surrounded the tree; "when dawn comes," thought they, "we have them!"

The eighty thousand monkeys saw these people, and were scared to death. Thought they, "No help have we but our Chief only;" so to him they came, and recited the first stanza:

"All around us see them stand, warriors armed with bow and quiver,
All around us, sword in hand: who is there who can deliver?"

[78] At this the monkey Chief answered: "Fear not; human beings have plenty to do. It is the middle watch now; there they stand, thinking—'We'll kill them!' but we will find some other business to hinder this business of theirs." And to console the Monkeys he repeated the second stanza:

"Men have many things to do; something will disperse the meeting;
See what still remains for you; eat, while fruit is left for eating."

The Great Being comforted the monkey troop. If they had not had this crumb of comfort they would have broken their hearts and perished. When the Great Being had consoled the monkeys, he cried, "Assemble all the monkeys together!" But in assembling them, there was one they could not find, his nephew, a monkey named Senaka. So they told him that Senaka was not among the troop. "If Senaka is not here," said he, "have no fear; he will find a way to help you."

Now at the time when the troop sallied forth, Senaka had been asleep. Later he awoke, and could not see any body about. So he followed their tracks, and by and bye he saw all the people hastening up. "Some danger for our troop," thought he. Just then he spied, in a hut on the outskirts of the village, an old woman, fast asleep, before a lighted fire. And making as though he were a village child going out to the fields, Senaka seized a firebrand, [79] and standing well to windward, set light to the village. Then did every man leave the monkeys, and hurried up to quench the fire. So the monkeys scampered away, and each brought one fruit for Senaka.

When this discourse came to an end, the Master identified the Birth: "Mahānāma Sakka was the nephew Senaka of those days; Buddha's followers were the monkey troop; and I myself was their Chief."

No. 178.

KACCHAPA-JĀTAKA.

"*Here was I born*," *etc.*—This story the Master told in Jetavana, how a man got rid of malaria[1].

It is said that malarial fever once broke out in a family of Sāvatthi. The parents said to their son: "Don't stay in this house, son; make a hole in the wall and escape somewhere, and save your life[2]. Then come back again—in this place a great hoard is buried; dig it up, and restore the family fortunes, and a happy life to you!" The young fellow did as he was bid; he broke through the wall, and made his escape. When his complaint was cured, he returned and dug the treasure up, with which he set up his household.

One day, laden with oil and ghee, clothes and raiment, and other offerings, he repaired to Jetavana, and greeted the Master, and took his seat. The Master entered into converse with him. "We hear," said he, "that you had cholera in your house. How did you escape it?" He told the Master all about it. Said he, "In days of yore, as now, friend layman, when danger arose, there were people who were too fond of home to leave it, and they perished thereby; while those who were not too fond of it, but departed elsewhere, saved themselves alive." And then at his request the Master told an old-world story.

Once on a time, when Brahmadatta was reigning in Benares, the Bodhisatta was born in a village as a potter's son. He plied the potter's trade, and had a wife and family to support.

At that time there lay a great natural lake close by the great river of Benares. When there was much water, river and lake were one; but when the water was low, [80] they were apart. Now fish and tortoises know by instinct when the year will be rainy and when there will be a drought. So at the time of our story the fish and tortoises which lived in that lake knew there would be a drought; and when the two were one water, they swam out of the lake into the river. But there was one Tortoise that would not go into the river, because, said he, "here I was born, and here I have grown up, and here is my parents' home: leave it I cannot!"

[1] *ahivātarogo* occurs in the Comm. on *Therīgāthā* (*P. T. S.* 1893), p. 120, line 20, but no hint as to its meaning is given. The word should mean, "snake-wind-disease," perhaps malarial fever, which e.g. in the Terai is believed to be due to snake's breath. Or is it possible that *ahi*, which may mean the navel, could here be the bowels, and some such disease as cholera be meant?

[2] It is noteworthy that here the same means is used to outwit the spirit of disease as is often taken to outwit the ghosts of the dead; who might be supposed to guard the door, but not the parts of the house where there was no outlet.

Then in the hot season the water all dried up. He dug a hole and buried himself, just in the place where the Bodhisatta was used to come for clay. There the Bodhisatta came to get some clay; with a big spade he dug down, till he cracked the tortoise' shell, turning him out on the ground as though he were a large piece of clay. In his agony the creature thought, "Here I am, dying, all because I was too fond of my home to leave it!" and in the words of these verses following he made his moan:—

"Here was I born, and here I lived; my refuge was the clay;
And now the clay has played me false in a most grievous way;
Thee, thee I call, O Bhaggava[1]; hear what I have to say!

"Go where thou canst find happiness, where'er the place may be;
Forest or village, there the wise both home and birthplace see;
Go where there's life; nor stay at home for death to master thee."

[81] So he went on and on, talking to the Bodhisatta, till he died. The Bodhisatta picked him up, and collecting all the villagers addressed them thus: "Look at this tortoise. When the other fish and tortoises went into the great river, he was too fond of home to go with them, and buried himself in the place where I get my clay. Then as I was digging for clay, I broke his shell with my big spade, and turned him out on the ground in the belief that he was a large lump of clay. Then he called to mind what he had done, lamented his fate in two verses of poetry, and expired. So you see he came to his end because he was too fond of his home. Take care not to be like this tortoise. Don't say to yourselves, 'I have sight, I have hearing, I have smell, I have taste, I have touch, I have a son, I have a daughter, I have numbers of men and maids for my service, I have precious gold'; do not cleave to these things with craving and desire. Each being passes through three stages of existence[2]." Thus did he exhort the crowd with all a Buddha's skill. The discourse was bruited abroad all over India, and for full seven thousand years it was remembered. All the crowd abode by his exhortation; and gave alms and did good until at last they went to swell the hosts of heaven.

When the Master had made an end, he declared the Truths, and identified the Birth:—at the conclusion of the Truths the young man was established in the Fruit of the First Path:—saying, "Ananda was then the Tortoise, and the Potter was I myself."

[1] "Addressing the potter." Schol.

[2] World of Sense, World of Form, World of formless Existence.

No. 179.

SATADHAMMA-JĀTAKA.

[82] "*What a trifle,*" *etc.*—This story the Master told while sojourning in Jetavana, about the twenty-one unlawful ways of earning a livelihood.

At one time there were a great many Brethren who used to get a living by being physicians, or runners, doing errands on foot, exchanging alms for alms[1], and the like, the twenty-one unlawful callings. All this will be set forth in the Sāketa Birth[2]. When the Master found out that they got their living thus, he said, "Now there are a great many Brethren who get their living in unlawful ways. Those who get their living thus will not escape birth as goblins or disembodied spirits; they will become beasts of burden; they will be born in hell; for their benefit and blessing it is necessary to hold a discourse which bears its own moral clear and plain." So he summoned the Community together, and said, "Brethren, you must not win your necessaries by the one-and-twenty unlawful methods. Food won unlawfully is like a piece of redhot iron, like a deadly poison. These unlawful methods are blamed and rebuked by disciples of all Buddhas and Pacceka-Buddhas. For those who eat food gained by unlawful means there is no laughter and no joy. Food got in this way, in my religion, is like the leavings of one of the lowest caste. To partake of it, for a disciple of the Religion of the Good, is like partaking of the leavings of the vilest of mankind." And with these words, he told an old-world story.

Once upon a time, when Brahmadatta was king of Benares, the Bodhisatta was born as the son of a man of the lowest caste. When he grew up, he took the road for some purpose, taking for his provision some rice grains in a basket.

At that time there was a young fellow in Benares, named Satadhamma. He was the son of a magnifico, a Northern brahmin. He also took the road for some purpose, but neither rice grains nor basket had he. The two met upon the highway. Said the young brahmin to the other, "What caste are you of?" He replied, "Of the lowest. And what are you?" [83] "Oh, I am a Northern brahmin." "All right, let us journey together;" and so together they fared along. Breakfast time came. The Bodhisatta sat down where there was some nice water, and washed his hands, and opened his basket. "Will you have some?" said he. "Tut, tut," says the other, "I want none, you low fellow." "All right,"

[1] The offence meant is giving a share of alms on one day, and receiving the like the next day, to save the trouble of seeking alms daily.

[2] No. 237, which however only refers to no. 68.

says the Bodhisatta. Careful to waste none, he put as much as he wanted in a leaf apart from the rest, fastened up his basket, and ate. Then he took a drink of water, washed his hands and feet, and picked up the rest of his rice and food. "Come along, young Sir," says he, and they started off again on their journey.

All day they tramped along; and at evening they both had a bath in some nice water. When they came out, the Bodhisatta sat down in a nice place, undid his parcel, and began to eat. This time he did not offer the other a share. The young gentleman was tired with walking all day, and hungry to the bottom of his soul; there he stood, looking on, and thinking, "If he offers me any, I'll take it." But the other ate away without a word. "This low fellow," thought the young man, "eats every scrap without a word. Well, I'll beg a piece; I can throw away the outside, which is defiled, and eat the rest." And so he did; he ate what was left. As soon as he had eaten, he thought—"How I have disgraced my birth, my clan, my family! Why, I have eaten the leavings of a low born churl!" Keen indeed was his remorse; he threw up the food, and blood came with it. "Oh, what a wicked deed I have done," he wept, "all for the sake of a trifle!" and he went on in the words of the first stanza: [84]

"What a trifle! and his leavings! given too against his will!
And I am a highborn brahmin! and the stuff has made me ill!"

Thus did the young gentleman make his lamentation; adding, "Why did I do such a wicked thing just for life's sake?" He plunged into the jungle, and never let any eye see him again, but there he died forlorn.

When this story was ended, the Master repeated, "Just as the young brahmin, Brethren, after eating the leavings of a low-caste man, found that neither laughter nor joy was for him, because he had taken improper food; so whosoever has embraced this salvation, and gains a livelihood by unlawful means, when he eats the food and supports his life in any way that is blamed and disapproved by the Buddha, will find that there is no laughter and no joy for him." Then, becoming perfectly enlightened, he repeated the second stanza:—

"He that lives by being wicked, he that cares not if he sins,
Like the brahmin in the story, has no joy of what he wins."

[85] When this discourse was concluded, the Master declared the Truths and identified the Birth:—at the conclusion of the Truths many Brethren entered upon the Paths and the Fruit thereof:—saying, "At the time of the story I was the low-caste man."

No. 180.

DUDDADA-JĀTAKA.

"*'Tis hard to do as good men do," etc.*—This story the Master told whilst in Jetavana, about alms given in common. Two friends at Sāvatthi, young men of good position, made a collection, providing all the necessaries to give the Buddha and his followers. They invited them all, provided bounty for seven days, and on the seventh presented them with all their requisites. The eldest of these saluted the Master, and said, sitting beside him, "Sir, amongst the givers some gave much and some gave little; but let it bear much fruit for all alike." Then he offered the gift. The Master's reply was: "In giving these things to the Buddha and his followers, you, my lay friends, have done a great deed. In days of old wise men gave their bounty thus, and thus offered their gifts." Then at his request he told a story.

Once upon a time, when Brahmadatta was king of Benares, the Bodhisatta was born into a brahmin family of Kāsi. When he grew up, he was thoroughly educated at Takkasilā; after which he renounced the world, and took up the religious life, and with a band of disciples went to live in Himalaya. There he lived a long time.

Once having need to procure salt and seasoning, he went on pilgrimage through the country-side, and in course of it he arrived at Benares. There he settled in the king's park; and on the following morning he and his company went a-begging to some village outside the gates. The people gave him alms. Next day he sought alms in the city. The people were all glad to give him their alms. They clubbed together and made a collection; and provided plenty for the band of anchorites. After the presentation their spokesman offered his gift with the same words as above. The Bodhisatta replied, "Friend, where faith[1] is, no gift is small." And he returned his thanks in these verses following: [86]

"'Tis hard to do as good men do, to give as they can give,
Bad men can hardly imitate the life which good men live.

"And so, when good and evil go to pass away from earth,
The bad are born in hell below, in heaven the good have birth."

This was his thanksgiving. He remained in the place for the four months of the rains, and then returned to Himalaya; where he practised all the modes of holy meditation, and without a single interruption continued in them until he joined the hosts of heaven.

When this discourse came to an end the Master identified the Birth: "At that time," said he, "the Buddha's company was the body of ascetics, and I myself was their leader."

[1] *Citta-pasādo.*

No. 181.

ASADISA-JĀTAKA[1].

"*Prince Peerless, skilled in archers' craft,*" *etc.*—This story the Master told at Jetavana, about the Great Renunciation. The Master said, "Not now alone, Brethren, has the Tathāgata made the Great Renunciation: in other days he also renounced the white parasol of royalty, and did the same." And he told a story of the past.

---

[87] Once upon a time, when Brahmadatta was king of Benares, the Bodhisatta was conceived as the son of the Queen Consort. She was safely delivered; and on his nameday they gave him the name of Asadisa-Kumāra, Prince Peerless. About the time he was able to walk, the Queen conceived one who was also to be a wise being. She was safely delivered, and on the nameday they called the babe Brahmadatta-Kumāra, or Prince Heaven-sent.

When Prince Peerless was sixteen, he went to Takkasilā for his education. There at the feet of a world-famed teacher he learnt the Three Vedas and the Eighteen Accomplishments; in the science of archery he was peerless; then he returned to Benares.

When the king was on his deathbed he commanded that Prince Peerless should be king in his stead, and Prince Brahmadatta heir apparent. Then he died; after which the kingship was offered to Peerless, who refused, saying that he cared not for it. So they consecrated Brahmadatta to be king by sprinkling him. Peerless cared nothing for glory, and wanted nothing.

While the younger brother ruled, Peerless lived in all royal state. The slaves came and slandered him to his brother; "Prince Peerless wants to be king!" said they. Brahmadatta believed them, and allowed himself to be deceived; he sent some men to take Peerless prisoner.

One of Prince Peerless' attendants told him what was afoot. He waxed angry with his brother, and went away into another country. When he was arrived there, he sent in word to the king that an archer was come, and awaited him. "What wages does he ask?" the king enquired. "A hundred thousand a year." "Good," said the king; "let him enter."

[1] Hardy, *Manual of Buddhism*, 114. The latter part of the story is given very briefly in *Mahāvastu* 2. 82—3, *Çarakṣepana Jātaka*. It is figured on the Bharhut Stupa, see Cunningham, p. 70, and plate XXVII. 13; and on the Sanchi Tope, see Fergusson, *Tree and Serpent Worship*, pl. XXXVI. p. 181.

Peerless came into the presence, and stood waiting. "Are you the archer?" asked the king. "Yes, Sire." "Very well, I take you into my service." After that Peerless remained in the service of this king. [88] But the old archers were annoyed at the wage which was given him; "Too much," they grumbled.

One day it so happened that the king went out into his park. There, at foot of a mango tree, where a screen had been put up before a certain stone seat of ceremony, he reclined upon a magnificent couch. He happened to look up, and there right at the treetop he saw a cluster of mango fruit. "It is too high to climb for," thought he; so summoning his archers, he asked them whether they could cut off yon cluster with an arrow, and bring it down for him. "Oh," said they, "that is not much for us to do. But your majesty has seen our skill often enough. The newcomer is so much better paid than we, that perhaps you might make him bring down the fruit."

Then the king sent for Peerless, and asked him if he could do it. "Oh yes, your Majesty, if I may choose my position." "What position do you want?" "The place where your couch stands." The king had the couch removed, and gave place.

Peerless had no bow in his hand; he used to carry it underneath his body-cloth; so he must needs have a screen. The king ordered a screen to be brought and spread for him, and our archer went in. He doffed the white cloth which he wore over all, and put on a red cloth next his skin; then he fastened his girdle, and donned a red waistcloth. From a bag he took out a sword in pieces, which he put together and girt on his left side. Next he put on a mailcoat of gold, fastened his bow-case over his back, and took out his great ramshorn bow, made in several pieces, which he fitted together, fixed the bowstring, red as coral; put a turban upon his head; twirling the arrow with his nails, he threw open the screen and came out, looking like a serpent prince just emerging from the riven ground. He went to the place of shooting, arrow set to bow, and then put this question to the king. "Your Majesty," said he, "am I to bring this fruit down with an upward shot, [89] or by dropping the arrow upon it?"

"My son," said the king, "I have often seen a mark brought down by the upward shot, but never one taken in the fall. You had better make the shaft fall on it."

"Your Majesty," said the archer, "this arrow will fly high. Up to the heaven of the Four Great Kings it will fly, and then return of itself. You must please be patient till it returns." The king promised. Then the archer said again, "Your Majesty, this arrow in its upshot will pierce the stalk exactly in the middle; and when it comes down, it will not swerve a hair's-breadth either way, but hit the same spot to a nicety, and bring down the cluster with it." Then he sped the arrow forth swiftly. As the arrow went up it pierced the exact centre of the mango stalk. By the time the archer knew his arrow had reached the place of the Four Great Kings, he let fly another arrow with greater speed than the first. This struck the feather of the first arrow, and turned it back; then itself went up as far as the heaven of the Thirty-three Archangels. There the deities caught and kept it.

The sound of the falling arrow as it cleft the air was as the sound of a thunderbolt. "What is that noise?" asked every man. "That is the arrow falling," our archer replied. The bystanders were all frightened to death, for fear the arrow should fall on them; but Peerless comforted them. "Fear nothing," said he, "and I will see that it does not fall on the earth." Down came the arrow, not a hairbreadth out either way, but neatly cut through the stalk of the mango cluster. The archer caught the arrow in one hand and the fruit in the other, so that they should not fall upon the ground. "We never saw such a thing before!" cried the onlookers, at this marvel. [90] How they praised the great man! how they cheered and clapped and snapped their fingers, thousands of kerchiefs waving in the air! In their joy and delight the courtiers gave presents to Peerless amounting to ten millions of money. And the king too showered gifts and honours upon him like rain.

While the Bodhisatta was receiving such glory and honour at the hands of this king, seven kings, who knew that there was no Prince Peerless in Benares, drew a leaguer around the city, and summoned its king to fight or yield. The king was frightened out of his life. "Where is my brother?" he asked. "He is in the service of a neighbouring king," was the reply. "If my dear brother does not come," said he, "I am a dead man. Go, fall at his feet in my name, appease him, bring him hither!" His messengers came and did their errand. Peerless took leave of his master, and returned to Benares. He comforted his brother and bade him fear nothing; then scratched[1] a message upon an arrow to this effect: "I, Prince Peerless, am returned. I mean to kill you all with one arrow which I will shoot at you. Let those who care for life make their escape." This he shot so that it fell upon the very middle of a golden dish, from which the seven kings were eating together. When they read the writing they all fled, half-dead with fright.

Thus did our Prince put to flight seven kings, without shedding even so much blood as a little fly might drink; then, looking upon his younger brother, he renounced his lusts, and forsook the world, cultivated the Faculties and the Attainments, and at his life's end came to Brahma's heaven.

---

[1] In the *Mahāvastu* it is wrapt round it (2. p. 82. 14, *pariveṭhitvā*); so in Hardy.

[91] "And this is the way," said the Master, "that Prince Peerless routed seven kings and won the battle; after which he took up the religious life." Then becoming perfectly enlightened he uttered these two verses:

"Prince Peerless, skilled in archers' craft, a doughty chief was he;
Swift as the lightning sped his shaft great warriors' bane to be.

"Among his foes what havoc done! yet hurt he not a soul;
He saved his brother; and he won the grace of self-control."

[92] When the Master had ended this discourse, he identified the Birth: "Ānanda was then the younger brother, and I was myself the elder."

No. 182.

SAṀGĀMĀVACARA-JĀTAKA.

"*O Elephant, a hero thou*," *etc.*—This story the Master told while staying at Jetavana, about Elder Nanda.

The Master, on his first return to Kapila city, had received into the Community Prince Nanda, his younger brother, and after returned to Sāvatthi and stayed there. Now Father Nanda, remembering how as he was leaving his home, after taking the Bowl, in the Master's company, Janapadakalyāṇī was looking out of a window, with her hair half combed, and she said—"Why, Prince Nanda is off with the Master!—Come back soon, dear lord!"—remembering this, I say, grew downcast and despondent, yellower and yellower, and the veins stood knotted over his skin.

When the Master learnt of this, he thought, "What if I could establish Nanda in sainthood!" To Nanda's cell he went, and sat on the seat which was offered him. "Well, Nanda," he asked, "are you content with our teaching?" "Sir," replied Nanda, "I am in love with Janapadakalyāṇī, and I am not content." "Have you been on pilgrimage in the Himalaya, Nanda?" "No, Sir, not yet." "Then we will go." "But, Sir, I have no miraculous power; how can I go?" "I will take you, Nanda." So saying, the Master took him by the hand, and thus passed through the air.

On the way they passed over a burnt field. There, upon the charred stump of a tree, with nose and tail half gone, hair scorched off, and hide a cinder, nothing but skin, all covered with blood, sat a she-monkey. "Do you see that monkey, Nanda?" the Master asked. "Yes, Sir." "Take a good look at her," said he. Then he pointed out, stretching over sixty leagues, the uplands of Manosilā, the seven great lakes, Anotatta and the rest, the five great rivers, the whole Himalaya highlands, with the magnificent hills named of Gold, of Silver, and of Gems, and hundreds of other lovely spots. Next he asked, "Nanda, have you ever seen the abode of the Thirty-three Archangels?" [93] "No, Sir, never," was the reply. "Come along, Nanda," said he, "and I will show you the abode of the Thirty-three." Therewith he brought him to the Yellowstone Throne[1], and made him sit on it. Sakka, king of the gods in two heavens, came with his host

[1] The throne of Sakka (Indra).

of gods, gave greeting and sat down on one side. His handmaids to the number of twenty-five million, and five hundred nymphs with doves' feet, came and made greeting, then sat down on one side. The Master made Nanda look at these five hundred nymphs again and again, with desire after them. "Nanda," said he, "do you see these dove's-foot nymphs?" "Yes, Sir." "Well, which is prettiest—they or Janapadakalyāṇī?" "Oh, Sir! as that wretched ape was in comparison with Janapadakalyāṇī, so is she compared with these!" "Well, Nanda, what are you going to do?" "How is it possible, Sir, to win these nymphs?" "By living as an ascetic, Sir," said the Master, "one may win these nymphs." The lad said, "If the Blessed One pledges his word that an ascetic life will win these nymphs, an ascetic life I will lead." "Agreed, Nanda, I pledge my word." "Well, Sir," said he, "don't let us make a long business of it. Let us be off, and I will become an ascetic."

The Master brought him to Jetavana back again. The Elder began to follow the ascetic life.

The Master recounted to Sāriputta, the Captain of the Faith, how his younger brother had made him pledge himself in the midst of the gods in the heaven of the Thirty-three about the nymphs. In the same manner, he told the story to Elder Mahāmoggallāna, to Elder Mahākassapa, to Elder Anuruddha, to Elder Ānanda, the Treasurer of the Faith, eighty great disciples in all; and then, one after the other, he told it to the other Brethren. The Captain of the Faith, Elder Sāriputta, asked Elder Nanda, "Is it true, as I hear, friend, that you have the Buddha's pledged word that you shall win the nymphs of the gods in the heaven of the Thirty-three, by passing your life as an ascetic? Then," he went on, "is not your holy life all bound up with womankind and lust? If you live chaste just for the sake of women, what is the difference between you and a labourer who works for hire?" [94] This saying quenched all the fire in him and made him ashamed of himself. In the same way all the eighty chief disciples, and all the rest of the Brethren, made this worthy father ashamed. "I have been wrong," thought he; in all shame and remorse, he screwed up his courage, and set to work to develope his spiritual insight. Soon he attained to sainthood. He came to the Master, and said, "Sir, I release the Blessed One from his promise." The Master said, "If you have attained sainthood, Nanda, I am thereby released from my promise."

When the Brethren heard of this, they began to talk it over in their Hall of Truth. "How docile yon Elder Nanda is, to be sure! Why, friend, one word of advice awakened his sense of shame; at once he began to live as an ascetic and now he is a Saint!" The Master came in, and asked what they were talking about together. They told him. "Brethren," said he, "Nanda was just as docile in former days as he is now;" and then he told them a story.

Once upon a time when Brahmadatta was reigning in Benares, the Bodhisatta was born as an elephant-trainer's son. When he grew up, he was carefully taught all that pertains to the training of elephants. He was in the service of a king who was an enemy to the king of Benares. He trained this king's elephant of state to perfection.

The king determined to capture Benares. Mounting upon his state elephant, he led a mighty host against Benares, and laid siege to it. Then he sent a letter to the king of the city: "Fight, or yield!" The king chose to fight. Walls and gates, towers and battlements he manned with a great host, and defied the foe.

The hostile king armed his state elephant, and clad himself in armour, took a sharp goad in his hand, and drove his beast city-wards; "Now," said he, "I'll storm this city, and kill my enemy, and get his realms into my hands!" But at sight of the defenders, who cast boiling mud, and stones from their catapults, and all kinds of missiles, the elephant was scared out of his wits and would not come near the place. Thereupon up came the trainer, crying, "Son, a hero like you is quite at home in the battle-field! [95] in such a place it is disgraceful to turn tail!" And to encourage his elephant, he uttered these two verses:

"O Elephant, a hero thou, whose home is in the field:
There stands the gate before thee now: why dost thou turn and yield?

"Make haste! break through the iron bar, and beat the pillars down!
Crash through the gates, made fast for war, and enter in the town!"

The Elephant listened; one word of advice was enough to turn him. Winding his trunk about the shafts of the pillars, he tore them up like so many toadstools: he beat against the gateway, broke down the bars, and forcing his way through entered the city and won it for his king.

When the Master had finished this discourse, he identified the Birth:—"In those days Nanda was the Elephant, Ānanda was the king, and the trainer was I myself."

No. 183.

VĀLODAKA-JĀTAKA[1].

"*This sorry draught*," *etc.*—This story the Master told whilst at Jetavana, about five hundred persons who ate broken meat.

At Sāvatthi, we learn, were five hundred persons who had left the stumbling-block of a worldly life to their sons and daughters, [96] and lived all together sitting under the Master's preaching. Of these, some were in the First Path, some in the Second, some in the Third: not a single one but had embraced salvation. They that invited the Master invited these also. But they had five hundred pages waiting upon them, to bring them toothbrushes, mouth-water, and garlands of flowers; these lads used to eat their broken meat. After their meal, and a nap, they used to run down to the Aciravatī, and on the river bank they would wrestle like very Mallians[2], shouting all the time. But the five hundred lay brethren were quiet, made very little noise, courted solitude.

[1] The introductory story is varied in *Dhammapada*, Comm. p. 271.

[2] The Mallians were a tribe of professional wrestlers.

The Master happened to hear the pages shouting. "What is that noise, Ānanda?" he asked. "The pages, who eat the broken meat," was the reply. The Master said: "Ānanda, this is not the only time these pages have fed on broken meat, and made a great noise after it; they used to do the same in the olden days; and then too these lay brethren were just as quiet as they are now." So saying, at his request, the Master told a story of the past.

Once upon a time, when Brahmadatta was king of Benares, the Bodhisatta was born as the son of one of his courtiers, and became the king's adviser in all things both temporal and spiritual. Word came to the king of a revolt on the frontier. He ordered five hundred chargers to be got ready, and an army complete in its four parts[1]. With this he set out, and quelled the rising, after which he returned to Benares.

When he came home, he gave order, "As the horses are tired, let them have some juicy food, some grape-juice to drink." The steeds took this delicious drink, then retired to their stables and stood quietly each in his stall.

But there was a mass of leavings, with nearly all the goodness squeezed out of it. The keepers asked the king what to do with that. "Knead it up with water," was his command, "strain through a towel, and give it to the donkeys who carry the horses' provender." This wretched stuff the donkeys drank up. It maddened them, and they galloped about the palace yard braying loudly.

From an open window the king saw the Bodhisatta, and called out to him. [97] "Look there! how mad these donkeys are from that sorry drink! how they bray, how they caper! But those fine thorobreds that drank the strong liquor, they make no noise; they are perfectly quiet, and jump not at all. What is the meaning of this?" and he repeated the first stanza:—

"This sorry draught, the goodness all strained out[2],
Drives all these asses in a drunken rout:
The thorobreds, that drank the potent juice,
Stand silent, nor skip capering about."

And the Bodhisatta explained the matter in the second stanza:—

"The low-born churl, though he but taste and try,
Is frolicsome and drunken by and by:
He that is gentle keeps a steady brain
Even if he drain most potent liquor dry."

When the king had listened to the Bodhisatta's answer, he had the donkeys driven out of his courtyard. Then, abiding by the Bodhisatta's

[1] Elephants, horse, chariots, infantry.

[2] *Dhammapada*, p. 275.

advice, he gave alms and did good until he passed away to fare according to his deserts.

When this discourse was ended, the Master identified the Birth as follows:—"At that time these pages were the five hundred asses, these lay brethren were the five hundred thorobreds, Ānanda was the king, and the wise courtier was I myself."

No. 184.

GIRIDANTA-JĀTAKA.

[98] "*Thanks to the groom,*" *etc.*—This story the Master told while staying in Veḷuvana Park, about keeping bad company. The circumstances have been already recounted under the Mahilāmukha Jātaka[1]. Again, as before, the Master said: "In former days this Brother kept bad company just as he does now." Then he told an old story.

Once upon a time, there was a king named Sāma, the Black, reigning in Benares. In those days the Bodhisatta was one of a courtier's family, and grew up to be the king's temporal and spiritual adviser. Now the king had a state horse named Paṇḍava, and one Giridanta was his trainer, a lame man. The horse used to watch him as he tramped on and on in front, holding the halter; and knowing him to be his trainer, imitated him and limped too.

Somebody told the king how the horse was limping. The king sent surgeons. They examined the horse, but found him perfectly sound; and so accordingly made report. Then the king sent the Bodhisatta. "Go, friend," said he, "and find out all about it." He soon found out that the horse was lame because he went about with a lame trainer. So he told the king what it was. "It's a case of bad company," said he, and went on to repeat the first stanza:—

"Thanks to the groom, poor Paṇḍava is in a parlous state:
No more displays his former ways, but needs must imitate."

[1] No. 26.

"Well, now, my friend," said the king, "what's to be done?" "Get a good groom," replied the Bodhisatta, "and the horse will be as good as ever." Then he repeated the second stanza:—[99]

"Find but a fit and proper groom, on whom you can depend,
To bridle him and exercise, the horse will quickly mend;
His sorry plight will be set right; he imitates his friend."

The king did so. The horse became as good as before. The king showed great honour to the Bodhisatta, being pleased that he knew even the ways of animals.

The Master, when this discourse was ended, identified the Birth:—"Devadatta was Giridanta in those days; the Brother who keeps bad company was the horse; and the wise counsellor was I myself."

No. 185.

ANABHIRATI-JĀTAKA.

"*Thick, muddy water,*" *etc.*—This story the Master told while staying in Jetavana, and it was about a young brahmin.

A young brahmin, as they say, belonging to Sāvatthi, had mastered the Three Vedas, and used to teach sacred verses to a number of young brahmins and kshatriyas. In time he settled down as a married man. His thoughts being now busy with wealth and ornaments, serving men and serving women, lands and substance, kine and buffaloes, sons and daughters, he became subject to passion, error, folly. This obscured his wits, so that he forgot how to repeat his formulæ in due order, and every now and then the charms did not come clear in his mind. This man one day procured a quantity of flowers and sweet scents, and these he took to the Master in Jetavana Park. After his greeting, he sat down on one side. [100] The Master talked pleasantly to him. "Well, young Sir, you are a teacher of the sacred verses. Do you know them all by heart?" "Well, Sir, I used to know them all right, but since I married my mind has been darkened, and I don't know them any longer." "Ah, young Sir," the Master said, "just the same happened before; at first your mind was clear, and you knew all your verses perfectly, but when your mind was obscured by passions and lusts, you could no longer clearly see them." Then at his request the Master told the following story.

Once upon a time, when Brahmadatta was king of Benares, the Bodhisatta was born in the family of a brahmin magnifico. When he grew up, he studied under a far-famed teacher of Takkasilā, where he learnt all magic charms. After returning to Benares he taught these charms to a large number of brahmin and kshatriya youths.

Amongst these youths was one young brahmin who had learnt the Three Vedas by heart; he became a master of ritual[1], and could repeat the whole of the sacred texts without stumbling in a single line. By and bye he married and settled down. Then household cares clouded his mind, and no longer could he repeat the sacred verses.

One day his teacher paid him a visit. "Well, young Sir," he enquired, "do you know all your verses off by heart?" "Since I have been the head of a household," was the reply, "my mind has been clouded, and I cannot repeat them." "My son," said his teacher, "when the mind is clouded, no matter how perfectly the scriptures have been learnt, they will not stand out clear. But when the mind is serene there is no forgetting them." And thereupon he repeated the two verses following:—

"Thick, muddy water will not show
Fish or shell or sand or gravel that may lie below[2]:
So with a clouded wit:
Nor your nor other's good is seen in it.

"Clear, quiet waters ever show
All, be it fish or shell, that lies below; [101]
So with unclouded wit:
Both your and other's good shows clear in it."

When the Master had finished this discourse, he declared the Truths, and identified the Birth:—at the conclusion of the Truths the young brahmin entered upon the Fruit of the First Path:—"In those days, this youth was the young brahmin, and I was his teacher."

No. 186.

DADHI-VĀHANA-JĀTAKA[3].

"*Sweet was once the mango's savour,*" *etc.*—This story the Master told whilst dwelling in Jetavana, on the subject of keeping bad company. The circumstances were the same as above. Again the Master said: "Brethren, bad

[1] Or it may mean 'a pupil-teacher.'

[2] There is an irregularity in this stanza, the Pali having an extra line. I have reproduced this by making line 2 of an irregular length.

[3] Fausbøll, *Five Jātakas*, pp. 1 and 20; Rhys Davids, *Buddhist Birth Stories*, p. xvi. This tale belongs to the same group as Grimm no. 36, *The Wishing Table, the Gold-Ass*, and *the Cudgel in the Sack*; no. 54, *The Knapsack, the Hat and the Horn* (to which see the bibliographical note in Hunt's edition).

company is evil and injurious; why should one talk of the evil effects of bad company on human beings? In days long gone by, even a vegetable, a mango tree, whose sweet fruit was a dish fit for the gods, turned sour and bitter through the influence of a noisome and bitter nimb tree." Then he told a story.

Once upon a time, when Brahmadatta was reigning in Benares, four brahmins, brothers, of the land of Kāsi, left the world and became hermits; they built themselves four huts in a row in the highlands of the Himalaya, and there they lived.

The eldest brother died, and was born as Sakka. Knowing who he had been, he used to visit the others every seven or eight days, and lend them a helping hand.

One day, he visited the eldest of the anchorites, and after the usual greeting, took his seat to one side. [102] "Well, Sir, how can I serve you?" he enquired. The hermit, who was suffering from jaundice, replied, "Fire is what I want." Sakka gave him a razor-axe. (A razor-axe is so called because it serves as razor or as axe according as you fit it into the handle.) "Why," said the hermit, "who is there to get me firewood with this?" "If you want a fire, Sir," replied Sakka, "all you have to do is to strike your hand upon the axe, and say—'Fetch wood and make a fire!' The axe will fetch the wood and make you the fire."

After giving him this razor-axe he next visited the second brother, and asked him the same question—"How can I serve you, Sir?" Now there was an elephant track by his hut, and the creatures annoyed him. So he told Sakka that he was annoyed by elephants, and wanted them to be driven away. Sakka gave him a drum. "If you beat upon this side, Sir," he explained, "your enemies will run away; but if you strike the other, they will become your firm friends, and will encompass you with an army in fourfold array." Then he handed him the drum.

Lastly he made a visit to the youngest, and asked as before how he could serve him. He too had jaundice, and what he said was—"Please give me some curds." Sakka gave him a milk-bowl, with these words: "Turn this over if you want anything, and a great river will pour out of it, and will flood the whole place, and it will be able even to win a kingdom for you." With these words he departed.

After this the axe used to make fire for the eldest brother, the second used to beat upon one side of his drum and drive the elephants away, and the youngest had his curds to eat.

About this time a wild boar, that lived in a ruined village, lit upon a gem possessed of magic power. Picking up the gem in his mouth, he rose in the air by its magic. From afar he could see an isle in mid-ocean, and there he resolved to live. So descending he chose a pleasant spot beneath a mango tree, [103] and there he made his abode.

One day he fell asleep under the tree, with the jewel lying in front of him. Now a certain man from the Kāsi country, who had been turned out of doors by his parents as a ne'er-do-well, had made his way to a seaport, where he embarked on shipboard as a sailors' drudge. In mid-sea the ship was wrecked, and he floated upon a plank to this island. As he wandered in search of fruit, he espied our boar fast asleep. Quietly he crept up, seized the gem, and found himself by magic rising through the air! He alighted on the mango tree, and pondered. "The magic of this gem," thought he, "has taught yon boar to be a sky-walker; that's how he got here, I suppose. Well! I must kill him and make a meal of him first; and then I'll be off." So he snapt off a twig, dropping it upon the boar's head. The boar woke up, and seeing no gem, ran trembling up and down. The man up in the tree laughed. The boar looked up, and seeing him ran his head against the tree, and killed himself.

The man came down, lit a fire, cooked the boar and made a meal. Then he rose up in the sky, and set out on his journey.

As he passed over the Himalaya, he saw the hermits' settlement. So he descended, and spent two or three days in the eldest brother's hut, entertaining and entertained, and he found out the virtue of the axe. He made up his mind to get it for himself. So he showed our hermit the virtue of his gem, and offered to exchange it for the axe. The hermit longed to be able to pass through mid-air[1], and struck the bargain. The man took the axe, and departed; but before he had gone very far, he struck upon it, and said—"Axe! smash that hermit's skull and bring the gem to me!" Off flew the axe, clove the hermit's skull, and brought the gem back.

Then the man hid the axe away, and paid a visit to the second brother. [104] With him the visitor stayed a few days, and soon discovered the power of his drum. Then he exchanged his gem for the drum, as before, and as before made the axe cleave the owner's skull. After this he went on to the youngest of the three hermits, found out the power of the milk-bowl, gave his jewel in exchange for it, and as before sent his axe to cleave the man's skull. Thus he was now owner of jewel, axe, drum, and milk-bowl, all four.

He now rose up and past through the air. Stopping hard by Benares, he wrote a letter which he sent by a messenger's hands, that the king must either fight him or yield. On receipt of this message the king sallied forth to "seize the scoundrel." But he beat on one side of his drum, and was promptly surrounded by an army in fourfold array. When he saw that the king had deployed his forces, he then overturned the milk-bowl, and a great river poured forth; multitudes were drowned

[1] This was one of the supernatural powers much coveted by Buddhists.

in the river of curds. Next he struck upon his axe. "Fetch me the king's head!" cried he; away went the axe, and came back and dropt the head at his feet. Not a man could raise hand against him.

So encompassed by a mighty host, he entered the city, and caused himself to be anointed king under the title of king Dadhi-vāhana, or Carried-on-the-Curds, and ruled righteously.

One day, as the king was amusing himself by casting a net into the river, he caught a mango fruit, fit for the gods, which had floated down from Lake Kaṇṇamuṇḍa. When the net was hauled out, the mango was found, and shown to the king. It was a huge fruit, as big as a basin, round, and golden in colour. The king asked what the fruit was: Mango, said the foresters. He ate it, and had the stone planted in his park, and watered with milk-water.

The tree sprouted up, and in three years it bore fruit. Great was the worship paid to this tree; milk-water was poured about it; perfumed garlands with five sprays[1] were hung upon it; wreaths were festooned about it; a lamp was kept burning, and fed with scented oil; and all round it was a screen of cloth. The fruit was sweet, and had the colour of fine gold. King Dadhi-vāhana, before sending presents of these mangoes to other kings, [105] used to prick with a thorn that place in the stone where the sprout would come from, for fear of their growing the like by planting it. When they ate the fruit, they used to plant the stone; but they could not get it to take root. They enquired the reason, and learnt how the matter was.

One king asked his gardener whether he could spoil the flavour of this fruit, and turn it bitter on the tree. Yes, the man said he could; so his king gave him a thousand pieces and sent him on his errand.

So soon as he had arrived in Benares, the man sent a message to the king that a gardener was come. The king admitted him to the presence. After the man had saluted him, the king asked, "You are a gardener?" "Yes, Sire," said the man, and began to sound his own praises. "Very well," said the king, "you may go and assist my park-keeper." So after that these used both to look after the royal grounds.

The new comer managed to make the park look more beautiful by forcing flowers and fruit out of their season. This pleased the king,

[1] The meaning of *gandhapañcaṅgulikaṁ* is uncertain. Perhaps a garland in which sprouts or twigs were arranged radiating like the fingers of a hand. See Morris in *J.P.T.S.*, 1884, *s.v.* See vol. i. p. 71 for a different rendering; but there *gandhena pañcaṅgulikaṁ datvā* seems rather to mean "making five-finger wreaths with scent." The spread hand is in many places a symbol used to avert the evil eye. In some villages of India it is marked on the house walls (*North Ind. N. and Q.*, i. 42); it is carved on Phoenician tombstones (see those in the Bibliothèque Nationale in Paris); and I have seen it in all parts of Syria, on the houses of Jews, Christians, and Moslems.

so that he dismissed the former keeper and gave the park into sole charge of the new one. No sooner had this man got the park into his own hands than he planted nimbs and creepers about the choice mango tree. By and by the nimbs sprouted up. Above and below, root with root, and branch with branch, these were all entangled with the mango tree. Thus this tree, with its sweet fruit, grew bitter as the bitter-leaved nimb by the company of this noxious and sour plant. As soon as the gardener knew that the fruit had gone bitter, he took to his heels.

King Dadhi-vāhana went a-walking in his pleasaunce, and took a bite of the mango fruit. The juice in his mouth tasted like a nasty nimb; swallow it he could not, so he coughed and spat it out. Now at that time the Bodhisatta was his temporal and spiritual counsellor. The king turned to him. "Wise Sir, this tree is as carefully cared for as ever, and yet its fruit has gone bitter. What's the meaning of it?" and asking this question, he repeated the first stanza:—[106]

"Sweet was once the mango's savour, sweet its scent, its colour gold:
What has caused this bitter flavour? for we tend it as of old."

The Bodhisatta explained the reason in the second stanza:—

"Round about the trunk entwining, branch with branch, and root with root,
See the bitter creeper climbing; that is what has spoilt your fruit;
And so you see bad company will make the better follow suit."

On hearing this the Bodhisatta caused all the nimbs and creepers to be removed, and their roots pulled up; the noxious soil was all taken away, and sweet earth put in its place; and the tree was carefully fed with sweet water, milk-water, scented water. Then by absorbing all this sweetness its fruit grew sweet again. The king put his former gardener in charge of the park, and after his life was done passed away to fare according to his deserts.

After this discourse was ended, the Master identified the Birth:—"In those days I was the wise counsellor."

No. 187.

CATUMAṬṬA-JĀTAKA.

"*Sit and sing,*" *etc.*—This story the Master told while staying at Jetavana, about an old Brother. Once, we are told, two of the chief disciples were sitting together, questioning and answering; when up came an old Brother, and made a third. [107] Taking a seat, he said, "I have a question too, Sirs, which I should like to ask you: and if you have any difficulty, you may put it to me." The Elders were disgusted; they rose up and left him. The congregation who listened to the discourse of the Elders, after the meeting broke up, came to the Master; he asked what brought them there untimely and they told him what had happened. He replied, "This is not the first time, Brethren, that Sāriputta and Moggallāna have been disgusted with this man, and left him without a word; it was just the same in olden days." And he proceeded to tell a story of the past.

Once upon a time, when Brahmadatta was king of Benares, the Bodhisatta became a tree-sprite that lived in a forest. Two young Geese flew down from Mount Cittakūṭa and perched upon this tree. They flew about in search of food, returned thither again, and after resting flew back to their mountain home. As time went on and on, the sprite struck up a friendship with them. Coming and going, they were great friends, and used to talk of religion to one another before they parted.

It happened one day as the birds sat on the treetop, talking with the Bodhisatta, that a Jackal, halting at the foot of the tree, addressed the young Geese in the words of the following stanza:—

"Sit and sing upon the tree
If in private you would be.
Sit upon the ground, and sing
Verses to the beasts' own king!"

Filled with disgust, the young Geese took wing and flew back to Cittakūṭa. When they were gone, the Bodhisatta repeated the second stanza for the Jackal's benefit:—

"Fairwing here to fairwing sings,
God to god sweet converse brings;
Perfect beauty[1], you must then
Back into your hole again!"

---

[108] When the Master had ended this discourse, he identified the Birth:—"In those times the old man was the Jackal, Sāriputta and Moggallāna the two young Geese, and I myself was the tree-sprite."

[1] Lit. 'lovely in four points,' i.e. as the schol. explains 'in form, in birth, in voice, in quality': said sarcastically.

No. 188.

SĪHAKOṬṬHUKA-JĀTAKA.

"*Lion's claws and lion's paws,*" *etc.*—This is a story told by the Master whilst at Jetavana, about Kokālika. They say that Kokālika one day hearing a number of wise Brethren preaching, desired to preach himself; all the rest is like the circumstances given in a previous tale[1]. This time again the Master on hearing of it said, "Not this once only has Kokālika been shown up for what he was worth by means of his own voice; the very same thing happened before." And he told a story.

Once on a time, when Brahmadatta was king of Benares, the Bodhisatta was a Lion in the Himalaya mountains, and he had a cub by a she-jackal who mated with him. The cub was just like his sire in toes, claws, mane, colour, figure—all these; but in voice he was like his dam.

One day, after a shower of rain, all the Lions were gambolling together and roaring; the cub thought he would like to roar too, and yelped like a jackal. On hearing which all the Lions fell silent at once! Another cub of the same sire, own brother of this one, heard the sound, and said, "Father, yon lion is like us in colour and everything except in voice. Who's he?" in asking which question he repeated the first stanza:—

"Lion's claws and lion's paws,
Lion's feet to stand upon;
But the bellow of this fellow
Sounds not like a lion's son!"

[109] In answer the Bodhisatta said, "It's your brother, the Jackal's cub; like me in form, but in voice like his dam." Then he gave a word of advice to the other cub—"My dear son, as long as you live here keep a quiet tongue in your head. If you give tongue again, they'll all find out that you are a Jackal." To drive the advice home he repeated the second stanza:—

"All will see what kind you be
If you yelp as once before;
So don't try it, but keep quiet:
Yours is not a lion's roar."

After this advice the creature never again so much as tried to roar.

When the Master had finished this discourse, he identified the Birth:—"In those days Kokālika was the Jackal, Rahula was the brother cub, and the king of beasts was I myself."

[1] No. 172; compare no. 189. Kokālika is often alluded to in this way; cp. nos. 117, 481. There is a story in the *Cullavagga* i. 18. 3, turning on a similar point; a hen has a chick by a crow, and when it would cry cock-a-doodle-doo it caws, and *vice versa* (*Vinaya Texts*, *S. B. E.*, ii. p. 362).

No. 189.

SĪHACAMMA-JĀTAKA[1].

"*Nor lion nor tiger I see,*" *etc.*—This story, like the last, was about Kokālika, told by the Master in Jetavana. This time he wanted to intone. The Master on hearing of it told the following story.

Once upon a time, when Brahmadatta was reigning in Benares, the Bodhisatta was born in a farmer's family, and when he grew up he got a livelihood by tillage.

At the same time there was a Merchant who used to go about hawking goods, which a donkey carried for him. Wherever he went, he used to take his bundle off the ass, and throw a lionskin over him, [110] and then turn him loose in the rice and barley fields. When the watchmen saw this creature, they imagined him to be a lion, and so durst not come near him.

One day this hawker stopped at a certain village, and while he was getting his own breakfast cooked, he turned the ass loose in a barley field with the lionskin on. The watchmen thought it was a lion, and durst not come near, but fled home and gave the alarm. All the villagers armed themselves, and hurried to the field, shouting and blowing on conchs and beating drums. The ass was frightened out of his wits, and gave a hee-haw! Then the Bodhisatta, seeing that it was a donkey, repeated the first stanza:—

> "Nor lion nor tiger I see,
> Not even a leopard is he:
> But a donkey—the wretched old hack!
> With a lionskin over his back!"

As soon as the villagers learnt that it was only an ass, they cudgelled him till they broke his bones, and then went off with the lionskin. When the Merchant appeared, and found that his ass had come to grief, he repeated the second stanza:—

> "The donkey, if he had been wise,
> Might long the green barley have eaten;
> A lionskin was his disguise:—
> But he gave a hee-haw, and got beaten!"

[1] Fausbøll, *Five Jātakas*, pp. 14 and 39; Rhys Davids, *Buddhist Birth Stories*, p. v. This is Aesop's *Ass in the Lion's Skin*.

As he was in the act of uttering these words, the ass expired. The Merchant left him, and went his way.

After this discourse was ended, the Master identified the Birth:—"At that time Kokālika was the ass, and the wise farmer was I myself."

No. 190.

SĪLĀNISAMSA-JĀTAKA.

[111] "*Behold the fruit of sacrifice,*" *etc.*—This story the Master told whilst staying in Jetavana, about a believing layman. This was a faithful, pious soul, an elect disciple. One evening, on his way to Jetavana, he came to the bank of the river Aciravatī, when the ferrymen had pulled up their boat on the shore in order to attend service; as no boat could be seen at the landing-stage, and our friend's mind being full of delightful thoughts of the Buddha, he walked into the river[1]. His feet did not sink below the water. He got as far as mid-river walking as though he were on dry land; but there he noticed the waves. Then his ecstasy subsided, and his feet began to sink. Again he strung himself up to high tension, and walked on over the water. So he arrived at Jetavana, greeted the Master, and took a seat on one side. The Master entered into conversation with him pleasantly. "I hope, good layman," said he, "you had no mishap on your way." "Oh, Sir," he replied, "on my way I was so absorbed in thoughts of the Buddha that I set foot upon the river; but I walked over it as though it had been dry ground!" "Ah, friend layman," said the Master, "you are not the only one who has kept safe by remembering the virtues of the Buddha. In olden days pious laymen have been shipwrecked in mid-ocean, and saved themselves by remembering the Buddha's virtues." Then, at the man's request, he told an old-world tale.

Once upon a time, in the days when Kassapa was Supreme Buddha, a disciple, who had entered on the Paths, took passage on board ship in company with a barber of some considerable property. The barber's wife had given him in charge of our friend, to look after him in better and in worse.

A week later, the ship was wrecked in mid-ocean. These two persons

[1] The resemblance to St Peter on the Sea of Galilee is striking.

clinging to one plank were cast up on an island. There the barber killed some birds, and cooked them, offering a share of his meal to the lay brother. "No, thank you," said he, "I have had enough." He was thinking to himself, "In this place there is no help for us except the Three Jewels[1]," and so he pondered upon the blessings of the Three Jewels. As he pondered and pondered, a Serpent-king who had been born in that isle changed his own body to the shape of a great ship. The ship was filled with the seven kinds of precious things. [112] A Spirit of the Sea was the helmsman. The three masts were made of sapphire, the anchor[2] of gold, the ropes of silver, and the planks were golden.

The Sea-spirit stood on board, crying—"Any passengers for India?" The lay brother said, "Yes, that's where we are bound for." "In with you then—on board with you!" He went aboard, and wanted to call his friend the barber. "You may come," says the helmsman, "but not he." "Why not?" "He is not a man of holy life, that's why," said the other; "I brought this ship for you, not for him." "Very well:—the gifts I have given, the virtues I have practised, the powers I have developed—I give him the fruit of all of them!" "I thank you, master!" said the barber. "Now," said the Sea-spirit, "I can take you aboard." So he conveyed them both oversea, and sailed upstream to Benares. There, by his power, he created a store of wealth for both of them, and bespoke them thus.

"Keep company with the wise and good. If this barber had not been in company with this pious layman, he would have perished in the midst of the deep." Then he uttered these verses in praise of good company:—

"Behold the fruit of sacrifice, virtue, and piety:
A serpent in ship-shape conveys the good man o'er the sea.

"Make friendship only with the good, and keep good company;
Friends with the good, this Barber could his home in safety see."

[113] Thus did the Spirit of the Sea hold forth, poised in mid-air. Finally he went to his own abode, taking the Serpent-king along with him.

The Master, after finishing this discourse, declared the Truths and identified the Birth:—at the conclusion of the Truths the pious layman entered on the Fruit of the Second Path:—"On that occasion the converted lay brother attained Nirvana; Sāriputta was the Serpent-king, and the Sea-spirit was I myself."

[1] The Three Jewels are Buddha, the Law, the Order. For the seven precious things (or jewels), see Childers, p. 402 *b*.

[2] *lakāro* or *laṅkāro*. I do not know what the word means. Prof. Cowell suggests "anchor," the Mod. Persian for which is *langar*.

No. 191.

RUHAKA-JĀTAKA.

"*Even a broken bowstring,*" *etc.*—This story the Master told while dwelling in Jetavana, about temptation arising from a former wife. The circumstances will be explained in the Eighth Book, in the Indriya-Jātaka[1]. Then the Master said to this brother, "That is a woman who does you harm. In former times, too, she put you to the blush before the king and his whole court, and gave you good reason to leave your home." And he told an old-world tale.

Once upon a time, when king Brahmadatta was reigning in Benares, the Bodhisatta was born of his chief queen. He came of age, and his father passed away; and then he became king and ruled in righteousness.

The Bodhisatta had a chaplain named Ruhaka, and this Ruhaka had an old brahmin woman to wife.

The king gave the brahmin a horse accoutred with all its trappings, and he mounted the horse and went to wait upon the king. As he rode along on the back of his richly caparisoned steed, the people on this side and that were loud in its praise: "See that fine horse!" they cried; "what a beauty!"

When he came home again, he went into his mansion and told his wife. [114] "Goodwife," said he, "our horse is passing fine! Right and left the people are all speaking in praise of it."

Now his wife was no better than she should be, and full of deceit; so she made reply to him thus.

"Ah, husband, you do not know wherein lies the beauty of this horse. It is all in his fine trappings. Now if you would make yourself fine like the horse, put his trappings on yourself and go down into the street, prancing along horse-fashion[2]. You will see the king, and he will praise you, and all the people will praise you."

This fool of a brahmin listened to it all, but did not know what she purposed. So he believed her, and did as she had said. All that saw him laughed aloud: "There goes a fine professor!" said they all. And the king cried shame on him. "Why, my Teacher," said he, "has your bile gone wrong? Are you crazy?" At this the brahmin thought that he must have behaved amiss, and he was ashamed. So he was wroth with his wife, and made haste home, saying to himself, "The woman has shamed me

[1] No. 423.

[2] Compare *Pañcatantra* iv. 6 (Benfey, ii. p. 307).

before the king and all his army: I will chastise her and turn her out of doors!"

But the crafty woman found out that he had come home in anger; she stole a march on him, and departed by a side door, and made her way to the palace, where she stayed four or five days. When the king heard of it, he sent for his chaplain, and said to him,

"My Teacher, all womankind are full of faults; you ought to forgive this lady;" and with intent to make him forgive he uttered the first stanza:—

"Even a broken bowstring can be mended and made whole:
Forgive your wife, and cherish not this anger in your soul."

[115] Hearing this, Ruhaka uttered the second:—

"While there is bark[1] and workmen too
'Tis easy to buy bowstrings now.
Another wife I will procure;
I've had enough of this one, sure."

So saying, he sent her away, and took him another brahmin woman to wife.

The Master, after finishing this discourse, declared the Truths and identified the Birth:—at the conclusion of the Truths the tempted Brother was established in the fruit of the First Path:—"On that occasion the former wife was the same, Ruhaka was the tempted brother, and I was the king of Benares."

No. 192.

SIRI-KĀḶAKAṆṆI-JĀTAKA[2].

"*Even though women may be fair,*" *etc.*—This story will be given in the Mahā-ummagga-Jātaka[3].

[1] Reading *mudūsu*, 'fresh (bark),' from the fibre of which bowstrings were sometimes made.

[2] Cf. *Thibetan Tales*, xxi. pp. 291—5, "How a Woman Requites Love."

[3] No. 538 in Westergaard.

No. 193[1].

CULLA-PADUMA-JĀTAKA.

"*'Tis I—no other*," *etc.*—This story the Master told while dwelling at Jetavana about a backsliding brother. The circumstances will be explained in the Ummadantī Birth[2]. When this brother was asked by the Master whether he were really a backslider, he replied that he was. "Who," said the Master, "has caused you to backslide?" He replied that he had seen a woman dressed up in finery, and overcome by passion he had backslidden. Then the Master said, "Brother, womankind are all ungrateful and treacherous; wise men of old were even so stupid as to give the blood from their own right knee for them to drink, and made them presents all their life long, and yet did not win their hearts." And he told an old-world tale.

---

[116] Once upon a time, when king Brahmadatta reigned over Benares, the Bodhisatta was born as his chief queen's son. On his name-day, they called him Prince Paduma, the Lotus Prince. After him came six younger brothers. One after another these seven came of age and married and settled down, living as the king's companions.

One day the king looked out into the palace courts, and as he looked he saw these men with a great following on their way to wait upon himself. He conceived the suspicion that they meant to slay him, and seize his kingdom. So he sent for them, and after this fashion bespake them.

"My sons, you may not dwell in this town. So go elsewhere, and when I die you shall return and take the kingdom which belongs to our family."

They agreed to their father's words; and went home weeping and wailing. "It matters not where we go!" they cried; and taking their wives with them, they left the city, and journeyed along the road. By and bye they came to a wood, where they could get no food or drink. And being unable to bear the pangs of hunger, they determined to save their lives at the women's cost. They seized the youngest brother's wife, and slew her; they cut up her body into thirteen parts, and ate it. But the Bodhisatta and his wife set aside one portion, and ate the other between them.

Thus they did six days, and slew and ate six of the women; and each day the Bodhisatta set one portion aside, so that he had six portions saved.

[1] See *Pañcatantra* iv. 5 (Benfey, ii. p. 305); *Thibetan Tales*, no. xxi. "How a Woman requites Love."

[2] No. 527.

On the seventh day the others would have taken the Bodhisatta's wife to kill her; but instead he gave them the six portions which he had kept. "Eat these," said he; "to-morrow I will manage." They all did eat the flesh; and when the time came that they fell asleep, the Bodhisatta and his wife made off together.

When they had gone a little space, the woman said, "Husband, I can go no further." So the Bodhisatta took her upon his shoulders, and at sunrise he came out of the wood. When the sun was risen, said she—"Husband, I am thirsty!"

"There is no water, dear wife!" said he.

But she begged him again and again, until he struck his right knee with his sword, [117] and said,

"Water there is none; but sit you down and drink the blood here from my knee." And so she did.

By and bye they came to the mighty Ganges. They drank, they bathed, they ate all manner of fruits, and rested in a pleasant spot. And there by a bend of the river they made a hermit's hut and took up their abode in it.

Now it happened that a robber in the regions of Upper Ganges had been guilty of high treason. His hands and feet, and his nose and ears had been cut off, and he was laid in a canoe, and left to drift down the great river. To this place he floated, groaning aloud with pain. The Bodhisatta heard his piteous wailing.

"While I live," said he, "no poor creature shall perish for me!" and to the river bank he went, and saved the man. He brought him to the hut, and with astringent lotions and ointments he tended his wounds.

But his wife said to herself, "Here is a nice lazy fellow he has fetched out of the Ganges, to look after!" and she went about spitting for disgust at the fellow.

Now when the man's wounds were growing together, the Bodhisatta had him to dwell there in the hut along with his wife, and he brought fruits of all kinds from the forest to feed both him and the woman. And as they thus dwelt together, the woman fell in love with the fellow, and committed sin. Then she desired to kill the Bodhisatta, and said to him, "Husband, as I sat on your shoulder when I came out from the forest, I saw yon hill, and I vowed that if ever you and I should be saved, and come to no harm, I would make offering to the holy spirit of the hill. Now this spirit haunts me: and I desire to pay my offering!"

"Very good," said the Bodhisatta, not knowing her guile. He prepared an offering, and delivering to her the vessel of offering, he climbed the hill-top. [118] Then his wife said to him,

"Husband, not the hill-spirit, but you are my chief of gods! Then in your honour first of all I will offer wild flowers, and walk reverently round you, keeping you on the right, and salute you: and after that I will make my offering to the mountain spirit." So saying, she placed him facing a precipice, and pretended that she was fain to salute him in reverent fashion. Thus getting behind him, she smote him on the back, and hurled him down the precipice. Then she cried in her joy, "I have seen the back of my enemy!" and she came down from the mountain, and went into the presence of her paramour.

Now the Bodhisatta tumbled down the cliff; but he stuck fast in a clump of leaves on the top of a fig tree where there were no thorns. Yet he could not get down the hill, so there he sat among the branches, eating the figs. It happened that a huge Iguana used to climb the hill from the foot of it, and would eat the fruit of this fig tree. That day he saw the Bodhisatta and took to flight. On the next day, he came and ate some fruit on one side of it. Again and again he came, till at last he struck up a friendship with the Bodhisatta.

"How did you get to this place?" he asked; and the Bodhisatta told him how.

"Well, don't be afraid," said the Iguana; and taking him on his own back, he descended the hill and brought him out of the forest. There he set him upon the high road, and showed him what way he should go, and himself returned to the forest.

The other proceeded to a certain village, and dwelt there till he heard of his father's death. Upon this he made his way to Benares. There he inherited the kingdom which belonged to his family, and took the name of King Lotus; the ten rules of righteousness for kings he did not transgress, and he ruled uprightly. He built six Halls of Bounty, one at each of the four gates, one in the midst of the city, and one before the palace; and every day he distributed in gifts six hundred thousand pieces of money.

Now the wicked wife took her paramour upon her shoulders, and came forth out of the forest; and she went a-begging among the people, and collected rice and gruel to support him withal. [119] If she was asked what the man was to her, she would reply, "His mother was sister to my father, he is my cousin[1]; to him they gave me. Even if he were doomed to death I would take my own husband upon my shoulders, and care for him, and beg food for his living!"

"What a devoted wife!" said all the people. And thenceforward they gave her more food than ever. Some of them also offered advice, saying, "Do not live in this way. King Lotus is lord of Benares; he has set all India in a stir by his bounty. It will delight him to see you; so delighted will he be, that he will give you rich gifts. Put your husband

[1] The Sanskrit version says "his kinsfolk persecuted him," which gives a reason for the state he was seen in.

in this basket, and make your way to him." So saying, they persuaded her, and gave her a basket of osiers.

The wicked woman placed her paramour in the basket, and taking it up she repaired to Benares, and lived on what she got at the Halls of Bounty. Now the Bodhisatta used to ride to an alms-hall upon the back of a splendid elephant richly dight; and after giving alms to eight or ten people, he would set out again for home. Then the wicked woman placed her paramour in the basket, and taking it up, she stood where the king was used to pass. The king saw her. "Who is this?" he asked. "A devoted wife," was the answer. He sent for her, and recognised who she was. He caused the man to be put down from the basket, and asked her, "What is this man to you?"—"He is the son of my father's sister, given me by my family, my own husband," she answered.

"Ah, what a devoted wife!" cried they all: for they knew not the ins and outs of it; and they praised the wicked woman.

"What—is the scoundrel your cousin? did your family give him to you?" asked the king; "your husband, is he?"

She did not recognise the king; and "Yes, my lord!" said she, as bold as you like.

"And is this the king of Benares' son? Are you not the wife of prince Lotus, the daughter of such and such a king, your name so and so? Did not you drink the blood from my knee? Did you not fall in love with this rascal, and throw me down a precipice? Ah, you thought that I was dead, and here you are with death written upon your own forehead—and here am I, alive!" [120] Then he turned to his courtiers. "Do you remember what I told you, when you questioned me? My six younger brothers slew their six wives and ate them; but I kept my wife unhurt, and brought her to Ganges' bank, where I dwelt in a hermit's hut: I hauled a condemned criminal out of the river, and supported him; this woman fell in love with him, and threw me down a precipice, but I saved my life by showing kindness. This is no other than the wicked woman who threw me off the crag: this, and no other, is the condemned wretch!" And then he uttered the following verses:

"'Tis I—no other, and this quean is she;
The handless knave, no other, there you see;
Quoth she—'This is the husband of my youth.'
Women deserve to die; they have no truth.

"With a great club beat out the scoundrel's life
Who lies in wait to steal his neighbour's wife.
Then take the faithful harlot by and bye,
And shear off nose and ears before she die."

[121] But although the Bodhisatta could not swallow his anger, and ordained this punishment for them, he did not do accordingly; but he

smothered his wrath, and had the basket fixed upon her head so fast that she could not take it off; the villain he had placed in the same, and they were driven out of his kingdom.

When the Master had ended this discourse, he declared the Truths and identified the Birth:—at the conclusion of the Truths the backsliding Brother entered on the Fruit of the First Path:—"In those days certain elders were the six brothers, the young lady Ciñcā was the wife, Devadatta was the criminal, Ānanda was the Iguana, and King Lotus was I myself."

No. 194.

MAṆICORA-JĀTAKA.

"*No gods are here,*" *etc.*—This story the Master told during a stay in Veḷuvana, how Devadatta tried to kill him. Hearing that Devadatta went about to kill him, he said, "Brethren, this is not the only time that Devadatta has been trying to kill me; he tried to do so before, and failed." Then he told them this story.

Once upon a time Brahmadatta was reigning in Benares, when the Bodhisatta came to life as the son of a householder who lived in a village not far from the city.

When he came to years, they fetched a young lady of family from Benares to marry him. She was a fair and lovely maiden, beautiful as a nymph divine, graceful like a twining creeper, ravishing as a sylph. Her name was Sujātā; she was faithful, virtuous, and dutiful. She always did duly her devoir to her lord and his parents. This girl was very dear and precious to the Bodhisatta. [122] So they two dwelt together in joy, and unity, and oneness of mind.

On a day Sujātā said to her husband, "I have a wish to see my mother and father."

"Very good, my wife," replied he; "make ready food sufficient for the journey." He caused food of all sorts to be cooked, and placed the provisions in a waggon; since he drove the vehicle, he sat in front, and his wife behind. To Benares they went; and there they unyoked the waggon, and washed, and ate. Then the Bodhisatta yoked the oxen again, and sat in front; and Sujātā, who had changed her dress and adorned herself, sat behind.

As the waggon entered the city, the king of Benares happened to be making a solemn circuit round the place mounted upon the back of a splendid elephant; and he passed by that place. Sujātā had come down out of the cart, and was walking behind on foot. The king saw her: her beauty so attracted his eye, that he became enamoured of her. He called one of his suite. "Go," said he, "and find out whether yon woman has a husband or no." The man did as he was bid, and came back to tell the king. "She has a husband, I am told," said he; "do you see that man sitting in the cart yonder? He is her husband."

The king could not smother his passion, and sin entered into his mind. "I will find some way of getting rid of this fellow," thought he, "and then I will take the wife myself." Calling to a man, he said, "Here, my good fellow, take this jewelled crest, and make as though you were passing down the street. As you go, drop it in the waggon of yonder man." So saying, he gave him a jewelled crest, and dismissed him. The man took it, and went; as he passed the waggon, he dropped it in; then he returned, and reported to the king that it was done.

"I have lost a jewelled crest!" cried the king: the whole place was in an uproar.

"Shut all the gates!" the king gave order: "cut off the outlets! hunt the thief!" The king's followers obeyed. The city was all confusion! The other man, taking some others with him, went up to the Bodhisatta, crying—"Hullo! stop your cart! [123] the king has lost a jewelled crest; we must search your cart!" And search it he did, till he found the jewel which he had put there himself. "Thief!" cried he, seizing the Bodhisatta; they beat him and kicked him; then binding his arms behind him they dragged him before the king, crying out—"See the thief who stole your jewel!" "Off with his head!" was the king's command. They scourged him with whips, and tormented him at every street corner, and cast him out of the city by the south gates.

Now Sujātā left the waggon, and stretching out her arms she ran after him, wailing as she went—"O my husband, it is I who brought you into this woful plight!" The king's servants threw the Bodhisatta upon his back, with the intent to cut off his head. When she saw this, Sujātā thought upon her own goodness and virtue, reflecting thus within herself; "I suppose there can be no spirit here strong enough to stay the hand of cruel and wicked men, who work mischief to the virtuous"; and weeping and wailing she repeated the first stanza:—

"No gods are here: they must be far away;—
No gods, who over all the world hold sway:
Now wild and violent men may work their will,
For here is no one who could say them nay."

As this virtuous woman thus lamented, the throne of Sakka[1], king of the Gods, grew hot as he sat upon it. [124] "Who is it that would make me fall from my godhead?" thought Sakka. Then he was ware of what was befalling. "The king of Benares," he thought, "is doing a very cruel deed. He is making the virtuous Sujātā miserable; now I must go thither!" So descending from the godworld, by his own power he dismounted the wicked king from the elephant on whose back he was riding, and laid him upon his back in the place of execution, but the Bodhisatta he caught up, and decked him with all kinds of ornaments, and made the king's dress come upon him, and set him on the back of the king's elephant. The servants lifted the axe and smote off a head—but it was the king's head; and when it was off, they knew that it was the head of the king.

Sakka took upon him a visible body, and came before the Bodhisatta, and consecrated him to be king; and caused the place of chief queen to be given to Sujātā. And as the courtiers, the brahmins and householders, and the rest, saw Sakka, king of the gods, they rejoiced, saying, "The unrighteous king is slain! now have we received from the hands of Sakka a king who is righteous!" And Sakka stood poised in the air, and declared, "This your righteous king from this time forth shall rule in righteousness. If a king be unrighteous, God sends rain out of season, and in season he sends no rain: and fear of famine, fear of pestilence, fear of the sword—these three fears come upon men for him." Thus did he instruct them, and spake this second verse:—

"For him no rain falls in the time of rain,
But out of season pours and pours amain.
A king comes down from heaven upon the earth.
Behold the reason why this man is slain."

[125] Thus did Sakka admonish a great concourse of folk, and then he went straight to his divine abode. And the Bodhisatta reigned in righteousness, and then went to swell the hosts of heaven.

The Master, having ended this discourse, thus identified the Birth:—"At that time Devadatta was the wicked king; Anuruddha was Sakka; Sujātā was Rāhula's mother; but the king by Sakka's gift was I myself."

[1] Indra.

No. 195.

PABBATŪPATTHARA-JĀTAKA.

"*A happy lake*," *etc.*—This story the Master told while dwelling at Jetavana, about the king of Kosala.

We are told that a certain courtier intrigued in the royal harem. The king inquired into the matter, and when he found it all out exactly he determined to tell the Master. So he came to Jetavana, and saluted the Master; told him how a courtier had intrigued, and asked what he was to do. The Master asked him whether he found the courtier useful to him, and whether he loved his wife. "Yes," was the reply, "the man is very useful; he is the mainstay of my court; and I do love the woman." "Sire," replied the Master, "when servants are useful, and women are dear, there is no harming them. In olden days too kings listened to the words of the wise, and were indifferent to such things." And he told an old-world tale.

Once upon a time, when Brahmadatta was king of Benares, the Bodhisatta was born into a courtier's family. When he came of age, he became the king's counsellor in things temporal and spiritual.

Now one of the king's court intrigued in the harem, and the king learnt all about it. "He is a most useful servant," thought he, "and the woman is dear to me. I cannot destroy these two. [126] I will put a question to some wise man of my court; and if I must put up with it, put up with it I will; if not, then I will not."

He sent for the Bodhisatta, and bade him be seated. "Wise sir," said he, "I have a question to ask you."

"Ask it, O king! I will make answer," replied the other. Then the king asked his question in the words of the first couplet:—

"A happy lake lay sheltered at the foot of a lovely hill,
But a jackal used it, knowing that a lion watched it still."

"Surely," thought the Bodhisatta, "one of his courtiers must have intrigued in the harem"; and he recited the second couplet:—

"Out of the mighty river all creatures drink at will:
If she is dear, have patience—the river's a river still."

[127] Thus did the Great Being advise the king.

And the king abode by this advice, and he forgave them both, bidding them go and sin no more. And from that time they ceased. And the king gave alms, and did good, till at his life's end he went to fill the hosts of heaven.

And the king of Kosala also, after hearing this discourse, forgave both these people and remained indifferent.

When the Master had ended this discourse, he identified the Birth:—"At that time Ānanda was the king, and I myself was the wise councillor."

No. 196.

VALĀHASSA-JĀTAKA.

"*They who will neglect*," *etc.*—This story the Master told while staying in Jetavana, about a Brother who had become a backslider.

When the Master asked him if it was really true that he was a backslider, the Brother replied that it was true. Being questioned for the reason, he replied that his passion had been aroused by seeing a finely dressed woman. Then the Master thus addressed him:

"Brother, these women tempt men by their figure and voice, scents, perfumes, and touch, and by their wiles and dalliance; thus they get men into their power; and as soon as they perceive that this is done, they ruin them, character, wealth and all, by their evil ways. This gives them the name of she-goblins. In former days also a troop of she-goblins tempted a caravan of traders, and got power over them; and afterwards, when they got sight of other men, they killed every one of the first, and then devoured them, crunching them in their teeth while the blood ran down over both cheeks." And then he told an old story.

Once upon a time, there was in the island of Ceylon a goblin town called Sirīsavatthu, peopled by she-goblins. When a ship is wrecked, these adorn and deck themselves, and taking rice and gruel, with trains of slaves, and their children on their hip, they come up to the merchants. [128] In order to make them imagine that theirs is a city of human beings, they make them see here and there men ploughing and tending kine, herds of cattle, dogs, and the like. Then approaching the merchants they invite them to partake of the gruel, rice, and other food which they bring. The merchants, all unaware, eat of what is offered. When they have eaten and drunken, and are taking their rest, the goblins address them thus: "Where do you live? where do you come from? whither are you going, and what errand brought you here?" "We were shipwrecked here," they reply. "Very good, noble sirs," the others make answer; "'tis three years ago since our own husbands went on board ship; they must have perished. You are merchants too; we will be your wives." Thus they lead them astray by their women's wiles, and tricks, and dalliance, until they get them into the goblin city; then, if they have any others already caught, they bind these with magic chains, and cast them into the house of torment. And if they find no shipwrecked men in the place where they dwell, they scour the coast as far as the river Kalyāṇi[1] on one side and the island of Nāgadīpa on the other. This is their way.

Now it happened once that five hundred shipwrecked traders were cast ashore near the city of these she-goblins. The goblins came up to them and enticed them, till they brought them to their city; those whom they had caught before, they bound with magic chains and cast them into the house of torment. Then the chief goblin took the chief man, and the others took the rest, till five hundred had the five hundred traders; and they made the men their husbands. Then in the night time, when her man was asleep, the chief she-goblin rose up, and made her way to the house of death, slew some of the men and ate them. The others did the same. When the eldest goblin returned from eating men's flesh, her body was cold. The eldest merchant embraced her, and perceived that she was a goblin. [129] "All the five hundred of them must be goblins!" he thought to himself: "we must make our escape!"

So in the early morning, when he went to wash his face, he bespake the other merchants in these words. "These are goblins, and not human beings! As soon as other shipwrecked men can be found, they will make them their husbands, and will eat us; come—let us escape!"

Two hundred and fifty of them replied, "We cannot leave them: go ye, if ye will, but we will not flee away."

Then the chief trader with two hundred and fifty, who were ready to obey him, fled away in fear of the goblins.

Now at that time, the Bodhisatta had come into the world as a flying horse[2], white all over, and beaked like a crow, with hair like muñja grass[3], possessed of supernatural power, able to fly through the air. From Himalaya he flew through the air until he came to Ceylon. There he passed over the ponds and tanks of Ceylon, and ate the paddy that grew wild there. As he passed on thus, he thrice uttered human speech filled with mercy, saying—"Who wants to go home? who wants to go home?" The traders heard his saying, and cried—"We are going home, master!" joining their hands, and raising them respectfully to their foreheads. "Then climb up on my back," said the Bodhisatta. Thereat some of

[1] The modern Kaelani-gaṅgā (*Journ. of the Pali Text Soc.*, 1888, p. 20).

[2] On one side of a pillar in a Buddhist railing at Mathura, is a flying horse with people clinging to it, perhaps intended for this scene (Anderson, *Catalogue of the Indian Museum*, i. p. 189).

[3] Saccharum Muñja.

them climbed up, some laid hold of his tail, and some remained standing, with a respectful salute. Then the Bodhisatta took up even those who stood still saluting him, and conveyed all of them, even two hundred and fifty, to their own country, and set down each in his own place; then he went back to his place of dwelling.

And the she-goblins, when other men came to that place, slew those two hundred and fifty who were left, and devoured them.

The Master now said, addressing the Brethren: "Brethren, even as these traders perished by falling into the hands of she-goblins, but the others by obeying the behest of the wonderful horse each returned safe home again; so, even so, they who neglect the advice of the Buddhas, both Brethren and Sisters, lay Brethren and lay Sisters, [130] come to great misery in the four hells, places where they are punished under the five fetters, and so forth. But those who abide by such advice come to the three kinds of fortunate birth, the six heavens of sense, the twenty worlds of Brahma, and reaching the state of imperishable Nirvana they attain great blessedness." Then, becoming perfectly enlightened, he recited the following verses:—

"They who will neglect the Buddha when he tells them what to do,
As the goblins ate the merchants, likewise they shall perish too.

"They who hearken to the Buddha when he tells them what to do,
As the bird-horse saved the merchants, they shall win salvation too."

When the Master had ended this discourse, he declared the Truths and identified the Birth:—at the conclusion of the Truths the backsliding Brother entered on the Fruit of the First Path, and many others entered on the Fruit of the First, Second, Third or Fourth:—"The Buddha's followers were the two hundred and fifty who followed the advice of the horse, and I was the horse myself."

No. 197.

MITTĀMITTA-JĀTAKA.

"*He smiles not*," *etc.*—This story the Master told whilst dwelling at Sāvatthi, about a certain Brother.

This Brother took a piece of cloth, deposited by his teacher, feeling confident that if he took it his teacher would not be angry. Then he made a shoe-bag of it, and took his leave. When this teacher asked why he took it, he replied he had felt confident, if he did, that his teacher would not be angry. The teacher flew into a passion, [131] got up and struck him a blow. "What confidence is there between you and me?" he asked.

This fact became known among the Brotherhood. One day the brothers were all together talking about it in the Hall of Truth. "Friend, young Brother

So-and-so felt so confident of his teacher's friendship, that he took a piece of cloth, and made it into a shoe-bag. Then the teacher asked him what confidence there was between them, flew into a passion, jumped up, and gave him a blow." The Master came in, and asked them what they were talking of as they sat there together. They told him. Then he said, "This is not the first time, Brothers, that this man has disappointed the confidence of his fellow. He did the same before." And then he told an old-world tale.

Once upon a time, when Brahmadatta was king of Benares, the Bodhisatta was born as a brahmin's son in the realm of Kāsi. When he came of age, he renounced the world; he caused to grow in him the Supernatural Faculties and the Attainments, and took up his abode in the region of Himalaya with a band of disciples. One of this band of ascetics disobeyed the voice of the Bodhisatta, and kept a young elephant which had lost its dam. This creature by and by grew big, then killed its master and made off into the forest. The ascetics did his obsequies; and then, coming about the Bodhisatta, they put this question to him.

"Sir, how may we know whether one is a friend or an enemy?"

This the Bodhisatta declared to them in the following stanzas:—

"He smiles not when he sees him, no welcome will he show,
He will not turn his eyes that way, and answers him with No.

"These are the marks and tokens by which your foe you see:
These if a wise man sees and hears he knows his enemy."

[132] In these words the Bodhisatta declared the marks of friend and foe. Thereafter he cultivated the Excellences, and entered the heaven of Brahma.

When the Master had ended this discourse, he identified the Birth:—"The Brother in question was he who kept the pet elephant, his teacher was the elephant, the Buddha's followers were then the band of hermits, and I myself was their chief."

No. 198[1].

"*I come, my son,*" *etc.*—This story the Master told whilst living at Jetavana, about a brother who was a backslider.

We hear that the Master asked him if he really were a backslider; and he replied, yes, he was. Being asked the reason, he replied, "Because my passions

[1] There are many variants of this story. Compare *Gesta Romanorum* (Early Eng. Text Soc.), no. 45, pp. 174 ff.; *Boke of the Knight de la Tour Landry* (same series), p. 22. Compare no. 145.

were aroused on seeing a woman in her finery." Then the Master said, "Brother, there is no watching women. In days of yore, watchers were placed to guard the doors, and yet they could not keep them safe; even when you have got them, you cannot keep them." And he told an old-world tale.

Once upon a time, when Brahmadatta was king of Benares, the Bodhisatta came into the world as a young parrot. His name was Rādha, and his youngest brother was named Poṭṭhapāda. While they were yet quite young, both of them were caught by a fowler and handed over to a brahmin in Benares. The brahmin cared for them as if they were his children. [133] But the brahmin's wife was a wicked woman; there was no watching her.

The husband had to go away on business, and addressed his young parrots thus. "Little dears, I am going away on business. Keep watch on your mother in season and out of season; observe whether or not any man visits her." So off he went, leaving his wife in charge of the young parrots.

As soon as he was gone, the woman began to do wrong; night and day the visitors came and went—there was no end to them. Poṭṭhapāda, observing this, said to Rādha—"Our master gave this woman into our charge, and here she is doing wickedness. I will speak to her."

"Don't," said Rādha. But the other would not listen. "Mother," said he, "why do you commit sin?"

How she longed to kill him! But making as though she would fondle him, she called him to her.

"Little one, you are my son! I will never do it again! Here, then, the dear!" So he came out; then she seized him crying,

"What! you preach to *me*! you don't know your measure!" and she wrung his neck, and threw him into the oven.

The brahmin returned. When he had rested, he asked the Bodhisatta: "Well, my dear, what about your mother—does she do wrong, or no?" and as he asked the question, he repeated the first couplet:—

"I come, my son, the journey done, and now I am at home again:
Come tell me; is your mother true? does she make love to other men?"

Rādha answered, "Father dear, the wise speak not of things which do not conduce to blessing, whether they have happened or not"; and he explained this by repeating the second couplet: [134]

"For what he said he now lies dead, burnt up beneath the ashes there:
It is not well the truth to tell, lest Poṭṭhapāda's fate I share."

Thus did the Bodhisatta hold forth to the brahmin; and he went on—"This is no place for me to live in either"; then bidding the brahmin farewell, he flew away to the woods.

When the Master had ended this discourse, he declared the Truths, and identified the Birth:—at the conclusion of the Truths the backsliding Brother reached the Fruit of the First Path:—"Ananda was Poṭṭhapāda, and I myself was Rādha."

No. 199.

GAHAPATI-JĀTAKA.

"*I like not this,*" *etc.*—This story the Master told, also about a backsliding Brother, during a sojourn in Jetavana, and in the course of his address he said, "Womankind can never be kept right; somehow or other they will sin and trick their husbands." And then he told the following story.

Once upon a time, in the reign of Brahmadatta, king of Benares, the Bodhisatta was born in the realm of Kāsi as a householder's son: and coming of age he married and settled down. Now his wife was a wicked woman, and she intrigued with the village headman. The Bodhisatta got wind of it, and bethought him how he might put her to the test. [135]

At that time all the grain had been carried away during the rainy season, and there was a famine. But it was the time when the corn had just sprouted; and all the villagers came together, and besought help of their headman, saying, "Two months from now, when we have harvested the grain, we will pay you in kind"; so they got an old ox from him, and ate it.

One day, the headman watched his chance, and when the Bodhisatta was gone abroad he visited the house. Just as the two were happy together, the Bodhisatta came in by the village gate, and set his face towards home. The woman was looking towards the village gate, and saw him. "Why, who's this?" she wondered, looking at him as he stood on the threshold. "It is he!" She knew him, and she told the headman. He trembled in terror.

"Don't be afraid," said the woman, "I have a plan. You know we have had meat from you to eat: make as though you were seeking the price of the meat; I will climb up into the granary, and stand at the door of it, crying, 'No rice here!' while you must stand in the middle of the room, and call out insisting, again and again, 'I have children at home; give me the price of the meat!'"

So saying, she climbed up to the granary, and sat in the door of it. The other stood in the midst of the house, and cried, "Give me the price of the meat!" while she replied, sitting at the granary door, "There is no rice in the granary; I will give it when the harvest is home: leave me now!"

The goodman entered the house, and saw what they were about. "This must be that wicked woman's plan," he thought, and he called to the headman.

"Sir Headman, when we had some of your old ox to eat, we promised to give you rice for it in two months' time. Not half a month has passed; then why do you try to make us pay now? That's not the reason you are here: you must have come for something else. I don't like your ways. That wicked and sinful woman yonder knows that there is no rice in the garner, but she has climbed up, and there she sits, crying [136] 'No rice here!' and you cry 'Give!' I don't like your doings, either of you!" and to make his meaning clear, he uttered these lines:—

"I like not this, I like not that; I like not her, I say,
Who stands beside the granary, and cries 'I cannot pay!'

"Nor you, nor you, Sir! listen now:—my means and store are small;
You gave me once a skinny cow, and two months' grace withal;
Now, ere the day, you bid me pay! I like it not at all."

So saying, he seized the headman by the lock of hair on the top of his head, dragged him out into the courtyard, threw him down, and as he cried, "I'm the Headman!" mocked him thus—"Damages, please, for injury done to the chattels under another man's watch and ward!" while he thrashed him till the man was faint. Then he took him by the neck and cast him out of the house. The wicked woman he seized by the hair of her head, pulled her away from the garner, knocked her down, and threatened her—"If you ever do this kind of thing again, I'll make you remember it!"

From that day forward the headman durst not even look at that house, and the woman did not dare to transgress even in thought.

---

[137] When this discourse was ended, the Master declared the Truths, at the conclusion of which the backsliding Brother reached the Fruit of the First Path:—"The goodman who punished that headman was I myself."

No. 200.

SĀDHUSĪLA-JĀTAKA.

"*One is good*," *etc.*—This story the Master told while dwelling at Jetavana, about a brahmin.

This man, we are told, had four daughters. Four suitors wooed them; one was fine and handsome, one was old and well advanced in years, the third a man of family, and the fourth was good. He thought to himself, "When a man is settling his daughters and disposing of them, whom should he give them to? the handsome man or the oldish man, or one of the other two, the highly born or the very virtuous man?" Ponder as he would, he could not decide. So he thought he would tell the matter to the Supreme Buddha, who would be sure to know; and then he would give the girls to the most suitable wooer. So he had a quantity of perfumes and garlands prepared, and visited the monastery. Saluting the Master, he sat on one side, and told him everything from beginning to end; then he asked, "To which of these four should I give my daughters?" To this the Master replied, "In olden days, as now, wise men asked this question; but now that re-birth has confused your memory, you cannot remember the case." And then at his request the Master told an old-world tale.

Once upon a time, when Brahmadatta ruled in Benares, the Bodhisatta was born as a brahmin's son. He came of age, and received his education at Takkasilā; then on returning he became a famous teacher.

Now there was a brahmin who had four daughters. These four were wooed by four persons as told above. The brahmin could not decide to whom to give them. "I will enquire of the teacher," he thought, "and then he shall have them to whom they should be given." So he came into the teacher's presence, and repeated the first couplet:—

"One is good, and one is noble; one has beauty, one has years.
Answer me this question, brahmin; of the four, which best appears?"

[138] Hearing this, the teacher replied, "Even though there be beauty and the like qualities, a man is to be despised if he fail in virtue. Therefore the former is not the measure of a man; those that I like are the virtuous." And in explanation of this matter, he repeated the second couplet:—

"Good is beauty: to the aged show respect, for this is right:
Good is noble birth; but virtue—virtue, that is my delight."

When the brahmin heard this, he gave all his daughters to the virtuous wooer.

The Master, when this discourse was ended, declared the Truths and identified the Birth:—at the conclusion of the Truths the brahmin attained the Fruit of the First Path:—"This brahmin was the brahmin then, and the famous teacher was I myself."

No. 201.

BANDHANĀGĀRA-JĀTAKA.

[139] "*Not iron fetters*," *etc.*—This story the Master told whilst staying in Jetavana, about the prison-house.

At the time of this story we hear that a gang of burglars, highwaymen, and murderers had been caught and haled before the king of Kosala. The king ordered them to be made fast with chains, and ropes, and fetters. Thirty country Brothers, desirous of seeing the Master, had paid him a visit and offered their salutations. Next day, as they were seeking alms, they passed the prison and noticed these rascals. In the evening, after their return from the day's rounds, they approached the Buddha: "Sir," they said, "to-day, as we were seeking alms, we saw in the prison-house a number of criminals bound fast in chains and fetters, being in great misery. They could not break these fetters, and run away. Is there any fetter stronger than these?"

The Master replied, "Brethren, those are fetters, it is true; but the fetters which consist of a craving for wealth, corn, sons, wives and children are stronger than they are an hundred-fold, nay a thousand-fold. Yet even those fetters, hard to break as they are, have been broken by wise men of the olden time, who went to Himalaya and became anchorites." Then he told them an old-world tale.

Once upon a time, while Brahmadatta ruled over Benares, the Bodhisatta was born into a poor man's family. When he grew up, his father died. He earned wages, and supported his mother. His mother, much against his will, brought a wife home for him, and soon after died. Now his wife conceived. Not knowing that she had conceived, he said to her, "Wife, you must earn your living; I will renounce the world." Then said she, "Nay, for I am with child. [140] Wait and see the child that is born of me, and then go and become a hermit." To this he agreed. So when she was delivered, he said, "Now, wife, you are safely delivered, and I must turn hermit." "Wait," said she, "till the time when the child is weaned." And after that she conceived again.

"If I agree to her request," thought the Bodhisatta, "I shall never get away at all. I will flee without saying a word to her, and become a hermit." So he told her nothing, but rose up in the night, and fled away.

The city guards seized him. "I have a mother to support," said he—"let me go!" thus he made them let him go free, and after staying in a certain place, he passed out by the chief gate and made his way to the Himalayas, where he lived as a recluse; and caused the Supernatural Faculties and the Attainments to spring up within him, as he dwelt in the rapture of meditation. As he dwelt there, he exulted, saying—"The bond of wife and child, the bond of passion, so hard to break, is broken!" and he uttered these lines:—

"Not iron fetters—so the wise have told—
Not ropes, or bars of wood, so fast can hold
As passion, and the love of child or wife,
Of precious gems and earrings of fine gold.

"These heavy fetters—who is there can find
Release from such?—these are the ties that bind:
These if the wise can burst, then they are free,
Leaving all love and all desire behind!"

[141] And the Bodhisatta, after uttering this aspiration, without breaking the charm of his ecstasy attained to Brahma's world.

When the Master had ended this discourse, he declared the Truths:—at the conclusion of the Truths, some entered the First Path, some the Second, some the Third, and some the Fourth:—"In the story, Mahāmāyā was the mother, King Suddhodana was the father, Rāhula's mother was the wife, Rāhula himself the son, and I was the man who left his family and became an anchorite."

No. 202.

KEḶI-SĪLA-JĀTAKA.

[142] "*Geese, herons, elephants,*" etc.—This story the Master told while dwelling at Jetavana, about Lakuṇṭaka the venerable and good.

Now this venerable Lakuṇṭaka, we learn, was well known in the faith of the Buddha, a famous man, speaking sweet words, a honeyed preacher, of keen discernment, with his passions perfectly subdued, but in stature the smallest of all the eighty Elders, no bigger than a novice, like a dwarf kept for amusement.

One day, he had been to the gate of Jetavana to salute the Buddha, when thirty brothers from the country arrived at the gate on their way to salute him too. When they saw the Elder, they imagined him to be some novice; they pulled the corner of his robe, they caught his hands, held his head, tweaked his nose, got him by the ears and shook him, and handled him very rudely; then after putting aside their bowl and robe, they visited the Master and saluted him. Next they asked him, "Sir, we understand that you have an Elder who goes by the name of Lakuṇṭaka the Good, a honeyed preacher. Where is he?" "Do you want to see him?" the Master asked. "Yes, Sir." "He is the man you saw by the gate, and twitched his robe and pulled him about with great rudeness before you came here." "Why, Sir," asked they, "how is it that a man devoted to prayer, full of high aspirations, a true disciple—how is it he is so insignificant?" "Because of his own sins," answered the Master; and at their request he told them an old-world tale.

Once upon a time, when king Brahmadatta reigned in Benares, the Bodhisatta became Sakka, king of the gods. Brahmadatta could not endure to look upon anything old or decrepit, whether elephant, horse, ox, or what not. He was full of pranks, and whenever he saw any such, he would chase them away; old carts he had broken up; any old women that he saw he sent for, and beat upon the belly, then stood them up again and gave them a scare; he made old men roll about and play on the ground like tumblers. If he saw none, but only heard that there was a greybeard in such and such a town, [143] he sent for him thence and took his sport with him.

At this the people for very shame sent their parents outside the boundaries of the kingdom. No more did men tend or care for their mother and father. The king's friends were as wanton as he. As men died, they filled up the four[1] worlds of unhappiness; the company of the gods grew less and less.

Sakka saw that there were no newcomers among the gods; and he cast about him what was to be done. At last he hit upon a plan. "I will humble him!" thought Sakka; and he took upon him the form of an old man, and placing two jars of buttermilk in a crazy old waggon, he yoked to it a pair of old oxen, and set out upon a feast day. Brahmadatta, mounted upon a richly caparisoned elephant, was making a solemn procession about the city, which was all decorated; and Sakka, clad in rags, and driving this cart, came to meet the king. When the king saw the old cart, he shouted, "Away with that cart, you!" But his people answered, "Where is it, my lord? we cannot see any cart!" (for Sakka by his power let it be seen by no one but the king). And, coming up to the king repeatedly, at last Sakka, still driving his cart, smashed one of the jars upon the king's head, and made him turn round; then he smashed the other in like manner. And the buttermilk trickled down on either side of his head. Thus was the king plagued and tormented, and made miserable by Sakka's doings.

[1] The four *apāye* = Hell, birth as an animal, birth as a *peta* (ghost), birth among the *asuras* (Titans or fallen spirits).

When Sakka saw his distress, he made the cart disappear, and took his proper shape again. Poised in mid-air, thunderbolt in hand, he upbraided him—"O wicked and unrighteous king! Will you never become old yourself? will not age assail you? Yet you sport and mock, and do despite to those who are old! It is through you alone, and these doings of yours, that men die on every hand, and fill up the four worlds of unhappiness, and that men cannot care for their parents' welfare! If you do not cease from this, I will cleave your head with my thunderbolt. Go, and do so no more."

With this rebuke, he declared the worth of parents, and made known the advantage of reverencing old age; after which discourse he departed to his own place. From that time forward the king never so much as thought of doing anything like what he had done before.

---

[144] This story ended, the Master, becoming perfectly enlightened, recited these two couplets:—

> "Geese, herons, elephants, and spotted deer
> Though all unlike, alike the lion fear.
>
> "Even so, a child is great if he be clever;
> Fools may be big, but great they can be never[1]."

When this discourse was ended, the Master declared the Truths and identified the Birth:—at the conclusion of the Truths some of those Brethren entered on the First Path, some on the Second, and some upon the Fourth:—"The excellent Lakuṇṭaka was the king in the story, who made people the butt for his jests and then became a butt himself, whilst I myself was Sakka."

No. 203[2].

KHANDHA-VATTA-JĀTAKA.

"[2]*Virūpakkha snakes I love," etc.*—This story the Master told whilst living at Jetavana, about a certain brother.

As he sat, we are told, at the door of his living room, chopping sticks, a snake crept out of a rotten log, and bit his toe; he died on the spot. All the monastery learnt how he had come by his sudden death. In the Hall of Truth

[1] These lines occur in Samyutta-Nikāya, pt. II. xxi. 6 (ii. p. 279, ed. *P. T. S.*).

[2] See *Cullavagga* v. 6 (iii. 75 in *Vinaya Texts, S.B.E.*), where the verses occur again. The verses partly recur in the 'Bower MS,' a Sanskrit MS lately found in the

they began talking about it; saying how Brother So-and-so was sitting at his door, chopping wood, when a snake bit him, and he died immediately of the bite.

[145] The Master came in, and wanted to know what they were discussing as they sat there together. They told him. Said he, "Brethren, if our brother had practised kindness towards the four royal races of serpents, that snake would not have bitten him: wise anchorites in by-gone days, before the Buddha was born, by using kindness to these four royal races, were released from the fear that sprang from these serpents." Then he told them an old-world tale.

Once upon a time, during the reign of Brahmadatta king of Benares, the Bodhisatta came into the world as a young brahmin of Kāsi. When he came of age, he quelled his passions and took upon him the life of an ascetic; he developed the Supernatural Faculties and the Attainments; he built an hermitage by the bend of the Ganges near the foot of Himalaya, and there he dwelt, surrounded by a band of ascetics, lost in the rapture of meditation.

At that time there were many kinds of snakes upon the Ganges bank, which did mischief to the hermits, and many of them perished by snake-bite. The ascetics told the matter to the Bodhisatta. He summoned all the ascetics to meet him, and thus addressed them: "If you showed goodwill to the four royal races of snakes, no serpents would bite you. Therefore from this time forward do you show goodwill to the four royal races." Then he added this verse:—

"Virūpakkha snakes I love,
Erāpatha snakes I love,
Chabbyāputta snakes I love,
Kaṇhāgotamas I love."

After thus naming the four royal families of the snakes, he added: "If you can cultivate goodwill towards these, no snake creature will bite you or do you harm." Then he repeated the second verse:—[146]

"Creatures all beneath the sun,
Two feet, four feet, more, or none—
How I love you, every one!"

Having declared the nature of the love within him, he uttered another verse by way of prayer:—

"Creatures all, two feet or four,
You with none, and you with more,
Do not hurt me, I implore!"

ruins of an ancient city in Kashgaria (see *J.P.T.S.*, 1893, p. 64). The kinds of snakes mentioned cannot be identified. Snake charms are extremely common in Sanskrit; there are many in the Atharva Veda.

Then again, in general terms, he repeated one verse more:—

"All ye creatures that have birth,
Breathe, and move upon the earth,
Happy be ye, one and all,
Never into mischief fall[1]."

[147] Thus did he set forth how one must show love and goodwill to all creatures without distinction; he reminded his hearers of the virtues of the Three Treasures, saying—"Infinite is the Buddha, infinite the Law, and the Order infinite." He said, "Remember the quality of the Three Treasures;" and thus having shown them the infinity of the Three Treasures, and wishing to show them that all beings are finite, he added, "Finite and measurable are creeping things, snakes, scorpions, centipedes, spiders, lizards, mice." Then again, "As the passions and lusts in these creatures are the qualities which make them finite and limited, let us be protected night and day against these finite things by the power of the Three Treasures, which are infinite: wherefore remember the worth of the Three Treasures." Then he recited this stanza:—

"Now I am guarded safe, and fenced around;
Now let all creatures leave me to my ground.
All honour to the Blessed One I pay,
And the seven Buddhas who have passed away."

[148] And bidding them also remember the seven Buddhas[2] whilst they did honour, the Bodhisatta composed this guardian charm and delivered it to his band of sages. Thenceforward the sages bore in mind the Bodhisatta's admonition, and cherished love and goodwill, and remembered the Buddha's virtues. As they did this, all the snake kind departed from them. And the Bodhisatta cultivated the Excellencies, and attained to Brahma's heaven.

When the Master had ended this discourse, he identified the Birth:—"The Buddha's followers were then the followers of the sage; and their Teacher was I myself."

[1] All the verses hitherto given match, and are to be taken together as the "First gāthā." The other is in a different metre, and is the "Second gāthā."

[2] For the seven Buddhas, see Wilson, *Select Works*, ii. 5.

No. 204.

VĪRAKA-JĀTAKA.

"*O have you seen*," *etc.*—This story the Master told, while dwelling at Jetavana, about imitating the Buddha.

When the Elders had gone with their followers to visit Devadatta[1], the Master asked Sāriputta what Devadatta had done when he saw them. The reply was that he had imitated the Buddha. The Master rejoined, "Not now only has Devadatta imitated me and thereby come to ruin; he did just the same before." Then, at the Elder's request, he told an old-world tale.

---

[149] Once upon a time, while Brahmadatta reigned as king in Benares, the Bodhisatta became a marsh crow, and dwelt by a certain pool. His name was Vīraka, the Strong.

There arose a famine in Kāsi. Men could not spare food for the crows, nor make offering to goblins and snakes. One by one the crows left the famine-stricken land, and betook them to the woods.

A certain crow named Saviṭṭhaka, who lived at Benares, took with him his lady crow and went to the place where Vīraka lived, making his abode beside the same pool.

One day, this crow was seeking food about the pool. He saw how Vīraka went down into it, and made a meal off some fish; and afterwards came up out of the water again, and stood drying his feathers. "Under the wing of that crow," thought he, "plenty of fish are to be got. I will become his servant." So he drew near.

"What is it, Sir?" asked Vīraka.

"I want to be your servant, my lord!" was the reply.

Vīraka agreed, and from that time the other served him. And from that time, Vīraka used to eat enough fish to keep him alive, and the rest he gave to Saviṭṭhaka as soon as he had caught them; and when Saviṭṭhaka had eaten enough to keep him alive, he gave what was over to his wife.

After a while pride came into his heart. "This crow," said he, "is black, and so am I: in eyes and beak and feet, too, there is no difference between us. I don't want his fish; I will catch my own!" So he told Vīraka that for the future he intended to go down to the water and catch fish himself. Then Vīraka said, "Good friend, you do not belong to a

[1] Sāriputta and Moggallāna visited the arch-heretic to try if they could win back his followers to the Master. The story of their visit, and how it succeeded, is told in the Vinaya, *Cullavagga*, vii. 4 foll. (translated in *S.B.E.*, *Vinaya Texts*, iii. 256). See also vol. i. no. 11.

tribe of such crows as are born to go into water and catch fish. Don't destroy yourself!"

But in spite of this attempt to dissuade him, Saviṭṭhaka did not take the warning to heart. Down he went to the pool, down into the water; but he could not make his way through the weeds and come out again—there he was, entangled in the weeds, with only the tip of his beak appearing above the water. So not being able to breathe he perished there beneath the water.

[150] His mate noticed that he did not return, and went to Vīraka to ask news of him. "My lord," she asked, "Saviṭṭhaka is not to be seen: where is he?" And as she asked him this, she repeated the first stanza:—

"O have you seen Saviṭṭhaka, O Vīraka, have you seen
My sweet-voiced mate whose neck is like the peacock in its sheen?"

When Vīraka heard it, he replied, "Yes, I know where he is gone," and recited the second stanza:—

"He was not born to dive beneath the wave,
But what he could not do he needs must try;
So the poor bird has found a watery grave,
Entangled in the weeds, and left to die."

When the lady-crow heard it, weeping, she returned to Benares.

After this discourse was ended, the Master identified the Birth:—"Devadatta was then incarnate as Saviṭṭhaka, and I myself was Vīraka."

No. 205.

GAṄGEYYA-JĀTAKA.

[151] "*Fine are the fish*," *etc.*—This story the Master told while dwelling at Jetavana, about two young Brethren.

These two young fellows, we are told, belonged to a good family of Sāvatthi, and had embraced the faith. But they, not realising the impurity of the body[1], sang the praises of their beauty, and went about bragging of it.

[1] Reading *an*-anuyuñjitvā.

One day they fell into a dispute on this point. "You're handsome, but so am I," said each of them; then, spying an aged Elder sitting not far away, they agreed that he was likely to know whether they were beautiful or not. Then they approached him with the question, "Sir, which of us is beautiful?" The Elder replied, "Friends, I am more beautiful than either of you." At this the young men reviled him, and went off, grumbling that he told them something they did not ask, but would not tell them what they did.

The Brotherhood became aware of this event; and one day, when they were all together in the Hall of Truth, they began talking about it. "Friend, how the old Elder shamed those two young fellows whose heads were full of their own beauty!" The Master came in, and asked what they were talking of now as they sat together. They told him. He rejoined, "This is not the only time, Brethren, that our friends were full of the praises of their own beauty. In olden times they used to go about boasting of it as they do now." And then he told them an old-world tale.

Once upon a time, during the reign of Brahmadatta, king of Benares, the Bodhisatta became a tree sprite on the bank of the Ganges. At the point where Ganges and Jumna meet, two fish met together, one from the Ganges and one from the Jumna. "I am beautiful!" said one, "and so are you!" and then they fell to quarrelling about their beauty. Not far from the Ganges they saw a Tortoise lying on the bank. "Yon fellow shall decide whether or no we are beautiful!" said they; and they went up to him. "Which of us is beautiful, friend Tortoise," they asked, "the Ganges fish or the Jumna fish?" The Tortoise answered, "The Ganges fish is beautiful, and the Jumna fish is beautiful: but I am more beautiful than you both." And to explain it, he uttered the first verse:—[152]

"Fine are the fish of Jumna stream, the Ganges fish are fine,
But a four-footed creature, with a tapering neck like mine,
Round like a spreading banyan tree, must all of them outshine."

When the fish heard this, they cried, "Ah, you rascally Tortoise! you won't answer our question, but you answer another one!" and they repeated the second verse:—

"We ask him this, he answers that: indeed a strange reply!
By his own tongue his praise is sung:—I like it not, not I!"

When this discourse was concluded, the Master identified the Birth:—"In those days the young Brothers were the two fish, the old man was the tortoise, and I was the tree-sprite who saw the whole thing from the Ganges bank."

No. 206[1].

KURUṄGA-MIGA-JĀTAKA.

"*Come, Tortoise,*" *etc.*—This story the Master told at Veḷuvana, about Devadatta. News came to the Master that Devadatta was plotting his death. "Ah, Brethren," said he, "it was just the same long ago; Devadatta tried then to kill me, as he is trying now." And he told them this story.

---

[153] Once upon a time, when Brahmadatta was king of Benares, the Bodhisatta became an Antelope, and lived within a forest, in a thicket near a certain lake. Not far from the same lake, sat a Woodpecker perched at the top of a tree; and in the lake dwelt a Tortoise. And the three became friends, and lived together in amity.

A hunter, wandering about in the wood, observed the Bodhisatta's footprint at the going down into the water; and he set a trap of leather, strong, like an iron chain, and went his way. In the first watch of the night the Bodhisatta went down to drink, and got caught in the noose: whereat he cried loud and long. Thereupon the Woodpecker flew down from her tree-top, and the Tortoise came out of the water, and consulted what was to be done.

Said the Woodpecker to the Tortoise, "Friend, you have teeth—bite this snare through; I will go and see to it that the hunter keeps away; and if we both do our best, our friend will not lose his life." To make this clear he uttered the first stanza:—

> "Come, Tortoise, tear the leathern snare, and bite it through and through,
> And of the hunter I'll take care, and keep him off from you."

The Tortoise began to gnaw the leather thong: the Woodpecker made his way to the hunter's dwelling. At dawn of day the hunter went out, knife in hand. As soon as the bird saw him start, he uttered a cry, flapped his wings, and struck him in the face as he left the front door. "Some bird of ill omen has struck me!" thought the hunter; he turned back, and lay down for a little while. Then he rose up again, and took his knife. The bird reasoned within himself, "The first time he went out by the front door, so now he will leave by the back:" and he sat him down behind the house. [154] The hunter, too, reasoned in the same way: "When I went out by the front door, I saw a bad omen, now will I

[1] Figured on the Bharhut Stupa (Cunningham, p. 67, and pl. xxvii. 9).

go out by the back!" and so he did. But the bird cried out again, and struck him in the face. Finding that he was again struck by a bird of ill omen, the hunter exclaimed, "This creature will not let me go!" and turning back he lay down until sunrise, and when the sun was risen, he took his knife and started.

The Woodpecker made all haste back to his friends. "Here comes the hunter!" he cried. By this time the Tortoise had gnawed through all the thongs but one tough thong: his teeth seemed as though they would fall out, and his mouth was all smeared with blood. The Bodhisatta saw the young hunter coming on like lightning, knife in hand: he burst the thong, and fled into the woods. The Woodpecker perched upon his tree-top. But the Tortoise was so weak, that he lay where he was. The hunter threw him into a bag, and tied it to a tree.

The Bodhisatta observed that the Tortoise was taken, and determined to save his friend's life. So he let the hunter see him, and made as though he were weak. The hunter saw him, and thinking him to be weak, seized his knife and set out in pursuit. The Bodhisatta, keeping just out of his reach, led him into the forest; and when he saw that they had come far away, gave him the slip and returned swift as the wind by another way. He lifted the bag with his horns, threw it upon the ground, ripped it open and let the Tortoise out. And the Woodpecker came down from the tree.

Then the Bodhisatta thus addressed them both: "My life has been saved by you, and you have done a friend's part to me. Now the hunter will come and take you; so do you, friend Woodpecker, migrate elsewhere with your brood, and you, friend Tortoise, dive into the water." They did so.

The Master, becoming perfectly enlightened, uttered the second stanza:—
[155]

"The Tortoise went into the pond, the Deer into the wood,
And from the tree the Woodpecker carried away his brood."

The hunter returned, and saw none of them. He found his bag torn; picked it up, and went home sorrowful. And the three friends lived all their life long in unbroken amity, and then passed away to fare according to their deeds.

When the Master had ended this discourse, he identified the Birth:—"Devadatta was the huntsman, Sāriputta the Woodpecker, Moggallāna the Tortoise, and I was the Antelope."

No. 207.

ASSAKA-JĀTAKA.

"*Once with the great king Assaka,*" *etc.*—This story the Master told whilst staying in Jetavana, about some one who was distracted by the recollection of a former wife. He asked the Brother whether he were really lovesick. The man said, Yes. "Whom are you in love with?" the Master continued. "My late wife," was the reply. Then the Master said, "Not this once only, Brother, have you been full of desire for this woman; in olden days her love brought you to great misery." And he told a story.

Once upon a time, there was a king Assaka reigning in Potali, which is a city of the kingdom of Kāsi. His queen consort, named Ubbarī, was very dear to him; she was charming, and graceful, and beautiful passing the beauty of women, though not so fair as a goddess. She died: and at her death the king was plunged in grief, and became sad and miserable. He had the body laid in a coffin, and embalmed with oil and ointment, and laid beneath the bed; and there he lay without food, weeping and wailing. [156] In vain did his parents and kinsfolk, friends and courtiers, priests and laymen, bid him not to grieve, since all things pass away; they could not move him. As he lay in sorrow, seven days passed by.

Now the Bodhisatta was at that time an ascetic, who had gained the Five Supernatural Faculties and the Eight Attainments; he dwelt at the foot of Himalaya. He was possessed of perfect supernatural insight, and as he looked round India with his heavenly vision, he saw this king lamenting, and straightway resolved to help him. By his miraculous power he rose in the air, and alighted in the king's park, and sat down on the ceremonial stone, like a golden image.

A young brahmin of the city of Potali entered the park, and seeing the Bodhisatta, he greeted him and sat down. The Bodhisatta began to talk pleasantly with him. "Is the king a just ruler?" he asked.

"Yes, Sir, the king is just," replied the youth; "but his queen is just dead; he has laid her body in a coffin, and lies down lamenting her; and to-day is the seventh day since he began.—Why do you not free the king from this great grief? Virtuous beings like you ought to overcome the king's sorrow."

"I do not know the king, young man," said the Bodhisatta; "but if he were to come and ask me, I would tell him the place where she has now come into the flesh again, and make her speak herself."

"Then, holy Sir, stay here until I bring the king to you," said the youth. The Bodhisatta agreed, and he hastened into the king's presence, and told him about it. "You should visit this being with the divine insight!" he told the king.

The king was overjoyed at the thought of seeing Ubbarī; and he entered his chariot and drove to the place. Greeting the Bodhisatta, he sat down on one side, and asked, "Is it true, as I am told, that you know where my queen has come into being again?"

"Yes, I do, my lord king," replied he.

Then the king asked where it was.

The Bodhisatta replied, "O king, she was intoxicated with her beauty, and so fell into negligence and did not do fair and virtuous acts; so now she has become a little dung-worm in this very park." [157]

"I don't believe it!" said the king.

"Then I will show her to you, and make her speak," answered the Bodhisatta.

"Please make her speak!" said the king.

The Bodhisatta commanded—"Let the two that are busy rolling a lump of cow-dung, come forth before the king!" and by his power he made them do it, and they came. The Bodhisatta pointed one out to the king: "There is your queen Ubbarī, O king! she has just come out of this lump, following her husband the dung-worm. Look and see."

"What! my queen Ubbarī a dung-worm? I don't believe it!" cried the king.

"I will make her speak, O king!"

"Pray make her speak, holy Sir!" said he.

The Bodhisatta by his power gave her speech. "Ubbarī!" said he.

"What is it, holy Sir?" she asked, in a human voice.

"What was your name in your former character?" the Bodhisatta asked her.

"My name was Ubbarī, Sir," she replied, "the consort of king Assaka."

"Tell me," the Bodhisatta went on, "which do you love best now—king Assaka, or this dung-worm?"

"O Sir, that was my former birth," said she. "Then I lived with him in this park, enjoying shape and sound, scent, savour and touch; but now that my memory is confused by re-birth, what is he? Why, now I would kill king Assaka, and would smear the feet of my husband the dung-worm with the blood flowing from his throat!" and in the midst of the king's company, she uttered these verses in a human voice:—

"Once with the great king Assaka, who was my husband dear,
Beloving and beloved, I walked about this garden here.

"But now new sorrows and new joys have made the old ones flee,
And dearer far than Assaka my Worm is now to me."

[158] When king Assaka heard this, he repented on the spot; and at once he caused the queen's body to be removed and washed his head. He saluted the Bodhisatta, and went back into the city; where he married another queen, and ruled in righteousness. And the Bodhisatta, having instructed the king, and set him free from sorrow, returned again to the Himalayas.

When the Master had ended this discourse, he declared the Truths and identified the Birth:—at the conclusion of the Truths, the lovesick Brother reached the Fruit of the First Path:—"Your late wife was Ubbarī; you, the lovesick Brother, were king Assaka; Sāriputta was the young brahmin; and the anchorite was I myself."

No. 208.

SUṀSUMĀRA-JĀTAKA[1].

"*Rose-apple, jack-fruit,*" *etc.*—This story the Master told at Jetavana, about Devadatta's attempts to murder him[2]. When he heard of these attempts, the Master said, "This is not the first time that Devadatta has tried to murder me;

[1] Cf. *Markaṭa-jātaka*, Mahāvastu ii. 208; *Cariyā-Piṭaka*, iii. 7; Morris, *Contemp. Rev.* vol. 39, quoting Griffis, *Japanese Fairy World*, p. 153. A monkey outwits a crocodile in No. 57, above.

The following variant, from Russia (Moscow district) may be of interest. It was given me by Mr I. Nestor Schnurmann, who heard it from his nurse (about 1860).—Once upon a time, the King of the Fishes was wanting in wisdom. His advisers told him that once he could get the heart of the fox, he would become wise. So he sent a deputation, consisting of the great magnates of the sea, whales and others. "Our king wants your advice on some state affairs." The fox, flattered, consented. A whale took him on his back. On the way the waves beat upon him; at last he asked what they really wanted. They said, what their king really wanted was to eat his heart, by which he hoped to become clever. He said, "Why didn't you tell me that before? I would gladly sacrifice my life for such a worthy object. But we foxes always leave our hearts at home. Take me back and I'll fetch it. Otherwise I'm sure your king will be angry." So they took him back. As soon as he got near the shore, he leaped on land, and cried "Ah you fools! Have you ever heard of an animal not carrying his heart with him?" and ran off. The fish had to return empty.

[2] These attempts of Devadatta, and how they were foiled, are set forth in *Cullavagga*, VII. iii. 6 foll., trans. in *S. B. E.*, *Vinaya Texts*, iii. 243 f.

he did the same before, and yet could not so much as make me afraid." Then he told this story.

Once upon a time, while Brahmadatta was king of Benares, the Bodhisatta came to life at the foot of Himalaya as a Monkey. He grew strong and sturdy, big of frame, well-to-do, and lived by a curve of the river Ganges in a forest haunt.

Now at that time there was a Crocodile dwelling in the Ganges. The Crocodile's mate saw the great frame of the monkey, [159] and she conceived a longing for his heart to eat. So she said to her lord: "Sir, I desire to eat the heart of that great king of the monkeys!"

"Good wife," said the Crocodile, "I live in the water and he lives on dry land: how can we catch him?"

"By hook or by crook," she replied, "caught he must be. If I don't get him, I shall die."

"All right," answered the Crocodile, consoling her, "don't trouble yourself. I have a plan; I will give you his heart to eat."

So when the Bodhisatta was sitting on the bank of the Ganges, after taking a drink of water, the Crocodile drew near, and said:

"Sir Monkey, why do you live on bad fruits in this old familiar place? On the other side of the Ganges there is no end to the mango trees, and labuja trees[1], with fruit sweet as honey! Is it not better to cross over and have all kinds of wild fruit to eat?"

"Lord Crocodile," the Monkey made answer, "deep and wide is the Ganges: how shall I get across?"

"If you will go, I will mount you on my back, and carry you over."

The Monkey trusted him, and agreed. "Come here, then," said the other, "up on my back with you!" and up the monkey climbed. But when the Crocodile had swum a little way, he plunged the Monkey under the water.

"Good friend, you are letting me sink!" cried the Monkey. "What is that for?"

Said the Crocodile, "You think I am carrying you out of pure good nature? Not a bit of it! My wife has a longing for your heart, and I want to give it her to eat!"

"Friend," said the Monkey, "it is nice of you to tell me. Why, if our heart were inside us when we go jumping among the tree-tops, it would be all knocked to pieces!"

"Well, where do you keep it?" asked the other.

The Bodhisatta pointed out a fig-tree, with clusters of ripe fruit,

[1] Artocarpus Lacucha (*Childers*).

standing not far off. "See," said he, "there are our hearts hanging on yon fig-tree." [160]

"If you will show me your heart," said the Crocodile, "then I won't kill you."

"Take me to the tree, then, and I will point it out to you hanging upon it."

The Crocodile brought him to the place. The Monkey leapt off his back, and climbing up the fig-tree sat upon it. "O silly Crocodile!" said he, "you thought that there were creatures that kept their hearts in a tree-top! You are a fool, and I have outwitted you! You may keep your fruit to yourself. Your body is great, but you have no sense." And then to explain this idea he uttered the following stanzas:—

"Rose-apple, jack-fruit, mangoes too across the water there I see;
Enough of them, I want them not; my fig is good enough for me!

"Great is your body, verily, but how much smaller is your wit!
Now go your ways, Sir Crocodile, for I have had the best of it."

The Crocodile, feeling as sad and miserable as if he had lost a thousand pieces of money, went back sorrowing to the place where he lived.

When the Master had ended this discourse, he identified the Birth:—"In those days Devadatta was the Crocodile, the lady Ciñcā was his mate, and I was the Monkey."

No. 209[1].

KAKKARA-JĀTAKA.

"*Trees a many have I seen,*" *etc.*—This story the Master told while dwelling at Jetavana, about a Brother who was one of the fellow-students of Elder Sāriputta, Captain of the Faith.

This fellow, as we learn, [161] was clever at taking care of his person. Food very hot or very cold he would not eat, for fear it should do him harm. He never went out for fear of being hurt by cold or heat; and he would not have rice which was either over-boiled or too hard.

The Brotherhood learnt how much care he took of himself. In the Hall of Truth, they all discussed it. "Friend, what a clever fellow Brother So-and-so is in knowing what is good for him!" The Master came in, and asked what they were talking of as they sat there together. They told him. Then he rejoined,

[1] Compare latter part of the Second *Çakuntaka Jātaka*, Mahāvastu ii. 250; the first line of the first verse and the whole of the second are nearly the same.

"Not only now is our young friend careful for his personal comfort. He was just the same in olden days." And he told them an old-world tale.

Once upon a time, in the reign of Brahmadatta, king of Benares, the Bodhisatta became a Tree-spirit in a forest glade. A certain fowler, with a decoy bird, hair noose, and stick, went into the forest in search of birds. He began to follow one old bird which flew off into the woods, trying to escape. The bird would not give him a chance of catching it in his snare, but kept rising and alighting, rising and alighting. So the fowler covered himself with twigs and branches, and set his noose and stick again and again. But the bird, wishing to make him ashamed of himself, sent forth a human voice and repeated the first stanza:—

"Trees a many have I seen
Growing in the woodland green:
But, O Tree, they could not do
Any such strange things as you!"

So saying, the bird flew off and went elsewhere. When it had gone, the fowler repeated the second verse:—[162]

"This old bird, that knows the snare,
Off has flown into the air;
Forth from out his cage has broken,
And with human voice has spoken!"

So said the fowler; and having hunted through the woods, took what he could catch and went home again.

When the Master had ended this discourse, he identified the Birth:—"Devadatta was the fowler then, the young dandy was the bird, and the tree-sprite that saw the whole thing was I myself."

No. 210.

KANDAGALAKA-JĀTAKA.

"*O friend,*" *etc.*—This was told by the Master, during a stay in Veḷuvana, about Devadatta's attempts to imitate him[1]. When he heard of these attempts to imitate him, the Master said, "This is not the first time Devadatta has destroyed himself by imitating me; the same thing happened before." Then he told this story.

---

[1] See above, note to no. 208.

Once upon a time, when Brahmadatta was king of Benares, the Bodhisatta entered into life as a Woodpecker. In a wood of acacia trees he lived, and his name was Khadiravaniya, the Bird of the Acacia Wood. He had a comrade named Kandagalaka, or Eatbulb, who got his food in a wood full of good fruit.

One day the friend went to visit Khadiravaniya. "My friend is come!" thought Khadiravaniya; and he led him into the acacia wood, and pecked at the tree-trunks until the insects came out, which he gave to his friend. As each was given him, the friend pecked it up, and ate it, as if it were a honey cake. As he ate, pride arose in his heart. [163] "This bird is a woodpecker," thought he, "and so am I. What need for me to be fed by him? I will get my own food in this acacia wood!" So he said to Khadiravaniya,

"Friend, don't trouble yourself,—I will get my own food in the acacia wood."

Then said the other, "You belong to a tribe of birds which finds its food in a forest of pithless silk-cotton trees, and trees that bear abundant fruit; but the acacia is full of pith, and hard. Please do not do so!"

"What!" said Kandagalaka—"am I not a woodpecker?" And he would not listen, but pecked at an acacia trunk. In a moment his beak snapped off, and his eyes bade fair to fall out of his head, and his head split. So not being able to hold fast to the tree, he fell to the ground, repeating the first verse:—

"O friend, what is this thorny, cool-leaved tree
Which at one blow has broke my beak for me?"

Having heard this, Khadiravaniya recited the second stanza:—

"This bird was good for rotten wood
And soft; but once he tried,
By some ill hap, hard trees to tap;
And broke his skull, and died."

[164] So said Khadiravaniya; and added, "O Kandagalaka, the tree where you broke your head is hard and strong!"

But the other perished then and there.

When the Master had ended this discourse, he identified the Birth:—"Devadatta was Kandagalaka, but Khadiravaniya was I myself."

No. 211[1].

SOMADATTA-JĀTAKA.

"*All the year long never ceasing,*" *etc.*—This story the Master told while dwelling at Jetavana, about Elder Lāḷudāyī, or Udāyī the Simpleton.

This man, we learn, was unable to get out a single sound in the presence of two or three people. He was so very nervous, that he said one thing when he meant another. It happened that the Brethren were speaking of this as they sat together in the Hall of Truth. [165] The Master came in, and asked what they were talking of as they sat there together. They told him. He answered, "Brethren, this is not the first time that Lāḷudāyī has been a very nervous man. It was just the same before." And he told an old-world tale.

Once on a time, while Brahmadatta was king of Benares, the Bodhisatta was born into a certain brahmin family in the kingdom of Kāsi. When he came of age, he went to study at Takkasilā. On returning he found his family poor; and he bade his parents farewell and set out to Benares, saying to himself, "I will set up my fallen family again!"

At Benares he became the king's attendant; and he grew very dear to the king and became a favourite.

Now his father lived by ploughing the land, but he had only one pair of oxen; and one of them died. He came before the Bodhisatta, and said to him, "Son, one of my oxen is dead, and the ploughing does not go on. Ask the king to give you one ox!"

"No, Father," answered he, "I have but just now seen the king; I ought not to ask him for oxen now:—you ask him."

"My son," said his father, "you do not know how bashful I am. If there are two or three people present I cannot get a word out. If I go to ask the king for an ox, I shall end by giving him this one!"

"Father," said the Bodhisatta, "what must be, must be. I cannot ask the king; but I will train you to do it." So he led his father to a cemetery where there were clumps of sweet grass; and tying up tufts of it, he scattered them here and there, and named them one by one, pointing them out to his father: "That is the King, that is the Viceroy, this is the Chief Captain. Now, Father, when you come before the king, you must first say—'Long live the king!' and then repeat this verse, to ask for an ox;" and this is the verse he taught him:—

"I had two oxen to my plough, with which my work was done,
But one is dead! O mighty prince, please give me another one!"

[1] Fausbøll, *Five Jātakas*, p. 31; Comm. on *Dhammapada* verse 152 (p. 317 of F.'s edition).

[166] For the space of a whole year the man learnt this couplet; and then he said to his son—"Dear Somadatta, I have learnt the lines! Now I can say it before any man! Take me to the king."

So the Bodhisatta, taking a suitable present, led his father into the king's presence. "Long live the king!" cried the brahmin, offering his present.

"Who is this brahmin, Somadatta?" the king asked.

"Great king, it is my father," he answered.

"Why has he come here?" asked the king. Then the brahmin repeated his couplet, to ask for the ox:—

"I had two oxen to my plough, with which my work was done,
But one is dead! O mighty prince, please take the other one!"

The king saw that there was some mistake. "Somadatta," said he, smiling, "you have plenty of oxen at home, I suppose?"

"If so, great king, they are your gift!"

At this answer the king was pleased. He gave the man, for a brahmin's offering, sixteen oxen, with fine caparison, and a village to live in, and sent him away with great honour. The brahmin ascended a car drawn by Sindh horses, pure white, and went to his dwelling in great pomp.

As the Bodhisatta sat beside his father in the chariot, said he, "Father, I taught you the whole year long, and yet when the moment came you gave your ox to the king!" and he uttered the first stanza:—

"All the year long never ceasing with unwearied diligence
Where the sweet grass grows in clusters day by day he practised it:
When he came amid the courtiers all at once he changed the sense;
Practice truly nought availeth if a man has little wit."

[167] When he heard this, the brahmin uttered the second stanza:—

"He that asks, dear Somadatta, takes his chance between the two—
May get more, or may get nothing: when you ask, 'tis ever so."

When the Master by this story had shown how Simpleton Udāyī had been just as bashful before as he was then, he identified the Birth:—"Lāḷudāyī was the father of Somadatta, and I was Somadatta myself."

No. 212.

UCCHIṬṬHA-BHATTA-JĀTAKA.

"*Hot at top*," *etc.* This is a story told by the Master while at Jetavana, about one who hankered after a lost wife. The Brother in question was asked by the Master if he really was lovesick. Yes, he said, so he was. "For whom?" was the next question. "For my late wife." "Brother," the Master said, "this same woman in former days was wicked, and made you eat the leavings of her paramour." Then he told this story of the past.

Once upon a time, while Brahmadatta was reigning in Benares, the Bodhisatta was born as one of a family of poor acrobats, that lived by begging. So when he grew up, he was needy and squalid, and by begging he lived.

There was at the time, in a certain village of Kāsi, a brahmin whose wife was bad and wicked, and did wrong. [168] And it befel that the husband went abroad one day upon some matter, and her lover watching his time went to visit the house. After she had received him, he said, "I will eat a bit before I go." So she made ready the food, and served up rice hot with sauce and curry, and gave it him, bidding him eat: she herself stood at the door, watching for the brahmin's coming. And while the lover was eating, the Bodhisatta stood waiting for a morsel.

At that moment the brahmin set his face for home. And his wife saw him drawing nigh, and ran in quickly—"Up, my man is coming!" and she made her lover go down into the store-room. The husband came in; she gave him a seat, and water for washing the hands; and upon the cold rice that was left by the other she turned out some hot rice, and set it before him. He put his hand into the rice, and felt that it was hot above and cold below. "This must be some one else's leavings," thought he; and so he asked the woman about it in the words of the first stanza:

"Hot at top, and cold at bottom, not alike it seems to be:
I would ask you for the reason: come, my lady, answer me!"

Again and again he asked, but she, fearing lest her deed should be discovered, held her peace. Then a thought came into our tumbler's mind. "The man down in the store-room must be a lover, and this is the master of the house: the wife says nothing, for fear that her deed be made manifest. Soho! I will declare the whole matter, and show the brahmin that a man is hidden in his larder!" [169] And he told him the whole matter: how that when he had gone out from his house, another had come in, and had done evil; how he had eaten the first rice, and the wife had stood by the door to watch the road; and how the other man had been hidden in the store-room. And in so saying, he repeated the second stanza:—

"I am a tumbler, Sir: I came on begging here intent;
He that you seek is hiding in the store-room, where he went!"

By his top-knot he haled the man out of the store-room, and bade him take care not to do the like again; and then he went away. The brahmin rebuked and beat them both, and gave them such a lesson that they were not likely to do the same again. Afterwards he passed away to fare according to his deserts.

When the Master had ended his discourse, he declared the Truths, and identified the Birth:—at the conclusion of the Truths the lovesick Brother reached the Fruit of the First Path:—"Your late wife was then the brahmin's lady; you, the lovesick Brother, were the brahmin himself; and I was the tumbler."

No. 213.

BHARU-JĀTAKA.

"*The king of Bharu,*" *etc.* This story the Master told while staying at Jetavana, about the king of Kosala.

Now we read that magnificent presents were made to the Blessed One and his company, and they were held in great respect, as it is written: "At that time the Blessed One was honoured and revered, respected, reverenced, highly esteemed, and received rich presents—robes, food, lodgement, drugs and medicines, and provisions; and the Brotherhood was honoured, etc. (as before); but the pilgrims of heterodox schools were not honoured, etc. (as before)[1]." Well, the sectaries, finding that honour and gifts diminished, convened a secret meeting for deliberation. "Since the appearance of the Priest Gotama," they said, [170] "honour and gifts come no more to us, but he has got the best of both. What can be the reason of his good fortune?" Then one of them spoke as follows. "Priest Gotama has the best and chiefest place in all India to live in, and that is the reason of his success." Then the others said, "If this is the reason, we will make a rival settlement above Jetavana, and then we shall receive presents." This was the conclusion they came to.

[1] This appears to be a regular formula; the Sanskrit equivalent occurs in *Divyāvadāna*, p. 91.

"But," thought they, "if we make our settlement unknown to the king, the Brethren will prevent us. If he accepts a present, he will not be disinclined to break up their settlement. So we had best bribe him to give us a place for ours."

So by the intervention of his courtiers, they offered an hundred thousand pieces to the king, with this message; "Great King, we want to make a rival settlement in Jetavana. If the Brethren tell you they won't permit it, please do not give them any answer." To this the king agreed, because he wanted the bribe.

After thus conciliating the king, the schismatics got an architect and put the work in hand. There was a good deal of noise about it.

"What is all this great noise and tumult, Ānanda?" the Master asked. "The noise," said he, "is some sectaries who are having a new settlement built." "That is not a fit place," he rejoined, "for them to settle. These sectaries are fond of noise; there's no living with them." Then he called the Brotherhood together, and bade them go inform the king, and have the building put a stop to.

The Brethren went and stood by the palace door. The king, as soon as he heard of their coming, knew they must be come about stopping the new settlement. But he had been bribed, and so he ordered his attendants to say the king was not at home. The Brethren went back and told the Master. The Master guessed that a bribe had been given, and sent his two chief disciples[1]. But the king, as soon as he heard of their coming, gave the same order as before; and they too returned and told the Master. The Master said, "Doubtless the king is not able to stay at home to-day; he must be out."

Next forenoon, he dressed himself, took his bowl and robe, and with five hundred brethren walked to the door of the palace. The king heard them come; he descended from the upper story, and took from the Buddha his alms-bowl. Then he gave rice and gruel to him and his followers, and with a salutation sat down on one side.

The Master began an exposition for the king's behoof, in these words. "Great King, other kings in by-gone days have taken bribes, and then by making virtuous people quarrel together have been dispossessed of their kingdom, and been utterly destroyed." And then, at his request, the Master told an old-world tale.

---

[171] Once upon a time, king Bharu was reigning over the kingdom of Bharu. At the same time the Bodhisatta was Teacher of a troop of monks. He was an ascetic who had acquired the Five Supernatural Faculties and the Eight Attainments; and he dwelt a long time in the region of Himalaya.

He came down from Himalaya to buy salt and seasoning, followed by five hundred ascetics; and they came by stages to the city of Bharu. He went a-begging through the city; and then coming forth from it, he sat down by the northern gate, at the root of a banyan tree all covered with twigs and branches. There he made a meal, and there he took up his abode.

Now when that band of hermits had dwelt there by the space of half a moon, there came another Teacher with another five hundred, who went seeking alms about the city, and then came out and sat beneath just such

[1] Sāriputta and Moggallāna.

another banyan tree by the south gate, and ate, and dwelt there. And the two bands abode there so long as they would, and then returned again to Himalaya.

When they had gone, the tree by the south gate withered away. Next time, they who had dwelt under it came first, and perceiving that their tree was withered, they first went on their rounds throughout the city, seeking alms, and then passing out by the northern gate, they ate and abode under the banyan tree that was by that gate. And the other band, coming afterwards, went their rounds in the city, and then made ready their meal and would have dwelt by their own tree. "This is not your tree, 'tis ours!" they cried; and they began to quarrel about the tree. The quarrel waxed great: these said—"Take not the place where we dwelt aforetime!" and those—"This time are we first come; do not you take it!" So crying aloud each that they were the owners of it, they all went to the king's palace.

The king ordained that they who had first dwelt there should hold it. [172] Then the others thought—"We will not allow ourselves to say that we have been beaten by these!" They looked about them with divine vision[1], and observing the body of a chariot fit for an emperor to use, they took it and offered it as a gift to the king, begging him to give them too possession of the tree. He took their gift, and ordained that both should dwell under the tree; and so they were there all masters together. Then the other hermits fetched the jewelled wheels of the same chariot, and offered them to the king, praying him, "O mighty king, make us to possess the tree alone!" And the king did so. Then the ascetics repented, and said: "To think that we, who have overcome the love of riches and the lust of the flesh, and have renounced the world, should fall to quarrelling by reason of a tree, and offer bribes for it! This is no seemly thing." And they went away in all haste till they came to Himalaya. And all the spirits that dwelt in the realm of Bharu with one mind were angry with the king, and they brought up the sea, and for the space of three hundred leagues they made the kingdom of Bharu as though it were not. And so for the sake of the king of Bharu alone, all the inhabitants of the kingdom perished thus.

When the Teacher had ended this tale, in his perfect wisdom, he uttered the following stanzas:—

"The king of Bharu, as old stories say,
Made holy hermits quarrel on a day:
For the which sin it fell that he fell dead,
And with him all his kingdom perished.

[1] One of the *Abhiññās* or Supernatural Faculties; see above.

"Wherefore the wise do not approve at all
When that desire into the heart doth fall.
He that is free from guile, whose heart is pure,
All that he says is ever true and sure[1]."

[173] When the Master had ended this story, he added, "Great King, one should not be under the power of desire. Two religious persons ought not to quarrel together." Then he identified the Birth:—"In those days, I was the leader of the sages."

When the king had entertained the Buddha, and he had departed, the king sent some men and had the rival settlement destroyed, and the sectaries became homeless.

No. 214.

PUṆṆA-NADĪ-JĀTAKA.

"*That which can drink*," *etc.*—This story the Master told while staying at Jetavana, about perfect wisdom.

On one occasion, the Brethren were gathered in the Hall of Truth, talking of the Buddha's wisdom. "Friend, the Supreme Buddha's wisdom is great, and wide, cutting, and quick, sharp, penetrating, and full of resource." The Master came in, and asked what they talked of as they sat there together. They told him. "Not now only," said he, "is the Buddha wise and resourceful; he was so in days of yore." And then he told them a story.

Once on a time, while Brahmadatta was king of Benares, the Bodhisatta came into the world as the son of the court chaplain. When he grew up, he studied at Takkasilā; and at his father's death he received the office of chaplain, and he was the king's counsellor in things human and divine.

Afterwards the king opened his ear to breedbates, and in anger bade the Bodhisatta dwell before his face no more, and sent him away from Benares. So he took his wife and family with him, and abode in a certain village of Kāsi. Afterward the king remembered his goodness, and said to himself:

[1] In commenting upon this line, the Scholiast says: "And those who at that time spoke the truth, blaming king Bharu for taking a bribe, found standing room upon a thousand islands which are yet to be seen to-day about the island of Nāḷikera."

"It is not meet that I should send a messenger to fetch my teacher. I will compose a verse of poetry, [174] and write it upon a leaf; I will cause crow's flesh to be cooked; and after I have tied up letter and meat in a white cloth, I will seal it with the king's seal, and send it to him. If he is wise, when he has read the letter and seen that it is crow's-meat, he will come; if not, then he will not come." And so he wrote on the leaf this stanza:—

"That which can drink when rivers are in flood;
That which the corn will cover out of sight;
That which forebodes a traveller on the road—
O wise one, eat! my riddle read aright[1]."

This verse did the king write upon a leaf, and sent it to the Bodhisatta. He read the letter, and thinking—"The king wishes to see me"—he repeated the second verse:—[175]

"The king does not forget to send me crow:
Geese, herons, peacocks,—other birds there are:
If he gives one, he'll give the rest, I know;
If he sent none at all 'twere worser far[2]."

Then he caused his vehicle to be made ready, and went, and looked upon the king. And the king, being pleased, set him again in the place of the king's chaplain.

This discourse ended, the Master identified the Birth:—"Ānanda was the king in those days, and I was his chaplain."

[1] *Kākapeyya*, both in Skr. and in Pali, is proverbial for rivers at the flood. For Skr. see Pāṇini, 2. 1. 33, where some comm. say 'deep,' some 'shallow.' The scholiast here says: "They call rivers *K.* when a crow standing on the bank can stretch out its neck and drink." Buddhaghosha, quoted by Rh. D. in note to *Buddhist Suttas*, *S. B. E.*, p. 178, says the same.—*Kākaguyha* is corn tall enough to hide a crow; see Pāṇ. 3. 2. 5 and the Kāçikā's comment, with the scholiast's note here.—In the dictionary of Vacaspati, vol. 2, p. 1846, col. 1, it is said "When the crow cries *Khare Khare*, a traveller is coming." The schol. here says: "If people wish to know whether an absent friend is coming back, they say—Caw, crow, if so-and-so is coming! and if the crows caw, they know that he will come."—This verse riddles on these three proverbs and beliefs. [For part of this note I am indebted to Prof. Cowell.]

[2] I am not sure of the meaning of these obscure lines, but this is the best I can make of it. The schol. says "When he gets crow's flesh he remembers to send me some; surely he will remember when he gets geese, etc." The phrase—"Geese, herons, peacocks," is a reminiscence of the verse quoted in No. 202, above.

No. 215[1].

KACCHAPA-JĀTAKA.

"*The Tortoise needs must speak*," etc.—This is a story told by the Master while staying in Jetavana, about Kokālika. The circumstances which gave rise to it will be set forth under the Mahātakkāri Birth[2]. Here again the Master said: "This is not the only time, Brethren, that Kokālika has been ruined by talking; it was the same before." And then he told the story as follows.

Once on a time Brahmadatta was king of Benares, and the Bodhisatta, being born to one of the king's court, grew up, and became the king's adviser in all things human and divine. But this king was very talkative; and when he talked there was no chance for any other to get in a word. [176] And the Bodhisatta, wishing to put a stop to his much talking, kept watching for an opportunity.

Now there dwelt a Tortoise in a certain pond in the region of Himalaya. Two young wild Geese, searching for food, struck up an acquaintance with him; and by and bye they grew close friends together. One day these two said to him: "Friend Tortoise, we have a lovely home in Himalaya, on a plateau of Mount Cittakūṭa, in a cave of gold! Will you come with us?"

"Why," said he, "how can I get there?"

"Oh, we will take you, if only you can keep your mouth shut, and say not a word to any body."

"Yes, I can do that," says he; "take me along!"

So they made the Tortoise hold a stick between his teeth; and themselves taking hold so of the two ends, they sprang up into the air.

The village children saw this, and exclaimed—"There are two geese carrying a tortoise by a stick!"

(By this time the geese flying swiftly had arrived at the space above the palace of the king, at Benares.) The Tortoise wanted to cry out—

[1] Fausbøll, *Five Jātakas*, p. 41; *Dhammapada*, p. 418; cp. Benfey's *Pantschatantra*, i. p. 239; Babrius, ed. Lewis, i. 122; Phaedrus, ed. Orelli, 55, 128; Rhys Davids, *Buddhist Birth Stories*, viii.; Jacobs, *Indian Fairy Tales*, pp. 100 and 245.

[2] *Takkāriya-jātaka*, No. 481.

"Well, and if my friends do carry me, what is that to you, you caitiffs?"—and he let go the stick from between his teeth, and falling into the open courtyard he split in two. What an uproar there was! "A tortoise has fallen in the courtyard, and broken in two!" they cried. The king, with the Bodhisatta, and all his court, came up to the place, and seeing the tortoise asked the Bodhisatta a question. "Wise Sir, what made this creature fall?"

"Now's my time!" thought he. "For a long while I have been wishing to admonish the king, and I have gone about seeking my opportunity. No doubt the truth is this: the tortoise and the geese became friendly; the geese must have meant to carry him to Himalaya, and so made him hold a stick between his teeth, and then lifted him into the air; then he must have heard some remark, and wanted to reply; and not being able to keep his mouth shut he must have let himself go; [177] and so he must have fallen from the sky and thus come by his death." So thought he; and addressed the king: "O king, they that have too much tongue, that set no limit to their speaking, ever come to such misfortune as this;" and he uttered the following verses:—

"The Tortoise needs must speak aloud,
Although between his teeth
A stick he bit: yet, spite of it,
He spoke—and fell beneath.

"And now, O mighty master, mark it well.
See thou speak wisely, see thou speak in season.
To death the Tortoise fell:
He talked too much: that was the reason."

"He is speaking of me!" the king thought to himself; and asked the Bodhisatta if it was so.

"Be it you, O great king, or be it another," replied he, "whosoever talks beyond measure comes by some misery of this kind;" and so he made the thing manifest. And thenceforward the king abstained from talking, and became a man of few words.

---

[178] This discourse ended, the Master identified the Birth:—"Kokālika was the tortoise then, the two famous Elders were the two wild geese, Ānanda was the king, and I was his wise adviser."

No. 216.

MACCHA-JĀTAKA.

"*'Tis not the fire,*" *etc.*—This story the Master told during a stay in Jetavana, about one who hankered after a former wife. The Master asked this Brother, "Is it true, Brother, what I hear, that you are lovesick?" "Yes, Sir." "For whom?" "For my late wife." Then the Master said to him: "This wife, Brother, has been the mischief to you. Long ago by her means you came near being spitted and roasted for food, but wise men saved your life." Then he told a tale of the past.

Once upon a time, when Brahmadatta was king of Benares, the Bodhisatta was his chaplain. Some fishermen drew out a Fish which had got caught in their net, and cast it upon hot sand, saying, "We will cook it in the embers, and eat." So they sharpened a spit. And the Fish fell a-weeping over his mate, and said these two verses:—

"'Tis not the fire that burns me, nor the spit that hurts me sore;
But the thought my mate may call me a faithless paramour.

"'Tis the flame of love that burns me, and fills my heart with pain;
Not death is the due of loving; O fishers, free me again!"

[179] At that moment the Bodhisatta approached the river bank; and hearing the Fish's lament, he went up to the fishermen and made them set the Fish at liberty.

This discourse ended, the Master declared the Truths and identified the Birth:—at the conclusion of the Truths the lovesick Brother reached the Fruit of the First Path:—"The wife was in those days the fish's mate, the lovesick Brother was the fish, and I myself was the chaplain."

No. 217.

SEGGU-JĀTAKA.

"*All the world's on pleasure bent,*" *etc.*—This story the Master told, while dwelling at Jetavana, about a greengrocer who was a lay-brother.

The circumstances have been already given in the First Book[1]. Here again the Master asked him where he had been so long; and he replied, "My daughter, Sir, is always smiling. After testing her, I gave her in marriage to a young gentleman. As this had to be done, I had no opportunity of paying you a visit." To this the Master answered, "Not now only is your daughter virtuous, but virtuous she was in days of yore; and as you have tested her now, so you tested her in those days." And at the man's request he told an old-world tale.

Once upon a time, when Brahmadatta was king of Benares, the Bodhisatta was a tree-spirit.

This same pious greengrocer took it into his head to test his daughter. He led her into the woods, [180] and seized her by the hand, making as though he had conceived a passion for her. And as she cried out in woe, he addressed her in the words of the first stanza:—

"All the world's on pleasure bent;
Ah, my baby innocent!
Now I've caught you, pray don't cry;
As the town does, so do I."

When she heard it, she answered, "Dear Father, I am a maid, and I know not the ways of sin:" and weeping she uttered the second stanza:—

"He that should keep me safe from all distress,
The same betrays me in my loneliness;
My father, who should be my sure defence,
Here in the forest offers violence."

And the greengrocer, after testing his daughter thus, took her home, and gave her in marriage to a young man. Afterwards he passed away according to his deeds.

When the Master had ended this discourse, he declared the Truths and identified the Birth:—at the end of the Truths the greengrocer entered on the Fruit of the First Path:—"In those days, father and daughter were the same as now, and the tree-spirit that saw it all was I myself."

[1] No. 102, *Paṇṇika-Jātaka*, where recurs the second stanza.

No. 218.

KŪṬA-VĀṆIJA-JĀTAKA.

"*Well planned indeed!" etc.*—[181] This story the Master told while staying in Jetavana, about a dishonest trader.

There were two traders of Sāvatthi, one pious and the other a cheat. These two joined partnership, and loaded five hundred waggons full of wares, journeying from east to west for trade; and returned to Sāvatthi with large profits.

The pious trader suggested to his partner that they should divide their stock. The rogue thought to himself, "This fellow has been roughing it for ever so long with bad food and lodging. Now he's at home again, he'll eat all sorts of dainties and die of a surfeit. Then I shall have all the stock for myself." What he said was, "Neither the stars nor the day are favourable; to-morrow or the next day we'll see about it;" so he kept putting it off. However, the pious trader pressed him, and the division was made. Then he went with scents and garlands to visit the Master; and after a respectful obeisance, he sat on one side. The Master asked when he had returned. "Just a fortnight ago, Sir," said he. "Then why have you delayed to visit the Buddha?" The trader explained. Then the Master said, "It is not only now that your partner is a rogue; he was just the same before;" and at his request told him an old-world tale.

Once upon a time, while Brahmadatta was king of Benares, the Bodhisatta came into this world as the son of one in the king's court. When he grew up he was made a Lord Justice.

At that time, two traders, one from a village and one of the town, were friends together. The villager deposited with the townsman five hundred ploughshares. The other sold these, and kept the price, and in the place where they were he scattered mouse dung. By and by came the villager, and asked for his ploughshare[1]. "The mice have eaten them up[2]!" said the cheat, and pointed out the mouse dung to him.

[1] Here, in the last sentence but one, and in the verses the singular *phālaṁ* is used. It is possible this may be a collective, but more likely that it harks back to a simpler and older version, where only one is spoken of. Readers cannot fail to have marked the fondness of the Jātaka editor for round numbers, especially five hundred.

[2] Things gnawed by mice or rats were unlucky; cp. vol. I. p. 372 (Pali), Tevijja-Sutta *Mahāsīlaṁ* i (trans. in *S. B. E.*, *Buddhist Suttas*, p. 196). The man here goes further than he need; if the mice had but nibbled the ploughshares perhaps he might throw them away.—We may also have a reference to an old proverb, found both in Greek and Latin: "where mice eat iron" meant "nowhere." Herondas 3. 76 *οὐδ' ὅκου χώρης οἱ μῦς ὁμοίως τὸν σίδηρον τρώγουσιν.* Seneca, *Apocolocyntosis* chap. 7 (to Claudius in heaven) venisti huc ubi mures ferrum rodunt.

"Well, well, so be it," replied the other: "what can be done with things which the mice have eaten?"

Now at the time of bathing he took the other trader's son, and set him in a friend's house, in an inner chamber, bidding them not suffer him to go out any whither. [182] And having washed himself he went to his friend's house.

"Where is my son?" asked the cheat.

"Dear friend," he replied, "I took him with me and left him on the river side; and when I was gone down into the water, there came a hawk, and seized your son in his extended claws, and flew up into the air. I beat the water, shouted, struggled—but could not make him let go."

"Lies!" cried the rogue. "No hawk could carry off a boy!"

"Let be, dear friend: if things happen that should not, how can I help it? Your son has been carried off by a hawk, as I say."

The other reviled him. "Ah, you scoundrel! you murderer! Now I will go to the judge, and have you dragged before him!" And he departed. The villager said, "As you please," and went to the court of justice. The rogue addressed the Bodhisatta thus:

"My lord, this fellow took my son with him to bathe, and when I asked where he was, he answered, that a hawk had carried him off. Judge my cause!"

"Tell the truth," said the Bodhisatta, asking the other.

"Indeed, my lord," he answered, "I took him with me, and a falcon has carried him off."

"But where in the world are there hawks which carry off boys?"

"My lord," he answered, "I have a question to ask you. If hawks cannot carry off boys into the air, can mice eat iron ploughshares?"

"What do you mean by that?"

"My lord, I deposited in this man's house five hundred ploughshares. The man told me that the mice had devoured them, and showed me the droppings of the mice that had done it. My lord, if mice eat ploughshares, then hawks carry off boys: but if mice cannot do this, neither will hawks carry the boy off. This man says the mice ate my ploughshares. Give sentence whether they are eaten or no. [183] Judge my cause!"

"He must have meant," thought the Bodhisatta, "to fight the trickster with his own weapons.—Well devised!" said he, and then he uttered these two verses:—

"Well planned indeed! The biter bit,
The trickster tricked—a pretty hit!
If mice eat ploughshares, hawks can fly
With boys away into the sky!

"A rogue out-rogued with tit for tat!
Give back the plough, and after that
Perhaps the man who lost the plough
May give your son back to you now!"[1]

[184] Thus he that had lost his son received him again, and he received his ploughshare that had lost it; and afterwards both passed away to fare according to their deeds.

When this discourse was ended, the Master identified the Birth:—"The cheat in both cases was the same, and so was the clever man; I myself was the Lord Chief Justice."

No. 219[2].

GARAHITA-JĀTAKA.

"*The gold is mine*," *etc.*—This story the Master told at Jetavana, about a brother who was downcast and discontent.

This man could not concentrate his mind on any single object, but his life was all full of discontent; and this was told to the Master. When asked by the Master if he really were discontented, he said yes; asked why, he replied that it was through his passions. "O Brother!" said the Master, "this passion has been despised even by the lower animals; and can you, a priest of such a doctrine, yield to discontent arising from the passion that even brutes despise?" Then he told him an old-world tale.

Once upon a time, when Brahmadatta reigned over Benares, the Bodhisatta came into the world as a Monkey, in the region of Himalaya. A woodranger caught him, brought him home and gave him to the king. For a long time he dwelt with the king, serving him faithfully, and he learnt a great deal about the manners of the world of men. The king was

[1] A like repartee is found in *North Ind. N. and Q.* iii. 214 (*The Judgement of the Jackal*); Swynnerton, *Ind. Nights Entertainments*, p. 142 (*The Traveller and the Oilman*); and a story of an oilman in Stumme's *Tunische Märchen*, vol. ii.

[2] *Folk-Lore Journal*, iii. 253.

pleased at his faithfulness. He sent for the woodranger, and bade him set the monkey free in the very place where he had been caught; and so he did.

All the monkey tribe gathered together upon the face of a huge rock, to see the Bodhisatta now that he had come back to them; and they spoke pleasantly to him.

"Sir, where have you been living this long time?"

"In the king's palace at Benares."

"Then how did you get free?"

"The king made me his pet monkey, and being pleased with my tricks, he let me go."

The monkeys went on—"You must know the manner of living in the world of men: [185] tell us about it too—we want to hear!"

"Don't ask me the manner of men's living," quoth the Bodhisatta.

"Do tell—we want to hear!" they said again.

"Mankind," said he, "both princes and Brahmans, cry out—'Mine! mine!' They know not of the impermanence, by which the things that be are not. Hear now the way of these blind fools;" and he spake these verses:—

"'The gold is mine, the precious gold!' so cry they, night and day:
These foolish folk cast never a look upon the holy way.

"There are two masters in the house; one has no beard to wear,
But has long breasts, ears pierced with holes, and goes with plaited hair;
His price is told in countless gold; he plagues all people there."

[186] On hearing this, all the monkeys cried out—"Stop, stop! we have heard what it is not meet to hear!" and with both hands they stopped their ears tight. And they liked not the place, because they said, "In this place we heard a thing not seemly;" so they went elsewhere. And this rock went by the name of Garahitapiṭṭhi Rock, or the Rock of Blaming.

When the Master had ended this discourse, he declared the Truths and identified the Birth:—at the conclusion of the Truths this Brother reached the Fruit of the First Path:—"The Buddha's present followers were that troop of monkeys, and their chief was I myself."

No. 220[1].

DHAMMADDHAJA-JĀTAKA.

"*You look as though*," *etc.*—This was told by the Master while staying at the Bamboo Grove, about attempts to murder him. On this occasion, as before, the Master said, "This is not the first time Devadatta has tried to murder me and has not even frightened me. He did the same before." And he told this story.

Once upon a time reigned at Benares a king named Yasapāṇi, the Glorious. His chief captain was named Kāḷaka, or Blackie. At that time the Bodhisatta was his chaplain, and had the name of Dhammaddhaja, the Banner of the Faith. There was also a man Chattapāṇi, maker of ornaments to the king. The king was a good king. But his chief captain swallowed bribes in the judging of causes; he was a backbiter; he took bribes, and defrauded the rightful owners.

On a day, one who had lost his suit was departing from the court, weeping and stretching out his arms, [187] when he fell in with the Bodhisatta as he was going to pay his service to the king. Falling at his feet, the man cried out, telling how he had been worsted in his cause: "Although such as you, my lord, instruct the king in the things of this world and the next, the Commander-in-Chief takes bribes, and defrauds rightful owners!"

The Bodhisatta pitied him. "Come, my good fellow," says he, "I will judge your cause for you!" and he proceeded to the court-house. A great company gathered together. The Bodhisatta reversed the sentence, and gave judgement for him that had the right. The spectators applauded. The sound was great. The king heard it, and asked—"What sound is this I hear?"

"My lord king," they answered, "it is a cause wrongly judged that has been judged aright by the wise Dhammaddhaja; that is why there is this shout of applause."

The king was pleased and sent for the Bodhisatta. "They tell me," he began, "that you have judged a cause?"

"Yes, great king, I have judged that which Kāḷaka did not judge aright."

[1] Here we have the "Hero's Tasks" in a new form.

"Be you judge from this day," said the king; "it will be a joy for my ears, and prosperity for the world!" He was unwilling, but the king begged him—"In mercy to all creatures, sit you in judgement!" and so the king won his consent.

From that time Kāḷaka received no presents; and losing his gains he spoke calumny of the Bodhisatta before the king, saying, "O mighty King, the wise Dhammaddhaja covets your kingdom!" But the king would not believe; and bade him say not so.

"If you do not believe me," said Kāḷaka, "look out of the window at the time of his coming. Then you will see that he has got the whole city into his own hands."

The king saw the crowd of those that were about him in his judgement hall. "There is his retinue," thought he. He gave way. "What are we to do, Captain?" he asked.

"My lord, he must be put to death." [188]

"How can we put him to death without having found him out in some great wickedness?"

"There is a way," said the other.

"What way?"

"Tell him to do what is impossible, and if he cannot, put him to death for that."

"But what is impossible to him?"

"My lord king," replied he, "it takes two years or twice two for a garden with good soil to bear fruit, being planted and tended. Send you for him, and say—'We want a garden to disport ourselves in to-morrow. Make us a garden!' This he will not be able to do; and we will slay him for that fault."

The king addressed himself to the Bodhisatta. "Wise Sir, we have sported long enough in our old garden; now we crave to sport in a new. Make us a garden! If you cannot make it, you must die."

The Bodhisatta reasoned, "It must be that Kāḷaka has set the king against me, because he gets no presents.—If I can," he said to the king, "O mighty king, I will see to it." And he went home. After a good meal he lay upon his bed, thinking. Sakka's palace grew hot[1]. Sakka reflecting perceived the Bodhisatta's difficulty. He made haste to him, entered his chamber, and asked him—"Wise Sir, what think you on?"—poised the while in mid-air.

"Who are you?" asked the Bodhisatta.

[1] This was supposed to happen when a good man was in straits. Some modern superstitions, turning upon the pity of a god for creatures in pain, may be seen in *North Ind. N. and Q.* iii. 285. As this: "Hot oil is poured into a dog's ear and the pain makes him yell. It is believed that his yells are heard by Raja Indra, who in pity stops the rain."

"I am Sakka."

"The king bids me make a garden: that is what I am thinking upon."

"Wise Sir, do not trouble: I will make you a garden like the groves of Nandana and Cittalatā! In what place shall I make it?"

"In such and such a place," he told him. Sakka made it, and returned to the city of the gods.

Next day, the Bodhisatta beheld the garden there in very truth, and sought the king's presence. "O king, the garden is ready: go to your sport!"

The king came to the place, and beheld a garden girt with a fence of eighteen cubits, vermilion tinted, having gates and ponds, [189] beautiful with all manner of trees laden heavy with flowers and fruit! "The sage has done my bidding," said he to Kāḷaka: "now what are we to do?"

"O mighty King!" replied he, "if he can make a garden in one night, can he not seize upon your kingdom?"

"Well, what are we to do?"

"We will make him perform another impossible thing."

"What is that?" asked the king.

"We will bid him make a lake possessed of the seven precious jewels!"

The king agreed, and thus addressed the Bodhisatta:

"Teacher, you have made a park. Make now a lake to match it, with the seven precious jewels. If you cannot make it, you shall not live!"

"Very good, great King," answered the Bodhisatta, "I will make it if I can."

Then Sakka made a lake of great splendour, having an hundred landing-places, a thousand inlets, covered over with lotus plants of five different colours, like the lake in Nandana.

Next day, the Bodhisatta beheld this also, and told the king: "See, the lake is made!" And the king saw it, and asked of Kāḷaka what was to be done.

"Bid him, my lord, make a house to suit it," said he.

"Make a house, Teacher," said the king to the Bodhisatta, "all of ivory, to suit with the park and the lake: if you do not make it, you must die!"

Then Sakka made him a house likewise. The Bodhisatta beheld it next day, and told the king. When the king had seen it, he asked Kāḷaka again, what was to do. Kāḷaka told him to bid the Bodhisatta make a jewel to suit the house. The king said to him, "Wise Sir, make a jewel to suit with this ivory house; I will go about looking at it by the light of the jewel: if you cannot make one, you must die!" Then Sakka made him a jewel too. Next day the Bodhisatta beheld it, and told the king. [190] When the king had seen it, he again asked Kāḷaka what was to be done.

"Mighty king!" answered he, "I think there is some sprite who does each thing that the Brahmin Dhammaddhaja wishes. Now bid him make something which even a divinity cannot make. Not even a deity can make a man with all four virtues[1]; therefore bid him make a keeper with these four." So the king said, "Teacher, you have made a park, a lake, and a palace, and a jewel to give light. Now make me a keeper with four virtues, to watch the park; if you cannot, you must die."

"So be it," answered he, "if it is possible, I will see to it." He went home, had a good meal, and lay down. When he awoke in the morning, he sat upon his bed, and thought thus. "What the great king Sakka can make by his power, that he has made. He cannot make a park-keeper with four virtues[1]. This being so, it is better to die forlorn in the woods, than to die at the hand of other men." So saying no word to any man, he went down from his dwelling and passed out of the city by the chief gate, and entered the woods, where he sat him down beneath a tree and reflected upon the religion of the good. Sakka perceived it; and in the fashion of a forester he approached the Bodhisatta, saying,

"Brahmin, you are young and tender: why sit you here in this wood, as though you had never seen pain before?" As he asked it, he repeated the first stanza:—

"You look as though your life must happy be;
Yet to the wild woods you would homeless go,
Like some poor wretch whose life was misery,
And pine beneath this tree in lonely woe."

[191] To this the Bodhisatta made answer in the second stanza:—

"I look as though my life must happy be;
Yet to the wild woods I would homeless go,
Like some poor wretch whose life was misery,
And pine beneath this tree in lonely woe,
Pondering the truth that all the saints do know."

Then Sakka said, "If so, then why, Brahmin, are you sitting here?"

"The king," he made answer, "requires a park-keeper with four good qualities; such an one cannot be found; so I thought—Why perish by the hand of man? I will off to the woods, and die a lonely death. So here I came, and here I sit."

Then the other replied, "Brahmin, I am Sakka, king of the gods. By

[1] *Caturaṅga-samannāgataṁ*; it is an odd coincidence that the Pythagoreans called the perfect man τετράγωνος, 'four-square' (see the poem of Simonides, in Plat. *Prot.* 339 B).

me was your park made, and those other things. A park-keeper possessed of four virtues cannot be made; but in your country there is one Chattapāṇi, who makes ornaments for the head, and he is such a man. If a park-keeper is wanted, go and make this workman the keeper." With these words Sakka departed to his city divine, after consoling him and bidding him fear no more.

[192] The Bodhisatta went home, and having broken his fast, he repaired to the palace gates, and there in that spot he saw Chattapāṇi. He took him by the hand, and asked him—"Is it true, as I hear, Chattapāṇi, that you are endowed with the four virtues?"

"Who told you so?" asked the other.

"Sakka, king of the gods."

"Why did he tell you?" He recounted all, and told the reason. The other said,

"Yes, I am endowed with the four virtues." The Bodhisatta taking him by the hand led him into the king's presence. "Here, mighty monarch, is Chattapāṇi, endowed with four virtues. If there is need of a keeper for the park, make him keeper."

"Is it true, as I hear," the king asked him, "that you have four virtues?"

"Yes, mighty king."

"What are they?" he asked.

> "I envy not, and drink no wine;
> No strong desire, no wrath is mine,"

said he.

"Why, Chattapāṇi," cried the king, "did you say you have no envy?"

"Yes, O king, I have no envy."

"What are the things you do not envy?"

"Listen, my lord!" said he; and then he told how he felt no envy in the following lines[1]:—

[1] The following is the commentary on these lines. The story is that of No. 120, where the first stanza of those which follow, is given.

"This is the meaning. In former days, I was a king of Benares like this, and for a woman's sake I imprisoned a chaplain.

> The free are bound, when folly has her say;
> When wisdom speaks, the bond go free away.

Just as in the Birth now spoken of, this Chattapāṇi became king. The queen intrigued with sixty-four of the slaves. She tempted the Bodhisatta, and when he would not consent she tried to ruin him by speaking calumny of him; then the king threw him into prison. The Bodhisatta was brought before him bound, and explained the real state of the case. Then he was set free himself; and then he got the king to release all those slaves who had been imprisoned, and advised him to forgive both

"A chaplain once in bonds I threw—
Which thing a woman made me do:
He built me up in holy lore;
Since when I never envied more."

[193] Then the king said, "Dear Chattapāṇi, why do you abstain from strong drink?" And the other answered in the following verse[1]:—

the queen and them. All the rest is to be understood exactly as explained above. It was in reference to this he said

"A chaplain once in bonds I threw—
Which thing a woman made me do:
He built me up in holy lore;
Since when I never envied more."

But then I thought, 'I have avoided sixteen thousand women, and I cannot satisfy this one in the way of passion. Such is the anger of women, hard to satisfy. It is like being angry, saying, 'Why is it dirty?' when a worn garment is dirty; it is like being angry, saying, 'Why does it become like this?' when after a meal some passes into the draught. I made a resolve that henceforth no envy should arise in me by way of passion, lest I should fail to become a saint. From that time I have been free from envy. This is the point of saying, '*Since when I never envied more.*'"

[1] The scholiast tells the following story to illustrate this verse.—"I was once," says the speaker, "a king of Benares; I could not live without strong drink and meat. Now in that city animals might not be slaughtered on the Sabbath (*uposatha-divasesu*); so the cook had prepared some meat for my Sabbath meal the day before (the 13th of the lunar fortnight). This, being badly kept, the dogs ate. The cook durst not come before the king on the Sabbath to serve his rich and varied repast in the upper chamber without meat, so he asked the queen's advice. "My lady, to-day I have no meat; and without it I dare not offer a meal to him, what am I to do?" Said she, "The king is very fond of my son. As he fondles him, he hardly knows whether he exists or not. [194] I will dress my son up, and give him into the king's hands, and while he plays with him you shall serve his dinner; he will not notice." So she dressed up her darling son, and put him into the king's hands. As he was playing with the lad, the cook served the dinner. The king, mad with drink, and seeing no meat upon the dish, asked where the meat was. The answer was that no meat was to be had that day because there was no killing on the Sabbath. "Meat is hard to get for me, is it?" he said; and then he wrung his dear son's neck as he sat in his arms, and killed him; threw him down before the cook, and told him to look sharp and cook it. The cook obeyed, and the king ate his own son's flesh. For dread of the king not a soul durst weep or wail or say a word. The king ate, and went to sleep. Next morning, having slept off his intoxication, he asked for his son. Then the queen fell weeping at his feet, and said, "Oh, sir, yesterday you killed your son and ate his flesh!" The king wept and wailed for grief, and thought, "This is because of drinking strong drink!" Then, seeing the mischief of drinking, I made a resolution that lest I should never become a saint, I would never touch this deadly liquor; taking dust, and rubbing it upon my mouth. From that time I have drunk no strong drink. This is the point of the lines, "*Once I was drunken.*"

"Once I was drunken, and I ate
My own son's flesh upon my plate;
Then, touched with sorrow and with pain,
Swore never to touch drink again."

[194] Then the king said, "But what, dear sir, makes you indifferent, without love?" The man explained it in these words[1]:—

"King Kitavāsa was my name;
A mighty king was I;
My boy the Buddha's basin broke
And so he had to die."

[195] Said the king then, "What was it, good friend, that made you to be without anger?" And the other made the matter clear in these lines:

"As Araka, for seven years
I practised charity;
And then for seven ages dwelt
In Brahma's heaven on high."

When Chattapāṇi had thus explained his four attributes, the king made a sign to his attendants. And in an instant all the court, [196] priests and laymen and all, rose up, and cried out upon Kāḷaka—"Fie, bribe-swallowing thief and scoundrel! You couldn't get your bribes, and so you would murder the wise man by speaking ill of him!" They seized him by hand and foot, and bundled him out of the palace; and catching up whatever

[1] The scholiast tells this story: "The meaning is, Once upon a time I was a king named Kitavāsa, and a son was born to me. The fortune-tellers said that the boy would perish of lack of water. So he was named Duṭṭhakumāra. When he grew up, he was viceroy. The king kept his son close to him, before or behind; and to break the prophecy had tanks made at the four city gates and here and there inside the city; he made halls in the squares and crossways, and set water jars in them. One day the young man, dressed finely, went to the park by himself. On his way he saw a Pacceka-Buddha in the road, and many people spoke to him, praised him, did obeisance before him. [195] 'What!' thought the prince, 'when such as I am passing by, do people show all this respect to yonder shavepate?' Angry, he dismounted from the elephant, and asked the Buddha if he had received his food. 'Yes,' was the reply. The prince took it from him, cast it on the ground, rice and bowl together, and crushed it to dust under his feet. 'The man is lost, verily!' said the Buddha, and looked into his face. 'I am Prince Duṭṭha, son of king Kitavāsa!' said the prince—'what harm will you do me, by looking angrily at me and opening your eyes?' The Buddha, having lost his food, rose up in the air and went off to a cave at the foot of Nanda, in Northern Himalaya. At that very moment the prince's evil-doing began to bear fruit, and he cried—'I burn! I burn!' His body burst into flame, and he fell down in the road where he was; all the water that there was near disappeared, the conduits dried up, then and there he perished, and passed into hell. The king heard it, and was overcome with grief. Then he thought—'This grief is come upon me because my son was dear to me. If I had had no affection, I had had no pain. From this time forward I resolve that I will fix my affection on nothing, animate or inanimate.'"

they could get hold of, this a stone, and this a staff, they broke his head and did him to death: and dragging him by the feet they cast him upon a dunghill.

Thenceforward the king ruled in righteousness, until he passed away according to his deserts.

This discourse ended, the Master identified the Birth:—"Devadatta was the Commander Kāḷaka, Sāriputta was the artisan Chattapāṇi, and I was Dhammaddhaja."

No. 221.

KĀSĀVA-JĀTAKA.

"*If any man,*" *etc.*—This story the Master told while staying at Jetavana, about Devadatta.

It was occasioned by something that happened at Rājagaha. At one period the Captain of the Faith was living with five hundred brethren at the Bamboo Grove. And Devadatta, with a body of men wicked like himself, lived at Gayāsīsa.

At that time the citizens of Rājagaha used to club together for the purpose of almsgiving. A trader, who had come there on business, brought a magnificent perfumed yellow robe, asking that he might become one of them, and give this garment as his contribution. The townspeople brought plenty of gifts. All that was contributed by those who had clubbed together consisted of ready money. There was this garment left. The crowd which had come together said, "Here is this beautiful perfumed robe left over. Who shall have it—Elder Sāriputta, or Devadatta?" Some were in favour of Sāriputta; others said, "Elder Sāriputta will stay here a few days, [197] and then go travelling at his own sweet will; but Devadatta always lives near our city; he is our refuge in good fortune or ill. Devadatta shall have it!" They made a division, and those who voted for Devadatta were in the majority. So to Devadatta they gave it. He had it cut in strips, and sewn together, and coloured like gold, and so he wore it upon him.

At the same time, thirty Brethren went from Sāvatthi to salute the Master. After greetings had been exchanged, they told him all this affair, adding, "And so, sir, Devadatta wears this mark of the saint, which suits him ill enough." "Brethren," said the Master, "this is not the first time that Devadatta has put on the garb of a saint, a most unsuitable dress. He did the same before." And then he told them an old-world tale.

Once upon a time, when Brahmadatta was king of Benares, the Bodhisatta came into this world as an Elephant in the Himalaya region.

Lord of a herd that numbered eighty thousand wild elephants, he dwelt in the forest land.

A poor man that lived in Benares, seeing the workers of ivory in the ivory bazaar making bangles and all manner of ivory trinkets, he asked them would they buy an elephant's tusks, if he should get them. To which they answered, Yes.

So he took a weapon, and clothing himself in a yellow robe, he put on the guise of a Pacceka-Buddha[1], with a covering band about his head. Taking his stand in the path of the elephants, he slew one of them with his weapon, and sold the tusks of it in Benares; and in this manner he made a living. After this he began always to slay the very last elephant in the Bodhisatta's troop. Day by day the elephants grew fewer and fewer. Then they went and asked the Bodhisatta how it was that their numbers dwindled. He perceived the reason. "Some man," thought he, "stands in the place where the elephants go, having made himself like a Pacceka-Buddha in appearance. Now can it be he that slays the elephants? I will find him out." So one day he sent the others on before him [198] and he followed after. The man saw the Bodhisatta, and made a rush at him with his weapon. The Bodhisatta turned and stood. "I will beat him to the earth, and kill him!" thought he: and stretched out his trunk,—when he saw the yellow robes which the man wore. "I ought to pay respect to those sacred robes!" said he. So drawing back his trunk, he cried—"O man! Is not that dress, the flag of sainthood, unsuitable to you? Why do you wear it?" and he repeated these lines :—

"If any man, yet full of sin, should dare
To don the yellow robe, in whom no care
    For temperance is found, or love of truth,
He is not worthy such a robe to wear.

He who has spued out sin, who everywhere
Is firm in virtue, and whose chiefest care
    Is to control his passions, and be true,
He well deserves the yellow robe to wear."

[199] With these words, the Bodhisatta rebuked the man, and bade him never come there again, else he should die for it. Thus he drove him away.

After this discourse was ended, the Master identified the Birth :—"Devadatta was the man who killed the elephants, and the head of the herd was I."

[1] One who has attained the knowledge needful for attaining Nirvana, but does not preach it to men.

No. 222.

CŪLA-NANDIYA-JĀTAKA[1].

"*I call to mind*," *etc.*—This story the Master told whilst dwelling in the Bamboo Grove, about Devadatta.

One day the brethren fell a-talking in the Hall of Truth: "Friend, that man Devadatta is harsh, cruel, and tyrannical, full of baneful devices against the Supreme Buddha. He flung a stone[2], he even used the aid of Nāḷāgiri[3]; pity and compassion there is none in him for the Tathāgata."

The Master came in, and asked what they were talking about as they sat there. They told him. Then he said, "This is not the first time, Brethren, that Devadatta has been harsh, cruel, merciless. He was so before." And he told them an old-world tale.

Once upon a time, when Brahmadatta was king of Benares, the Bodhisatta became a Monkey named Nandiya, or Jolly; and dwelt in the Himalaya region; and his youngest brother bore the name of Jollikin. They two headed a band of eighty thousand monkeys, and they had a blind mother in their home to care for.

They left their mother in her lair in the bushes, and went amongst the trees to find sweet wild fruit of all kinds, which they sent back home to her. The messengers did not deliver it; and, tormented with hunger, she became nothing but skin and bone. Said the Bodhisatta to her,

"Mother, we send you plenty of sweet fruits: then what makes you so thin?"

"My son, I never get it!" [200]

The Bodhisatta pondered. "While I look after my herd, my mother will perish! I will leave the herd, and look after my mother alone." So calling his brother, "Brother," said he, "do you tend the herd, and I will care for our mother."

"Nay, brother," replied he, "what care I for ruling a herd? I too will care for only our mother!" So the two of them were of one mind, and leaving the herd, they brought their mother down out of Himalaya, and took up their abode in a banyan tree of the border-land, where they took care of her.

[1] *Questions of Milinda*, iv. 4. 24 (trans. in *S. B. E.*, xxxv. 287).

[2] For the stone-throwing see *Cullavagga* vii. 3. 9; Hardy, *Manual*, p. 320.

[3] A fierce elephant, let loose at Devadatta's request to kill the Buddha. See *Cullavagga* vii. 3. 11 f. (*Vinaya Texts*, *S. B. E.*, iii. 247 f.); *Milinda*, iv. 4. 44 (where he is called *Dhanapālaka*, as *supra* vol. i. 57); Hardy, *Manual*, p. 320.

Now a certain Brahmin, who lived at Takkasilā, had received his education from a famous teacher, and afterward he took leave of him, saying that he would depart. This teacher had the power of divining from the signs on a man's body; and thus he perceived that his pupil was harsh, cruel, and violent. "My son," said he, "you are harsh, and cruel, and violent. Such persons do not prosper at all seasons alike; they come to dire woe and dire destruction. Be not harsh, nor do what you will afterwards repent." With this counsel, he let him go.

The youth took leave of his teacher, and went his way to Benares. There he married and settled down; and not being able to earn a livelihood by any other of his arts, he determined to live by his bow. So he set to work as a huntsman; and left Benares to earn his living. Dwelling in a border village, he would range the woods girt with bow and quiver, and lived by sale of the flesh of all manner of beasts which he slew.

One day, as he was returning homewards after having caught nothing at all in the forest, he observed a banyan tree standing on the verge of an open glade. "Perhaps," thought he, "there may be something here." And he turned his face towards the banyan tree. Now the two brothers had just fed their mother with fruits, and were sitting behind her in the tree, when they saw the man coming. "Even if he sees our mother," said they, "what will he do?" and they hid amongst the branches. Then this cruel man, as he came up to the tree and saw the mother monkey weak with age, and blind, thought to himself, "Why should I return empty-handed? I will shoot this she-monkey first!" [201] and lifted up his bow to shoot her. This the Bodhisatta saw, and said to his brother, "Jollikin, my dear, this man wants to shoot our mother! I will save her life. When I am dead, do you take care of her." So saying, down he came out of the tree, and called out,

"O man, don't shoot my mother! she is blind, and weak for age. I will save her life; don't kill her, but kill me instead!" and when the other had promised, he sat down in a place within bowshot. The hunter pitilessly shot the Bodhisatta; when he dropped, the man prepared his bow to shoot the mother monkey. Jollikin saw this, and thought to himself, "Yon hunter wants to shoot my mother. Even if she only lives a day, she will have received the gift of life; I will give my life for hers." Accordingly, down he came from the tree, and said,

"O man, don't shoot my mother! I give my life for hers. Shoot me—take both us brothers, and spare our mother's life!" The hunter consented, and Jollikin squatted down within bowshot. The hunter shot this one too, and killed him—"It will do for my children at home," thought he—and he shot the mother too; hung them all three on his carrying pole, and set his face homewards. At that moment a thunderbolt fell upon the house of this wicked man, and burnt up his wife and two children with the house: nothing was left but the roof and the bamboo uprights.

A man met him at the entering in of the village, and told him of it. Sorrow for his wife and children overcame him: down on the spot he dropped his pole with the game, and his bow, threw off his garments, and naked he went homewards, wailing with hands outstretched. Then the bamboo uprights broke, and fell upon his head, and crushed it. The earth yawned, flame rose from hell. As he was being swallowed up in the earth, he thought upon his master's warning: [202] "Then this was the teaching that the Brahmin Pārāsariya gave me!" and lamenting he uttered these stanzas:—

"I call to mind my teacher's words: so this was what he meant!
Be careful you should nothing do of which you might repent.

"Whatever a man does, the same he in himself will find;
The good man, good; and evil he that evil has designed;
And so our deeds are all like seeds, and bring forth fruit in kind."

Lamenting thus, he went down into the earth, and came to life in the depths of hell.

When the Master had ended this discourse, by which he showed how in other days, as then, Devadatta had been harsh, cruel, and merciless, he identified the Birth in these words: "In those days Devadatta was the hunter, Sāriputta was the famous teacher, Ānanda was Jollikin, the noble Lady Gotamī was the mother, and I was the monkey Jolly."

No. 223.

PUṬA-BHATTA-JĀTAKA.

"*Honour for honour*," *etc.*—This story the Master told in Jetavana, about a landed proprietor.

Tradition has it that once a landowner who was a citizen of Sāvatthi did business with a landowner from the country. [203] Taking his wife with him, he visited this man, his debtor; but the debtor averred that he could not pay. The other, in anger, set out for home without having broken his fast. On the road, some people met him; and seeing how famished the man was, gave him food, bidding him share it with his wife.

When he got this, he grudged his wife a share. So addressing her he said, "Wife, this is a well-known haunt of thieves, so you had better go in front." Having thus got rid of her, he ate all the food, and then showed her the pot empty, saying—"Look here, wife! they gave me an empty pot!" She guessed that he had eaten it all up himself, and was much annoyed.

As they both passed by the monastery in Jetavana, they thought they would go into the park and get a drink of water. There sat the Master, waiting on purpose to see them, like a hunter on the trail, seated under the shade of his perfumed cell. He greeted them kindly, and said, "Lay Sister, is your husband kind and loving?" "I love him, sir," she replied, "but he does not love me; let alone other days, this very day he was given a pot of food on the way, and gave not a bit to me, but ate it all himself." "Lay Sister, so it has always been—you loving and kind, and he loveless; but when by the help of the wise he learns your worth, he will do you all honour." Then, at her request, he told an old-world tale.

On a time, while Brahmadatta was king in Benares, the Bodhisatta was the son of one of the king's court. On coming of age he became the king's adviser in things temporal and spiritual. It happened that the king was afraid of his son, lest he might injure him; and sent him away. Taking his wife, the son departed from that city, and came to a village of Kāsi, where he dwelt. By and by when the father died, his son hearing of it set out to go back to Benares; "that I may receive the kingdom which is my birthright," said he. On his way one gave him a mess of pottage, saying, "Eat, and give to your wife also." But he gave her none, and did eat it all himself. [204] Thought she—"A cruel man this, indeed!" and she was full of sorrow.

When he had come to Benares, and received his kingdom, he made her the queen consort; but thinking—"A little is enough for her," he showed her no other consideration or honour, not so much as to ask her how she did.

"This queen," thought the Bodhisatta, "serves the king well, and loves him; but the king spends not a thought upon her. I will make him show her respect and honour."

So he came to the queen, and made salutation, and stood aside. "What is it, dear sir?" she asked.

"Lady," he asked, "how can we serve you? ought you not to give the old Fathers a piece of cloth or a dish of rice?"

"Dear sir, I never receive anything myself; what shall I give to you? When I received, did I not give? But now the king gives me nothing at all: let alone giving anything else, as he was going along the road he received a bowl of rice, and never gave me a bit—he ate it all himself."

"Well, madam, will you be able to say this in the king's presence?"

"Yes," she replied.

"Very well then. To-day, when I stand before the king, when I ask my question do you give the same answer: this very day will I make your goodness known." So the Bodhisatta went on before, and stood in the king's presence. And she too went and stood near the king.

Then said the Bodhisatta, "Madam, you are very cruel. Ought you not to give the Fathers a piece of cloth or a dish of food?" And she made answer, "Good sir, I myself receive nothing from the king: what can I give to you?"

"Are you not the queen consort?" quoth he.

"Good sir," said she, "what boots the place of a queen consort, when no respect is paid? What will the king give me now? When he received a dish of rice on the road, [205] he gave me none, but ate it all himself." And the Bodhisatta asked him, "Is it so, O king?" And the king assented. When the Bodhisatta saw that the king assented, "Then lady," quoth he, "why dwell here with the king after he has become unkindly? In the world, union without love is painful. While you dwell here, loveless union with the king will bring you sorrow. These folk honour him that honours, and when one honours not—as soon as you see it, you should go elsewhither; they that dwell in the world are many." And he repeated the stanzas following:—

"Honour for honour, love for love is due:
Do good to him who does the same to you:
Observance breeds observance; but 'tis plain
None need help him who will not help again.

"Return neglect for negligence, nor stay
To comfort him whose love is past away.
The world is wide; and when the birds descry
That trees have lost their fruit—away they fly."

Hearing this, the king gave his queen all honour; and from that time forward they dwelt together in friendship and harmony.

---

[206] When the Master had ended this discourse, he declared the Truths, and identified the Birth:—at the conclusion of the Truths the husband and wife entered on the Fruit of the First Path:—"The husband and wife are the same in both cases, and the wise counsellor was I myself."

No. 224.

KUMBHĪLA-JĀTAKA.

"*O Ape,*" *etc.*—This story the Master told at the Bamboo Grove, about Devadatta.

"O Ape, these virtues four bring victory:
 Truth, Wisdom, Self-control, and Piety.

"Without these blessings is no victory—
 Truth, Wisdom, Self-control, and Piety."

No. 225.

KHANTI-VAṆṆANA-JĀTAKA.

"*There is a man,*" *etc.*—This story the Master told at Jetavana, about the king of Kosala. A very useful subordinate intrigued in the harem. Even though he knew the culprit, the king pocketed the affront, because the fellow was useful, and told the Master of it. The Master said, "Other kings in days long gone by have done the same;" and at his request, told the following story.

Once upon a time, when Brahmadatta was king of Benares, a man of his court fell into an intrigue in the king's harem, and an attendant of this courtier did the same thing in the courtier's house. The man could not endure to be thus affronted. So he led the other before the king, saying, "My lord, [207] I have a servant who does all manner of work, and he has made me a cuckold: what must I do with him?" and with the question he uttered this first verse following:—

"There is a man within my house, a zealous servant too;
He has betrayed my trust, O king! Say—what am I to do?"

On hearing this, the king uttered the second verse:—

"I too a zealous servant have; and here he stands, indeed!
Good men, I trow, are rare enow: so patience is my rede."

The courtier saw that these words of the king were aimed at him; and for the future durst do no wrong in the king's house. And the servant likewise, having come to know that the matter had been told to the king, durst for the future do that thing no more.

This discourse ended, the Master identified the Birth:—"I was the king of Benares." And the courtier on this occasion found out that the king had told of him to the Master, and never did such a thing again.

No. 226.

KOSIYA-JĀTAKA.

[208] "*There is a time,*" *etc.*—A story told by the Master at Jetavana, about the king of Kosala. This king started to quell a border rising at a bad season of the year. The circumstances have been described already[1]. The Master as before told the king a story.

Once on a time, the king of Benares having started for the field of war at an unseasonable time, set up a camp in his park. At that time an Owl entered a thicket of bamboos, and hid in it. There came a flock of Crows: "We will catch him," said they, "so soon as he shall come out." And they compassed it around. Out he came before his time, nor did he wait until the sun should set; and tried to make his escape. The crows surrounded him, and pecked him with their beaks till he fell to the ground. The king asked the Bodhisatta: "Tell me, wise sir, why are the crows attacking this owl?" And the Bodhisatta made answer, "They that leave their dwelling before the right time, great king, fall into just such misery as this. Therefore before the time one should not leave one's

[1] See no. 176, p. 51 above.

dwelling place." And to make the matter clear, he uttered this pair of verses:

"There is a time for every thing: who forth from home will go
One man or many, out of time, will surely meet some woe;
As did the Owl, unlucky fowl! pecked dead by many a crow.

"Who masters quite each rule and rite; who others' weakness knows;
Like wise owls, he will happy be, and conquer all his foes."

[209] When the king heard this, he turned back home again.

This discourse ended, the Master identified the Birth:—"Ānanda was then the king, and the wise courtier was I myself."

No. 227.

GŪTHA-PĀṆA-JĀTAKA.

"*Well matched*," etc.—This story the Master told while dwelling at Jetavana, about one of the Brethren.

There stood at that time, about three-quarters[1] of a league from Jetavana, a market town, where a great deal of rice was distributed by ticket, and special meals were given. Here lived an inquisitive lout, who pestered the young men and novices who came to share in the distribution—[210] "Who are for solid food? who for drink? who for moist food?" And he made those who could not answer feel ashamed, and they dreaded him so much that to that village they would not go.

One day, a brother came to the ticket-hall, with the question, "Any food for distribution in such-and-such a village, sir?" "Yes, friend," was the answer, "but there's a lubber here asking questions; if you can't answer them, he abuses and reviles you. He is such a pest that nobody will go near the place." "Sir," said the other, "give me an order on the place, and I'll humble him, and make him modest, and so influence him that whenever he sees you after this, he'll feel inclined to run away."

The brothers agreed, and gave the necessary order. The man walked to our village, and at the gate of it he put on his robe. The loafer spied him—was at him like a mad ram, with "Answer me a question, priest!" "Layman, let me go first about the village for my broth, and then come back with it to the waiting hall."

When he returned with his meal, the man repeated his question. The brother answered, "Leave me to finish my broth, to sweep the room, and to fetch my ticket's worth of rice." So he fetched the rice; then placing his bowl in this very man's hands, he said, "Come, now I'll answer your question."

[1] *Gārutaddhayojanamatte*. It may possibly mean 'an eighth.'

Then he led him outside the village, folded his outer robe, put it on his shoulder, and taking the bowl from the other, stood waiting for him to begin. The man said, "Priest, answer me one question." "Very well, so I will," said the brother; and with one blow he felled him to the ground, bruised his eyes, beat him, dropped filth in his face, and went off, with these parting words to frighten him, "If ever again you ask a question of any Brother who comes to this village, I'll see about it!"

After this, he took to his heels at the mere sight of a Brother.

By and bye all this became known among the Brotherhood. One day they were talking about it in the Hall of Truth: "Friend, I hear that Brother So-and-so dropped filth in the face of that loafer, and left him!" The Master came in, and wanted to know what they were all talking about as they sat there. They told him. Said he, "Brethren, this is not the first time this brother attacked the man with dirt, but he did just the same before." Then he told them an old-world tale.

---

[211] Once on a time, those citizens of the kingdoms of Aṅga and Magadha who were travelling from one land to the other, used to stay in a house on the marches of the two kingdoms, and there they drank liquor and ate the flesh of fishes, and early in the morning they yoked their carts and went away. At the time when they came, a certain dung-beetle, led by the odour of dung, came to the place where they had drunken, and saw some liquor shed upon the ground, and for thirst he drank it, and returned to his lump of dung intoxicated. When he climbed upon it the moist dung gave way a little. "The world cannot bear my weight!" he bawled out. At that very instant a maddened Elephant came to the spot, and smelling the dung went back in disgust. The Beetle saw it. "You creature," he thought, "is afraid of me, and see how he runs away!—I must fight with him!" and so he challenged him in the first stanza:—

"Well matched! for we are heroes both: here let us issue try:
Turn back, turn back, friend Elephant! Why would you fear and fly?
Let Magadha and Aṅga see how great our bravery!"

The Elephant listened, and heard the voice; he turned back towards the Beetle, and said the second stanza, by way of rebuke:—

"Non pede, longinquave manu, non dentibus utar:
Stercore, cui stercus cura, perisse decet."

[212] And so, dropping a great piece of dung upon him, and making water, he killed him then and there; and scampered into the forest, trumpeting.

When this discourse was ended, the Master identified the Birth:—"In those days, this lout was the dung-beetle, the Brother in question was the elephant, and I was the tree-sprite who saw it all from that clump of trees."

No. 228.

KĀMANĪTA-JĀTAKA.

"*Three forts,*" *etc.*—This story the Master told at Jetavana about a brahmin named Kāmanīta. The circumstances will be explained in the Twelfth Book, and the Kāma-Jātaka[1].

[The king of Benares had two sons.] And of these two sons the elder went to Benares, and became king: the youngest was the viceroy. He that was king was given over to the desire of riches, and the lust of the flesh, and greedy of gain.

At the time, the Bodhisatta was Sakka, king of the gods. And as he looked out upon India, and observed that the king of it was given over to these lusts, he said to himself, "I will chastise that king, and make him ashamed." So taking the semblance of a young brahmin, he went to the king and looked at him.

"What wants this young fellow?" the king asked.

Said he, "Great king, I see three towns, prosperous, fertile, having elephants, horses, chariots and infantry in plenty, full of ornaments of gold and fine gold. These may be taken with a very small army. I have come hither to offer to get them for you!"

"When shall we go, young man?" asked the king.

"To-morrow, Sire."

"Then leave me now; to-morrow early shall you go."

"Good, my king: hasten to prepare the army!" And so saying [213] Sakka went back again to his own place.

Next day the king caused the drum to beat, and an army to be made ready; and having summoned his courtiers, he thus bespoke them:—

"Yesterday a young brahmin came and said that he would conquer for me three cities—Uttarapañcāla, Indapatta, and Kekaka. Wherefore now we will go along with that man and conquer those cities. Summon him in all haste!"

"What place did you assign him, my lord, to dwell in?"

"I gave him no place to dwell in," said the king.

"But you gave him wherewith to pay for a lodging?"

[1] No. 467.

"Nay, not even that."

"Then how shall we find him?"

"Seek him in the streets of the city," said the king.

They sought, but found him not. So they came before the king, and told him, "O king, we cannot see him."

Great sorrow fell upon the king. "What glory has been snatched from me!" he groaned; his heart became hot, his blood became disordered, dysentery attacked him, the physicians could not cure him.

After the space of three or four days, Sakka meditated, and was ware of his illness. Said he, "I will cure him:" and in the semblance of a brahmin he went and stood at his door. He caused it to be told the king, "A brahmin physician is come to cure you."

On hearing it, the king answered, "All the great physicians of the court have not been able to cure me. Give him a fee, and let him go."

Sakka listened, and made reply: "I want not even money for my lodging, nor will I take fee for my leechcraft. I will cure him: let the king see me!"

"Then let him come in," said the king, on receiving this message. Then Sakka went in, and wishing victory to the king, sat on one side.

"Are you going to cure me?" the king asked.

He replied, "Even so, my lord."

"Cure me, then!" said the king.

"Very good, Sire. Tell me the symptoms of your disease, and how it came about,—what you have eaten or drunken, to bring it on, or what you have heard or seen."

"Dear friend, my disease was brought upon me by something that I heard."

Then the other asked, "What was it?" [214]

"Dear Sir, there came a young brahmin who offered to win and give me power over three cities: and I gave him neither lodging, nor wherewithal to pay for one. He must have grown angry with me, and gone away to some other king. So when I bethought me how great glory had been snatched away from me, this disease came upon me; cure, if you can, this which has come upon me for my covetousness." And to make the matter clear he uttered the first stanza:—

> "Three forts, each builded high upon a mount,
> I want to take, whose names I here recount[1]:
> And there is one thing further that I need—
> Cure me, O brahmin, me the slave of greed!"

Then Sakka said, "O king, by simples made with roots you cannot

[1] The names of Pañcāla, Kuru, and Kekaka are given.

be cured, but you must be cured with the simple of knowledge:" and he uttered the second verse as follows: [215]

"There are, who cure the bite of a black snake;
The wise can heal the wounds that goblins make.
The slave of greed no doctor can make whole;
What cure is there for the backsliding soul?"

So spake the great Being to explain his meaning, and he added this yet beyond: "O king, what if you were to get those three cities, then while you reigned over these four cities, could you wear four pairs of robes at once, eat out of four golden dishes, lie on four state beds? O king, one ought not to be mastered by desire. Desire is the root of all evil; when desire is increased, he that cherishes her is cast into the eight great hells, and the sixteen lowest hells, and into all kinds and manner of misery." So the great Being terrified the king with fear of hell and misery, and discoursed to him. And the king, by hearing his discourse, got rid of his heartbreak, and in a moment he became whole of his disease. [216] And Sakka after giving him instruction, and establishing him in virtue, went away to the world of gods. And the king thenceforward gave alms and did good, and he passed away to fare according to his deserts.

When this discourse was ended, the Master identified the Birth:—"The Brother who is a slave to his desires was at that time the king; and I myself was Sakka."

No. 229.

PALĀYI-JĀTAKA.

"*Lo, my elephants,*" *etc.*—This story the Master told at Jetavana, about a mendicant, with vagrant tastes.

He traversed the whole of India for the purpose of arguing, and found no one to contradict him. At last he got as far as Sāvatthi, and asked was there any one there who could argue with him. The people said, "There is One who could argue with a thousand such—all-wise, chief of men, the mighty Gotama, lord of the faith, who bears down all opposition, there is no adversary in all India who can dispute with Him. As the billows break upon the shore, so all arguments break against his feet, and are dashed to spray." Thus they described the qualities of the Buddha.

"Where is he now?" asked the mendicant. He was at Jetavana, they replied. "Now I'll get up a disputation with him!" said the mendicant. So attended by a large crowd he made his way to Jetavana. On seeing the gate towers of Jetavana[1], which Prince Jeta had built at a cost of ninety millions of money, he asked whether that was the palace where the Priest Gotama lived. The gateway of it, they said. "If this be the gateway, what will the dwelling be like!" he cried. "There's no end to the perfumed chambers!" the people said. "Who could argue with such a priest as this?" he asked; and hurried off at once.

The crowd shouted for joy, and thronged into the park. "What brings you here before your time?" asked the Master. They told him what had happened. Said he, "This is not the first time, laymen, that he hurried away at the mere sight of the gateway of my dwelling. He did the same before." And at their request, he told an old-world tale.

---

[217] Once upon a time, it befel that the Bodhisatta reigned king in Takkasilā, of the realm of Gandhāra, and Brahmadatta in Benares. Brahmadatta resolved to capture Takkasilā; wherefore with a great host he set forth, and took up a position not far from the city, and set his army in array: "Here be the elephants, here the horses, the chariots here, and here the footmen: thus do ye charge and hurl with your weapons; as the clouds pour forth rain, so pour ye forth a rain of arrows!" and he uttered this pair of stanzas:—

"Lo, my elephants and horses, like the storm-cloud in the sky!
Lo, my surging sea of chariots shooting arrow-spray on high!
Lo, my host of warriors, striking sword in hand, with blow and thrust,
Closing in upon the city, till their foes shall bite the dust!

"Rush against them—fall upon them! shout the war-cry—loudly sing!
While the elephants in concert raise a clamorous trumpeting!
As the thunder and the lightning flash and rumble in the sky,
So be now your voice uplifted in the loud long battle-cry!"

[218] So cried the king. And he made his army march, and came before the gate of the city; and when he saw the towers on the city gate, he asked whether was that the king's dwelling. "That," said they, "is the gate tower." "If the gate tower be such as this, of what sort will the king's palace be?" he asked. And they replied, "Like to Vejayanta, the palace of Sakka!" On hearing it, the king said, "With so glorious a king we shall never be able to fight!" And having seen no more than the tower set upon the city gate, he turned and fled away, and came again to Benares.

This discourse ended, the Master identified the Birth:—"Our mendicant gadabout was then the king of Benares, and I was the king of Takkasilā myself."

[1] The Jetavana monastery is represented on the Bhārhut Stupa (Cunningham, pl. LVII); for the *gandhakuṭi*, see pl. XXVIII, fig. 3.

No. 230.

DUTIYA-PALĀYI-JĀTAKA.

"*Countless are my banners*," *etc.*—[219] This story the Master told whilst living at Jetavana, about this same gadabout mendicant.

At that time, the Master, with a large company round him, sitting on the beautifully adorned throne of the truth, upon a vermilion dais, was discoursing like a young lion roaring with a lion's roar. The mendicant, seeing the Buddha's form like the form of Brahma, his face like the glory of the full moon, and his forehead like a plate of gold, turned round where he had come, in the midst of the crowd, and ran off, saying, "Who could overcome a man like this?"

The crowd went in chase, then came back and told the Master. He said, "Not only now has this mendicant fled at the mere sight of my golden face; he did the same before." And he told an old-world tale.

Once on a time, the Bodhisatta was king in Benares, and in Takkasilā reigned a certain king of Gandhāra. This king, desiring to capture Benares, went and compassed the city about with a complete army of four divisions. And taking his stand at the city gate, he looked upon his army, and said he, "Who shall be able to conquer so great an army as this?" and describing his army, he uttered the first stanza:—

"Countless are my banners: rival none they own:
Flocks of crows can never stem the rolling sea—
Never can the storm-blast beat a mountain down:—
So, of all the living none can conquer me!"

[220] Then the Bodhisatta disclosed his own glorious countenance, in fashion as the full moon; and threatening him, thus spoke: "Fool, babble not vainly! Now will I destroy your host, as a maddened elephant crushes a thicket of reeds!" and he repeated the second stanza:—

"Fool! and hast thou never yet a rival found?
Thou art hot with fever, if thou seekst to wound
Solitary savage elephants like me!
As they crush a reed-stalk so will I crush thee!"

When the king of Gandhāra heard him threaten thus, [221] he looked up, and beholding his wide forehead like a plate of gold, for fear of being captured himself he turned and ran away, and came again even unto his own city.

This discourse ended, the Master identified the Birth:—"The vagrant gadabout was at that time the king of Gandhāra, and the king of Benares was I myself."

No. 231.

UPĀHANA-JĀTAKA.

"*As when a pair of shoes,*" *etc.*—This story the Master told in the Bamboo Grove, about Devadatta. The Brethren gathered together in the Hall of Truth, and began to discuss the matter. "Friend, Devadatta having repudiated his teacher, and become the foe and adversary of the Tathāgata, has come to utter destruction." The Master came in, and asked what they were talking about as they sat there. They told him. The Master said, "Brethren, this is not the first time that Devadatta has repudiated his teacher, and become my enemy, and come to utter destruction. The same thing happened before." Then he told them an old-world tale.

Once on a time, while Brahmadatta was king of Benares, the Bodhisatta was born as the son of an elephant trainer. When he grew up, he was taught all the art of managing the elephant. And there came a young villager from Kāsi, and was taught of him. Now when the future Buddhas teach any, they do not give a niggardly dole of learning; but according to their own knowledge so teach they, keeping nothing back. So this youth learnt all the branches of knowledge from the Bodhisatta, without omission; and when he had learnt, said he to his master: [222]

"Master, I will go and serve the king."

"Good, my son," said he: and he went before the king, and told him how that a pupil of his would serve the king. Said the king, "Good, let him serve me." "Then do you know what fee to give?" says the Bodhisatta.

"A pupil of yours will not receive so much as you; if you receive an hundred, he shall have fifty; if you receive two, to him shall one be given." So the Bodhisatta went home, and told all this to his pupil.

"Master," said the youth, "all your knowledge do I know, piece for piece. If I shall have the like payment, I will serve the king; but if not, then I will not serve him." And this the Bodhisatta told to the king. Said the king,

"If the young man could do even as you—if he is able to show skill for skill with you, he shall receive the like." And the Bodhisatta told this to the pupil, and the pupil made answer, "Very good, I will." "To-morrow," said the king, "do you make exhibition of your skill." "Good, I will; let proclamation be made by beat of drum." And the king caused it to be proclaimed, "To-morrow the master and the pupil will make show together of their skill in managing the elephant. To-morrow let all that wish to see gather together in the courtyard of the palace, and see it."

"My pupil," thought the teacher to himself, "does not know all my resources." So he chose an elephant, and in one night he taught him to do all things awry. He taught him to back when bidden go forward, and to go on when told to back; to lie down when bidden rise, and to rise when bidden lie down; to drop when told to pick up, and to pick up when told to drop.

Next day mounting his elephant he came to the palace yard. And his pupil also was there, mounted upon a beautiful elephant. There was a great concourse of people. They both showed all their skill. But the Bodhisatta made his elephant reverse orders; [223] "Go on!" said he, and it backed; "Back!" and it ran forward; "Stand up!" and it lay down; "Lie!" and it stood up; "Pick it up!" and the creature dropped it; "Drop it!" and he picked it up. And the crowd cried, "Go to, you rascal! do not raise your voice against your master! You do not know your own measure, and you think you can match yourself against him!" and they assailed him with clods and staves, so that he gave up the ghost then and there. And the Bodhisatta came down from his elephant, and approaching the king, addressed him thus—

"O mighty king! for their own good men get them taught; but there was one to whom his learning brought misery with it, like an ill-made shoe;" and he uttered these two stanzas:—

"As when a pair of shoes which one has bought
For help and comfort cause but misery,
Chafing the feet till they grow burning hot
And making them to fester by and bye:

"Even so an underbred ignoble man,
Having learnt all that he can learn from you,
By your own teaching proves your very bane[1]:
The lowbred churl is like the ill-made shoe."

[224] The king was delighted, and heaped honours upon the Bodhisatta.

When this discourse was ended, the Master identified this Birth as follows:—"Devadatta was the pupil, and I myself was the teacher."

[1] The schol. would take *tam* as for *attānam*, "he hurts himself," not "thee," but this is hardly possible. The verses do not seem to fit the story very exactly.

No. 232.

VĪṆĀ-THŪṆA-JĀTAKA.

"*Your own idea,*" *etc.*—This story the Master told while staying at Jetavana, about a young lady.

She was the only daughter of a rich merchant of Sāvatthi. She noticed that in her father's house a great fuss was made over a fine bull, and asked her nurse what it meant. "Who is this, nurse, that is honoured so?" The nurse replied that it was a right royal bull.

Another day she was looking from an upper storey down the street, when lo, she spied a hunchback. [225] Thought she, "In the cow tribe, the leader has a hump. I suppose it's the same with men. That must be a right royal man, and I must go and be his humble follower." So she sent her maid to say that the merchant's daughter wished to join herself to him, and he was to wait for her in a certain spot. She collected her treasures together, and disguising herself, left the mansion and went off with the hunchback.

By and bye all this became known in the town and among the Brotherhood. In the Hall of Truth, brothers discussed its bearings: "Friend, there is a merchant's daughter who has eloped with a hunchback!" The Master came in, and asked what they were all talking about together. They told him. He replied, "This is not the first time, Brethren, that she has fallen in love with a hunchback. She did the same before." And he told them an old-world tale.

Once on a time, while Brahmadatta was king of Benares, the Bodhisatta was born of a rich man's family in a certain market town. When he came of age, he lived as a householder, and was blessed with sons and daughters, and for his son's wife he chose the daughter of a rich citizen of Benares, and fixed the day.

Now the girl saw in her home honour and reverence offered to a bull. She asked of her nurse, "What is that?"—"A right royal bull," said she. And afterward the girl saw a hunchback going through the street. "That must be a right royal man!" thought she; and taking with her the best of her belongings in a bundle, she went off with him.

The Bodhisatta also, having a mind to fetch the girl home, set out for Benares with a great company; and he travelled by the same road.

The pair went along the road all night long. All night long the hunchback was overcome with thirst; and at the sunrise, he was attacked by colic, and great pain came upon him. So he went off the road, dizzy with pain, and fell down, like a broken lute-stick, huddled together; the girl too sat down at his feet. The Bodhisatta observed her sitting at the hunchback's feet, and recognised her. Approaching, he talked with her, repeating the first stanza: [226]

"Your own idea! this foolish man can't move without a guide,
This foolish hunchback! 'tis not meet you should be by his side."

And hearing his voice, the girl answered by the second stanza:—

"I thought the crookback king of men, and loved him for his worth,—
Who, like a lute with broken strings, lies huddled on the earth."

And when the Bodhisatta perceived that she had only followed him in disguise, he caused her to bathe, and adorned her, and took her into his carriage and went to his home.

When this discourse was ended, the Master identified the Birth:—"The girl is the same in both cases; and the merchant of Benares was I myself."

No. 233.

VIKAṆṆAKA-JĀTAKA.

[227] "*The barb is in your back*," *etc.*—This story the Master told while dwelling in Jetavana, about a backsliding brother.

He was brought into the Hall of Truth, and asked if he were really backsliding; to which he replied yes. When asked why, he replied "Because of the quality of desire." The Master said, "Desire is like twy-barbed arrows for getting lodgement in the heart; once there, they kill, as the barbed arrows killed the crocodile." Then he told them an old-world tale.

Once upon a time, the Bodhisatta was king of Benares, and a good king he was. One day he entered his park, and came to the side of a lake. And those who were clever with dance and song began to dance and to sing. The fish and tortoises, eager to hear the sound of song, flocked together and went along beside the king. And the king, seeing a mass of fish as long as a palm trunk, asked his courtiers,

"Now why do these fish follow me?"

Said the courtiers, "They are coming to offer their services to their lord."

The king was pleased at this saying, that they were come to serve him, and ordered rice to be given to them regularly. At the time of feeding some of the fish came, and some did not; and rice was wasted. They told the king of it. "Henceforward," said the king, "at the time for the giving of rice let a drum be sounded; and at the sound of the drum, when the fish flock together, give the food to them." From thenceforth the feeder caused a drum to sound, and when they flocked together gave rice to the fish. As they were gathered thus, eating the food, came a crocodile and ate some of the fish. The feeder told the king. The king listened. "When the crocodile is eating the fish," said he, "pierce him with a harpoon, and capture him." [228]

"Good," the man said. And he went aboard a boat, and so soon as the crocodile was come to eat the fish, he pierced him with a harpoon. It went into his back. Mad with pain, the crocodile went off with the harpoon. Perceiving that he was wounded, the feeder spake to him by this stanza:—

"The barb is in your back, go where you may.
The beat of drum, calling my fish to feed,
Brought you, pursuing, greedy, on the way
Which brought you also to your direst need."

When the crocodile got to his own place, he died.

To explain this matter, the Master having become perfectly enlightened spake the second verse as follows:

"So, when the world tempts any man to sin
Who knows no law but his own will and wish,
He perishes amid his friends and kin,
Even as the Crocodile that ate the fish."

[229] When this discourse was ended, the Master declared the Truths and identified the Birth:—at the conclusion of the Truths, the backsliding Brother reached the Fruit of the First Path:—"In those days I was the king of Benares."

No. 234.

ASITĀBHŪ-JĀTAKA.

"*Now desire has gone,*" *etc.*—This story the Master told while staying at Jetavana, about a young girl.

Tradition tells us that a certain man at Sāvatthi, a servant of the Master's two chief disciples, had one beautiful and happy daughter. When she grew up, she married into a family as good as her own. The husband, without consulting anybody, used to enjoy himself elsewhere at his own sweet will. She took no notice of his disrespect; but invited the two chief disciples, made them presents, and listened to their preaching, until she reached the Fruit of the First Path. After this she spent all her time in the enjoyment of the Path and the Fruit; at last, thinking that as her husband did not want her, there was no need for her to remain in the household, she determined to embrace the religious life. She informed her parents of her plan, carried it out, and became a saint.

Her story became known amongst the Brotherhood; and one day they were discussing it in the Hall of Truth. "Friend, the daughter of such and such a family strives to attain the highest good. Finding that her husband did not care for her, she made rich presents to the chief disciples, listened to their preaching, and gained the Fruit of the First Path; she took leave of her parents, became a religious, and then a saint. So, friend, the girl sought the highest good."

While they were talking, the Master came in and asked what it was all about. They told him. He said, "This is not the first time, Brethren, that she seeks the highest; she did so in olden days as well." And he told an old-world tale.

Once on a time, when Brahmadatta was king in Benares, the Bodhisatta was living as an ascetic, in the Himalaya region; and he had cultivated the Faculties and the Attainments. Then the king of Benares, observing how magnifical was the pomp of his son Prince Brahmadatta, was filled with suspicion, and banished his son from the realm.

[230] The youth with his wife Asitābhū made his way to Himalaya, and took up his abode in a hut of leaves, with fish to eat, and all manner of wild fruits. He saw a woodland sprite, and became enamoured of her. "Her will I make my wife!" said he, and nought recking of Asitābhū, he followed after her steps. His wife seeing that he followed after the sprite, was wroth. "The man cares nought for me," she thought; "what have I to do with him?" So she came to the Bodhisatta, and did him reverence: she learnt what she must needs do to be initiated, and gazing at the mystic object, she developed the Faculties and the Attainments, bade the Bodhisatta farewell, and returning stood at the door of her hut of leaves.

Now Brahmadatta followed the sprite, but saw not by what way she went; and baulked of his desire he set his face again for the hut. Asitābhū saw him coming, and rose up in the air; and poised upon a plane in the air of the colour of a precious stone, she said to him—"My young lord! 'tis through you that I have attained this ecstatic bliss!" and she uttered the first stanza:—

"Now desire has gone,
  Thanks to you, and found its ending:
Like a tusk, once sawn,
  None can make it one by mending."

So saying, as he looked, she rose up and departed to another place. And when she had gone, he uttered the second stanza, lamenting:—[231]

"Greed that knows no stay,
  Lust, the senses all confusing,
Steals our good away,
  Even as now my wife I'm losing."

And having made his moan in this stanza, he dwelt alone in the forest, and at his father's death he received the sovereignty.

After this discourse was ended, the Master identified the Birth:—"These two people were then the prince and princess, and I was the hermit."

No. 235.

VACCHA-NAKHA-JĀTAKA.

"*Houses in the world are sweet*," *etc.*—This story the Master told at Jetavana, about Roja the Mallian.

We learn that this man, who was a lay friend of Ānanda's, sent the Elder a message that he should come to him. The Elder took leave of the Master, and went. He served the Elder with all sorts of food, and sat down on one side, engaging him in a pleasant conversation. Then he offered the Elder a share of his house, tempting him by the five channels of desire. "Ananda, Sir, I have at home great store of live and dead stock. I will divide it and give you half; let us live in one house together!" The Elder declared to him the suffering which is involved in desire; then rose from his seat, and returned to the monastery.

When the Master asked whether he had seen Roja, he replied that he had. "What did he say to you?" "Sir, Roja invited me to return to the world; then I explained to him the suffering involved in desires and the worldly life." The Master said, "Ānanda, this is not the first time that Roja the Mallian has invited anchorites to return to the world; he did the same before;" and then, at his request, he told a story of the olden time.

---

[232] Once upon a time, when Brahmadatta was king of Benares, the Bodhisatta was one of a family of brahmins who lived in a certain market town. Coming to years, he took up the religious life, and dwelt for a long time amid the Himalayas.

He went to Benares to purchase salt and seasoning, and abode in the king's grounds; next day he entered Benares.

Now a certain rich man of the place, pleased at his behaviour, took him home, gave him to eat, and receiving his promise to abide with him, caused him to dwell in the garden and attended to his wants. And they conceived a friendship each for the other.

One day, the rich man, by reason of his love and friendship for the Bodhisatta, thought this within himself: "The life of an ascetic is unhappy. I will persuade my friend Vacchanakha to unfrock himself; I will part my wealth in two, and give half to him, and we both will dwell together." So one day, when the meal was done, he spake sweetly to his friend and said—

"Good Vacchanakha, unhappy is the hermit's life; 'tis pleasant to live in a house. Come now, let us both together take our pleasure as we will." So saying, he uttered the first stanza:—

"Houses in the world are sweet,
  Full of food, and full of treasure;
There you have your fill of meat—
  Eating, drinking at your pleasure."

The Bodhisatta on hearing him, thus replied: "Good Sir, from ignorance you have become greedy in desire, and call the householder's life good, and the life of the ascetic bad; listen now, and I will tell you how bad is the householder's life;" and he uttered the second stanza: [233]

"He that hath houses peace can never know,
He lies and cheats, he must deal many a blow
  On others' shoulders: nought this fault can cure:
Then who into a house would willing go?"

With these words the great Buddha told the defects of a householder's life, and went into the garden again.

When the Master had ended this discourse, he identified the Birth:—"Roja the Mallian was the Benares merchant, and I was Vacchanakha the mendicant."

No. 236.

BAKA-JĀTAKA.

"*See that twice-born bird*," *etc.*—This story the Master told while staying in Jetavana, about a hypocrite. When he was brought before the Master, the Master said, "Brethren, he was a hypocrite of old just as he is now," and told the following story.

---

[234] Once on a time, when Brahmadatta was king of Benares, the Bodhisatta became a Fish in a certain pond in the Himalaya region, and a great shoal went with him. Now a Crane desired to eat the fish. So in a place near the pond he drooped his head, and spread out his wings, and looked vacantly, vacantly at the fish, waiting till they were off their guard[1]. At the same moment the Bodhisatta with his shoal came to that place in search of food. And the shoal of fish on seeing the crane uttered the first stanza:—

"See that twice-born[2] bird, how white—
Like a water-lily seeming;
Wings outspread to left and right—
Oh, how pious! dreaming, dreaming!"

Then the Bodhisatta looked, and uttered the second stanza:—

"What he is ye do not know,
Or you would not sing his praises.
He is our most treacherous foe;
That is why no wing he raises."

Thereupon the fish splashed in the water and drove the crane away.

When this discourse was ended, the Master identified the Birth:—"This hypocrite was the Crane, and I was the chief of the shoal of fish."

No. 237.

SĀKETA-JĀTAKA.

"*Why are hearts cold,*" *etc.*—This story the Master told during a stay near Sāketa, about a brahmin named Sāketa. Both the circumstances that suggested the story and the story itself have already been given in the First Book[3].

---

[1] "A crane's sleep" is an Indian proverb for trickery.

[2] *dijo* is used of a bird as born in the egg and from the egg. It is also applied to Brahmins, and so conveys an additional notion of piety.

[3] No. 68.

[235]...And when the Tathāgata had gone to the monastery, the Brother asked, "How, Sir, did the love begin?" and repeated the first stanza:—

"Why are hearts cold to one—O Buddha, tell!—
And love another so exceeding well?"

The Master explained the nature of love by the second stanza:—

"Those love they who in other lives were dear,
As sure as grows the lotus in the mere."

After this discourse was ended, the Master identified the Birth:—"These two people were the brahmin and his wife in the story; and I was their son."

No. 238.

EKAPADA-JĀTAKA.

[236] "*Tell me one word,*" *etc.*—This story the Master told in Jetavana, about a certain landowner.

We are told that there was a landowner who lived at Sāvatthi. One day, his son sitting on his hip asked him what is called the "Door[1]" question. He replied, "That question requires a Buddha; nobody else can answer it." So he took his son to Jetavana, and saluted the Master. "Sir," said he, "as my son sat on my hip, he asked me the question called the 'Door.' I didn't know the answer, so here I am to ask you to give it." Said the Master, "This is not the first time, layman, that the lad has been a seeker after the way to accomplish his ends, and asked wise men this question; he did so before, and wise men in olden days gave him the answer; but by reason of the dimness caused by re-birth, he has forgotten it." And at his request the Master told a tale of the olden time.

Once upon a time, when Brahmadatta was reigning in Benares, the Bodhisatta came into this world as a rich merchant's son. He grew up, and when in course of time the father died, he took his father's place as a merchant.

[1] This question referred to the means of entering on the Paths.

And his son, a young boy, sitting on his hip, asked him a question. "Father," said he, "tell me a thing in one word which embraces a wide range of meaning;" and he repeated the first stanza:—

"Tell me one word that all things comprehends:
By what, in short, can we attain our ends?"

His father replied with the second:—

"One thing for all things precious—that is skill:
Add virtue and add patience, and you will
Do good to friends and to your foes do ill."

[237] Thus did the Bodhisatta answer his son's question. The son used the way which his father pointed out to accomplish his purposes, and by and bye he passed away to fare according to his deserts.

When this discourse was ended, the Master declared the Truths and identified the Birth:—at the conclusion of the Truths father and son reached the Fruit of the First Path:—"This man was then the son, and I was the merchant of Benares myself."

No. 239.

HARITA-MĀTA-JĀTAKA.

"*When I was in their cage*," *etc.*—This story the Master told while dwelling in the Bamboo-grove, about Ajātasattu.

Mahā-Kosala, the king of Kosala's father, when he married his daughter to king Bimbisāra, had given her a village in Kāsi for bath-money. After Ajātasattu murdered Bimbisāra, his father, the queen very soon died of love for him. Even after his mother's death, Ajātasattu still enjoyed the revenues of this village. But the king of Kosala determined that no parricide should have a village which was his by right of inheritance, and made war upon him. Sometimes the uncle got the best of it, and sometimes the nephew. And when Ajātasattu was victor, he raised his banner and marched through the country back to his capital in triumph; but when he lost, all downcast he returned without letting any one know.

It happened on a day that the Brethren sat talking about it in the Hall of Truth. "Friend"—so one would say—"Ajātasattu is delighted when he beats his uncle, and when he loses he is cast down." The Master, entering the Hall, asked what they were discussing this time; [238] and they told him. He said, "Brethren, this is not the first time that the man has been happy when he conquered, and miserable when he did not." And he told them an old-world tale.

Once upon a time, when Brahmadatta was king of Benares, the Bodhisatta became a Green Frog. At the time people set wicker cages in all pits and holes of the rivers, to catch fish withal. In one cage were a large number of fish. And a Water-snake, eating fish, went into the trap himself. A number of the fish thronging together fell to biting him, until he was covered with blood. Seeing no help for it, in fear of his life he slipped out of the mouth of the cage, and lay down full of pain on the edge of the water. At the same moment, the Green Frog took a leap and fell into the mouth of the trap. The Snake, not knowing to whom he could appeal, asked the Frog that he saw there in the trap—"Friend Frog, are you pleased with the behaviour of yonder Fish?" and he uttered the first stanza:—

"When I was in their cage, the fish did bite
Me, though a snake. Green Frog, does that seem right?"

Then the Frog answered him, "Yes, friend Snake, it does: why not? if you eat fish which get into your demesne, [239] the fish eat you when you get into theirs. In his own place, and district, and feeding ground no one is weak." So saying, he uttered the second stanza:—

"Men rob as long as they can compass it;
And when they cannot—why, the biter's bit!"

The Bodhisatta having pronounced his opinion, all the fish observing the Snake's weakness, cried, "Let us seize our foe!" and came out of the cage, and did him to death then and there, and then departed.

When the Master had ended this discourse, he identified the Birth:—"Ajātasattu was the Water-snake, and the Green Frog was I."

No. 240.

MAHĀPIṄGALA-JĀTAKA[1].

"*The Yellow King,*" *etc.*—This story the Master told at the Jetavana Park, about Devadatta the heretic.

Devadatta for nine months had tried to compass the destruction of the future Buddha, and had sunk down into the earth by the gateway of Jetavana.

[1] *Folk-Lore Journal*, iii. 126.

Then they that dwelt at Jetavana and in all the country round about were delighted, saying, "Devadatta the enemy of Buddha has been swallowed up in the earth: the adversary is slain, and the Master has become perfectly enlightened!" [240] And hearing these words spoken many a time and oft, the people of all the continent of India, and all the goblins, and living creatures, and gods were delighted likewise. One day, all the brethren were talking together in the Hall of Truth, and thus would they say: "Brother, since Devadatta sank into the earth, what a number of people are glad, saying, Devadatta is swallowed up by the earth!" The Teacher entered, and asked, "What are ye all talking about here, brethren?" They told him. Then said he, "This is not the first time, O brethren, that multitudes have rejoiced and laughed aloud at the death of Devadatta. Long ago they rejoiced and laughed as they do now." And he told them an old-world tale.

Once upon a time reigned at Benares a wicked and unjust king named Mahā-piṅgala, the Great Yellow King, who did sinfully after his own will and pleasure. With taxes and fines, and many mutilations[1] and robberies, he crushed the folk as it were sugar-cane in a mill; he was cruel, fierce, ferocious. For other people he had not a grain of pity; at home he was harsh and implacable towards his wives, his sons and daughters, to his brahmin courtiers and the householders of the country. He was like a speck of dust that falls in the eye, like gravel in the broth, like a thorn sticking in the heel.

Now the Bodhisatta was a son of king Mahā-piṅgala. After this king had reigned for a long time, he died. When he died all the citizens of Benares were overjoyed and laughed a great laugh; they burnt his body with a thousand cartloads of logs, and quenched the place of burning with thousands of jars of water, and consecrated the Bodhisatta to be king: they caused a drum of rejoicing to beat about the streets, for joy that they had got them a righteous king. They raised flags and banners, and decked out the city; at every door was set a pavilion, and scattering parched corn and flowers, they sat them down upon the decorated platforms under fine canopies, and did eat and drink. The Bodhisatta himself sat upon a fine divan [241] on a great raised dais, in great magnificence, with a white parasol stretched above him. The courtiers and householders, the citizens and the doorkeepers stood around their king.

But one doorkeeper, standing not far from the king, was sighing and sobbing. "Good Porter," said the Bodhisatta, observing him, "all the people are making merry for joy that my father is dead, but you stand weeping. Come, was my father good and kind to you?" And with the question he uttered the first stanza:—

[1] *-jaṁghakahāpaṇādigahanena* I take to mean 'the taking away of legs, money, etc.' Possibly *jaṁghā* (taking it independently) may mean something like 'boot' or 'stocks,' but I can find no authority for this.

"The Yellow King was cruel to all men;
Now he is dead, all freely breathe again.
Was he, the yellow-eyed, so very dear?
Or, Porter, why do you stand weeping here?"

The man heard, and answered: "I am not weeping for sorrow that Piṅgala is dead. My head would be glad enough. For King Piṅgala, every time he came down from the palace, or went up into it, would give me eight blows over the head with his fist, like the blows of a blacksmith's hammer. So when he goes down to the other world, he will deal eight blows on the head of Yama, the gatekeeper of hell, as though he were striking me. Then the people there will cry—He is too cruel for us! and will send him up again. And I fear he will come and deal fisticuffs on my head again, and that is why I weep." To explain the matter he uttered the second stanza:—[242]

"The Yellow King was anything but dear:
It is his coming back again I fear.
What if he beat the king of Death, and then
The king of Death should send him back again?"

Then said the Bodhisatta: "That king has been burnt with a thousand cartloads of wood; the place of his burning has been soaked with water from thousands of pitchers, and the ground has been dug up all round; beings that have gone to the other world, except by force of fate[1], do not return to the same bodily shape as they had before; do not be afraid!" and to comfort him, he repeated the following stanza:—

"Thousands of loads of wood have burnt him quite,
Thousands of pitchers quenched what still did burn;
The earth is dug about to left and right—
Fear not—the king will never more return.

After that, the porter took comfort. And the Bodhisatta ruled in righteousness; and after giving gifts and doing other good acts, he passed away to fare according to his deserts.

When the Master had ended this discourse, he identified the Birth:-"Devadatta was Piṅgala; and his son was I myself."

[1] Reading *aññatra gativasā*, 'except by the power of re-birth.'

No. 241[1].

SABBADĀṬHA-JĀTAKA.

"*Even as the Jackal*," etc. This story the Master told while staying in the Bamboo-grove, about Devadatta.

Devadatta, having won favour in the eyes of Ajātasattu, yet could not make the repute and support which he received last any time. Ever since they saw the miracle[2] done when Nālāgiri was sent against him, the reputation and receipts of Devadatta began to fall off. [243]

So one day, the Brethren were all talking about it in the Hall of Truth: "Friend, Devadatta managed to get reputation and support, yet could not keep it up. This happened in olden days in just the same way." And then he told them an old-world tale.

Once upon a time, Brahmadatta was king of Benares, and the Bodhisatta was his chaplain; and he had mastered the three Vedas and the eighteen branches of knowledge. He knew the spell entitled 'Of subduing the World.' (Now this spell is one which involves religious meditation.)

One day, the Bodhisatta thought that he would recite this spell; so he sat down in a place apart upon a flat stone, and there went through his reciting of it. It is said that this spell could be taught to no one without use of a special rite; for which reason he recited it in the place just described. It so happened that a Jackal lying in a hole heard the spell at the time that he was reciting it, and got it by heart. We are told that this jackal in a previous existence had been some brahmin who had learnt the charm 'Of subduing the World.'

The Bodhisatta ended his recitation, and rose up, saying—"Surely I have that spell by heart now." Then the Jackal arose out of his hole, and cried—"Ho, brahmin! I have learnt the spell better than you know it yourself!" and off he ran. The Bodhisatta set off in chase, and followed some way, crying—"Yon jackal will do a great mischief—catch him, catch him!" But the jackal got clear off into the forest.

The Jackal found a she-jackal, and gave her a little nip upon the body. "What is it, master?" she asked. "Do you know me," he asked, "or do you not?" "[3]I do not know you." He repeated the spell, and thus had

[1] *Folk-Lore Journal*, iv. 60.

[2] A great elephant was let loose for the purpose of destroying the Buddha, but only did him reverence: *Cullavagga*, vii. 3. 11 (*S. B. E.*, *Vinaya Texts*, iii. 247); Hardy, *Manual of Buddhism*, p. 320; *Milinda-pañha* iv. 4. 30 (trans. in *S. B. E.*, i. 288).

[3] Perhaps *ājānāmi* "I do know you."

under his orders several hundreds of jackals, and gathered round him all the elephants and horses, lions and tigers, swine and deer, and all other fourfooted creatures; [244] and their king he became, under the title of Sabbadāṭha, or Alltusk, and a she-jackal he made his consort. On the back of two elephants stood a lion, and on the lion's back sat Sabbadāṭha, the jackal king, along with his consort the she-jackal; and great honour was paid to them.

Now the Jackal was tempted by his great honour, and became puffed up with pride, and he resolved to capture the kingdom of Benares. So with all the fourfooted creatures in his train, he came to a place near to Benares. His host covered twelve leagues of ground. From his position there he sent a message to the king, "Give up your kingdom, or fight for it." The citizens of Benares, smitten with terror, shut close their gates and stayed within.

Then the Bodhisatta drew near the king, and said to him, "Fear not, mighty king! leave me the task of fighting with the jackal king, Sabbadāṭha. Except only me, no one is able to fight with him at all." Thus he gave heart to the king and the citizens. "I will ask him at once," he went on, "what he will do in order to take the city." So he mounted the tower over one of the gates, and cried out—"Sabbadāṭha, what will you do to get possession of this realm?"

"I will cause the lions to roar, and with the roaring I will frighten the multitude: thus will I take it!"

"Oh, that's it," thought the Bodhisatta, and down he came from the tower. He made proclamation by beat of drum that all the dwellers in the great city of Benares, over all its twelve leagues, must stop up their ears with flour. The multitude heard the command; they stopped up their own ears with flour, so that they could not hear each other speak:—nay, they even did the same to their cats and other animals.

Then the Bodhisatta went up a second time into the tower, and cried out "Sabbadāṭha!"

"What is it, Brahmin?" quoth he.

"How will you take this realm?" he asked.

"I will cause the lions to roar, and I will frighten the people, and destroy them; thus will I take it!" he said.

"You will not be able to make the lions roar; these noble lions, with their tawny paws and shaggy manes, will never do the bidding of an old jackal like you!"

The jackal, stubborn with pride, [245] answered, "Not only will the other lions obey me, but I'll even make this one, upon whose back I sit, roar alone!"

"Very well," said the Bodhisatta, "do it if you can."

So he tapped with his foot on the lion which he sat upon, to roar.

And the lion resting his mouth upon the Elephant's temple, roared thrice, without any manner of doubt. The elephants were terrified and dropped the Jackal down at their feet; they trampled upon his head and crushed it to atoms. Then and there Sabbadāṭha perished. And the elephants, hearing the roar of the lion, were frightened to death, and wounding one another, they all perished there. The rest of the creatures, deer and swine, down to the hares and cats, perished then and there, all except the lions; and these ran off and took to the woods. There was a heap of carcases covering the ground for twelve leagues.

The Bodhisatta came down from the tower, and had the gates of the city thrown open. By beat of drum he caused proclamation to be made throughout the city: "Let all the people take the flour from out of their ears, and they that desire meat, meat let them take!" The people all ate what meat they could fresh, and the rest they dried and preserved.

It was at this time, according to tradition, that people first began to dry meat.

The Master having finished this discourse, identified the Birth by the following verses, full of divine wisdom:—

"Even as the Jackal, stiff with pride,
Craved for a mighty host on every side,
And all toothed creatures came
Flocking around, until he won great fame:

"Even so the man who is supplied
With a great host of men on every side,
As great renown has he
As had the Jackal in his sovranty."

[246] "In those days Devadatta was the Jackal, Ānanda was the king, and I was the chaplain."

No. 242.

SUNAKHA-JĀTAKA.

"*Foolish Dog*," etc. This story the Master told whilst living in Jetavana, about a dog that used to be fed in the resting hall by the Ambala tower.

It is said that from a puppy this dog had been kept there and fed by some water-carriers. In course of time it grew up there to be a big dog. Once a villager happened to see him; and he bought him from the water-carriers for an upper garment and a rupee; then, fastening him to a chain, led the dog away. The dog was led away, unresisting, making no sound, and followed and followed the new master, eating whatever was offered. "He's fond of me, no doubt," thought the man; and let him free from the chain. No sooner did the dog find himself free, than off he went, and never stopped until he came back to the place he started from.

Seeing him, the Brethren guessed what had happened; and in the evening, when they were gathered in the Hall of Truth, they began talking about it. "Friend—here's the dog back again in our resting hall! how clever he must have been, to get rid of his chain! No sooner free, than back he ran!" The Master, entering, asked what they were all talking about as they sat together. They told him. He rejoined, "Brethren, this is not the first time our dog was clever at getting rid of his chain; he was just the same before." And he told them an old-world tale.

Once upon a time, when Brahmadatta was king of Benares, the Bodhisatta was born in a rich family of the kingdom of Kāsi; and when he grew up, he set up a house of his own. There was a man in Benares who had a dog which had been fed on rice till it grew fat. [247] And a certain villager who had come to Benares saw the dog; and to the owner he gave a fine garment and a piece of money for the dog, which he led off bound by a strap. Arrived at the outskirts of a forest, he entered a hut, tied up the dog, and lay down to sleep. At that moment the Bodhisatta entered the forest on some errand, and beheld the dog made fast by a thong; whereat he uttered the first stanza:—

"Foolish Dog! why don't you bite
Through that strap that holds you tight?
In a trice you would be free,
Scampering off merrily!"

On hearing this stanza, the Dog uttered the second:—

"Resolute—determined, I
Wait my opportunity:
Careful watch and ward I keep
Till the people are asleep."

So spake he; and when the company were asleep, he gnawed through the strap, and returned to his master's house in great glee.

---

[248] When this discourse was ended, the Master identified the Birth:— "The dogs are the same, and I was the wise man."

No. 243.

GUTTILA-JĀTAKA.

"*I had a pupil once*," *etc.*—This story the Master told in the Bamboo-grove, about Devadatta.

On this occasion the Brethren said to Devadatta: "Friend Devadatta, the Supreme Buddha is your teacher; of him you learnt the Three Piṭakas and how to produce the Four kinds of Ecstasy; you really should not act the enemy to your own teacher!" Devadatta replied: "Why, friends,—Gotama the Ascetic my teacher? Not a bit: was it not by my own power that I learnt the Three Piṭakas, and produced the Four Ecstasies?" He refused to acknowledge his teacher.

The Brethren fell a-talking of this in the Hall of Truth. "Friend! Devadatta repudiates his teacher! he has become an enemy of the Supreme Buddha! and what a miserable fate has befallen him!" In came the Master, and enquired what they were all talking of together. They told him. "Ah, Brethren," said he, "this is not the first time that Devadatta has repudiated his teacher, and shown himself my enemy, and come to a miserable end. It was just the same before." And then he told the following story.

Once upon a time, when Brahmadatta was reigning in Benares, the Bodhisatta was born in a musician's family. His name was Master Guttila. When he grew up, he mastered all the branches of music, and under the name of Guttila the Musician he became the chief of his kind in all India. He married no wife, but maintained his blind parents[1].

At that time certain traders of Benares made a journey to Ujjeni for trade. A holiday was proclaimed; they all clubbed together; they procured scents and perfumes and ointments, and all manner of foods and meats. "Pay the hire," they cried, "and fetch a musician!"

It happened that at the time a certain Mūsila [249] was the chief musician in Ujjeni. Him they sent for, and made him their musician. Mūsila was a player on the lute; and he tuned his lute up to the highest key, to play upon. But they knew the playing of Guttila the Musician, and his music seemed to them like scratching on a mat. So not one of them showed pleasure. When Mūsila saw that they expressed no pleasure, he said to himself—"Too sharp, I suppose," and tuning his lute down to the middle tone, he played it so. Still they sat indifferent. Then thought he, "I suppose they know nothing about it;" and making as though he

[1] Guttila is one of the four men who "even in their earthly bodies attained to glory in the city of the gods." *Milinda*, iv. 8. 25 (trans. in *S. B. E.*, ii. 145).

too were ignorant, he played with the strings all loose. As before, they made no sign. Then Mūsila asked them, "Good merchants, why do you not like my playing?"

"What! are you playing?" cried they. "We imagined that you must be tuning up."

"Why, do you know any better musician," he asked, "or are you too ignorant to like my playing?"

Said the merchants, "We have heard the music of Guttila the Musician, at Benares; and yours sounds like women crooning to soothe their babies."

"Here, take your money back," said he, "I don't want it. Only when you go to Benares, please take me with you."

They agreed, and took him back to Benares with them; they pointed out the dwelling of Guttila, and departed every man to his own house.

Mūsila entered the Bodhisatta's dwelling; he saw his beautiful lute where it stood, tied up: he took it down, and played upon it. At this the old parents, who could not see him because they were blind, [250] cried out—

"The mice are gnawing at the lute! Shoo! shoo! the rats are biting the lute to pieces!"

At once Mūsila put down the lute, and greeted the old folks.

"Where do you come from?" asked they.

He replied, "I come from Ujjeni to learn at the feet of the teacher."

"Oh, all right," said they. He asked where the teacher was.

"He is out, father; but he will be back to-day," came the answer. Mūsila sat down and waited until he came; then after some friendly words, he told his errand. Now the Bodhisatta was skilled in divining from the lineaments of the body. He perceived that this was not a good man; so he refused. "Go, my son, this art is not for you." Mūsila clasped the feet of the Bodhisatta's parents, to help his suit, and prayed them—"Make him teach me!" Again and again his parents besought the Bodhisatta to do so; until he could not stand it any longer, and did as he was asked. And Mūsila went along with the Bodhisatta into the king's palace.

"Who is this, master?" asked the king, on seeing him.

"A pupil of mine, great king!" was the reply.

By and bye he got the ear of the king.

Now the Bodhisatta did not stint his knowledge, but taught his pupil everything which he knew himself. This done, he said, "Your knowledge is now perfect."

Thought Mūsila, "I have now mastered my art. This city of Benares is the chief city in all India. My teacher is old; here therefore must I stay." So he said to his teacher, "Sir, I would serve the king." "Good, my son," replied he, "I will tell the king of it."

He came before the king, and said, "My pupil is wishful to serve your Highness. Fix what his fee shall be."

The king answered, "His fee shall be the half of yours." And he came and told it to Mūsila. Mūsila said, "If I receive the same as you, I will serve; but if not, then I will not serve him." [251]

"Why?" "Say: do I not know all that you know?" "Yes, you do." "Then why does he offer me the half?"

The Bodhisatta informed the king what had passed. The king said,

"If he is as perfect in his art as you, he shall receive the same as you do." This saying of the king the Bodhisatta told to his pupil. The pupil consented to the bargain; and the king, being informed of this, replied—"Very good. What day will you compete together?" "Be it the seventh day from this, O king."

The king sent for Mūsila. "I understand that you are ready to try issue with your master?"

"Yes, your Majesty," was the reply.

The king would have dissuaded him. "Don't do it," said he, "there should be never rivalry between master and pupil."

"Hold, O king!" cried he—"yes, let there be a meeting between me and my teacher on the seventh day; we shall know which of us is master of his art."

So the king agreed; and he sent the drum beating round the city with this notice:—"Oyez! on the seventh day Guttila the Teacher, and Mūsila the Pupil, will meet at the door of the royal palace, to show their skill. Let the people assemble from the city, and see their skill!"

The Bodhisatta thought within himself, "This Mūsila is young and fresh, I am old and my strength is gone. What an old man does will not prosper. If my pupil is beaten[1], there is no great credit in that. If he beats me, death in the woods is better than the shame which will be my portion." So to the woods he went, but he kept returning through fear of death and going back to the wood through fear of shame. And in this way six days passed by. The grass died as he walked, and his feet wore away a path.

At that time, Sakka's throne became hot. Sakka meditated, and perceived what had happened. "Guttila the Musician is suffering much sorrow in the forest by reason of his pupil. [252] I must help him!" So he went in haste and stood before the Bodhisatta. "Master," said he, "why have you taken to the woods?"

"Who are you?" asked the other.

[1] Reading *antevāsike*.

"I am Sakka."

Then said the Bodhisatta, "I was in fear of being worsted by my pupil, O king of the gods; and therefore did I flee to the woods." And he repeated the first stanza[1]:—

> "I had a pupil once, who learnt of me
> The seven-stringed lute's melodious minstrelsy;
> He now would fain his teacher's skill outdo.
> O Kosiya[2]! do thou my helper be!"

"Fear not," said Sakka, "I am your defence and refuge:" and he repeated the second stanza:—

> "Fear not, for I will help thee at thy need;
> For honour is the teacher's rightful meed.
> Fear not! thy pupil shall not rival thee,
> But thou shalt prove the better man indeed."

"As you play, you shall break one of the strings of your lute, and play upon six; and the music shall be as good as before. Mūsila too shall break a string, and he shall not be able to make music with his lute; then shall he be defeated. And when you see that he is defeated, you shall break the second string of your lute, and the third, even unto the seventh, and you shall go on playing with nothing but the body; and from the ends of the broken strings the sound shall go forth, and fill all the land of Benares for a space of twelve leagues." [253] With these words he gave the Bodhisatta three playing-dice, and went on: "When the sound of the lute has filled all the city, you must throw one of these dice into the air; and three hundred nymphs shall descend and dance before you. While they dance throw up the second, and three hundred shall dance in front of your lute; then the third, and then three hundred more shall come down and dance within the arena. I too will come with them; go on, and fear not!"

In the morning the Bodhisatta returned home. At the palace door a pavilion was set up, and a throne was set apart for the king. He came down from the palace, and took his seat upon the divan in the gay pavilion. All around him were thousands of slaves, women beauteously apparelled, courtiers, brahmins, citizens. All the people of the town had come together. In the courtyard they were fixing the seats circle on circle, tier above tier. The Bodhisatta, washed and anointed, had eaten of all manner of finest meats; and lute in hand he sat waiting in his appointed place. Sakka was there, invisible, poised in the air, surrounded

[1] These stanzas, together with those which follow on page 255, and others, occur in the *Vimāna-vatthu*, no. 33 (p. 28 in the *P. T. S.* ed.), *Guttila-vimāna*.

[2] A title of Indra; the word means an Owl (Skr. *Kauçika*): it is one of the many Indian clan names that are also names of animals.

by a great company. However, the Bodhisatta saw him. Mūsila too was there, and sat in his own seat. All around was a great concourse of people.

First the two played each the same piece. When they played, both the same, the multitude was delighted, and gave abundant applause. Sakka spoke to the Bodhisatta, from his place in the air: "Break one of the strings!" said he. Then the Bodhisatta brake the bee-string; and the string, though broken, gave out a sound from its broken end; it seemed like music divine. Mūsila too broke a string; but after that no sound came out of it. His teacher broke the second, and so on to the seventh string: he played upon the body alone, and the sound continued, and filled the town:—the multitude in thousands waved and waved their kerchiefs in the air, in thousands they shouted applause. [254] The Bodhisatta threw up one of the dice into the air, and three hundred nymphs descended and began to dance. And when he had thrown the second and third in the same manner, there were nine hundred nymphs a-dancing as Sakka had said. Then the king made a sign to the multitude; up rose the multitude, and cried—"You made a great mistake in matching yourself against your teacher! You know not your measure!' Thus they cried out against Mūsila; and with stones and staves, and anything that came to hand, they beat and bruised him to death, and seizing him by the feet, they cast him upon a dustheap.

The king in his delight showered gifts upon the Bodhisatta, and so did they of the city. Sakka likewise spake pleasantly to him, and said, "Wise Sir, I will send anon my charioteer Mātali with a car drawn by a thousand thoroughbreds; and you shall mount upon my divine car, drawn by a thousand steeds, and travel to heaven"; and he departed.

When Sakka was returned, and sat upon his throne, made all of a precious stone, the daughters of the gods asked him, "Where have you been, O king?" Sakka told them in full all that had happened, and praised the virtues and good parts of the Bodhisatta. Then said the daughters of the gods,

"O king, we long to look upon this teacher; fetch him hither!"

Sakka summoned Mātali. "The nymphs of heaven," said he, "desire to look upon Guttila the Musician. Go, seat him in my divine car, and bring him hither." The charioteer went and brought the Bodhisatta. Sakka gave him a friendly greeting. "The maidens of the gods," said he, "wish to hear your music, Master."

"We musicians, O great king," said he, "live by practice of our art. For a recompense I will play."

"Play on, and I will recompense you."

"I care for no other recompense but this. Let these daughters of the gods tell me what acts of virtue brought them here; then will I play." [255]

Then said the daughters of the gods, "Gladly will we tell you after of the virtues that we have practised; but first do you play to us, Master."

For the space of a week the Bodhisatta played to them, and his music surpassed the music of heaven. On the seventh day he asked the daughters of the gods of their virtuous lives, beginning from the first. One of them, in the time of the Buddha Kassapa, had given an upper garment to a certain Brother; and having renewed existence as an attendant of Sakka, had become chief among the daughters of the gods, with a retinue of a thousand nymphs: of her the Bodhisatta asked—"What did you do in a previous existence, that has brought you here?" The manner of his question and the gift she had given have been told in the Vimāna story: they spoke as follows:—

"O brilliant goddess, like the morning star,
Shedding thy light of beauty near and far[1],
Whence springs this beauty? whence this happiness?
Whence all the blessings that the heart can bless?
I ask thee, goddess excellent in might,
Whence comes this all-pervading wondrous light?
When thou wert mortal woman, what didst thou
To gain the glory that surrounds thee now?"

"Chief among men and chief of women she
Who gives an upper robe in charity.
She that gives pleasant things is sure to win
A home divine and fair to enter in.
Behold this habitation, how divine!
As fruit of my good deeds this home is mine:
A thousand nymphs stand ready at my call;
Fair nymphs—and I the fairest of them all.
And therefore am I excellent in might;
Hence comes this all-pervading wondrous light!"

[256] Another had given flowers for worship to a Brother who craved an alms. Another had been asked for a scented wreath of five sprays for the shrine, and gave it. Another had given sweet fruits. Another had given fine essences. Another had given a scented five-spray to the shrine of the Buddha Kassapa. Another had heard the discourse of Brethren or Sisters in wayfaring, or such as had taken up their abode in the house of some family. Another had stood in the water, and given water to a Brother who had eaten his meal on a boat. Another living in the world had done her duty by mother-in-law and father-in-law, never losing her temper. Another had divided even the share that she received, and so did eat, and was virtuous. Another, who had been a slave in some household, without anger and without pride had given away a share of her own portion, and had been born again as an attendant upon the king of

[1] These two lines occur in the Comm. to the *Dhammapada*, p. 99. See also note on the First Stanza, above.

the gods. So also all those who are written in the story of Guttila-vimāna, thirty and seven daughters of the gods, were asked by the Bodhisatta what each had done to come there, and they too told what they had done in the same way by verses.

On hearing all this, the Bodhisatta exclaimed: "'Tis good for me, in sooth, truly 'tis very good for me, that I came here, and heard by how very small a merit great glory has been attained. Henceforward, when I return to the world of men, I will give all manner of gifts, and perform good deeds." And he uttered this aspiration:—

"O happy dawn! O happy must I be![1]
O happy pilgrimage, whereby I see
These daughters of the gods, divinely fair, [257]
And hear their sweet discourse! Henceforth I swear
Full of sweet peace, and generosity,
Of temperance, and truth my life shall be,
Till I come there where no more sorrows are."

Then after seven days had passed, the king of heaven laid his commands upon Mātali the charioteer, and he seated Guttila in the chariot and sent him to Benares. And when he came to Benares, he told the people what he had seen with his own eyes in heaven. From that time the people resolved to do good deeds with all their might.

When this discourse was ended, the Master identified the Birth: "In those days Devadatta was Mūsila, Anuruddha was Sakka, Ānanda was the king, and I was Guttila the Musician."

No. 244.

VĪTICCHA-JĀTAKA.

"*What he sees*," *etc.*—This story the Master told at Jetavana, about a turntail vagrant who wandered about the country.

It is said that this man could not find any one to argue with him in all India; till he came to Sāvatthi, and asked whether any one could dispute with him. Yes—he was told—the Supreme Buddha; hearing which, he and a multitude with him repaired to Jetavana, and put a question to the Master,

[1] *Vimāna-vatthu*, p. 31.

whilst he was discoursing in the midst of the four kinds of disciples. The Master answered his question, and then put one to him in return. This the man failed to answer, got up, and turned tail. The crowd sitting round exclaimed, "One word, Sir, vanquished the itinerant!" Said the Master, "Yes, Brethren, and just as I have vanquished him now with one word, so I did before." Then he told a story of olden days.

Once upon a time, when Brahmadatta was king of Benares, the Bodhisatta was born a brahmin in the kingdom of Kāsi. He grew up, and mastered his passions; and embracing the religious life, [258] he dwelt a long time in the Himalayas.

He came down from the highlands, and took up his abode near a considerable town, in a hut of leaves built beside a bend of the river Ganges.

A certain pilgrim, who found no one that could answer him throughout all India, came to that town. "Is there anyone," asked he, "who can argue with me?"

Yes, they said, and told him the power of the Bodhisatta. So, followed by a great multitude, he made his way to the place where the Bodhisatta dwelt, and after greeting him, took a seat.

"Will you drink," he asked, "of the Ganges water, infused with wild wood odours?"

The pilgrim tried to catch him in his words. "What is Ganges? Ganges may be sand, Ganges may be water, Ganges may be the near bank, Ganges may be the far bank!"

Said the Bodhisatta to the pilgrim, "Besides the sand, the water, the hither and the further bank, what other Ganges can you have?" The pilgrim had no answer for this; he rose up, and went away. When he had gone the Bodhisatta spake these verses by way of discourse to the assembled multitude:—

"What he sees, he will not have;
What he sees not he will crave.
He may go a long way yet—
What he wants he will not get.

"He contemns what he has got;
Once 'tis gained, he wants it not.
He craves everything always:
Who craves nothing earns our praise."

---

[259] When this discourse was ended, the Master identified the Birth: "The vagrant is the same in both cases, and I myself was then the ascetic."

No. 245.

MŪLA-PARIYĀYA-JĀTAKA.

"*Time all consumes,*" *etc.*—This is a story told by the Master while he stayed near Ukkaṭṭhā, in the Subhagavana Park, in connexion with the Chapter on the Succession of Causes.

At that time, it is said, five hundred brahmins who had mastered the three Vedas, having embraced salvation, studied the Three Piṭakas. These learnt, they became intoxicated with pride, thinking to themselves—"The Supreme Buddha knows just the Three Piṭakas, and we know them too. So what is the difference between us?" They discontinued their waiting upon the Buddha, and went about with an equal following of their own.

One day the Master, when these men were seated before him, repeated the Chapter on the Succession of Causes, and adorned it with the Eight Stages of Knowledge. They did not understand a word. The thought came into their mind—"Here we have been believing that there were none so wise as we, and of this we understand nothing. There is none so wise as the Buddhas: O the excellence of the Buddhas!" After this they were humbled, as quiet as serpents with their fangs extracted.

When the Master had stayed as long as he wished in Ukkaṭṭhā, he departed to Vesāli; and at Gotama's shrine he repeated the Chapter on Gotama. There was a quaking of a thousand worlds! Hearing this, these Brothers became saints.

But however, after the Master had finished repeating the Chapter on the Succession of Causes, during his visit to Ukkaṭṭhā [260] the Brethren discussed the whole affair in the Hall of Truth. "How great is the power of the Buddhas, friend! Why, these brahmin mendicants, who used to be so drunk with pride, have been humbled by the lesson on the Succession of Causes!" The Master entered and asked what their talk was about. They told him. He said, "Brethren, this is not the first time that I have humbled these men, who used to carry their heads so high with pride; I did the same before." And then he told them a tale of the olden time.

Once upon a time, when Brahmadatta reigned in Benares, the Bodhisatta was born a brahmin; who when he grew up, and mastered the Three Vedas, became a far-famed teacher, and instructed five hundred pupils in sacred verses. These five hundred, having given their best energy to their work, and perfected their learning, said within themselves,

"We know as much as our teacher: there is no difference."

Proud and stubborn, they would not come before their teacher's face, nor do their round of duty.

One day, they saw their master seated beneath a jujube tree; and desiring to mock him, they tapped upon the tree with their fingers. "A worthless tree!" said they.

The Bodhisatta observed that they were mocking him. "My pupils," he said, "I will ask you a question."

They were delighted. "Speak on," said they, "we will answer."

Their teacher asked the question by repeating the first stanza:—

"Time all consumes, even time itself as well.
Who is't consumes the all-consumer?—tell[1]!"

[261] The youths listened to the problem; but not one amongst them could answer it. Then said the Bodhisatta,

"Do not imagine that this question is in the Three Vedas. You imagine that you know all that I know, and so you act like the jujube tree[2]. You don't know that I know a great deal which is unknown to you. Leave me now: I give you seven days—think over this question for so long."

So they made salutation, and departed each to his own house. There for a week they pondered, yet they could make neither head nor tail of the problem. On the seventh day, they came to their teacher, and greeted him, sitting down.

"Well, ye of auspicious speech, have you solved the question?"

"No, we have not," said they.

Again the Bodhisatta spoke in reproof, uttering the second stanza:—

"Heads grow on necks, and hair on heads will grow:
How many heads have ears, I wish to know?"

"Fools are ye," he went on, rebuking the youths: "ye have ears with holes in them, but not wisdom;" and he solved the problem. [262] They listened. "Ah," said they, "great are our Teachers!" and they craved his pardon, and quenching their pride they waited upon the Bodhisatta.

When the Master had ended this discourse, he identified the Birth: "At that time these Brothers were the five hundred pupils; and I myself was their teacher."

[1] *Kālaghaso*, the 'consumer of time,' is he who, by destroying the thirst for existence, so lives as not to be born again (Scholiast's explanation).

[2] The jujube fruit is often contrasted with the cocoa nut, as being only externally pleasing, see *Hitop.* i. 95.

No. 246.

TELOVĀDA-JĀTAKA.

"*The wicked kills,*" *etc.*—This is a story which the Master told while staying in his gabled chamber near Vesāli, about Sīhasenāpati.

It is said that this man, after he had fled to the Refuge, offered hospitality and then gave food with meat in it. The naked ascetics on hearing this were angry and displeased; they wanted to do the Buddha a mischief; "The priest Gotama," sneered they, "with his eyes open, eats meat prepared on purpose for him."

The Brethren discussed this matter in their Hall of Truth: "Friend, Nāthaputta the Ascetic[1] goes about sneering, because, he says, 'Priest Gotama eats meat prepared on purpose for him, with his eyes open'." Hearing this, the Master rejoined:—"This is not the first time, Brethren, that Nāthaputta has been sneering at me for eating meat which was got ready for me on purpose; he did just so in former times." And he told them an old-world tale.

Once on a time, when Brahmadatta was king of Benares, the Bodhisatta was born a brahmin. When he came of age he embraced the religious life.

He came down from Himalaya to get salt and seasoning, and next day walked the city, begging alms. A certain wealthy man designed to annoy the ascetic. So he brought him to his dwelling, and pointed out a seat, and then served him with fish. After the meal, the man sat on one side, and said,

"This food was prepared on purpose for you, by killing living creatures. Not upon my head is this wrong, but upon yours!" And he repeated the first stanza:—

> "The wicked kills, and cooks, and gives to eat:
> He is defiled with sin that takes such meat."

[263] On hearing this, the Bodhisatta recited the second stanza:—

> "The wicked may for gift slay wife or son,
> Yet, if the holy eat, no sin is done[2]."

[1] He is one of the six *titthiyas* (Heretics), and generally called *Nātaputta* (which is probably the right spelling here). The 'naked ascetics' were probably the Jains.

[2] "...Those who take life are in fault, but not the persons who eat the flesh; my priests have permission to eat whatever food it is customary to eat in any place or country, so that it be done without the indulgence of the appetite, or evil desire." Hardy, *Manual*, p. 327.

And the Bodhisatta with these words of instruction rose from his seat and departed.

This discourse ended, the Master identified the Birth: "Nāthaputta the Naked Ascetic was this wealthy man, and I was the ascetic."

No. 247.

PĀDAÑJALI-JĀTAKA.

"*Surely this lad*," *etc.*—This story the Master told while dwelling in Jetavana, about the Elder Lāḷudāyi.

One day, it is said, the two chief disciples were discussing a question. The Brethren who heard the discussion praised the Elders. Elder Lāḷudāyi, who sat amongst the company, curled his lip with the thought—"What is their knowledge compared with mine?" When the Brethren noticed this, they left him. The company broke up.

The Brethren were talking about it in the Hall of Truth. "Friend, did you see how Lāḷudāyi curled his lip in scorn of the two chief disciples?" On hearing which the Master said, "Brethren, in olden days, as now, Lāḷudāyi had no other answer but a curl of the lip." Then he told them an old-world tale.

---

[264] Once upon a time, when king Brahmadatta was reigning in Benares, the Bodhisatta was his adviser in things spiritual and temporal. Now the king had a son, Pādañjali by name, an idle lazy loafer. By and bye the king died. His obsequies over, the courtiers talked of consecrating his son Pādañjali to be king. But the Bodhisatta said,

"'Tis a lazy fellow, an idle loafer,—shall we take and consecrate him king?"

The courtiers held a trial. They sat the youth down before them, and made a wrong decision. They adjudged something to the wrong owner, and asked him, "Young sir, do we decide rightly?"

The lad curled his lip.

"He is a wise lad, I think," thought the Bodhisatta; "he must know that we have decided wrongly:" and he recited the first verse:—

> "Surely the lad is wise beyond all men.
> He curls his lip—he must see through us, then!"

Next day, as before, they arranged a trial, but this time judged it aright. Again they asked him what he thought of it.

Again he curled his lip. Then the Bodhisatta perceived that he was a blind fool, and repeated the second verse :—

"Not right from wrong, nor bad from good he knows :
He curls his lip—but no more sense he shows."

The courtiers became aware that the young man Pādañjali was a fool, and they made the Bodhisatta king.

When the Master had ended this discourse, he identified the Birth : "Lāḷudāyi was Pādañjali, and I was the wise courtier."

No. 248.

KIṀSUKOPAMA-JĀTAKA.

[265] "*All have seen,*" *etc.*—This story the Master told whilst staying at Jetavana, on the Chapter about the Judas tree[1].

Four Brothers, approaching the Tathāgata, asked him to explain the means by which ecstasy may be induced. This he explained. This done, they dispersed to the several places where they spent their nights and days. One of them, having learnt the Six Spheres of Touch, became a saint ; another did so after learning the Five Elements of Being, the third after learning the Four Principal Elements, the fourth after learning the Eighteen Constituents of Being. Each of them recounted to the Master the particular excellence which he had attained. A thought came into the mind of one of them ; and he asked the Master, "There is only one Nirvana for all these modes of meditation ; how is it that all of them lead to sainthood?" Then the Master asked, "Is not this like the people who saw the Judas tree?" As they requested him to tell them about it, he repeated a tale of bygone days.

Once on a time Brahmadatta the king of Benares had four sons. One day they sent for the charioteer, and said to him,

"We want to see a Judas tree ; show us one!"

[1] *Kiṁsuka = Butea Frondosa.*

"Very well, I will," the charioteer replied. But he did not show it to them all together. He took the eldest at once to the forest in the chariot, and showed him the tree at the time when the buds were just sprouting from the stem. To the second he showed it when the leaves were green, to the third at the time of blossoming, and to the fourth when it was bearing fruit.

After this it happened that the four brothers were sitting together, and some one asked, "What sort of a tree is the Judas tree?" Then the first brother answered,

"Like a burnt stump!"

And the second cried, "Like a banyan tree!"

And the third—"Like a piece of meat[1]!"

And the fourth said, "Like the acacia!"

They were vexed at each other's answers, and ran to find their father. "My lord," they asked, "what sort of a tree is the Judas tree?"

"What did you say to that?" he asked. They told him the manner of their answers. Said the king,

"All four of you have seen the tree. Only when the charioteer showed you the tree, you did not ask him 'What is the tree like at such a time?' [266] or 'at such another time?' You made no distinctions, and that is the reason of your mistake." And he repeated the first stanza:—

"All have seen the Judas tree—
What is your perplexity?
No one asked the charioteer
What its form the livelong year!"

The Master, having explained the matter, then addressed the Brethren: "Now as the four brothers, because they did not make a distinction and ask, fell in doubt about the tree, so you have fallen in doubt about the right": and in his perfect wisdom he uttered the second verse:—

"Who know the right with some deficiency
Feel doubt, like those four brothers with the tree."

When this discourse was ended, the Master identified the Birth: "At that time I was the king of Benares."

[1] It has pink flowers.

No. 249.

SĀLAKA-JĀTAKA.

"*Like my own son,*" *etc.*—This story the Master told whilst living in Jetavana, about a distinguished Elder.

It is said that he had ordained a youth, whom he treated unkindly. The novice at last could stand it no longer, and returned to the world. Then the Elder tried to coax him. [267] "Look here, lad," said he, "your robe shall be your own, and your bowl too; I have another bowl and robe which I'll give you. Join us again!" At first he refused, but at last after much asking he did so. From the day he joined the brotherhood the Elder maltreated him as before. Again the lad found it too much, and left the order. As the Elder begged him again several times to join, the lad replied, "You can neither do with me nor without me; let me alone—I will not join!"

The Brethren got talking about this in the Hall of Truth. "Friend," said they, "a sensitive lad that! He knew the Elder too well to join us." The Master came in and asked what they were talking about. They told him. He rejoined, "Not only is the lad sensitive now, Brethren, but he was just the same of old; when once he saw the faults of that man, he would not accept him again." And he told a story of the olden time.

Once upon a time, in the reign of Brahmadatta king of Benares, the Bodhisatta was born into a landowner's family, and gained a living by selling corn. Another man, a snake-charmer, had trained a monkey, made him swallow an antidote, and making a snake play with the monkey he gained his livelihood in this way.

A merrymaking had been proclaimed; this man wished to make merry at the feast, and he entrusted the monkey to this merchant, bidding him not neglect it. Seven days after he came to the merchant, and asked for his monkey. The monkey heard his master's voice, and came out quickly from the grain shop. At once the man beat him over the back with a piece of bamboo; then he took him off to the woods, tied him up and fell asleep. So soon as the monkey saw that he was asleep, he loosed his bonds, scampered off and climbed a mango tree. He ate a mango, and dropped the stone upon the snake-charmer's head. The man awoke, and looked up: there was the monkey. "I'll wheedle him!" he thought, "and when he comes down from the tree, I'll catch him!" So to wheedle him, he repeated the first verse:—

"Like my own son you shall be,
Master in our family:
[268] Come down, Nuncle[1] from the tree—
Come and hurry home with me?"

[1] *sālaka*, lit. 'brother-in-law,' often used as a term of abuse.

The monkey listened, and repeated the second verse:—

"You are laughing in your sleeve!
Have you quite forgot that beating?
Here I am content to live
(So good-bye) ripe mangoes eating."

Up he arose, and was soon lost in the wood; while the snake-charmer returned to his house in high dudgeon.

When this discourse was ended, the Master identified the Birth: "Our novice was the Monkey. The Elder was the snake-charmer, and I myself was the corn-merchant."

No. 250.

KAPI-JĀTAKA.

"*A holy sage*," *etc.*—This story was told by the Master whilst living at Jetavana, about a hypocritical Brother.

The Brotherhood found out his hypocrisy. In the Hall of Truth they were talking it over: "Friend, Brother So-and-so, after embracing the Buddha's religion, which leads to salvation, still practises hypocrisy." The Master on coming in [269] asked what they were discussing together. They told him. Said he, "Brethren, it is not the only time this Brother has been a hypocrite; for a hypocrite he was before, when he shammed simply for the sake of warming himself at the fire." Then he told them an old-world tale.

Once on a time, when Brahmadatta was king in Benares, the Bodhisatta was born one of a brahmin family. When he grew up, and his own son was of an age to run about, his wife died; he took the child on his hip, and departed into the Himalayas, where he became an ascetic, and brought up his son to the same life, dwelling in a hut of leaves.

It was the rainy season, and the heaven poured down its floods incessantly: a Monkey wandered about, tormented with the cold, chattering and rattling his teeth. The Bodhisatta fetched a great log, lit a fire, and lay down upon his pallet. His son sat by him, and chafed his feet.

Now the Monkey had found a dress belonging to some dead anchorite. He clad himself in the upper and lower garment, throwing the skin over one shoulder; he took the pole and waterpot, and in this sage's dress he came to the leaf-hut for the fire: and there he stood, in his borrowed plumes.

The lad caught sight of him, and cried out to his father, "See, father—there is an ascetic, trembling with cold! Call him hither; he shall warm himself." Thus addressing his father, he uttered the first stanza:—

"A holy sage stands shivering at our gate,
A sage, to peace and goodness consecrate.
O father! bid the holy man come in,
That all his cold and misery may abate."

The Bodhisatta listened to his son; he rose up, and looked; then he knew it was a monkey, and repeated the second stanza: [270]

"No holy sage is he: it is a vile
And loathsome Monkey, greedy all to spoil
That he can touch, who dwells among the trees;
Once let him in, our home he will defile."

With these words, the Bodhisatta seized a firebrand, and scared away the monkey; and he leaped up, and whether he liked the wood or whether he didn't, he never returned to that place any more. The Bodhisatta cultivated the Faculties and the Attainments, and to the young ascetic he explained the process of the mystic trance; and he too let the Faculties and the Attainments spring up within him. And both of them, without a break in their ecstasy, became destined to Brahma's world.

Thus did the Master discourse by way of shewing how this man was not then only, but always, a hypocrite. This ended, he declared the Truths, and identified the Birth:—at the conclusion of the Truths some reached the First Path, some the Second, and yet some the Third:—"The hypocritical Brother was the Monkey, Rāhula was the son, and I was the hermit myself."

BOOK III.—TIKA-NIPATA.

No. 251.

SAṀKAPPA-JĀTAKA.

[271] "*No archer,*" *etc.*—This story the Master told at Jetavana, about a backsliding Brother.

A young nobleman, living in Sāvatthi, gave his heart to the doctrine of the Treasures[1], and embraced the religious life. But one day, as he went his rounds in Sāvatthi, he happened to see a woman dressed in gay apparel. Passion sprang up in his heart; he became disconsolate. When his teachers, counsellors and friends saw him thus, they at once asked him the cause. Seeing that he longed to return to the world, they said to one another, "My friend, the Master can remove the sins of those who are tormented by the sin of lust and the like, and by declaring the Truths, he brings them to enjoy the fruition of sanctity. Come, let us lead him to the Master." So to the Master they brought him. Said he, "Why do you bring me this youth against his will, Brothers?" They told him the reason. "Is this true," he asked, "that you are a backslider, as they say?" He assented. The Master asked the reason, and he recounted what had happened. Said he, "O Brother, it has happened before that these women have caused impurity to spring up even in pure beings whose sins have been stayed by the power of ecstasy. Why should not vain men like you be defiled, when defilement comes even to the pure? Even men of the highest repute have fallen into dishonour; how much more the unpurified! Shall not the wind that shakes Mount Sineru also stir a heap of old leaves? [272] This sin has troubled the enlightened Buddha himself, sitting on his throne, and shall it not trouble such an one as you?" and at their request he told them an old-world tale.

Once upon a time, when Brahmadatta was king of Benares, the Bodhisatta was born into a great brahmin family, which had wealth to the amount of eight hundred millions of money. He grew up, and received his education at Takkasilā, and returned to Benares. There he married a wife; and on his parents' death, he performed their obsequies.

[1] Buddha, the Law, the Order.

Then, as he inspected his treasure, he reflected—"The treasure is still here, but they who gathered it are here no more!" He was overcome with grief, and the sweat poured from his body.

He lived a long time at home, and gave much in alms; he mastered his passions; then he left his weeping friends, and went into the Himalayas, where he built a hut in a delightful spot, and lived upon the wild fruits and roots of the forest, which he found in his goings to and fro. Ere long he cultivated the Faculties and the Attainments, and lived awhile in the bliss of joyous meditation.

Then a thought came to him. He would go amongst mankind, to buy salt and seasoning; thus his body would grow strong, and he would wander about on foot. "All that shall give alms to a virtuous man like me," thought he, "and greet me with respect, shall fill the heavenly regions." So down he came from Himalaya, and by and bye, as he tramped onwards, he came to Benares at the time of the sun-setting. He looked about for a place to bide in, and spied the royal park. "Here," said he, "is a place fit for retirement; here will I dwell." So he entered the park, and sat at the foot of a tree, and spent the night in the joy of meditation.

Next day in the forenoon, having seen to his bodily needs, and adjusted his matted hair, his skin and robes of bark, he took up his alms-bowl; all his senses were quiet, his pride was calmed, he bore himself nobly, looking no more than a plough's length before him; by the glory of his appearance, which was perfect in every way, [273] he drew upon him the eyes of the world. In this fashion he entered the city, and begged from door to door, till he came to the king's palace.

Now the king was upon his terrace, walking to and fro. He spied the Bodhisatta through a window. He was pleased with his bearing; "If," thought he, "there is such a thing as perfect quietude, it must be found in this man." So he sent one of his courtiers, bidding him fetch the ascetic. The man came up with a greeting, and took his alms-bowl, saying, "The king sends for you, Sir."

"Noble friend," replied the Bodhisatta, "the king does not know me!"

"Then, Sir, please remain here until I return." So he told the king what the beggar had said. Then said the king,

"We have no confidential priest: go, fetch him;" and at the same time he beckoned out of the window, calling to him—"Here, come in, Sir!"

The Bodhisatta gave up his alms-bowl to the courtier, and mounted upon the terrace. Then the king greeted him, and set him upon the king's couch, and offered him all the foods and meats prepared for himself. When he had eaten, he put a few questions to him; and the answers which were given pleased him ever more and more, so that with a word of respect, he asked,

"Good Sir, where do you live? whence did you come hither?"

"I dwell in Himalaya, mighty king, and from Himalaya have I come."

The king asked, "Why?"

"In the rainy season, O king, we must seek a fixed abode."

"Then," the king said, "abide here in my royal park, you shall not lack for the four things needful; I shall acquire the merit which leads to heaven."

The promise was given; and having broken his fast he went with the Bodhisatta into the grounds, and caused a hut of leaves to be built there. A covered walk he had made, and prepared all the places for his living by night and by day. All the furniture and requisites for an anchorite's life he had brought, and bidding him be comfortable he gave him in charge to the park-keeper.

For twelve years after this, [274] the Bodhisatta had his dwelling in that place.

Once it so happened that a frontier district rose in rebellion. The king desired to go himself to quell it. Calling his queen, he said—"Lady, either you or I must stay behind."

"Why do you say that, my lord?" she asked.

"For the sake of the good ascetic."

"I will not neglect him," said she. "Mine be it to attend upon the holy father; do you go away without anxiety."

So the king departed; and then the queen waited attentively upon the Bodhisatta.

Now the king was gone; at the fixed season the Bodhisatta came. When it pleased him, he would come to the palace, and take his meal there. One day, he tarried a long time. The queen had made ready all his food; she bathed and adorned herself, and prepared a low seat; with a clean robe thrown loosely over her, she reclined, waiting for the Bodhisatta to come. Now the Bodhisatta noted the time of day; he took up his alms-bowl, and passing through the air, came up to the great window. She heard his bark robes rustle, and as she rose hastily, her yellow dress slipped. The Bodhisatta let this unusual sight penetrate his senses, and looked upon her with desire. Then the evil passion that had been calmed by the power of his ecstasy, rose as a cobra rises spreading his hood, from the basket in which he is kept: he was like a milky tree struck by the axe. As his passion gained force, his ecstatic calm gave way, his senses lost their purity; he was as it were a crow with a broken wing. He could not sit down as before, and take his meal; not though she begged him to be seated, could he take his seat. So the queen placed all the food together in his alms-bowl; [275] but that day he could not do as he used to do after his meal, and go out of the window through the air; taking the food, he went down by the great staircase, and so into the grove.

When he came there, he could eat nothing. He set down the food at the foot of his bench, murmuring, "What a woman! lovely hands, lovely feet! what a waist, what thighs!" and so forth. Thus he lay for seven days. The food all went bad, and was covered with a cloud of black flies.

Then the king returned, having reduced his frontier to order. The city was all decorated; he went round it in solemn procession, keeping it always on the right, and then proceeded to the palace. Next he entered the grove, wishing to see the Bodhisatta. He noticed the dirt and rubbish about the hermitage, and thinking he must be gone, he pushed back the hut door, and stepped in. There lay the anchorite. "He must be ill," thought the king. So he had the putrid food thrown away, and the hut set in order, and then asked,

"What is the matter, Sir?"

"Sire, I am wounded!"

Then the king thought, "I suppose my enemies must have done this. They could not get a chance at me, so they determined to do a mischief to what I love." So he turned him over, looking for the wound; but no wound could he see. Then he asked, "Where's the place, Sir?"

"No one has hurt me," replied the Bodhisatta, "only I have wounded my own heart." And he rose, and sat upon a seat, and repeated the following verses:

"No archer drew an arrow to his ear
To deal this wound; no feathered shaft is here
Plucked from a peacock's wing, and decked out fine
By skilful fletchers:—'tis this heart of mine,

"Once cleansed from passion by my own firm will,
And keen intelligence, which through desire
Hath dealt the wound that bids me fair to kill,
And burns through all the limbs of me like fire.

[276] "I see no wound from which the blood might flow:
My own heart's folly 'tis that pierces so."

Thus did the Bodhisatta explain matters to the king by these three stanzas. Then he made the king retire from the hut, and induced the mystic trance; and so he recovered his interrupted ecstasy. Then he left the hut, and sitting in the air, exhorted the king. After this he declared that he would go up to Himalaya. The king would have dissuaded him, but he said,

"O king, see what humiliation has come upon me while I dwelt here! I cannot live here." And although the king entreated him, he uprose in the air, and departed to Himalaya, where he abode his life long, and then went to Brahma's world.

---

[277] When the Master had ended this discourse, he declared the Truths and identified the Birth:—at the conclusion of the Truths the backsliding Brother became a Saint, and some entered the First Path, some the Second, and some the Third:—"Ānanda was the king, and I was the hermit."

No. 252.

TILA-MUṬṬHI-JĀTAKA.

"*Now I bethink me*," *etc.*—This story the Master told in Jetavana, about a passionate man. We learn that there was a Brother who was full of bitterness. No matter how little was said to him, he fell in a rage and spoke roughly; showing wrath, hatred, and mistrust. In the Hall of Truth the Brethren discussed the matter. "Friend, how angry and bitter is Brother So-and-so! He goes snapping about for all the world like salt in the fire. Though he has adopted this peaceful religion, yet he cannot even restrain his anger." The Master heard this and sent a brother to fetch the man in question. "Are you really as passionate as they say?" he asked. The man said he was. Then the Master added, "This is not the first time, Brethren, that this man has been passionate. He was just the same before;" and he told them an old-world tale.

Once on a time, Brahmadatta the king of Benares had a son named Prince Brahmadatta. Now kings of former times, though there might be a famous teacher living in their own city, often used to send their sons to foreign countries afar off to complete their education, that by this means they might learn to quell their pride and highmindedness, and endure heat or cold, and be made acquainted with the ways of the world. So did this king. Calling his boy to him—now the lad was sixteen years old—he gave him one-soled sandals, a sunshade of leaves, and a thousand pieces of money, with these words:

"My son, get you to Takkasilā, and study there."

[278] The boy obeyed. He bade his parents farewell, and in due course arrived at Takkasilā. There he enquired for the teacher's dwelling, and reached it at the time when the teacher had finished his lecture, and

was walking up and down at the door of the house. When the lad set eyes upon the teacher, he loosed his shoes, closed his sunshade, and with a respectful greeting stood still where he was. The teacher saw that he was weary, and welcomed the new-comer. The lad ate, and rested a little. Then he returned to the teacher, and stood respectfully by him.

"Where have you come from?" he asked.

"From Benares."

"Whose son are you?"

"I am the son of the king of Benares."

"What brings you here?"

"I come to learn," replied the lad.

"Well, have you brought a teacher's fee? or do you wish to attend on me in return for teaching you?"

"I have brought a fee with me:" and with this he laid at the teacher's feet his purse of a thousand pieces.

The resident pupils attend on their teacher by day, and at night they learn of him: but they who bring a fee are treated like the eldest sons in his house, and thus they learn. And this teacher, like the rest, gave schooling to the prince on every light and lucky day[1]. Thus the young prince was taught.

Now one day, he went to bathe along with his teacher. There was an old woman, who had prepared some white seeds, and strewed them out before her: there she sat, watching them. The youth looked upon these white seeds, and desired to eat; he picked up a handful, and ate them.

"Yon fellow must be hungry," thought she; but she said nothing, and sat silent.

Next day the same thing happened at the same time. Again the woman said nothing to him. On the third day, he did it again; then the old dame cried out, saying,

"The great Teacher is letting his pupils rob me!" and uplifting her arms she raised a lamentation.

The Teacher turned back. [279] "What is it, mother?" he asked.

"Master, I have been parching some seeds, and your pupil took a handful and ate them! This he has done to-day, he did it yesterday, and he did it the day before! Surely he will eat me out of house and home!"

"Don't cry, mother: I will see that you are paid."

"Oh, I want no payment, master: only teach your pupil not to do it again."

"See here, then, mother," said he; and he caused two lads to take the

[1] There are four *nakkhattas* called *lahu*, 'light'; there is another reading *subhanakkhattena*, 'every fair day'. The meaning is by no means clear.

young fellow by his two hands, and smote him thrice upon the back with a bamboo stick, bidding him take care not to do it again.

The prince was very angry with his teacher. With a bloodshot glare, he eyed him from his head to foot. The teacher observed how angry he was, and how he eyed him.

The youth applied himself to his work, and finished his courses. But the offence he hid away in his heart, and determined to murder his teacher. When the time came for him to go away, he said to him,

"O my Teacher, when I receive the kingdom of Benares, I will send for you. Then come to me, I pray." And so he exacted a promise most affectionately.

He returned to Benares, and visited his parents, and showed proof of what he had learnt. Said the king, "I have lived to see my son again, and while I yet live, I will see the magnificence of his rule." So he made his son king in his stead.

When the prince enjoyed the splendour of royalty, he remembered his grudge, and anger rose within him. "I will be the death of that fellow!" he thought, and sent off a messenger to fetch his teacher.

"I shall never be able to appease him while he is young," thought the teacher; so he came not. But when the prince's time of rule was half over, he thought he could appease him then; and he came, and stood at the king's door, and sent to say that the teacher from Takkasilā had arrived. The king was glad, and caused the brahmin to be led in. Then his anger rose, and his eyes grew bloodshot. He beckoned to those about him. "Ha, the place which my teacher struck still hurts me to-day! He has come here with death written upon his forehead, [280] to die! To-day his life must end!" and he repeated the first two verses:—

"Now I bethink me, for a few poor seeds, in days of yore,
You seized me by the arm, and beat me with a stick full sore.
Brahmin, are you in love with death, and do you nothing fear
For seizing me and beating me, that now you venture here?"

Thus he threatened him with death. As he heard, the teacher uttered the third verse:—

"The gently born[1] who uses blows ungentleness to quell—
This is right discipline, not wrath: the wise all know it well."

[1] The Scholiast explains what 'gentle breeding' means. It may be used of conduct, both in men and animals; as—

"'Tis gentle to respect old age, red Goose:
Go where you will: I set your husband loose:"

"And so, great king, understand this yourself. Know that this is no just cause for anger. Indeed, if you had not been taught this lesson by me, you would have gone on taking cakes and sweets, fruit, and the like, until you became covetous through these acts of theft; then by degrees you would have been lured on to house-breaking, highway robbery, and murder about the villages; the end would have been, that you would have been taken red-handed and haled before the king for a public enemy and a robber; and you would have come in fear of public punishment, when the king should say, 'Take this man, and punish him according to his crimes.' Whence could have come all this prosperity which you now enjoy? Is it not through me that you have attained to such magnificence?"

Thus did his teacher talk over the king. [282] And the courtiers, who stood round, said when they heard his speech, "Of a truth, my lord, all your magnificence really belongs to your teacher!"

At once the king recognised the goodness of his teacher, and said to him,

"All my power I give to you, my teacher! receive the kingdom!"

But the other refused, saying, "No, my lord king; I have no wish for the kingdom."

And the king sent to Takkasilā for the teacher's wife and family; he gave them great power, and made him the royal priest; he treated him like a father, and obeyed his admonitions; and after bestowing gifts and doing good deeds he became destined for paradise.

When the Master had ended this discourse, he declared the Truths:—at the conclusion of the Truths the passionate brother attained the Fruit of the Third Path, and many others entered on the First, or Second, or Third:—"At that time the passionate Brother was the king; but the Teacher was I myself."

or of form, 'noble,' 'thoroughbred': as—[281]

> "Your mien shows breeding, and your clear calm eye:
> You must have left some noble family.
> What made you wish to leave your home and wealth
> To be an anchorite for your soul's health?"

and adds yet this other:

> "Clad in a semblance of fair piety
> But all deceitful, boldly forth leapt he,
> A babbler of vain sayings, mean and base,
> Intemperate, the ruin of his race."

(The last four lines occur in Sutta Nipāta, verse 89.)

No. 253.

MAṆI-KAṆṬHA-JĀTAKA[1].

"*Rich food and drink*," etc.—This story the Master told while he was dwelling at the shrine of Aggālava, near Ālavī, about the rules for building cells.

Some Brethren who lived in Ālavī[2] were begging[3] from all quarters the materials for houses which they were getting made for themselves. They were for ever dinning and dunning; "Give us a man, give us somebody to do servant's work," and so forth. Everybody was annoyed at this begging and solicitation. So much annoyed were they, that at sight of these Brethren they were startled and scared away.

It happened that the reverend father Mahākassapa entered Ālavī, and traversed the place in quest of alms. The people, as soon as they saw the Elder, ran away as before[4]. After mealtime, having returned from his rounds, he summoned the brethren, and thus addressed them: "Once Ālavī was a capital place for alms; why is it so poor now?" They told him the reason.

Now the Blessed One was at the time dwelling at the Aggālava shrine. To the Blessed One came the Elder, and told him all about it. The Master convened the Brethren touching this matter. [283] "I hear," said he, "that you are building houses and worrying everybody for help. Is this true?" They said it was. Then the Master rebuked them, adding these words: "Even in the serpent world, Brethren, full as it is of the seven precious stones, this kind of begging is distasteful to the serpents. How much more to men, from whom it is as hard to get a rupee as it is to skin a flint!" and he told an old-world tale.

Once upon a time, when Brahmadatta reigned in Benares, the Bodhisatta was born as a rich brahmin's son. When he was old enough to run about, his mother gave birth to another wise being. Both the brothers, when they grew up, were so deeply pained at their parents' death, that they became anchorites, and dwelt in leaf-huts which they made them at a bend of the Ganges river. The elder had his lodge by the upper Ganges, and the younger by the lower river.

One day, a Serpent-King (his name was Maṇikaṇṭha, or Jewel-throat) left his dwelling-place, and taking the shape of a man, walked along the river bank until he came to the younger brother's hermitage. He greeted

[1] I think this Jātaka is represented on the Stupa of Bharbut. In pl. XLII. 1 we see a man sitting before a hut, apparently conversing with a great five-headed cobra. The story is also told in the Vinaya Piṭaka, *Suttavibhaṅga*, VI. 1. 3.

[2] The introductory story occurs in the Vinaya, *Suttavibhaṅga*, *Saṃghādisesa*, vi. 1. The sin was importunity.

[3] Reading *saṃyācikāya* (as in *Suttavibhaṅga*).

[4] Reading *paṭipajjisu*.

the owner, and sat down at one side. They conversed pleasantly together; and such friends did they become, that there was no living apart for them. Often and often came Jewel-throat to visit the younger recluse, and sat talking and chatting; and when he left, so much did he love the man, he put off his shape, and encircled the ascetic with snake's folds, and embraced him, with his great hood upon his head; there he lay a little, till his affection was satisfied; then he let go his friend's body, and bidding him farewell, returned to his own place. For fear of him, the hermit grew thin; he became squalid, lost his colour, grew yellower and yellower, and the veins stood out upon his skin.

It happened one day that he paid a visit to his brother. "Why, brother," said he, "what makes you thin? how did you lose your colour? why are you so yellow, and why do your veins stand out like this upon your skin?"

The other told him all about it.

"Come tell me," said the first, "do you like him to come or not?"

[284]. "No, I don't."

"Well, what ornament does the Serpent-King wear when he visits you?"

"A precious jewel!"

"Very well. When he comes again, before he has time to sit down, ask him to give you the jewel. Then he will depart without embracing you in his snaky folds. Next day stand at your door, and ask him for it there; and on the third ask him just as he emerges from the river. He will never visit you again."

The younger promised so to do, and returned to his hut. On the morrow, when the Serpent had come, as he stood there the hermit cried, "Give me your beautiful jewel!" The Serpent hurried away without sitting down. On the day following, the hermit stood at his door, and called out as the Serpent came—"You would not give me your jewel yesterday! now to-day you must!" And the Serpent slipt off without entering the hut. On the third day, the man called out just as the Serpent was emerging from the water—"This is the third day that I have asked you for it: come, give this jewel to me!" And the Serpent, speaking from his place in the water, refused, in the words of these two stanzas:—

"Rich food and drink in plenty I can have
By means of this fine jewel which you crave:
You ask too much; the gem I will not give;
Nor visit you again while I shall live.

"Like lads who wait with tempered sword in hand,
You scare me as my jewel you demand,
You ask too much—the gem I will not give,
Nor ever visit you while I shall live!"

[285] With these words, the King of the Serpents plunged beneath the water, and went to his own place, never to return.

Then the ascetic, not seeing his beautiful Serpent-King again, became thinner and thinner still; he grew more squalid, lost his colour worse than before, and grew more yellow, and the veins rose thicker on his skin!

The elder brother thought he would go and see how his brother was getting on. He paid him a visit, and found him yellower than he had been before.

"Why, how is this? worse than ever!" said he.

His brother replied, "It is because I never see the lovely King of Serpents!"

"This hermit," said the elder, on hearing his answer, "cannot live without his Serpent-King;" and he repeated the third verse:—

"Importune not a man whose love you prize,
For begging makes you hateful in his eyes.
The brahmin begged the Serpent's gem so sore
He disappeared and never came back more."

Then he counselled his brother not to grieve, and with this consolation, left him and returned to his own hermitage. And after that [286] the two brothers cultivated the Faculties and the Attainments, and became destined for the heaven of Brahma.

The Master added, "Thus, Brethren, even in the world of serpents, where are the seven precious stones in plenty, begging is disliked by the serpents: how much more by men!" And, after teaching them this lesson, he identified the Birth:—"At that time, Ānanda was the younger brother, but the elder was I myself."

No. 254.

KUṆḌAKA-KUCCHI-SINDHAVA-JĀTAKA.

"*Grass and the scum of gruel,*" *etc.*—This story the Master told at Jetavana about the Elder Sāriputta.

It once fell out that the Buddha had been spending the rainy season in Sāvatthi, and afterwards had been on alms-pilgrimage. On his return, the inhabitants determined to welcome his home-coming; and they made their gifts to the Buddha and his following. They posted the clerk who used to sound the call for preaching, to distribute the Brethren amongst all comers, according to the number they wished to provide for.

There was one poor old woman, who had prepared one portion. The Brethren were assigned, some to this giver, some to that. At sunrise, the poor woman came to the clerk, and said, "Give a Brother to me!" He answered, "I have already distributed them all; but Elder Sāriputta is still in the monastery, and you may give your portion to him." At this she was delighted, and waited by the gate of Jetavana until the Elder came out. She gave him greeting, took his bowl from his hand, and leading him to her house, offered him a seat.

Many pious families heard a rumour that some old woman had got Sāriputta to sit down at her door. Amongst those who heard it was king Pasenadi the Kosala. He at once sent her food of all sorts, together with a garment and a purse of a thousand pieces, with the request, "Let her who is entertaining the priest, put on this robe, and spend this money, and thus entertain the Elder." As the king did, so did Anātha-piṇḍika, [287] the younger Anātha-piṇḍika, the lay sister Visākhā (a great lady),—all sent the same: other families sent one hundred, two hundred or so, as their means allowed. Thus in a single day the old woman got as much as a hundred thousand pieces of money.

Our Elder drank the broth which she gave him, and ate her food, and the rice that she cooked; then he thanked her, and so edified her that she was converted. Then he returned to the monastery.

In the Hall of Truth, the brethren discussed the Elder's goodness. "Friend, the Captain of the Faith has rescued an old housewife from poverty. He has been her mainstay. The food she offered he did not disdain to eat."

The Master entered, and asked what they were talking of now as they sat together. They told him. And he said, "This is not the first time, Brethren, that Sāriputta has been the refuge of this old woman; nor the first time he did not disdain to eat the food she offered. He did the same before." And he told an old-world tale.

It happened once upon a time, when Brahmadatta was king of Benares, that the Bodhisatta was born into a trader's family in the Northern province. Five hundred people of that country, horse-dealers, used to convey horses to Benares, and sell them there.

Now a certain dealer took the road to Benares with five hundred horses for sale. On this road, not far off Benares, there is a town, where had formerly lived a rich merchant. A vast dwelling once was his; but his family had gradually gone down in the world, and only one old woman was left, who lived in the family house. The dealer took up his lodging for a certain hire in that house, and kept his horses hard by.

On that very day, as luck would have it, a thoroughbred mare of his foaled. He tarried two or three days, and then taking his horses with him went off to visit the king. Thereat the old woman asked him for the hire of the house.

"All right, mother, I'll pay you," said he. [288]

"When you pay me, my son," she said then, "give me this foal, and deduct its value from the hire." The dealer did as she asked and went his way. The woman loved the foal like a son; and she fed him upon parched rice drippings, on broken meats, and grass.

Some time after, the Bodhisatta, on his way with five hundred horses, took lodging in this house. But the horses scented this highbred foal, that fed on red rice-powder, and not one of them would enter the place. Then said the Bodhisatta to the dame,

"There seems to be some horse in the place, mother?"

"Oh, my son, the only horse there is a young foal which I keep here as tenderly as it were my son!"

"Where is he, mother?"

"Gone out to graze."

"When will he return?"

"Oh, he'll soon come back."

The Bodhisatta kept the horses without, and sat down to wait until the foal should come in; and soon the foal returned from his walk. When he set eyes on the fine foal with his belly full of rice powder, the Bodhisatta noted his marks, and thought he, "This is a priceless thoroughbred; I must buy him of the old woman."

By this time the foal had entered the house and gone to his own stable. At once all the horses were able to go in too.

There abode the Bodhisatta for a few days, and attended to his horses. Then as he made to go, "Mother," said he to the old woman, "let me buy this foal of you."

"What are you saying! one mustn't sell one's own foster child!"

"What do you give him to eat, mother?"

"Rice boiled, and rice gruel, and parched rice; broken meats and grass; and rice-broth to drink."

"Well, mother, if I get him, I'll feed him on the daintiest of fare; [289] when he stands, he shall have a cloth awning spread over him; I will give him a carpet to stand on."

"Will you, my son? Then take this child of mine, and go, and may he be happy!"

And the Bodhisatta paid a separate price for the foal's four feet, for his tail and for his head; six purses of a thousand pieces of money he laid down, one for each; and he caused the dame to robe herself in a new dress, and decked her with ornaments, and set her in front of the foal. And the foal opened his eyes, and looked upon his mother, and shed tears. She stroked his back, and said, "I have received the recompense for what I have done for thee: go, my son!" and then he departed.

Next day the Bodhisatta thought he would make trial of the foal, whether he knew his own power or no. So after preparing common food, he caused red rice gruel to be poured out, presented to him in a bucket. But this he could not swallow; and refused to touch any such food. Then the Bodhisatta to test him, uttered the first verse:—

"Grass and the scum of gruel you thought good
In former times: why don't you eat your food?"

On hearing which, the Foal answered with the two other couplets following:—

"When people do not know one's birth and breed,
Rice-scum is good enough to serve one's need.

"But I am chief of steeds, as you are ware;
Therefore from you I will not take this fare."

[290] Then answered the Bodhisatta, "I did this to try you; do not be angry"; and he cooked the fine food and offered it to him. When he came to the king's courtyard, he set the five hundred horses on one side, and on the other an embroidered awning, under which he laid a carpet, with a canopy of stuff over it; and here he lodged the foal.

The king coming to inspect the horses asked why this horse was housed apart.

"O king," was the reply, "if this horse be not kept apart, he will let loose these others."

"Is he a beautiful horse?" the king asked.

"Yes, O king."

"Then let me see his paces."

The owner caparisoned him, and mounted on his back. Then he cleared the courtyard of men, and rode the horse about in it. The whole place appeared to be encircled with lines of horses, without a break!

Then said the Bodhisatta, "See my horse's speed, O king!" and let him have his head. Not a man could see him at all! Then he fastened a red leaf upon the horse's flank; and they saw just the leaf. And then he rode him over the surface of a pond in a certain garden of the city. Over he went, and not even the tips of his hoofs were wet. Again, he galloped over lotus leaves, [291] without even pushing one of them under water.

When his master had thus showed off the steed's magnificent paces, he dismounted, clapped his hands, and held out one, palm upwards. The horse got upon it, and stood on the palm of his master's hand, with his four feet close together. And the Bodhisatta said, "O mighty king! not even the whole circle of the ocean would be space enough for this horse to show off all his skill." The king was so pleased that he gave him the half of his kingdom: the horse he installed as his horse of state, sprinkling him with ceremonial water. Dear was he and precious to the king, and great honour was done him; and his dwelling place was made like the chamber where the king dwelt, all beautiful: the floor was sprinkled with all the four manners of perfumes, the walls were hung with wreaths of flowers and frequent garlands; up in the roof was an awning of cloth spangled with golden stars; it was all like a lovely pavilion round about. A lamp of scented oil burnt always; and in the retiring closet was set a golden jar. His food was always fit for a king. And after he came there, the lordship over all India came into this king's hand. And the king did good deeds and almsgiving according to the Bodhisatta's admonition, and became destined for paradise.

When the Master had ended this discourse, he declared the Truths, and identified the Birth: (now at the conclusion of the Truths many entered the First Path, or the Second, or the Third:) "At that time the old woman was the same, Sāriputta was the thoroughbred, Ānanda was the king, and the horsedealer was I myself."

No. 255.

SUKA-JĀTAKA.

"*What time the bird,*" *etc.*—This story the Master told while dwelling at Jetavana, about a Brother who died of over-eating.

[292] On his death, the brethren assembled in the Hall of Truth, and discussed his demerits on this fashion: "Friend, Brother So-and-so was ignorant how much he could safely eat. So he ate more than he could digest, and died in consequence." The Master entered, and asked what they talked of now as they sat together; and they told him. "Brethren," he said, "this is not the first time our friend died of surfeit; the same has happened before." Then he told them an old-world tale.

Once on a time, when king Brahmadatta reigned over Benares, the Bodhisatta became a Parrot, and dwelt in the Himalaya region. He was king over several thousands of his kind, who lived on the seaward side of the Himalayas; and one son was his. When his son grew up to be strong, the father Parrot's eyes became weak. The truth is, that parrots fly with great swiftness; wherefore when they be old it is the eye that weakens first. His son kept his parents in the nest, and would bring them food to feed them.

It happened one day that our young Parrot went to the place where he found his food, and alighted upon a mountain-top. Thence he looked over the ocean, and beheld an island, in which was a mango grove full of sweet golden fruit. So next day, at the time of the fetching of food, he rose in the air and flew to this grove of mangoes, where he sucked the mango juice, and took of the fruit, and bore it home to his mother and father. As the Bodhisatta ate of it, he knew the taste.

"My son," said he, "this is a mango of such and such an island," naming it.

"Even so, father!" replied the young Parrot.

"Parrots that go thither, my son, have not length of life," he said. "Go not to that island again!"—But the son obeyed him not, and went yet again.

Then one day it befel that he went as usual, and drank much of the mango juice. With a mango in his beak [293] he was passing over the ocean, when he grew worn out with so long carrying, and sleep mastered him; sleeping he flew on, and the fruit which he carried fell from out of his beak. And by degrees he left his path, and sinking down skimmed the surface of the water, till in the end he fell in. And then a fish caught and devoured him. When he should have returned, he returned not, and the Bodhisatta knew that he must have fallen into the water. Then his parents, receiving no sustenance, pined away and died.

The Master, having told this tale, in his perfect wisdom, uttered the following stanzas:—

"What time the bird without excess did eat,
He found the way, and brought his mother meat.

"But once he ate too much, forgot the mean,
He fell; and afterward was no more seen.

"So be not greedy; modest be in all.
To spare is safe; greed goeth before a fall[1]."

[1] The Scholiast adds the following lines:

"Be moderate in eating wet or dry,
And this thy hunger's need will satisfy.
Who eats with care, whose belly is not great,
Will be a holy hermit soon or late.
[294] Four or five mouthfuls,—then a drink is right;
Enough for any earnest eremite.
A careful moderate eater has small pain,
Slowly grows old, lives twice as long again."

And these:

"When sons bring meat to fathers in the wood,
Like ointment to the eye, 'tis very good.
Thus for bare life, with weariness forspent,
He nourished him upon such nourishment."

When the Master had ended this discourse, he declared the Truths (at the conclusion of which many persons entered the First Path, or the Second, or Third, or Fourth), and identified the Birth: "At that time, the brother who has over-eaten was the young Parrot, and the king of the Parrots was I myself."

No. 256.

JARUDAPĀNA-JĀTAKA.

"*Some merchants*," *etc.*—This story the Master told while living at Jetavana, about some traders whose home was at Sāvatthi.

The tradition is that these men had acquired wares in Sāvatthi, which they loaded on carts. When the time came for them to set about their business, they gave an invitation to the Blessed One, and offered him rich alms; they received the Refuges, were strengthened in the Precepts, and took their leave of the Master with these words, "Sir, we are going a long way. When we have parted with our wares, if we are fortunate and return in safety, we will come and wait upon you again." Then they set off on their journey.

In a difficult part of their road they observed a disused well. There was no water in it that they could see, and they were athirst; so they resolved to dig deeper. As they dug, [295] they came upon successive layers of minerals of all sorts, from iron to lapis lazuli. This find contented them; they filled their waggons with these treasures, and got back safe to Sāvatthi. They stowed away the treasure which they had brought; and then bethought them, that having been so lucky they would give food to the brotherhood. So they invited the Blessed One, and made him presents; and when they had respectfully greeted him, and sat down on one side, they recounted how they had found their treasure. Said he, "You, good laymen, are content with your find, and accept your wealth and your livelihood with all moderation. But in other days there were men not content, immoderate, who refused to do as wise men advised them, and so lost their life." And he told at their request an old-world tale.

Once on a time, when Brahmadatta was reigning in Benares, the Bodhisatta was born into the family of a business man; and grew up to be a great merchant. At one time he had filled his waggons with goods, and in company with a large caravan he came to this very same wood and saw this very same well. No sooner had the traders seen it, than they wanted to drink, and began to dig, and as they dug they came upon a quantity of metal and gems. But though they got a great deal of treasure, they were discontented. "There must be another treasure here, better than this!" they thought, and they dug and dug.

Then said the Bodhisatta to them, "Merchants, greed is the root of destruction. Ye have won a great deal of wealth; with this be ye content, and dig no more." But they digged yet the more notwithstanding.

Now this well was haunted by serpents. The Serpent-king, incensed at the falling of clods and earth, slew them with the breath of his nostrils[1], all saving the Bodhisatta, [296] and destroyed them; and he came up from the serpent world, and put the oxen to the carts, filled them with jewels, and seating the Bodhisatta upon a fine waggon, he made certain young serpents drive the carts, and brought him to Benares. He led him into his house, set the treasure in order, and went away again to his own place in the serpent land. And the Bodhisatta spent his treasure, so that he made much stir throughout all India by his almsgiving, and, having undertaken the deeds of virtue, and kept the holy day, at the end of his life he came to paradise.

The Master, after telling this tale, in his perfect wisdom, uttered the following lines:—

"Some merchants, wanting water, dug the ground
In an old well, and there a treasure found:—
Tin, iron, copper, lead, silver and gold,
Beryls and pearls and jewels manifold.

"But not content, still more they did desire,
And fiery serpents slew them all with fire.
Dig if thou wilt, but dig not to excess;
For too much digging is a wickedness.

"Digging bestowed a treasure on these men;
But too much digging lost it all again."

When the Master had finished this discourse, he identified the Birth:—"At that time, Sāriputta was the Serpent-king, and the master of the caravan was I myself."

[1] *Nāsikavātena.* Perhaps this throws light on the disease *ahivātarogo*, p. 55 *note*.

No. 257.

GĀMAṆI-CAṆḌA-JĀTAKA[1].

[297] "*It is not a clever builder,*" *etc.*—This story the Master told while sojourning at Jetavana, about the praise of wisdom. In the Hall of Truth sat the Brethren, praising the wisdom of the Buddha: "The Blessed One has wisdom great and wide, wisdom witty and quick, wisdom sharp and penetrating. He excels this world and the world of gods in wisdom."

The Master entered, and asked what they were talking of now as they sat there. They told him. He answered, "This is not the first time, Brethren, that the Blessed One has been wise; he was the same before." And he told an old-world tale.

Once upon a time, Brethren, when Janasandha was reigning in Benares, the Bodhisatta came to life as the son of his chief queen. His face was resplendent, wearing a look of auspicious beauty, like a golden mirror well polished. On the day of his naming they called him Ādāsa-mukha, Prince Mirror-face.

Within the space of seven years his father caused him to be taught the Three Vedas, and all the duties of this world; and then he died, when the lad was seven years old. The courtiers performed the king's obsequies with great pomp, and made the offerings for the dead; and on the seventh day they gathered together in the palace court, and talked together. The prince was very young, they thought, and he could not be made king.

Before they made him king, they would test him. So they prepared a court of justice, and set a divan. Then they came into the prince's presence, and said they, "You must come, my lord, to the law-court." To this the prince agreed; and with a great company he repaired thither, and sat upon the dais.

Now at the time when the king sat down for judgement, the courtiers had dressed up a monkey, in the garb of a man who is skilled in the lore which tells what are good sites for a building. They made him go upon two feet, and brought him into the judgement hall.

[1] See Morris, *Folk-Lore Journal*, iii. 337; Tawney, *Phil. Journ.* xii. 112—119; *Academy*, Aug. 6, 1887, no. 796. Problems to be solved are a common part of the machinery of fairy tales; *e.g.* Grimm, no. 29, *The Devil with the Three Golden Hairs*, and the editors' notes.

"My lord," said they, "in the time of the king your father this man was one who divined by magic as to desirable sites, and well did he know his art. [298] Down in the earth as deep as seven cubits he can see a fault. By his help there was a place chosen for the king's house; let the king provide for him, and give him a post."

The prince scanned him from head to foot. "This is no man, but a monkey," he thought; "and monkeys can destroy what others have made, but of themselves can neither make anything nor carry out such a thing." And so he repeated the first stanza to his court:—

"It is not a clever builder, but an ape with a wrinkled face;
He can destroy what others make; that is the way of his race."

"It must be so, my lord!" said the courtiers, and took him away. But after a day or two they dressed this same creature in grand clothes, and brought him again to the judgement hall. "In the king your father's time, my lord, this was a judge who dealt justice. Him should you take to help you in the awarding of justice."

The prince looked at him. Thought he, "A man with mind and reason is not so hairy as all that. This witless ape cannot dispense justice;" and he repeated the second stanza:—

"There's no wit in this hairy creature; he breeds no confidence;
He knows nought, as my father taught: the animal has no sense!"

[299] "So it must be, my lord!" said the courtiers, and led him away. Yet once again did they dress up the very same monkey, and bring him to the hall of judgement. "Sire," said they, "in the time of the king your father this man did his duty to father and mother, and paid respect to old age in his family. Him you should keep with you."

Again the prince looked at him, and thought—"Monkeys are fickle of mind; such a thing they cannot do." And then he repeated the third stanza:—

"One thing Dasaratha[1] has taught me: no help such a creature would send
To father or mother, to sister or brother, or any who call him friend!"

"So must it be, my lord!" answered they, and took him away again. And they said amongst themselves, "'Tis a wise prince; he will be able to rule"; [300] and they made the Bodhisatta king; and throughout the city by beat of drum they made proclamation, saying, "The edicts of king Mirror-face!"

From that time the Bodhisatta reigned righteously; and his wisdom was noised abroad throughout all India. To show forth the matter of

[1] Dasaratha is another name for his father (*Schol.*).

this wisdom of his, these fourteen problems were brought to him to decide:—

> "An ox, a lad, a horse, a basket-knight,
> A squire, a light-o'-love, and a young dame,
> A snake, a deer, a partridge, and a sprite,
> A snake, ascetics, a young priest I name."

This happened as we shall now explain. When the Bodhisatta was inaugurated king, a certain servant of king Janasandha, named Gāmaṇi-caṇḍa, thus considered within himself: "This kingdom is glorious if it be governed by aid of those who are of an age with the king. Now I am old, and I cannot wait upon a young prince: so I will get me a living by farming in the country." So he departed from the city a distance of three leagues, and abode in a certain village. But he had no oxen for farming. And so, after rain had fallen, he begged the loan of two oxen from a friend; all day long he ploughed with them, and then he gave them grass to eat, and went to the owner's house to give them back again. At the moment it happened that the owner sat at meat with his wife; and the oxen entered the house, quite at home. As they entered, the master was raising his plate, and the wife putting hers down. Seeing that they did not invite him to share the meal, Gāmaṇi-caṇḍa departed without formally making over the oxen. During the night, thieves broke into the cow-pen, and stole the oxen away.

Early on the morrow, the owner of these oxen entered the cow-shed, but cattle there were none; he perceived that they had been stolen away by thieves. "I'll make Gāmaṇi pay for it!" thought he, and to Gāmaṇi he went. [301]

"I say, return me my oxen!" cried he.

"Are not they in their stall?"

"Now did you return them to me?"

"No, I didn't."

"Here's the king's officer: come along!"

Now this people have a custom that they pick up a bit of stone or a potsherd, and say—"Here's the king's officer; come along!" If any man refuses to go, he is punished. So when Gāmaṇi heard the word "officer," he went along.

So they went together towards the king's court. On the way, they came to a village where dwelt a friend of Gāmaṇi's. Said he to the other,

"I say, I'm very hungry. Wait here till I go in and get me something to eat!" and he entered his friend's house.

But his friend was not at home. The wife said,

"Sir, there is nothing cooked. Wait but a moment; I will cook at once and set before you."

She climbed a ladder to the grain store, and in her haste she fell to the ground. And as she was seven months gone with child, a miscarriage followed.

At that moment, in came the husband, and saw what had happened. "You have struck my wife," cried he, "and brought her labour upon her untimely! Here's a king's officer for you—come along!" and he carried him off. After this they went on, the two of them, with Gāmaṇi between.

As they went, there was a horse at a village gate; and the groom could not stop it, but it ran along with them. The horsekeeper called out to Gāmaṇi—

"Uncle[1] Caṇḍagāmaṇi, hit the horse with something, and head him back!" Gāmaṇi picked up a stone, and threw it at the horse. The stone struck his foot, and broke it like the stalk of a castor-oil plant. Then the man cried,

"Oh, you've broken my horse's leg! Here's a king's officer for you!" and he laid hold of him.

Gāmaṇi was thus three men's prisoner. As they led him along, he thought: "These people will denounce me to the king; [302] I can't pay for the oxen; much less the fine for causing an untimely birth; and then where shall I get the price of the horse? I were better dead." So, as they went along, he saw a wood hard by the road, and in it a hill with a precipice on one side of it. In the shadow of it were two basket-makers, father and son, weaving a mat. Said Gāmaṇi,

"I say, I want to retire for a moment: wait here, while I go aside"; and with these words he climbed the hill, and threw himself down the precipice. He fell upon the back of the elder basket-maker, and killed him on the spot. Gāmaṇi got up, and stood still.

"Ah, you villain! you've murdered my father!" cried the younger basket-maker; "here's the king's officer!" He seized Gāmaṇi's hands, and came out of the thicket.

"What's this?" asked the others.

"The villain has murdered my father!"

So on they went, the four of them, with Gāmaṇi in the middle.

They came to the gate of another village. The headman was there, who hailed Gāmaṇi: "Uncle[1] Caṇḍa, whither away?"

"To see the king," says Gāmaṇi.

"Oh indeed, to see the king. I want to send him a message; will you take it?"

"Yes, that I will."

"Well—I am usually handsome, rich, honoured, and healthy; but now I am miserable and have the jaundice too. Ask the king why this is.

[1] It is worth noting that this term of affection means a *mother's* brother.

He is a wise man, so they say; he will tell you, and you can bring me his message again."

To this the other agreed.

At another village a light-o'-love called out to him—"Whither bound, Uncle[1] Caṇḍa?"

"To see the king," says he.

"They say the king is a wise man; take him a message from me," says the woman. [303] "Aforetime I used to make great gains; now I don't get the worth of a betel-nut, and nobody courts me. Ask the king how this may be, and then you can tell me."

At a third village, there was a young woman who told Gāmaṇi, "I can live neither with my husband nor with my own family. Ask the king how this is, and then tell me."

A little further on there was a snake living in an ant-hill near the road. He saw Gāmaṇi, and called out,

"Whither away, Caṇḍa?"

"To see the king."

"The king is wise; take him a message from me. When I go out to get my food, I leave this ant-hill faint and famishing, and yet I fill the entrance hole with my body, and I get out with difficulty, dragging myself along. But when I come in again, I feel satisfied, and fat, yet I pass quickly through the hole without touching the sides. How is this? ask the king, and bring me his answer."

And further on a deer saw him, and said—"I can't eat grass anywhere but underneath this tree. Ask the king the reason." And again a partridge said, "When I sit at the foot of this ant-heap, and utter my note, I can make it prettily; but nowhere else. Ask the king why." And again, [304] a tree spirit saw him, and said,

"Whither away, Caṇḍa?"

"To the king."

"The king's a wise man, they say. In former times I was highly honoured; now I don't receive so much as a handful of twigs. Ask the king what the reason is."

And further on again he was seen by a serpent-king, who spoke to him thus: "The king is said to be a wise man: then ask him this question. Heretofore the water in this pool has been clear as crystal. Why is it that now it has become turbid, with scum all over it?"

Further on, not far from a town, certain ascetics who dwelt in a park saw him, and said, in the same way, "They say the king is wise. Of yore there were in this park sweet fruits in plenty, now they have grown tasteless and dry. Ask him what the reason is." Further on again, he was accosted by some brahmin students who were in a hall at the gate of a town. They said to him,

[1] See note, p. 210.

"Where are you going, Caṇḍa, eh?"

"To the king," says Caṇḍa.

"Then take a message for us. Till now, whatever passage we learnt was bright and clear; now it does not stay with us, it is not understood, but all is darkness,—it is like water in a leaky jar. Ask the king what the reason is."

Gāmaṇi-caṇḍa came before the king with his fourteen questions. When the king saw him, he recognised him. "This is my father's servant, who used to dandle me in his arms. Where has he been living all this time?" And "Caṇḍa," said he, "where have you been living all this time? [305] We have seen nothing of you for a long while; what brings you here?"

"Oh, my lord, when my lord the late king went to heaven, I departed into the country and kept myself by farming. Then this man summoned me for a suit regarding his cattle, and here he has brought me."

"If you had not been brought here, you had never come; but I'm glad that you were brought anyhow. Now I can see you. Where is that man?"

"Here, my lord."

"It is you that summoned our friend Caṇḍa?"

"Yes, my lord."

"Why?"

"He refuses to give back my pair of oxen!"

"Is this so, Caṇḍa?"

"Hear my story too, my lord!" said Caṇḍa; and told him the whole. When he had heard the tale, the king accosted the owner of the oxen. "Did you see the oxen," said he, "entering the stall?"

"No, my lord," the man replied.

"Why, man, did you never hear my name? They call me king Mirror-face. Speak out honestly."

"I saw them, my lord!" said he.

"Now, Caṇḍa," said the king, "you failed to return the oxen, and therefore you are his debtor for them. But this man, in saying that he had not seen them, told a direct lie. Therefore you with your own hands shall pluck his eyes out, and you shall yourself pay him twenty-four pieces of money as the price of the oxen." Then they led the owner of the oxen out of doors.

"If I lose my eyes, what do I care for the money?" thought he. And he fell at Gāmaṇi's feet, and besought him—"O master Caṇḍa, keep those twenty-four pieces, and take these too!" and he gave him other pieces, and ran away.

The second man said, "My lord, this fellow struck my wife, [306] and made her miscarry." "Is this true, Caṇḍa?" asked the king. Caṇḍa begged for a hearing, and told the whole story.

"Did you really strike her, and cause her to miscarry?" asked the king.

"No, my lord! I did no such thing."

"Now, can you"—to the other—"can you heal the miscarriage which he has caused?"

"No, my lord, I cannot."

"Now, what do you want to do?"

"I ought to have a son, my lord."

"Now then, Caṇḍa—you take the man's wife to your house; and when a son shall be born to you, hand him over to the husband."

Then this man also fell at Caṇḍa's feet, crying, "Don't break up my home, master!" threw down some money, and made off.

The third man then accused Caṇḍa of laming his horse's foot. Caṇḍa as before told what had happened. Then the king asked the owner,

"Did you really bid Caṇḍa strike the horse, and turn him back?"

"No, my lord, I did not." But on being pressed, he admitted that he had said so.

"This man," said the king, "has told a direct lie, in saying that he did not tell you to head back the horse. You may tear out his tongue; and then pay him a thousand pieces for the horse's price, which I will give you." But the fellow even gave him another sum of money, and departed.

Then the basket-maker's son said,

"This fellow is a murderer, and he killed my father!"

"Is it so, Caṇḍa?" asked the king. "Hear me, my lord," said Caṇḍa, and told him about it.

"Now, what do you want?" asked the king.

"My lord, I must have my father." [307]

"Caṇḍa," said the king, "this man must have a father. But you cannot bring him back from the dead. Then take his mother to your house, and do you be a father to him."

"Oh, master!" cried the man, "don't break up my dead father's home!" He gave Gāmaṇi a sum of money, and hurried away.

Thus Gāmaṇi won his suit, and in great delight he said to the king,

"My lord, I have several questions for you from several persons; may I tell you them?"

"Say on," said the king.

So Gāmaṇi told them all in reverse order, beginning with the young brahmins. The king answered them in turn. To the first question, he answered: "In the place where they lived there used to be a crowing cock that knew the time. When they heard his crow, they used to rise up, and repeat their texts, until the sun rose, and thus they did not forget what they learnt. But now there is a cock that crows out of season; he crows at dead of night, or in broad day. When he crows in the depth of night, up they rise, but they are too sleepy to repeat the text. When he crows in broad day, they rise up, but they have not the chance to repeat their texts. Thus it is, that whatever they learn, they soon forget."

To the second question, he answered: "Formerly these men used to do all the duties of the ascetic, and they induced the mystic trance. Now they have neglected the ascetic's duties, and they do what they ought not to do; the fruits which grow in the park they give to their attendants; they live in a sinful way, exchanging their alms[1]. This is why this fruit does not grow sweet. [308] If they once more with one consent do their duty as ascetics, again the fruit will grow sweet for them. Those hermits know not the wisdom of kings; tell them to live the ascetic life."

He heard the third question, and answered, "Those serpent chiefs quarrel one with another, and that is why the water becomes turbid. If they make friends as before, the water will be clear again." After hearing the fourth, "The tree-spirit," said he, "used formerly to protect men passing through the wood, and therefore she received many offerings. Now she gives them no protection, and so she receives no offerings. If she protects them as before, she will receive choice offerings again. She knows not that there are kings in the world. Tell her, then, to guard the men who go up into that wood." And on hearing the fifth, "Under the ant-hill where the partridge finds himself able to utter a pleasant cry is a crock of treasure; dig it up and get it." To the sixth he answered, "On the tree under which the deer found he could eat grass, is a great honey-comb. He craves the grass on which this honey has dropped, and so he can eat no other. You get the honeycomb, send the best of it to me, and eat the rest yourself." Then on hearing the seventh, "Under the snake's ant-heap lies a large treasure-crock, and there he lives guarding it. So when he goes out, from greed for this treasure his body sticks fast; but after he has fed, his desire for the treasure prevents his body from sticking, and he goes in quickly and easily. Dig up the treasure, and keep it." Then he replied to the eighth question, "Between the villages where dwell the young woman's husband and her parents [309] lives a lover of hers in a certain house. She remembers him, and her desire is toward him; therefore she cannot stay in her husband's house, but says she will go and see her parents, and on the way she stays a few days with her lover. When she has been at home a few days, again she remembers him, and saying she will return to her husband, she goes again to her lover. Go, tell her there are kings in the land; say, she must dwell with her husband,

[1] Some staying at home, while others beg for all, to save trouble. See p. 57, *note* 1.

and if she will not, let her have a care, the king will cause her to be seized, and she shall die." He heard the ninth, and to this he said, "The woman used formerly to take a price from the hand of one, and not to go with another until she was off with him[1], and that is how she used to receive much. Now she has changed her manner, and without leave of the first she goes with the last, so that she receives nothing, and none seek after her. If she keeps to her old custom, it will be as it was before. Tell her that she should keep to that." On hearing the tenth, he replied, "That village headman used once to deal justice indifferently, so that men were pleased and delighted with him; and in their delight they gave him many a present. This is what made him handsome, rich, and honoured. Now he loves to take bribes, and his judgement is not fair; so he is poor and miserable, and jaundiced. If he judges once again with righteousness, he will be again as he was before. He knows not that there are kings in the land. Tell him that he must use justice in giving judgement."

And Gāmaṇi-caṇḍa told all these messages, as they were told to him. And the king having resolved all these questions by his wisdom, like Buddha omniscient, [310] gave rich presents to Gāmaṇi-caṇḍa; and the village where Caṇḍa dwelt he gave to him, as a brahmin's gift, and let him go. Caṇḍa went out of the city, and told the king's answer to the brahmin youths, and the ascetics, to the serpent and to the tree-spirit; he took the treasure from the place where the partridge sat, and from the tree beneath which the deer did eat, he took the honeycomb, and sent honey to the king; he broke into the snake's ant-hill, and gathered the treasure out of it; and to the young woman, and the light-o'-love, and the village headman he said even as the king had told him. Then he returned to his own village, and dwelt there so long as he lived, and afterward passed away to fare according to his deserts. And king Mirror-face also gave alms, and wrought goodness, and finally after his death went to swell the hosts of heaven.

When the Master had ended this discourse, to show that not now only is the Blessed One wise, but wise he was before, he declared the Truths, and identified the Birth: (now at the conclusion of the Truths many persons entered on the First Path, or the Second, or the Third, or the Fourth:) "At that time Ānanda was Gāmaṇi-Caṇḍa; but king Mirror-face was I myself."

[1] Literally, "until she had made him enjoy his money's worth," *ajīrāpetvā*.

No. 258[1].

MANDHĀTU-JĀTAKA.

"*Wherever sun and moon*," *etc.* This story the Master told during a stay at Jetavana, about a backsliding brother.

We are told that this brother, in traversing Sāvatthi for his alms, saw a finely dressed woman and fell in love with her. Then the Brethren led him to the Hall of Truth, and informed the Master that he was a backslider. The Master asked whether it were true; and was answered, yes, it was. [311]

"Brother," said the Master, "when will you ever satisfy this lust, even while you are a householder? Such lust is as deep as the ocean, nothing can satisfy it. In former days there have been supreme monarchs, who attended by their retinue of men held sway over the four great continents encircled by two thousand isles, ruling even in the heaven of the four great kings, even when they were kings of the gods in the Heaven of the Thirty Three, even in the abode of the Thirty Six Sakkas,—even these failed to satisfy their lust, and died before they could do so; when will you be able to satisfy it?" And he told an old-world tale.

Long ago, in the early ages of the world, there lived a king named Mahāsammata, and he had a son Roja, who had a son Vararoja, who had a son Kalyāṇa, who had a son Varakalyāṇa, and Varakalyāṇa had a son named Uposatha, and Uposatha had a son Mandhātā. Mandhātā was endowed with the Seven Precious Things and the Four Supernatural Powers; and he was a great monarch. When he clenched his left hand, and then touched it with his right, there fell a rain of seven kinds of jewels, knee-deep, as though a celestial rain-cloud had arisen in the sky; so wondrous a man was he. Eighty-four thousand years he was a prince, the same number he took some share in ruling the kingdom, and even so many years he ruled as supreme king; his life lasted for countless ages.

One day, he could not satisfy some desire, so he showed signs of discontent.

"Why are you cast down, my lord?" the courtiers asked him.

"When the power of my merit is considered, what is this kingdom? Which place seems worth desiring?"

"Heaven, my lord."

[1] See *Divyāvadāna*, p. 210; Thibetan Tales, p. 1—20, *King Māndhātar.* This king is named as one of the four persons who have attained in their earthly bodies to glory in the city of the gods; *Milinda*, iv. 8. 25 (ii. p. 145 in the trans., *S. B. E.*).

So rolling along the Wheel of Empire, with his suite [312] he went to the heaven of the four great kings. The four kings, with a great throng of gods, came to meet him in state, bearing celestial flowers and perfumes; and having escorted him into their heaven, gave him rule over it. There he reigned in state, and a long time went by. But not there either could he satisfy his craving; and so he began to look sick with discontent.

"Why, mighty king," said the four monarchs, "are you unsatisfied?" And the king replied,

"What place is more lovely than this heaven?"

They answered, "My lord, we are like servants. The Heaven of the Thirty-three is more lovely than this!"

Mandhātā set the Wheel of Empire a-rolling, and with his court all round him turned his face to the Heaven of the Thirty-three. And Sakka, king of the Gods, bearing celestial flowers and perfumes, in the midst of a great throng of gods, came to meet him in state, and taking charge of him showed him the way he should go. At the time when the king was marching amidst the throng of gods, his eldest son took the Wheel of Empire, and descending to the paths of men, came to his own city. Sakka led Mandhātā into the Heaven of the Thirty-three, and gave him the half of his own kingdom. After that the two of them ruled together. Time went on, until Sakka had lived for sixty times an hundred thousand years, and thirty millions of years, then was born on earth again; another Sakka grew up, and he too reigned, and lived his life, and was born on earth. In this way six and thirty Sakkas followed one after another. Still Mandhātā reigned with his crowd of courtiers round him. As time went on, the force of his passion and desire grew stronger and stronger. "What is half a realm to me?" said he in his heart; "I will kill Sakka, and reign alone!" But kill Sakka he could not. This desire and greed of his was the root of his misfortune. The power of his life began to wane; old age seized upon him; [313] but a human body does not disintegrate in heaven. So from heaven he fell, and descended in a park. The gardener made known his coming to the royal family; they came and appointed him a resting-place in the park; there lay the king in lassitude and weariness. The courtiers asked him,

"My lord, what word shall we take from you?"

"Take from me," quoth he, "this message to the people: Mandhātā, king of kings, having ruled supreme over the four quarters of the globe, with all the two thousand islands round about, for a long time having reigned over the people of the four great kings, having been king of Heaven during the lifetime of six and thirty Sakkas, now lies dead." With these words he died, and went to fare according to his deserts.

This tale ended, the Master became perfectly enlightened and uttered the following stanzas:—

"Wherever sun and moon their courses run
All are Mandhātā's servants, every one:
Where'er earth's quarters see the light of day,
There king Mandhātā holds imperial sway.

"Not though a rain of coins fall from the sky [1]
Could anything be found to satisfy.
Pain is desire, and sorrow is unrest:
He that knows this is wise, and he is blest.

"Where longing is, there pleasure takes him wings,
Even though desire be set on heavenly things.
Disciples of the Very Buddha try
To crush out all desire eternally."

[314] When the Master had ended this discourse, he declared the Four Truths, and identified the Birth:—at the conclusion of the Truths the backsliding Brother and many others attained to the Fruit of the First Path:—"At that time, I was the great king Mandhātā."

No. 259.

TIRĪṬA-VACCHA-JĀTAKA.

"*When all alone*," *etc.* This story the Master told whilst living at Jetavana, about the gift of a thousand garments, how the reverend Ānanda received five hundred garments from the women of the household of the king of Kosala, and five hundred from the king himself. The circumstances have been described above, in the Sigāla Birth, of the Second Book [2].

Once on a time, while Brahmadatta was king of Benares, the Bodhisatta was born as the son of a brahmin in Kāsi. On his nameday they called him Master Tirīṭavaccha. In due time he grew up, and studied at Takkasilā. He married and settled down, but his parents' death so distressed him [315] that he became an ascetic, and lived in a woodland dwelling, feeding upon the roots and fruits of the forest.

[1] See *Dhammapada*, verses 186 and 187, which are the last two of these stanzas.

[2] No. 152, page 4, where however there is no word of this incident; it really occurs in No. 156, p. 17 of this volume.

Whilst he lived there, arose a disturbance on the frontiers of Benares. The king repaired thither, but was worsted in the fight; fearing for his life, he mounted an elephant, and fled away covertly through the forest. In the morning, Tirīṭavaccha had gone abroad to gather wild fruit, and meanwhile the king came upon his hut. "A hermit's hut!" quoth he; down he came from his elephant, weary with wind and sun, and athirst; he looked about for a waterpot, but none could he find. At the end of the covered walk he spied a well, but he could see no rope and bucket for the drawing of water. His thirst was too great to bear; he took off the girth which passed under the elephant's belly, made it fast on the edge, and let himself down into the well. But it was too short; so he tied on to the end of it his lower garment, and let himself down again. Still he could not reach the water. He could just touch it with his feet: he was very thirsty! "If I can but quench my thirst," thought he, "death itself will be sweet!" So down he dropped, and drank his fill; but he could not get up again, so he remained standing there in the well. And the elephant, so well trained was he, stood still, waiting for the king.

In the evening, the Bodhisatta returned, laden with wild fruits, and espied the elephant. "I suppose," thought he, "the king is come; but nothing is to be seen save the armed elephant. What's to do?" And he approached the elephant, which stood and waited for him. He went to the edge of the well, and saw the king at the bottom. "Fear nothing, O king!" he called out; then he placed a ladder, and helped the king out; he chafed the king's body, and anointed him with oil; after which he gave him of the fruits to eat [316], and loosed the elephant's armour. Two or three days the king rested there; then he went away, after making the Bodhisatta promise to pay him a visit.

The royal forces were encamped hard by the city; and when the king was perceived coming, they flocked around him.

After a month and half a month, the Bodhisatta returned to Benares, and settled in the park. Next day he came to the palace to ask for food. The king had opened a great window, and stood looking out into the courtyard; and so seeing the Bodhisatta, and recognising him, he descended and gave him greeting; he led him to a dais, and set him upon the throne under a white umbrella; his own food the king gave him to eat, and ate himself of it. Then he took him to the garden, and caused a covered walk and a dwelling to be made for him, and furnished him with all the necessaries of an ascetic; then giving him in charge of a gardener, he bade farewell, and departed. After this, the Bodhisatta took his food in the king's dwelling: great was the respect and honour paid to him.

But the courtiers could not endure it. "If a soldier," said they, "were to receive such honour, how would he behave?" They betook them to the viceroy: "My lord, our king is making too much of an ascetic! What can he have seen in the man? You speak with the king about it." The viceroy consented, and they all went together before the king. And the viceroy greeted the king, and uttered the first stanza:

> "There is no wit in him that I can see;
> He is no kinsman, nor a friend of thee;
> Why should this hermit with three bits of wood[1],
> Tirīṭavaccha, have such splendid food?"

[317] The king listened. Then he said, addressing his son,

"My son, you remember how once I went to the marches, and how I was conquered in war, and came not back for a few days?"

"I remember," said he.

"This man saved my life," said the king; and he told him all that had happened. "Well, my son, now that this my preserver is with me, I cannot requite him for what he has done, not even were I to give him my kingdom." And he recited the two stanzas following:—

> "When all alone, in a grim thirsty wood,
> He, and no other, tried to do me good;
> In my distress he lent a helping hand;
> Half-dead he drew me up and made me stand.
>
> "By his sole doing I returned again
> Out of death's jaws back to the world of men.
> To recompense such kindness is but fair;
> Give a rich offering, nor stint his share."

[318] So spake the king, as though he were causing the moon to rise up in the sky; and as the virtue of the Bodhisatta was declared, so was declared his own virtue everywhere; and his takings increased, and the honour shown to him. After that neither his viceroy nor his courtiers nor any one else durst say anything against him to the king. The king abode in the Bodhisatta's admonition; and he gave alms and did good, and at the last went to swell the hosts of heaven. And the Bodhisatta, having cultivated the Perfections and the Attainments, became destined to the world of Brahma.

Then the Master added, "Wise men of old gave help too;" and having thus concluded his discourse, he identified the Birth as follows: "Ānanda was the king, and I was the hermit."

[1] To hang his waterpot upon.

No. 260.

DŪTA-JĀTAKA[1].

"*O king, the Belly's messenger,*" *etc.* This story the Master told while staying at Jetavana, about a Brother who was addicted to covetousness. The circumstances will be given at large under the Kāka[2] Birth, in Book the Ninth. Here again the Master told the Brother, [319] "You were greedy before, Brother, as you are now; and in olden days for your greed you had your head cleft with a sword." Then he told an old-world story.

Once on a time, when Brahmadatta was king over Benares, the Bodhisatta was born as his son. He grew up, and finished his education at Takkasilā. On his father's death, he inherited the kingdom, and he was very dainty in his eating; accordingly he earned the name of King Dainty. There was so much extravagance about his eating, that on one dish he spent an hundred thousand pieces. When he ate, he ate not within doors; but as he wished to confer merit[3] upon many people by showing them the costly array of his meals, he caused a pavilion adorned with jewels to be set up at the door, and at the time of eating, he had this decorated, and there he sat upon a royal dais made all of gold, under a white parasol with princesses all around him, and ate the food of an hundred delicate flavours from a dish which cost an hundred thousand pieces of money.

Now a certain greedy man saw the king's manner of eating, and desired to have a taste. Unable to master his craving, he girt up his loins tight, and ran up to the king, calling out loudly—"Messenger! messenger! O king"—with his hands held up. (At that time and in that nation, if a man called out "Messenger!" no one would stay him; and so it was that the multitude divided and gave him way to pass.)

The man ran up swiftly, and catching a piece of rice from the king's dish, he put it in his mouth. The swordsman drew his sword, to cleave the man's head. But the king stayed him. "Smite not," said he;—then to the man, "fear nothing, eat on!" He washed his hands, and sat down.

[1] See Morris, *Folk-lore Journal*, iv. 54.

[2] There is no such heading in Book IX. There is a Kāka-Jātaka in Book VI. no. 395, where the Introd. Story is not given, but said to be "the same as before."

[3] The Talmud says that one should always run to meet the kings of Israel and even gentile kings.

[320] After the meal, the king caused his own drinking water and betel nut to be given to the man, and then said—

"Now my man, you had tidings, you said. What are your tidings?"

"O king, I am a messenger from Lust and the Belly. Says Lust to me, Go! and sent me here as her messenger;" and with these words he spake the first two stanzas:—

"O king, the Belly's messenger you see:
O lord of chariots, do not angry be!
For Belly's sake men very far will go,
Even to ask a favour of a foe.

"O king, the Belly's messenger you see;
O lord of chariots, do not angry be!
The Belly holds beneath his puissant sway
All men upon the earth both night and day."

When this the king heard, he said, "That is true; Belly-messengers are these; urged by lust they go to and fro, and lust makes them go. How prettily this man has put it!" he was pleased with him, and uttered the third stanza:—

"Brahmin, a thousand red kine I present
To thee; thereto the bull, for complement.
One messenger may to another give;
For Belly's messengers are all that live."

So said the king; and continued, "I have heard something I never heard before, or thought of, said by this great man." And so pleased was he, that he showered honours upon him.

---

[321] When the Master had ended this discourse, he declared the Truths and identified the Birth:—at the conclusion of the Truths the greedy Brother reached the Fruit of the Third Path, and many others entered the other Paths:—"The greedy man is the same in both stories, and I was King Dainty."

No. 261.

PADUMA-JĀTAKA.

"*Cut, and cut, and cut again,*" *etc.* This story the Master told at Jetavana, about some Brethren who made offering of garlands under Ānanda's tree. The circumstances will be given in the Kāliṅga-bodhi Birth[1]. This was called

[1] No. 479.

Ānanda's tree, because Ānanda planted it. All India heard tell how the Elder had planted this tree by the gate of Jetavana.

Some Brethren who lived in the country thought they would make offerings before Ānanda's tree. They journeyed to Jetavana, did their devoirs to the Master, and next day wended their way to Sāvatthi, to the Lotus Street; but not a garland could they get. So they told Ananda, how they had wished to make an offering to the tree, but that not a garland was to be had in all the Lotus Street. The Elder promised to fetch some; so he went off to the Lotus Street, and returned with many handfuls of blue lotus, which he gave them. With these they made their offering to the tree.

When the Brethren got wind of this, they began discussing the Elder's merits in the Hall of Truth: "Friend, some brothers of little merit from the country could not get a single nosegay in the Lotus Bazaar; but the Elder went and fetched them some." The Master entered, and asked what they were talking of as they sat there; and they told him. Said he, [322] "Brethren, this is not the first time that the clever tongue has gained a garland for clever speaking; it was the same before." And he told them an old-world tale.

Once on a time, when Brahmadatta reigned in Benares, the Bodhisatta was a rich merchant's son. In the town was a tank, in which the lotus flowered. A man who had lost his nose looked after the tank.

It happened one day that they proclaimed holiday in Benares; and the three sons of this rich man thought that they would put wreaths upon them, and go a merrymaking. "We'll flatter up the old lacknose fellow, and then we'll beg some flowers of him." So at the time when he used to pluck the lotus flowers, to the tank they went, and waited. And one of them uttered the first stanza:—

"Cut, and cut, and cut again,
Hair and whiskers grow amain;
And your nose will grow like these.
Give me just one lotus, please!"

But the man was angry, and gave none. Then the second said the second stanza:—

"In the autumn seeds are sown
Which ere long are fully grown;
May your nose sprout up like these.
Give me just one lotus, please!"

Again the man was angry, and gave no lotus. Then the third of them repeated the third stanza:—

"Babbling fools! to think that they
Can get a lotus in this way.
Say they yes, or say they no,
Noses cut no more will grow.
See, I ask you honestly:
Give a lotus, sir, to me!"

[323] On hearing this the lake keeper said, "The other two lied, but you have spoken the truth. You deserve to have some lotuses." So he gave him a great bunch of lotus, and went back to his lake.

When the Master had ended this discourse, he identified the Birth: "The boy who got the lotus was I myself."

No. 262.

MUDU-PĀṆI-JĀTAKA.

"*A soft hand*," *etc.* This story the Master told at Jetavana, about a backsliding Brother. They brought him to the Hall of Truth, and the Master asked him if he were really a backslider? He replied, yes, he was. Then said the Master, "O Brethren! It is impossible to keep women from going after their desires. In olden days, even wise men could not guard their own daughters; while they stood holding their fathers' hand, without their fathers' knowing, they went away wrong-doing with a paramour"; and he told them an old-world tale.

Once upon a time, while king Brahmadatta reigned in Benares, the Bodhisatta was born as the son of his Queen Consort. Growing up, he was educated at Takkasilā, and on his father's death he became king in his stead, and reigned righteously.

There dwelt with him a daughter and a nephew, both together in his house. One day as he sat with his court, he said,

"When I am dead my nephew will be king, [324] and my daughter will be his chief queen."

Afterwards, when they were grown up, he was sitting again amidst his court; and he said to them,

"I will bring home some other man's daughter for my nephew, and my own daughter will I marry into another king's family. In this way I shall have many relations." The courtiers agreed. Then the king assigned to the nephew a house outside the palace, and forbade his coming to the palace.

But these two were in love with each other. Thought the youth, "How shall I get the king's daughter outside the house?—Ah, I have it." He gave a present to the nurse.

"What am I to do for this, master?" she asked.

"Well, mother, I want to get a chance of bringing the princess out of doors."

"I will talk it over with the princess," said she, "and then tell you."

"Very good, mother," he replied.

To the princess she came. "Let me pick the insects out of your head," said she.

She sat the princess upon a low stool, and herself sitting on a higher one, she put the princess's head upon her lap, and in looking for the insects, she scratched the princess's head. The princess understood. She thought, "She has scratched me with my cousin the prince's nail, not her own.—Mother," asked she, "have you been with the prince?"

"Yes, my daughter."

"And what did he say?"

"He asked how he could find a way of getting you out of doors."

"If he is wise, he will know," said the princess; and she recited the first stanza, bidding the old woman learn it and repeat it to the prince:—

> "A soft hand, and a well-trained elephant,
> And a black rain-cloud, gives you what you want."

The woman learnt it, and returned to the prince.

"Well, mother, what did the princess say?" he asked.

"Nothing, [325] but only sent you this stanza," replied she; and she repeated it. The prince took it in, and dismissed her.

The prince understood exactly what was meant. He found a beautiful and soft-handed page lad, and prepared him. He bribed the keeper of a state elephant, and having trained the elephant to be impassive, he bided his time. Then, one fast-day of the dark fortnight, just after the middle watch, rain fell from a thick black cloud. "This is the day the princess meant," thought he; he mounted the elephant, and placed the lad of the soft hands on its back, and set out. Opposite the palace he fastened the elephant to the great wall of an open courtyard, and stood before a window getting drenched.

Now the king watched his daughter, and let her rest nowhere but upon a little bed, in his presence. She thought to herself, "To-day the prince will come!" and lay down without going to sleep.

"Father," said she, "I want to bathe."

"Come along, my daughter," said the king. Holding her hands, he led her to the window; he lifted her, and placed her on a lotus ornament outside it, holding her by one hand. As she bathed herself, she held out a hand to the prince. He loosed off the bangles from her arm, and fastened them on the arm of his page boy; then he lifted the lad, and placed him upon the lotus beside the princess. [326] She took his hand, and placed it in her father's, who took it, and let go his daughter's hand. Then she loosed the ornaments from her other arm, and fastened them on the other hand of the lad, which she placed in her father's, and went away with the prince. The king thought the lad to be his own daughter; and when the bathing was over, he put him to sleep in the royal bedchamber, shut to the door, and set his seal on it; then setting a guard, he retired to his own chamber, and lay down to rest.

When the daylight came, he opened the door, and there he saw this lad. "What's this?" cried he. The lad told how she was fled along with the prince. The king was cast down. "Not even if one goes along and holds hands," thought the king, "can one guard a woman. Thus women it is impossible to guard;" and he uttered these other two stanzas:—

"Though soft of speech, like rivers hard to fill,
Insatiate, nought can satisfy their will:
Down, down they sink: a man should flee afar
From women, when he knows what kind they are.
Whomso they serve for gold or for desire,
They burn him up like fuel in the fire[1]."

[327] So saying, the great Being added, "I must support my nephew;" so with great honour he gave his daughter to this very man, and made him viceroy. And the nephew at his uncle's death became king himself.

When the Master had ended this discourse, he declared the Truths and identified the Birth:—at the conclusion of the Truths, the backsliding Brother was firmly established in the Fruit of the First Path:—"In those days, I was the king."

[1] The following verses are given by the commentator:

"Where women rule, the seeing lose their sight,
The strong grow weak, the mighty have no might.
Where women rule, virtue and wisdom fly:
Reckless the prisoners in durance lie.
Like highway robbers, all they steal away
From their poor victims, careless come what may—
Reflection, virtue, truth, and reasoning
Self-sacrifice, and goodness—everything.
As fire burns fuel, for each careless wight
They burn fame, glory, learning, wit, and might."

The word for fire is the archaic *jātaveda*, used already in no. 35. See note in vol. i. p. 90.

No. 263.

CULLA-PALOBHANA-JĀTAKA.

[328] "*Not through the sea,*" *etc.* This story the Master told at Jetavana, also about a backsliding Brother. The Master had him brought into the Hall of Truth, and asked if it were true that he was a backslider. Yes, said he, it was. "Women," said the Master, "in olden days made even believing souls to sin." Then he told a story.

Once on a time Brahmadatta, the king of Benares, was childless. He said to his queen, "Let us offer prayer for a son." They offered prayer. After a long time, the Bodhisatta came down from the world of Brahma, and was conceived by this queen. So soon as he was born, he was bathed, and given to a serving woman to nurse. As he took the breast, he cried. He was given to another; but while a woman held him, he would not be quiet. So he was given to a man servant; and as soon as the man took him, he was quiet. After that men used to carry him about. When they suckled him, they would milk the breast for him, or they gave him the breast from behind a screen. Even when he grew older, they could not show him a woman. The king caused to be made for him a separate place for sitting or what not, and a separate room for meditation, all by himself.

When the lad was sixteen years old, the king thought thus within himself. "Other son have I none, and this one enjoys no pleasures. He will not even wish for the kingdom. What's the good of such a son?"

And there was a certain dancing girl, clever at dance and song and music, young, able to gain ascendancy over any man she came across. She approached the king, and asked what he was thinking about; the king told her what it was. [329]

"Let be, my lord," said she: "I will allure him, I will make him love me."

"Well, if you can allure my son, who has never had any dealings whatsoever with women, he shall be king, and you shall be his chief queen!"

"Leave that to me, my lord," said she; "and don't be anxious." So she came to the people of the guard, and said, "At dawn of day I will go to the sleeping place of the prince, and outside the room where he meditates apart I will sing. If he is angry, you must tell me, and I will go away; but if he listens, speak my praises." This they agreed to do.

So in the morning time she took her stand in that place, and sang with a voice of honey, so that the music was as sweet as the song, and the song as sweet as the music. The prince lay listening. Next day, he commanded that she should stand near and sing. The next day, he commanded her to stand in the private chamber, and the next, in his own presence; and so by and bye desire arose in him; he went the way of the world, and knew the joy of love. "I will not let another have this woman," he resolved; and taking his sword, he ran amuck through the street, chasing the people. The king had him captured, and banished him from the city along with the girl.

Together they journeyed to the jungle, away down the Ganges. There, with the river on one side and the sea on the other, they made a hut, and there they lived. She sat indoors, and cooked the roots and bulbs; the Bodhisatta brought wild fruits from the forest.

One day, when he was away in search of fruits, a hermit from an island in the sea, who was going his rounds to get food, saw smoke as he passed through the air, and alighted beside this hut.

"Sit down until it is cooked," said the woman; then her woman's charms seduced his soul, and brought it down from his mystic trance, making a breach in his purity. And he, like a crow with broken wing, [330] unable to leave her, sat there the whole day till he saw the Bodhisatta coming, and then ran off quickly in the direction of the sea. "This must be an enemy," thought he, and drawing his sword set off in chase. But the ascetic, making as though he would rise in the air, fell down into the sea. Then thought the Bodhisatta,

"Yon man is doubtless an ascetic who came hither through the air; and now that his trance is broken, he has fallen into the sea. I must go help him." And standing on the shore he uttered these verses:—

"Not through the sea, but by your magic power,
You journeyed hither at an earlier hour;
Now by a woman's evil company
You have been made to plunge beneath the sea.

"Full of seductive wiles, deceitful all,
They tempt the most pure-hearted to his fall.
Down—down they sink: a man should flee afar
From women, when he knows what kind they are.

"Whomso they serve, for gold or for desire,
They burn him up like fuel in the fire[1]."

[1] The Scholiast gives the following lines in his note:

Hallucination, sorrow, and disease,
Mirage, distress (and solid bonds are these),
The snare of death, deep-seated in the mind—
Who trusts in these is vilest of his kind.

When the ascetic heard these words which the Bodhisatta spake, he stood up in the midst of the sea, and resuming his interrupted trance, he rose through the air, and went away to his dwelling place. Thought the Bodhisatta, "Yon ascetic, with so great a burden, goes through the air like a fleck of cotton. [331] Why should not I like him cultivate the trance, and pass through the air?" So he returned to his hut, and led the woman among mankind again; then he told her to be gone, and himself went into the jungle, where he built him a hut in a pleasant spot, and became an ascetic; he prepared for the mystic trance, cultivated the Faculties and the Attainments, and became destined for the world of Brahma.

When this discourse was ended, the Master declared the Truths: (now at the conclusion of the Truths the backsliding Brother became established in the Fruit of the First Path:) "At that time," said he, "I was myself the youth that had never had anything to do with women."

No. 264.

MAHĀ-PANĀDA-JĀTAKA[1].

"*'Twas king Panāda,*" *etc.*—This story the Master told when he was settled on the bank of the Ganges, about the miraculous power of Elder Bhaddaji.

On one occasion, when the Master had passed the rains at Sāvatthi, he thought he would show kindness to a young gentleman named Bhaddaji. So with all the Brethren who were with him, he made his way to the city of Bhaddiya, and stayed three months in Jātiyā Grove, waiting until the young man should mature and perfect his knowledge. Now young Bhaddaji was a magnificent person, the only son of a rich merchant in Bhaddiya, with a fortune of eight hundred millions. He had three houses for the three seasons, in each of which he stayed four months; and after spending this period in one of them, he used to migrate with all his kith and kin to another in the greatest pomp. On these occasions all the town was a-flutter to see the young man's magnificence; and between these houses used to be erected seats in circles on circles and tiers above tiers.

When the Master had been there three months, he informed the townspeople that he intended to leave. Begging him to wait until the morrow, the townsfolk on the following day collected magnificent gifts for the Buddha and his attendant Brethren; and set up a pavilion in the midst of the town, decorating it and laying out seats; then they announced that the hour had come. The Master

[1] Cp. *Divyāvadāna*, p. 57.

with his company went and took their seats there. Everybody gave generously to them. After the meal was over, the Master in a voice sweet as honey returned thanks to them.

At this moment, young Bhaddaji was passing from one of his residences to another. [332] But that day not a soul came to see his splendour; only his own people were about him. So he asked his people how it was. Usually all the city was in a flutter to see him pass from house to house; circles on circles and tiers above tiers the seats were built; but just then there was nobody but his own followers! What could be the reason?

The reply was, "My lord, the Supreme Buddha has been spending three months near the town, and this day he leaves. He has just finished his meal, and is holding a discourse. All the town is there listening to his words."

"Oh, very well, we will go and hear him too," said the young man. So, in a blaze of ornaments, with his crowd of followers about him, he went and stood on the skirt of the crowd; as he heard the discourse, he threw off all his sins, and attained to high fruition and sainthood.

The Master, addressing the merchant of Bhaddiya, said, "Sir, your son, in all his splendour, while hearing my discourse has become a saint; this very day he should either embrace the religious life, or enter Nirvana."

"Sir," replied he, "I do not wish my son to enter Nirvana. Admit him to the religious order; this done, come with him to my house to-morrow."

The Blessed One accepted this invitation; he took the young gentleman to the monastery, admitted him to the brotherhood, and afterward to the lesser and greater orders. For a week the youth's parents showed generous hospitality to him.

After remaining these seven days, the Master went on alms-pilgrimage, taking the young man with him, and arrived at a village called Koṭi. The villagers of Koṭi gave generously to the Buddha and his followers. At the end of this meal, the Master began to express his thanks. While this was being done, the young gentleman went outside the village, and by a landing-place of the Ganges he sat down under a tree, and plunged in a trance, thinking that he would rise as soon as the Master should come. When the Elders of greatest age approached, he did not rise, but he rose as soon as the Master came. The unconverted folk were angry because he behaved as though he were a Brother of old standing, not rising up even when he saw the eldest Brethren approach.

The villagers constructed rafts. This done, [333] the Master asked where Bhaddaji was. "There he is, Sir." "Come, Bhaddaji, come aboard my raft." The Elder rose, and followed him to his raft. When they were in mid-river, the Master asked him a question.

"Bhaddaji, where is the palace you lived in when Great Panāda was king?" "Here, under the water," was the reply. The unconverted said one to the other, "Elder Bhaddaji is showing that he is a saint!" Then the Master bade him disperse the doubt of his fellow-students.

In a moment, the Elder, with a bow to his Master, moving by his mysterious power, took the whole pile of the palace on his finger, and rose in the air bearing the palace with him (it covered a space of twenty-five leagues); then he made a hole in it and showed himself to the present inhabitants of the palace below, and tossed the building above the water first one league, then two, then three. Then those who had been his kinsfolk in this former existence, who had now become fish or tortoises, water-snakes or frogs, because they loved the palace so much, and had come to life in the very same place, wriggled out of it when it rose up, and tumbled over and over into the water again. When the Master saw this, he said, "Bhaddaji, your relations are in trouble." At his Master's words the Elder let the palace go, and it sank to the place where it had been before.

The Master passed to the further side of the Ganges. Then they prepared

[1] For an explanation of this phrase, *aññaṁ vyākaroti*, see *Mahāvagga* I. v. 19 with the translators' note (*S. B. E.*, *Vinaya Texts* ii. p. 10).

him a seat just on the river bank. On the seat prepared for the Buddha, he sat, like the sun fresh risen pouring forth his rays. Then the Brethren asked him when it was that Elder Bhaddaji had lived in that palace. The Master answered, "In the days of king Great Panāda," and went on to tell them an old-world tale.

Once upon a time, a certain Suruci was king of Mithilā, which is a town in the kingdom of Videha. He had a son, named Suruci likewise, and he again had a son, the Great Panāda. They obtained possession of that mansion. They obtained it by a deed done in a former existence. A father and son made a hut of leaves with canes and branches of the fig-tree, as a dwelling for a Paccekabuddha.

The rest of the story will be told in the Suruci Birth, Book XIV.[1]

[334] The Master, having finished telling this story, in his perfect wisdom uttered these stanzas here following:—

"'Twas king Panāda who this palace had,
 A thousand bowshots high, in breadth sixteen,
A thousand bowshots high, in banners clad;
 An hundred storeys, all of emerald green.

"Six thousand men of music to and fro
 In seven companies did dance withal:
As Bhaddaji has said, 'twas even so:
 I, Sakka, was your slave, at beck and call."

[335] At that moment the unconverted people became resolved of their doubt.

When the Master had ended this discourse, he identified the Birth:—"Bhaddaji was the Great Panāda, and I was Sakka."

No. 265.

KHURAPPA-JĀTAKA.

"*When many a bow,*" *etc.*—This story the Master told in Jetavana, about a Brother who had lost all energy. The Master asked, was it true that this Brother had lost his energy. Yes, he replied. "Why," asked he, "have you slackened your energy, after embracing this doctrine of salvation? In days of yore, wise men were energetic even in matters which do not lead to salvation;" and so saying he told an old-world tale.

---

[1] No. 489.

Once on a time, while Brahmadatta was king of Benares, the Bodhisatta was born into the family of a forester. When he grew up, he took the lead of a band of five hundred foresters, and lived in a village at the entrance to the forest. He used to hire himself out to guide men through it.

Now one day a man of Benares, a merchant's son, arrived at that village with a caravan of five hundred waggons. Sending for the Bodhisatta, he offered him a thousand pieces to be his guide through the forest. He agreed, and received the money from the merchant's hand; and as he took it, he mentally devoted his life to the merchant's service. Then he guided him into the forest.

In the midst of the forest, up rose five hundred robbers. As for the rest of the company, no sooner did they see these robbers, than they grovelled upon their belly: the head forester alone, shouting and leaping and dealing blows, put to flight all the five hundred robbers, and led the merchant across the wood in safety. Once across the forest, the merchant encamped his caravan; [336] he gave the chief forester choice meats of every kind, and himself having broken his fast, sat pleasantly by him, and talked with him thus: "Tell me," said he, "how it was that even when five hundred robbers, with arms in their hands, were spread all around, you felt not even any fear in your heart?" And he uttered the first stanza:

"When many a bow the shaft at speed let fly—
Hands grasping blades of tempered steel were nigh—
When Death had marshalled all his dread array—
Why, 'mid such terror, felt you no dismay?"

On hearing this the forester repeated the two verses following:

"When many a bow the shaft at speed let fly—
Hands grasping blades of tempered steel were nigh—
When Death had marshalled all his dread array—
I felt a great and mighty joy this day.

"And this my joy gave me the victory;
I was resolved to die, if need should be;
He must contemn his life, who would fulfil
Heroic deeds and be a hero still."

[337] Thus did he send forth his words like a shower of arrows; and having explained how he had done heroically through being free from the desire to live, he parted from the young merchant, and returned to his own village; where after giving alms and doing good he passed away to fare according to his deserts.

When the Master had ended this discourse, he declared the Truths, and identified the Birth:—at the conclusion of the Truths the disheartened Brother attained to Sainthood:—"At that time I was the chief of the foresters."

No. 266.

VĀTAGGA-SINDHAVA-JĀTAKA.

"*He for whose sake,*" *etc.*—This story the Master told at Jetavana, about a certain land-owner.

At Sāvatthi, we learn, a handsome woman saw this man, who was also handsome, and fell in love. The passion within her was like a fire burning her body through and through. She lost her senses, both of body and of mind; she cared nothing for food; she only lay down hugging the frame of the bedstead.

Her friends and handmaidens asked her what troubled her at heart that she lay hugging the bedstead; what was the matter, they wished to know. The first few times she answered nothing; but as they continued pressing her, she told them what it was.

"Don't worry," said they, "we'll bring him to you;" and they went and had a talk with the man. At first he refused, but by their much asking he at last consented. They got his promise to come at a certain hour on a fixed day, and told the woman.

She prepared her chamber, and dressed herself in her finery, and sat on the bed waiting until he came. He sat down beside her. Then a thought came into her mind. [338] "If I accept his addresses at once, and make myself cheap, my pride will be humbled. To let him have his will the very first day he comes would be out of place. I will be capricious to-day, and afterwards I will give way." So no sooner had he touched her, and begun to dally, she caught his hands, and spoke roughly to him, bidding him go away, as she did not want him. He shrank back angrily, and went off home.

When the women found out what she had done, and that the man had gone off, they reproached her. "Here you are," they said, "in love with somebody, and lie down refusing to take nourishment; we had great difficulty in persuading the man, but at last we bring him; and then you'll have nothing to say to him!" She told them why it was, and they went off, warning her that she would get talked about.

The man never even came to look at her again. When she found she had lost him, she would take no nourishment, and soon died. When the man heard of her death, he took a quantity of flowers, scents, and perfumes, and went to Jetavana, where he saluted the Master and sat on one side.

The Master asked him, "How is it, lay brother, that we never see you here?" He told him the whole story, adding that he had avoided waiting on the Buddha all this time for shame. Said the Master, "Layman, on this occasion the woman sent for you through her passion, and then would have nothing to do with you and sent you away angry; and just so in olden days, she fell in love with wise persons, sent for them, and when they came refused to have anything to do with them, and thus plagued them and sent them to the right-about." Then at his request the Master told an old-world tale.

Once upon a time, when Brahmadatta was king of Benares, the Bodhisatta was a Sindh horse, and they called him Swift-as-the-Wind; and he was the king's horse of ceremony. The grooms used to take him to bathe in the Ganges. There a certain she-ass saw him, and fell in love.

Trembling with passion, [339] she neither ate grass nor drank water; but pined away and became thin, until she was nothing but skin and bone. Then a foal of hers, seeing her pining away, said, "Why do you eat no grass, mother, and drink no water; and why do you pine away, and lie trembling in this place or that? What is the matter?" She would not say; but after he had asked again and again, she told him the matter. Then her foal comforted her, saying,

"Mother, do not be troubled; I will bring him to you."

So when Swift-as-the-Wind went down to bathe, the foal said, approaching him,

"Sir, my mother is in love with you: she takes no food, and she is pining away to death. Give her life!"

"Good, my lad, I will," said the horse. "When my bath is over, the grooms let me go awhile to exercise on the river bank. Do you bring your mother to that place."

So the foal fetched his mother, and turned her loose in the place; then he hid himself hard by.

The groom let Swift-as-the-Wind go for a run; he spied the she-ass, and came up to her.

Now when the horse came up and began to sniff at her, thought the ass to herself, "If I make myself cheap, and let him have his way as soon as he has come here, my honour and pride will perish. I must make as though I did not wish it." So she gave him a kick on the lower jaw, and scampered away. It broke his jaw, and half killed him. "What does she matter to me?" thought Swift-as-the-Wind; [340] he felt ashamed and made off.

Then the ass repented, and lay down on the spot in grief. And her son the foal came up, and asked her a question in the following lines:

"He for whose sake you thin and yellow grew,
    And would not eat a bite,
That dear beloved one is come to you;
    Why do you take to flight?"

Hearing her son's voice, the ass repeated the second verse:

"If at the very first, when by her side
    He stands, without delay
A woman yields, all humbled is her pride:
    Therefore I ran away."

In these words she explained the feminine nature to her son.

The Master, in his perfect wisdom, repeated the third stanza:

> "If she refuse a suitor nobly born
> Who by her side would stay,
> As Kundalī mourned Windswift, she must mourn
> For many a long day."

When this discourse was ended, the Master declared the Truths and identified the Birth:—at the conclusion of the Truths, this land-owner entered on the Fruit of the First Path:—"This woman was the she-ass, and I was Swift-as-the-Wind."

No. 266.

KAKKAṬĀ-JĀTAKA[1].

"*Gold-clawed creature,*" *etc.*—[341] This story the Master told while dwelling at Jetavana, about a certain woman.

We are told that a certain land-owner of Sāvatthi, with his wife, was on a journey into the country for the purpose of collecting debts, when he fell among robbers. Now the wife was very beautiful and charming. The robber chief was so taken by her that he purposed killing the husband to get her. But the woman was good and virtuous, a devoted wife. She fell at the robber's feet, crying, "My lord, if you kill my husband for love of me, I will take poison, or stop my breath, and kill myself too! With you I will not go. Do not kill my husband uselessly!" In this way she begged him off.

They both got back safe to Sāvatthi. Then it occurred to them as they passed the monastery in Jetavana, that they would visit it and salute the Master. So to the perfumed cell they went, and after salutation sat down on one side. The Master asked them where they had been. "To collect our debts," they replied. "Did your journey pass off without mishap?" he asked next. "We were captured by robbers on the way," said the husband, "and the chief wanted to murder me; but my wife here begged me off, and I owe my life to her." Then said the Master, "You are not the only one, layman, whose life she has saved. In days of yore she saved the lives of other wise men." And then at his request the Master told an old-world tale.

Once on a time, when Brahmadatta was king of Benares, there was a great lake in Himalaya, wherein was a great golden Crab. Because he lived there, the place was known as the Crab Tarn. The Crab was very large, as big round as a threshing floor; it would catch elephants, and kill

[1] Cf. Morris in *Contemp. Rev.* 1881, vol. 39, p. 742; Cunningham, *Stupa of Bharhut*, pl. xxv. 2 (frontispiece to this volume).

and eat them; and from fear of it [342] the elephants durst not go down and browse there.

Now the Bodhisatta was conceived by the mate of an elephant, the leader of a herd, living hard by this Crab Tarn. The mother, in order to be safe till her delivery, sought another place on a mountain, and there she was delivered of a son; who in due time grew to years of wisdom, and was great and mighty, and prospered, and he was like a purple mountain of collyrium.

He chose another elephant for his mate, and he resolved to catch this Crab. So with his mate and his mother, he sought out the elephant herd, and finding his father, proposed to go and catch the Crab.

"You will not be able to do that, my son," said he.

But he begged the father again and again to give him leave, until at last he said, "Well, you may try."

So the young Elephant collected all the elephants beside the Crab Tarn, and led them close by the lake. "Does the Crab catch them when they go down, or while they are feeding, or when they come up again?"

They replied, "When the beasts come up again."

"Well then," said he, "do you all go down to the lake and eat whatever you see, and come up first; I will follow last behind you." And so they did. Then the Crab, seeing the Bodhisatta coming up last, caught his feet tight in his claw, like a smith who seizes a lump of iron in a huge pair of tongs. The Bodhisatta's mate did not leave him, but stood there close by him. The Bodhisatta pulled at the Crab, but could not make him budge. Then the Crab pulled, and drew him towards himself. At this in deadly fear the Elephant roared and roared; hearing which all the other elephants, in deadly terror, ran off trumpeting, and dropping excrement. Even his mate could not stand, but began to make off. [343] Then to tell her how he was held a prisoner, he uttered the first stanza, hoping to stay her from her flight:

"Gold-clawed[1] creature with projecting eyes,
Tarn-bred, hairless, clad in bony shell,
He has caught me! hear my woful cries!—
Mate! don't leave me—for you love me well!"

Then his mate turned round, and repeated the second stanza to his comfort:

"Leave you? never! never will I go—
Noble husband, with your years threescore.
All four quarters of the earth can show
None so dear as thou hast been of yore."

[1] *Siṅgī* means either 'horned' or 'gold,' and the scholiast gives both interpretations. As the word suggested both to the writer, I use a word which expresses both in English.

In this way she encouraged him; and saying, "Noble sir, now I will talk to the Crab a while to make him let you go," she addressed the Crab in the third stanza: [344]

"Of all the crabs that in the sea,
Ganges, or Nerbudda be,
You are best and chief, I know:
Hear me—let my husband go!"

As she spoke thus, the Crab's fancy was smitten with the sound of the female voice, and forgetting all fear he loosed his claws from the Elephant's leg, and suspected nothing of what he would do when he was set free. Then the Elephant lifted his foot, and stepped upon the Crab's back; and at once his eyes started out. The Elephant shouted the joy-cry. Up ran the other elephants all, pulled the Crab along and set him upon the ground, and trampled him to mincemeat. His two claws broken from his body lay apart. And this Crab Tarn, being near the Ganges, when there was a flood in the Ganges, was filled with Ganges water; when the water subsided it ran from the lake into the Ganges. Then these two claws were lifted and floated along the Ganges. One of them reached the sea, the other was found by the ten royal brothers while playing in the water, and they took it and made of it the little drum called Anaka. The Titans found that which reached the sea, and made it into the drum called Āḷambara. These afterwards being worsted in battle with Sakka, ran off and left it behind. Then Sakka caused it to be kept for his own use; and it is of this they say, "There is thunder like the Āḷambara cloud!"

When this discourse was ended, the Master declared the Truths, and identified the Birth:—at the conclusion of the Truths both husband and wife attained the Fruit of the First Path:—[345] "In those days, this lay sister was the she-elephant, and I myself was her mate."

No. 268[1].

ĀRĀMA-DŪSA-JĀTAKA.

"*Best of all*," *etc.*—This story the Master told whilst dwelling in the country near Dakkhiṇāgiri, about a gardener's son.

After the rains, the Master left Jetavana, and went on alms-pilgrimage in the

[1] This is the same story as No. 46 (vol. i. of the translation, p. 118): it is briefer, and the verses are not the same. See *Folk-Lore Journal*, iii. 251; Cunningham, *Bharhut*, XLV. 5 (frontispiece to vol. i.).

district about Dakkhiṇāgiri. A layman invited the Buddha and his company, and made them sit down in his grounds till he gave them of rice and cakes. Then he said, "If any of the holy Fathers care to see over the grounds, they might go along with the gardener;" and he ordered the gardener to supply them with any fruit they might fancy.

By and bye they came upon a bare spot. "What is the reason," they asked, "that this spot is bare and treeless?" "The reason is," answered the gardener, "that a certain gardener's son, who had to water the saplings, thought he had better give them water in proportion to the length of the roots; so he pulled them all up to see, and watered them accordingly. The result was that the place became bare."

The Brethren returned, and told this to their Master. Said he, "Not now only has the lad destroyed a plantation; he did just the same before;" and then he told them an old-world tale.

Once upon a time, when a king named Vissasena was reigning over Benares, proclamation was made of a holiday. The park keeper thought he would go and keep holiday; so calling the monkeys that lived in the park, he said:

"This park is a great blessing to you. I want to take a week's holiday. Will you water the saplings on the seventh day?" "Oh, yes," said they; he gave them the watering-skins, and went his way.

The monkeys drew water, and began to water the roots.

The eldest monkey cried out: "Wait, now! It's hard to get water always. We must husband it. Let us pull up the plants, [346] and notice the length of their roots; if they have long roots, they need plenty of water; but short ones need but a little." "True, true," they agreed; then some of them pulled up the plants; then others put them in again, and watered them.

The Bodhisatta at the time was a young gentleman living in Benares. Something or other took him to this park, and he saw what the monkeys were doing.

"Who bids you do that?" asked he.

"Our chief," they replied.

"If that is the wisdom of the chief, what must the rest of you be like!" said he; and to explain the matter, he uttered the first stanza:

"Best of all the troop is this:
What intelligence is his!
If he was chosen as the best,
What sort of creatures are the rest!"

Hearing this remark, the monkeys rejoined with the second stanza:

"Brahmin, you know not what you say
Blaming us in such a way!
If the root we do not know,
How can we tell the trees that grow?"

To which the Bodhisatta replied by the third, as follows:

"Monkeys, I have no blame for you,
Nor those who range the woodland through.
The monarch is a fool, to say
'Please tend my trees while I'm away.'"

[347] When this discourse was ended, the Master identified the Birth: "The lad who destroyed the park was the monkey chief, and I was the wise man."

No. 269.

SUJĀTA-JĀTAKA.

"*Those who are dowered,*" *etc.*—This story the Master told while living in Jetavana about one Sujātā, a daughter-in-law of Anātha-piṇḍika, daughter of the great merchant Dhanañjaya, and youngest sister of Visākhā.

We are told that she entered the house of Anātha-piṇḍika full of haughtiness, thinking how great a family she had come from, and she was obstinate, violent, passionate, and cruel; refused to do her part towards her new father and mother, or her husband; and went about the house with harsh words and hard blows for everyone.

One day, the Master and five hundred brothers visited Anātha-piṇḍika's house, and took their seats. The great merchant sat beside the Blessed One, hearkening to his discourse. At the same time Sujātā happened to be scolding the servants.

The Master ceased speaking, and asked what that noise was. The merchant explained that it was his rude daughter-in-law; that she did not behave properly towards her husband or his parents, she gave no alms, and had no good points; faithless and unbelieving, she went about the house scolding day and night. The Master bade send for her.

The woman came, and after saluting the Master, she stood on one side. Then the Master addressed her thus:

"Sujātā, there are seven kinds of wife a man may have; of which sort are you?" She replied, "Sir, you speak too shortly for me to understand; please explain." "Well," said the Master, "listen attentively," and he uttered the following verses:

"One is bad-hearted, nor compassionates
The good; loves others, but her lord she hates.
Destroying all that her lord's wealth obtains[1],
This wife the title of Destroyer gains.

[1] It is not clear whether *vadhena kītassa* is 'the thing bought by his wealth,' or the 'person'; probably both.

"Whate'er the husband gets for her by trade,
Or skilled profession, or the farmer's spade,
[348] She tries to filch a little out of it.
For such a wife the title Thief is fit.

"Careless of duty, lazy, passionate,
Greedy, foul-mouthed, and full of wrath and hate,
Tyrannical to all her underlings—
All this the title High and Mighty brings.

"Who evermore compassionates the good,
Cares for her husband as a mother would,
Guards all the wealth her husband may obtain—
This wife the title Motherly will gain.

"She who respects her husband in the way
Young sisters reverence to elders pay,
Modest, obedient to her husband's will,
The Sisterly is this wife's title still.

"She whom her husband's sight will always please
As friend that friend after long absence sees,
High-bred and virtuous, giving up her life
To him—this one is called the Friendly wife.

"Calm when abused, afraid of violence,
No passion, full of dogged patience,
True-hearted, bending to her husband's will,
Slave is the title given to her still."

[349] "These, Sujātā, are the seven wives a man may have. Three of these, the Destructive wife, the Dishonest wife, and Madam High and Mighty are reborn in hell; the other four in the Fifth Heaven.

"They who are called Destroyer in this life,
The High and Mighty, or the Thievish wife,
Being angry, wicked, disrespectful, go
Out of the body into hell below.

"They who are called the Friendly in this life,
Motherly, Sisterly, or Slavish wife,
By virtue and their long self-mastery
Pass into heaven when their bodies die."

Whilst the Master was explaining these seven kinds of wives, Sujātā attained to the Fruit of the First Path; and when the Master asked to which class she belonged, she answered, "I am a slave, Sir!" and respectfully saluting the Buddha, gained pardon of him.

Thus by one admonition the Master tamed the shrew; and after the meal, when he had declared their duties amidst the Brotherhood, he entered his scented chamber.

Now the Brethren gathered together in the Hall of Truth, and sang the Master's praises. "Friend, by a single admonition the Master has tamed a shrew, and raised her to Fruition of the First Path!" The Master entered, and asked what they were talking of as they sat together. They told him. Said he, "Brethren, this is not the first time that I have tamed Sujātā by a single admonition." And he proceeded to tell an old-world tale.

Once upon a time, while Brahmadatta reigned over Benares, the Bodhisatta was born as the son of his Queen Consort. When he grew up he received his education at Takkasilā, and after the death of his father, became king and ruled in righteousness.

His mother was a passionate woman, cruel, harsh, shrewish, ill-tongued. The son wished to admonish his mother; but he felt he must not do anything so disrespectful; so he kept on the look-out for a chance of dropping a hint.

One day he went down into the grounds, and his mother went with him. [350] A blue jay screeched on the road. At this all the courtiers stopped their ears, crying—

"What a harsh voice, what a shriek!—don't make that noise!"

While the Bodhisatta was walking through the park with his mother, and a company of players, a cuckoo, perched amid the thick leaves of a sāl[1] tree, sang with a sweet note. All the bystanders were delighted at her voice; clasping their hands, and stretching them out, they besought her—"Oh, what a soft voice, what a kind voice, what a gentle voice!—sing away, birdie, sing away!" and there they stood, stretching their necks, eagerly listening.

The Bodhisatta, noting these two things, thought that here was a chance to drop a hint to the queen-mother. "Mother," said he, "when they heard the jay's cry on the road, every body stopped their ears, and called out—Don't make that noise! don't make that noise! and stopped up their ears: for harsh sounds are liked by no body." And he repeated the following stanzas:—

"Those who are dowered with a lovely hue,
Though ne'er so fair and beautiful to view,
Yet if they have a voice all harsh to hear
Neither in this world nor the next are dear.

"There is a bird that you may often see;
Ill-favoured, black, and speckled though it be,
Yet its soft voice is pleasant to the ear:
How many creatures hold the cuckoo dear!

"Therefore your voice should gentle be and sweet,
Wise-speaking, not puffed up with self-conceit.
And such a voice—how sweet the sound of it!—
Explains the meaning of the Holy Writ[2]."

When the Bodhisatta had thus admonished his mother with these three verses, he won her over to his way of thinking; and ever afterwards she followed a right course of living. And he having by one word made his mother a self-denying woman afterwards passed away to fare according to his deeds.

---

[1] *Shorea Robusta.*

[2] The last stanza comes from *Dhammapada*, v. 363, not quoted word for word, but adapted to the context.

[351] When the Master had ended this discourse, he thus identified the Birth: "Sujātā was the mother of the king of Benares, and I was the king himself."

No. 270.

ULŪKA-JĀTAKA.

"*The owl is King,*" *etc.*—This story the Master told while living at Jetavana, about a quarrel between Crows and Owls.

At the period in question, the Crows used to eat Owls during the day, and at night, the Owls flew about, nipping off the heads of the Crows as they slept, and thus killing them. There was a certain brother who lived in a cell on the outskirts of Jetavana. When the time came for sweeping, there used to be a quantity of crows' heads to throw away, which had dropt from the tree, enough to fill seven or eight pottles. He told this to the brethren. In the Hall of Truth the Brethren began to talk about it. "Friend, Brother So-and-so finds ever so many crows' heads to throw away every day in the place where he lives!" [352] The Master came in, and asked what they were talking about as they sat together. They told him. They went on to ask how long it was since the Crows and Owls fell a-quarrelling. The Master replied, "Since the time of the first age of the world;" and then he told them an old-world tale.

Once upon a time, the people who lived in the first cycle of the world gathered together, and took for their king a certain man, handsome, auspicious, commanding, altogether perfect. The quadrupeds also gathered, and chose for king the Lion; and the fish in the ocean chose them a fish called Ānanda. Then all the birds in the Himalayas assembled upon a flat rock, crying,

"Among men there is a king, and among the beasts, and the fish have one too; but amongst us birds king there is none. We should not live in anarchy; we too should choose a king. Fix on some one fit to be set in the king's place!"

They searched about for such a bird, and chose the Owl; "Here is the bird we like," said they. And a bird made proclamation three times to all that there would be a vote taken on this matter. After patiently hearing this announcement twice, on the third time up rose a Crow, and cried out,

"Stay now! If that is what he looks like when he is being consecrated king, what will he look like when he is angry? If he only looks at us in anger, we shall be scattered like sesame seeds thrown on a hot plate. I don't want to make this fellow king!" and enlarging upon this he uttered the first stanza:—[353]

"The owl is king, you say, o'er all bird-kind:
With your permission, may I speak my mind?"

The Birds repeated the second, granting him leave to speak:—

"You have our leave, Sir, so it be good and right:
For other birds are young, and wise, and bright."

Thus permitted, he repeated the third:—

"I like not (with all deference be it said)
To have the Owl anointed as our Head.
Look at his face! if this good humour be,
What will he do when he looks angrily?"

Then he flew up into the air, cawing out "I don't like it! I don't like it!" The Owl rose and pursued him. Thenceforward those two nursed enmity one towards another. And the birds chose a golden Goose for their king, and dispersed.

---

[354] When the Master had ended this discourse, he declared the Truths and identified the Birth:—"At that time, the wild Goose chosen for king was I myself."

No. 271.

UDAPĀNA-DŪSAKA-JĀTAKA.

"*This well a forest-anchorite,*" *etc.*—This story the Master told whilst dwelling at Isipatana, about a Jackal that fouled a well.

We learn that a Jackal used to foul a well where the Brethren used to draw water, and then used to make off. One day the novices pelted him with clods of earth, and made it uncomfortable for him. After that he never came to look at the place again.

The Brethren heard of this and began to discuss it in the Hall of Truth. "Friend, the jackal that used to foul our well has never come near it since the novices chased him away with clods!" The Master came in, and asked what they were talking about now as they sat together. They told him. Then he replied, "Brethren, this is not the first time that this jackal fouled a well. He did the same before;" and then he told an old-world tale.

Once on a time, in this place near Benares called Isipatana was that very well. At that time the Bodhisatta was born of a good family. When he grew up he embraced the religious life, and with a body of followers dwelt at Isipatana. A certain Jackal fouled the well as has been described, and took to his heels. One day, the ascetics surrounded him, and having caught him somehow, they led him before the Bodhisatta. He addressed the Jackal in the lines of the first stanza:—

"This well a forest-anchorite has made
Who long has lived a hermit in the glade.
And after all his trouble and his toil
Why did you try, my friend, the well to spoil?"

[355] On hearing this, the Jackal repeated the second stanza:—

"This is the law of all the Jackal race,
To foul when they have drunk in any place:
My sires and grandsires always did the same;
So there is no just reason for your blame."

Then the Bodhisatta replied with the third:—

"If this is 'law' in jackal polity
I wonder what their 'lawlessness' can be!
I hope that I have seen the last of you,
Your actions, lawful and unlawful too."

Thus the Great Being admonished him, and said, "Do not go there again." Thenceforward he did not even pause to look at it.

When the Master had ended this discourse he declared the Truths and identified the Birth:—"The Jackal that fouled the well is the same in both cases; and I was the chief of the ascetic band."

No. 272.

VYAGGHA-JĀTAKA.

"*What time the nearness,*" *etc.*—[356] This story the Master told whilst living at Jetavana, about Kokālika[1]. The circumstances of this story will be given in the Thirteenth Book, and the Takkāriya-jātaka[2]. Here again Kokālika said, "I will take Sāriputta and Moggallāna with me." So having left Kokālika's country, he travelled to Jetavana, greeted the Master, and went on to the

[1] Kokālika was a follower of Devadatta.

[2] No. 481.

Elders. He said, "Friends, the citizens of Kokālika's country summon you. Let us go thither!" "Go yourself, friend, we won't," was the answer. After this refusal he went away by himself.

The Brethren got talking about this in the Hall of Truth. "Friend! Kokālika can't live either with Sāriputta and Moggallāna, or without them! He can't put up with their room or their company!" The Master came in, and enquired what they were all talking about together. They told him. He said, "In olden days, just as now, Kokālika couldn't live with Sāriputta and Moggallāna, or without them." And he told a story.

Once upon a time, when Brahmadatta was king of Benares, the Bodhisatta was a tree-spirit living in a wood. Not far from his abode lived another tree-spirit, in a great monarch of the forest. In the same forest dwelt a lion and a tiger. For fear of them no one durst till the earth, or cut down a tree, no one could even pause to look at it. And the lion and tiger used to kill and eat all manner of creatures; and what remained after eating, they left on the spot and departed, so that the forest was full of foul decaying stench.

The other spirit, being foolish and knowing neither reason nor unreason, one day bespoke thus the Bodhisatta:

"Good friend, the forest is full of foul stench all because of this lion and this tiger. I will drive them away."

Said he, "Good friend, it is just these two creatures [357] that protect our homes. Once they are driven off, our homes will be made desolate. If men see not the lion and the tiger tracks, they will cut all the forest down, make it all one open space, and till the land. Please do not do this thing!" and then he uttered the first two stanzas:

"What time the nearness of a bosom friend
Threatens your peace to end,
If you are wise, guard your supremacy
Like the apple of your eye.

"But when your bosom friend does more increase
The measure of your peace,
Let your friend's life in everything right through
Be dear as yours to you."

When the Bodhisatta had thus explained the matter, the foolish sprite notwithstanding did not lay it to heart, but one day assumed an awful shape, and drove away the lion and tiger. The people, no longer seeing the footmarks of these, divined that the lion and tiger must have gone to another wood, and cut down one side of this wood. Then the sprite came up to the Bodhisatta [358] and said to him,

"Ah, friend, I did not do as you said, but drove the creatures away; and now men have found out that they are gone, and they are cutting down the wood! What is to be done?" The reply was, that they were gone to live in such and such a wood; the sprite must go and fetch them back. This the sprite did; and, standing in front of them, repeated the third stanza, with a respectful salute:

"Come back, O Tigers! to the wood again,
And let it not be levelled with the plain;
For, without you, the axe will lay it low;
You, without it, for ever homeless go."

This request they refused, saying, "Go away! we will not come." The sprite returned to the forest alone. And the men after a very few days cut down all the wood, made fields, and brought them under cultivation.

When the Master had ended this discourse, he declared the Truths and identified the Birth:—"Kokālika was then the foolish Sprite, Sāriputta the Lion, Moggallāna the Tiger, and the wise Sprite was I myself."

No. 273.

KACCHAPA-JĀTAKA.

[359] "*Quis paterum extendens,*" *etc.*—This story the Master told during a stay in Jetavana, how a quarrel was made up between two magnates of the king's court in Kosala[1]. The circumstances have been told in the Second Book.

Brahmadatta quondam Benari regnante, Bodisatta sacerdotali genere regno Kasensi natus, postquam ad puberem aetatem pervenit, in urbe Takkasila studiis se dedit, et mox, cum lubidines tandem compressisset, solitarius homo in agro Himavanto prope ripam Gangae frondibus ramisque arborum mapale contexit ubi habitaret, Facultates Potentiasque magicas foveret, gaudium perpetuae cogitationis perciperet. Tum quidem hoc modo nato ita mens erat placida placataque ut ad summam patientiam unus pervenerit.

[1] Compare Nos. 154, 165.

Quem in limine casae sedentem visitabat Simius quidam impudentissimus pessimusque, inque aurem eius semen emittere solebat, neque tamen eum commovere poterat, sed sedebat porro summa animi tranquillitate Bodisatta. Accidit quondam ut ex aqua Testudo egressa somnum ore aperto captaret, in sole apricans. Quam cum vidisset Simius ille impudens, nec mora, pene in os inserto incepit futuere. Continuo Testudo experrecta os velut cistellam conclusit dentibusque comprendit id quod insertum erat. Simius cum nequiret nimium dolorem mulcere 'quo eam,' inquit, 'cui persuadeam ut hoc dolore me liberet?' Fore ut liberaretur ratus si ad Bodisattam pervenisset, Testudine ambabus manibus sublata ad Bodisattam pergit: qui ludos fecit Simium versibus his: [360]

"quis pateram extendens[1] nostram mendicat ad aulam?
unde venis? precibus quae, precor, esca datast?"

Quibus auditis Simius respondit:

"quod tetigisse nefas, tetigi: sum simius amens:
eripe me! ereptus mox nemora alta petam."

Continuo pergit Bodisatta, Simium allocutus:

"Cassapa testudo genus est: Condannus at ille:
Cassapa Condannum mitte fututa precor[2]."

[361] His verbis valde delectata Testudo Simium omisit: qui Bodisattae dicta salute, se in fugam dedit, neque umquam postea eum locum ne oculis quidem usurpavit. Testudo quoque cum salutem dixisset abiit, at Bodisatta, defixo in contemplatione perpetua animo, tandem in eum locum, cuius dominus Brahma deus, pervenit.

When this discourse was ended, the Master declared the Truths and identified the Birth: "The two magnates were the Monkey and Tortoise, and I was the hermit."

[1] The tortoise looked like a begging bowl.

[2] A curious verse, as bearing on the laws of marriage. *Kassapa* means 'belonging to the Tortoise clan' (for which see e.g. Muir, *Sanskrit Texts*, i. 438). The scholiast's note is: "The Tortoises are of the Kassapa clan, monkeys of the Koṇḍañña" = Skr. *Kauṇḍinya*, "between which two clans there is intermarriage (*āvāhavivāhasambandho*); now that it is consummated, let go."

No. 274.

LOLA-JĀTAKA[1].

"*Who is this tufted crane*," etc.—This story the Master told in Jetavana about a greedy Brother. He too was brought to the Audience Hall, when the Master said—"It is not only now that he is greedy; greedy he was before, and his greed lost him his life; and by his means wise men of old were driven out of house and home." Then he told a story.

Once upon a time, when Brahmadatta was king of Benares, a rich merchant's cook of that town hung up a nest-basket in the kitchen to win merit by it. The Bodhisatta at that time was a Pigeon; and he came and lived in it.

Now a greedy Crow as he flew over the kitchen was attracted by the fish which lay about in great variety. He fell a-hungering after it. "How in the world can I get some?" [362] thought he. Then his eye fell upon the Bodhisatta. "I have it!" thinks he, "I'll make this creature my cat's-paw." And this is how he carried out his resolve.

When the Pigeon went out to seek his day's food, behind him, following, following, came the Crow.

"What do you want with me, Mr Crow?" says the Pigeon. "You and I don't feed alike."

"Ah, but I like you," says the Crow. "Let me be your humble servant, and feed with you."

The Pigeon agreed. But when they went feeding together, the Crow only pretended to eat with him; ever and anon he would turn back, peck to bits some lump of cow-dung, and get a worm or two. When he had had his bellyful, up he flies—"Hullo, Mr Pigeon! what a time you take over your meal! You never know where to draw the line. Come, let's be going back before it is too late." And so they did. When they got back together, the Cook, seeing that their Pigeon had brought a friend, hung up another basket.

In this way things went on for four or five days. Then a great purchase of fish came to the rich man's kitchen. How the Crow longed

[1] The same story occurs in vol. i. p. 112 (no. 42). It has been also translated and slightly shortened by the writer, in Jacobs' *Indian Fairy Tales*, page 222. The two birds and the nest-basket seem to be figured on the Bharhut Stupa (Cunningham, pl. XLV. 7).

for some! There he lay, from early morn, groaning and making a great noise. In the morning, says the Pigeon to the Crow:

"Come along, old fellow,—breakfast!"

"You can go," says he, "I have such a fit of indigestion!"

"A Crow with indigestion? Nonsense!" says the Pigeon. "Even a lamp-wick hardly stays any time in your stomach; and anything else you digest in a trice, as soon as you eat it. Now you do what I tell you. [363] Don't behave in this way just for seeing a little fish!"

"Why, Sir, what are you saying? I tell you I have a bad pain inside!"

"All right, all right," says the Pigeon; "only do take care." And away he flew.

The Cook got all the dishes ready, and then stood at the kitchen door, mopping the sweat off him. "Now's my time!" thinks Mr Crow, and alights on a dish with some dainty food in it. Click! The cook heard the noise, and looked round. Ah! in a twinkling he caught the Crow, and plucked off all his feathers, except one tuft on the top of his head; then he powdered ginger and cinnamon, and mixt it up with buttermilk, and rubbed it in well all over the bird's body. "That's for spoiling my master's dinner, and making me throw it away!" said he, and threw him into his basket. Oh, how it hurt!

By and by, in came the Pigeon from his hunt. The first thing he saw was our Crow, making a great to-do. What fun he did make of him, to be sure! He dropt into poetry, as follows:—

"Who is this tufted crane[1] I see
Where she has no right to be?
Come out! my friend the Crow is near,
Who will do you harm, I fear!"

[364] To this the Crow answered with another verse:—

"No tufted crane am I—no, no!
Nothing but a greedy Crow.
I would not do as I was told
So I'm plucked, as you behold."

And the Pigeon rejoined with a third:—

"You'll come to grief again, I know--
It is your nature to do so.
If people make a dish of meat,
'Tis not for little birds to eat."

[1] The epithet "whose grandfather is the cloud (*lit.* swift one)" is added. I hope the reader will pardon its omission; it is unmanageable. The scholiast explains it by the curious superstition:—Cranes are conceived at the sound of thunder. Hence thunder is called their father, and the thundercloud their grandfather.

Then the Pigeon flew away, saying—"I can't live with this creature." And the Crow lay there groaning until he died.

When the Master had ended this discourse, he declared the Truths and identified the Birth:—at the conclusion of the Truths the greedy Brother reached the Fruit of the Third Path:—"The greedy Brother in those days was the greedy Crow; and I was the Pigeon."

No. 275.

[365] "*Who is this pretty Crane,*" *etc.*—This story the Master told at Jetavana about some greedy Brother. The two stories are just the same as the last. And these are the verses:—

"Who is this pretty Crane, and why
Does he in my Crow's basket lie?
An angry bird, my friend the Crow!
This is his nest, I'd have you know!"

"Do you not know me, friend, indeed?
Together we were used to feed!
I would not do as I was told,
So now I'm plucked, as you behold."

"You'll come to grief again, I know—
It is your nature to do so.
When people make a dish of meat
'Tis not for little birds to eat."

As before, the Bodhisatta said—"I can't live here any more," and flew away some whither.

When this discourse was ended, the Master declared the Truths and identified the Birth:—at the conclusion of the Truths, the greedy Brother attained the Fruit of the Third Path:—"The greedy Brother was the Crow, and I was the Pigeon."

No. 276.

KURUDHAMMA-JĀTAKA[1].

"*Knowing thy faith*," *etc.*—This story the Master told whilst dwelling in Jetavana, about a Brother that killed a wild goose. [366] Two Brothers, great friends, who came from Sāvatthi, and had embraced the religious life, after taking the higher orders used generally to go about together. One day they came to Aciravatī. After a bath, they stood on the sand, basking in the sunlight and talking pleasantly together. At this moment two wild geese flew over their heads. One of the young fellows picked up a stone. "I'm going to hit that goose bird in the eye!" says he. "You can't," says the other. "That I can," says the first, "and not only that—I can hit either this eye or that eye, as I please." "Not you!" says the other. "Look here, then!" says the first; and picking up a three-cornered stone, threw it after the bird. The bird turned its head on hearing the pebble whizz through the air. Then the other, seizing a round pebble, threw it so that it hit the near eye and came out of the other. The goose with a loud cry turned over and over and fell at their very feet.

The Brothers who were standing about saw what had occurred, and ran up, reproaching him. "What a shame," said they, "that you, who have embraced such a doctrine as ours, should take the life of a living creature!" They made him go before the Tathāgata with them. "Is what they say true?" asked the Master. "Have you really taken the life of a living creature?" "Yes, Sir," replied the Brother. "Brother," said he, "how is it that you have done this thing, after embracing so great salvation? Wise men of old, before the Buddha appeared, though they lived in the world, and the worldly life is impure, felt remorse about mere trifles; but you, who have embraced this great doctrine, have no scruples. A Brother ought to hold himself in control in deed, word, and thought." Then he told a story.

Once upon a time, when Dhanañjaya was king of Indapatta City, in the Kuru kingdom, the Bodhisatta was born as a son of his Queen Consort. By and bye he grew up, and was educated at Takkasilā. His father made him Viceroy, [367] and afterwards on his father's death he became king, and grew in the Kuru righteousness, keeping the ten royal duties. The Kuru righteousness means the Five Virtues; these the Bodhisatta observed, and kept pure; as did the Bodhisatta, even so did queen-mother, queen-consort, younger brother, viceroy, family priest, brahmin, driver, courtier, charioteer, treasurer, master of the granaries, noble, porter, courtesan, slave-girl—all did the same.

> King, mother, consort, viceroy, chaplain too,
> Driver and charioteer and treasurer,
> And he that governed the king's granaries,
> Porter, and courtesan, eleven in all,
> Observed the rules of Kuru righteousness.

[1] Cf. *Cariyā-Piṭaka*, I. 3; *Dhammapada*, p. 416.—In this story the king appears as a rain-maker, and on certain occasions dresses like the gods.

Thus all these did observe the Five Virtues, and kept them untarnished. The king built six Almonries,—one at each of the four city gates, one in the midst of the city, and one at his own door; daily he distributed 600,000 pieces of money in alms, by which he stirred up the whole of India. All India was overspread by his love and delight in charity.

At this period there was in the city of Dantapura, in the kingdom of Kāliṅga, a king named King Kāliṅga. In his realms the rain fell not, and because of the drought there was a famine in the land. The people thought that lack of food might produce a pestilence; and there was fear of drought, and fear of famine—these three fears were ever present before them. The people wandered about destitute hither and thither, leading their children by the hand. All the people in the kingdom gathered together, and came to Dantapura; and there at the king's door they made outcry.

As the king stood, by the window, he heard the noise, and asked why the people were making all that noise. [368]

"Oh, Sire," was the reply, "three fears have seized upon all your kingdom: there falls no rain, the crops fail, there is a famine. The people, starving, diseased, and destitute, are wandering about with their little ones by the hand. Make rain for us, O king!"

Said the king, "What used former monarchs to do, if it would not rain?"

"Former monarchs, O king, if it would not rain, used to give alms, to keep the holy day, to make vows of virtue, and to lie down seven days in their chamber on a grass pallet: then the rain would fall."

"Very good," the king said; and even so did he. Still even so there came no rain. The king said to his court,

"As you bade me, so I have done; but there is no rain. What am I to do?"

"O king, in the city of Indapatta, there is a state elephant, named Añjana-vasabho, the Black Bull. It belongs to Dhanañjaya, the Kuru king. This let us fetch; then the rain will come."

"But how can we do that? The king and his army are not easy to overcome."

"O king, there is no need to fight him. The king is fond of giving, he loves giving: were he but asked, he would even cut off his head in all its magnificence, or tear out his gracious eyes, or give up his very kingdom. There will be no need even to plead for the elephant. He will give it without fail."

"But who is able to ask him?" said the king.

"The Brahmins, great king!"

The king summoned eight Brahmins from a Brahmin village, and with all honour and respect sent them to ask for the elephant. They took money for their journey, and donned travelling garb, and without resting past one night in a place, travelled quickly until after a few days they took their meal at the almshall in the city gate. When they had satisfied their bodily wants, they asked, "When does the king come to the Almonry?"

The answer was, [369] "On three days in the fortnight—fourteenth, fifteenth, and eighth; but to-morrow is the full moon, so he will come to-morrow also."

So early the next morning, the brahmins went, and entered by the eastern gate. The Bodhisatta also, washed and anointed, all adorned and rarely arrayed, mounted upon a fine elephant richly caparisoned, came with a great company to the Almshall at the eastern gate. There he dismounted, and gave food to seven or eight people with his own hand. "In this manner give," said he, and mounting his elephant departed to the south gate. At the eastern gate the brahmins had had no chance, owing to the force of the royal guard; so they proceeded to the south, and watched when the king should come. When the king reached a rising ground not far from the gate, they raised their hands, and hailed the king victorious. The king guided his animal with the sharp goad to the place where they were. "Well, Brahmins, what is your wish?" asked he. Then the brahmins declared the virtues of the Bodhisatta in the first stanza:—

"Knowing thy faith and virtue, Lord, we come;
For this beast's sake our wealth we spent at home[1].

[370] To this the Bodhisatta made answer, "Brahmins, if all your wealth has been exhausted in getting this elephant, never mind—I give him to you with all his splendour." Thus comforting them, he repeated these two verses:—

"Whether or no ye serve for livery,
Whatever creature shall come here to me,
As my preceptors taught me long ago,
All that come here shall always welcome be.

"This elephant to you for gift I bring:
'Tis a king's portion, worthy of a king!
Take him, with all his trappings, golden chain,
Driver and all, and go your ways again."

[371] Thus spake the great Being, mounted upon his elephant's back; then, dismounting, he said to them—"If there is a spot on him unadorned, I will adorn it and then give him to you." Thrice he went about the creature, turning towards the right, and examined him; but he found no spot on him without adornment. Then he put the trunk into the brahmins'

[1] i.e. we spent all we had on food, trusting that you would give us the elephant when we asked for it.

hands; he besprinkled him with scented water from a fine golden vase, and made him over to them. The brahmins accepted the elephant with his belongings, and seating themselves upon his back rode to Dantapura, and handed him over to their king. But although the elephant was come, no rain fell yet.

Then the king asked again—"What can be the reason?"

They said, "Dhanañjaya, the Kuru King, observes the Kuru righteousness; therefore in his realms it rains every ten or fifteen days. That is the power of the king's goodness. If in this animal there is any good, how little it must be!" Then said the king, "Take this elephant, caparisoned as he is, with all his belongings, and give it back to the king. Write upon a golden plate the Kuru righteousness which he observes, and bring it hither." With these words he despatched the brahmins and courtiers.

These came before the king, and restored his elephant, saying, "My lord, even when your elephant came, [372] no rain fell in our country. They say that you observe the Kuru righteousness. Our king is wishful himself to observe it; and he has sent us, bidding us write it upon a golden plate, and bring it to him. Tell us this righteousness!"

"Friends," says the king, "indeed I did once observe this righteousness; but now I am in doubt about this very point. This righteousness does not bless my heart now: therefore I cannot give it you."

Why, you may ask, did not virtue bless the king any longer? Well, every third year, in the month of Kattika[1] the kings used to hold a festival, called the Kattika Feast. While keeping this feast, the kings used to deck themselves out in great magnificence, and dress up like gods; they stood in the presence of a goblin named Cittarāja, the King of Many Colours, and they would shoot to the four points of the compass arrows wreathed in flowers, and painted in divers colours. This king then, in keeping the feast, stood on the bank of a lake, in the presence of Cittarāja, and shot arrows to the four quarters. They could see whither three of the arrows went; but the fourth, which was shot over the water, this they saw not. Thought the king, "Perchance the arrow which I have shot has fallen upon some fish!" As this doubt arose, the sin of life-taking made a flaw in his virtue; that is why his virtue did not bless him as before. This the king told them; and added, "Friends, I am in doubt about myself, whether or no I do observe the Kuru righteousness; but my mother keeps it well. You can get it from her."

"But, O king," said they, "you had no intent to take life. Without the intent of the heart there is no taking of life. Give us the Kuru righteousness which you have kept!"

[1] October—November.

"Write, then," said he. And he caused them to write upon the plate of gold: "Slay not the living; take not what is not given; [373] walk not evilly in lust; speak no lies; drink no strong drink." Then he added,

"Still, it does not bless me; you had better learn it from my mother."

The messengers saluted the king, and visited the Queen-mother. "Lady," said they, "they say you keep the Kuru righteousness: pass it on to us!"

Said the Queen-mother, "My sons, indeed I did once keep this righteousness, but now I have my doubts. This righteousness does not make me happy, so I cannot give it to you." Now we are told that she had two sons, the elder being king and the younger viceroy. A certain king sent to the Bodhisatta perfumes of fine sandal wood worth an hundred thousand pieces, and a golden neckband worth an hundred thousand. And he, thinking to do his mother honour, sent the whole to her. Thought she: "I do not perfume myself with sandal-wood, I do not wear necklets. I will give them to my sons' wives." Then the thought occurred to her—"My elder son's wife is my lady; she is the chief queen: to her will I give the gold necklet; but the wife of the younger is a poor creature,—to her I will give the sandal perfume." And so to the one she gave the necklet, and the perfume gave she to the other. Afterward she bethought her, "I keep the Kuru righteousness; whether they be poor or whether they be not poor is no matter. It is not seemly that I should pay court to the elder. Perchance by not doing this I have made a flaw in my virtue!" And she began to doubt; that is why she spoke as she did.

The messengers said, "When it is in your hands, a thing is given even as you will. If you have scruples about a thing so small as that, what other sin would you ever do? Virtue is not broken by a thing of that kind. [374] Give us the Kuru righteousness!" And from her also they received it, and wrote it upon the golden plate.

"All the same, my sons," said the Queen-mother, "I am not happy in this righteousness. But my daughter-in-law observes it well. Ask her for it."

So they took their leave respectfully, and asked the daughter in the same way as before. And, as before, she replied, "I cannot, for I keep it myself no longer!"—Now one day as she sat at the lattice, looking down she saw the king making a solemn procession about the city; and behind him on the elephant's back sat the viceroy. She fell in love with him, and thought, "What if I were to strike up a friendship with him, and his brother were to die, and then he were to become king, and take me to wife!" Then it flashed across her mind—"I who keep the Kuru righteousness, who am married to a husband, I have looked with love upon another man! Here is a flaw in my virtue!" Remorse seized upon her. This she told the messengers.

Then they said, "Sin is not the mere uprising of a thought. If you feel remorse for so small a thing as this, what transgression could you ever commit? Not by such a small matter is virtue broken; give us this righteousness!" And she likewise told it to them, and they wrote it upon a golden plate. But she said, "However, my sons, my virtue is not perfect. But the viceroy observes these rules well; go ye and receive them from him."

Then again they repaired to the viceroy, and as before asked him for the Kuru righteousness.—Now the viceroy used to go and pay his devoirs to the king at evening; and when they came to the palace courtyard, in his car, if he wished to eat with the king, and spend the night there, he would throw his reins and goad upon the yoke; and that was a sign for the people to depart; and next morning early they would come again, and stand awaiting the viceroy's departure. And the charioteer [375] would attend the car, and come again with it early in the morning, and wait by the king's door. But if the viceroy would depart at the same time, he left the reins and goad there in the chariot, and went in to wait upon the king. Then the people, taking it for a sign that he would presently depart, stood waiting there at the palace door. One day he did thus, and went in to wait upon the king. But as he was within, it began to rain; and the king, remarking this, would not let him go away, so he took his meal, and slept there. But a great crowd of people stood expecting him to come out, and there they stayed all night in the wet. Next day the viceroy came out, and seeing the crowd standing there drenched, thought he—"I, who keep the Kuru righteousness, have put all this crowd to discomfort! Surely here is a flaw in my virtue!" and he was seized with remorse. So he said to the messengers: "Now doubt has come upon me if indeed I do keep this righteousness; therefore I cannot give it to you;" and he told them the matter.

"But," said they, "you never had the wish to plague those people. What is not intended is not counted to one's score. If you feel remorse for so small a thing, in what would you ever transgress?" So they received from him too the knowledge of this righteousness, and wrote it on their golden plate. "However," said he, "this righteousness is not perfected in me. But my chaplain keeps it well; go, ask him for it." Then again they went on to the chaplain.

Now the chaplain one day had been going to wait upon the king. On the road he saw a chariot, sent to the king by another king, coloured like the young sun. "Whose chariot?" he asked. "Sent for the king," they said. Then he thought, "I am an old man; if the king were to give me that chariot, how nice it would be to ride about in it!" When he came before the king, and stood by after greeting him with the prayer for prosperity, [376] they showed the chariot to the king. "That is a most beautiful car," said the king; "give it to my teacher." But the chaplain did not like taking it; no, not though he was begged again and again. Why was this? Because the thought came into his mind—"I, who practise the Kuru righteousness, have coveted another's goods. Surely this is a flaw in my virtue!" So he told the story to these messengers, adding, "My sons, I am in doubt about the Kuru righteousness; this righteousness does not bless me now; therefore I cannot teach it to you."

But the messengers said, "Not by mere uprising of covetise is virtue broken. If you feel a scruple in so small a matter, what real transgression would you ever do?" And from him also they received the righteousness, and wrote it on their golden plate. "Still, this goodness does not bless me now," said he; "but the royal driver[1] carefully practises it. Go and ask him." So they found the royal driver, and asked him.

Now the driver one day was measuring a field. Tying a cord to a stick, he gave one end to the owner of the field to hold, and took the other himself. The stick tied to the end of the cord which he held came to a crab's lurk-hole. Thought he, "If I put the stick in the hole, the crab in the hole will be hurt: if I put it on the other side, the king's property will lose; and if I put it on this side, the farmer will lose. What's to be done?" Then he thought again—"The crab ought to be in his hole; but if he were, he would show himself;" so he put the stick in the hole. The crab made a click! inside. Then he thought, "The stick must have struck upon the crab, and it must have killed him! I observe the Kuru righteousness, and now here's a flaw in it!" [377] So he told them this, and added, "So now I have my doubts about it, and I cannot give it to you."

Said the messengers, "You had no wish to kill the crab. What is done without intent is not counted to the score; if you feel a scruple about so small a matter, what real transgression would you ever do?" And they took the righteousness from his lips likewise, and wrote it on their golden plate. "However," said he, "though this does not bless me, the charioteer practises it carefully; go and ask him."

So they took their leave, and sought out the charioteer. Now the charioteer one day drove the king into his park in the car. There the king took his pleasure during the day, and at evening returned, and entered the chariot. But before he could get back to the city, at the time of sunset a storm cloud arose. The charioteer, fearing the king might get wet, touched up the team with the goad: the steeds sped swiftly home.

[1] Some difference there must be between *rajjugāhakaamacco* and *sāratthi* (the same words occur in *Dhp.* p. 416). I would suggest that the former is the more important, and may answer to the Greek *παραιβάτης*, Skr. *savyēṣṭhar*.

Ever since, going to the park or coming from it, from that spot they went at speed. Why was this? Because they thought there must be some danger at this spot, and that was why the charioteer had touched them with the goad. And the charioteer thought, "If the king is wet or dry, 'tis no fault of mine; but I have given a touch of the goad out of season to these well-trained steeds, and so they run at speed again and again till they are tired, all by my doing. And I observe the Kuru righteousness! Surely there's a flaw in it now!" This he told the messengers, and said, "For this cause I am in doubt about it, and I cannot give it to you." "But," said they, "you did not mean to tire the horses, and what is done without meaning is not set down to the score. If you feel a scruple about so small a matter, what real transgression could you ever commit?" And they learnt the righteousness from him also, [378] and wrote it down upon their golden plate. But the charioteer sent them in search of a certain wealthy man, saying, "Even though this righteousness does not bless me, he keeps it carefully."

So to this rich man they came, and asked him. Now he one day had gone to his paddy field, and seeing a head of rice bursting the husk, went about to tie it up with a wisp of rice; and taking a handful of it, he tied the head to a post. Then it occurred to him—"From this field I have yet to give the king his due, and I have taken a handful of rice from an untithed field! I, who observe the rules of Kuru righteousness! Surely I must have broken them!" And this matter he told to the messengers, saying, "Now I am in doubt about this righteousness, and so I cannot give it to you."

"But," said they, "you had no thought of thieving; without this one cannot be proclaimed[1] guilty of theft. If you feel scruples in such a small matter, when will you ever take what belongs to another man?" And from him too they received the righteousness, and wrote it down on their golden plate. He added, "Still, though I am not happy in this matter, the Master of the Royal Granaries keeps these rules well. Go, ask him for them." So they betook them to the Master of the Granaries.

Now this man, as he sat one day at the door of the granary, causing the rice of the king's tax to be measured, took a grain from the heap which was not yet measured, and put it down for a marker. At that moment rain began to fall. The official counted up the markers, so many, and then swept them all together and dropt them upon the heap which had been measured. Then he ran in quickly and sat in the gate-house. "Did I throw the markers on the measured heap or the unmeasured?" he wondered; and the thought came into his mind—[379] "If I threw them on what was already measured, the king's property has been increased,

[1] I.e. in the *saṅgha* (*ñatti* is a 'resolution').

and the owners have lost; I keep the Kuru righteousness; and now here's a flaw!" So he told this to the messengers, adding that therefore he had his doubts about it, and could not give it to them. But the messengers said, "You had no thought of theft, and without this no one can be declared guilty of dishonesty. If you feel scruples in a small matter like this, when would you ever steal any thing belonging to another?" And from him too they received the righteousness, and wrote it on their golden plate. "But," added he, "although this virtue is not perfect in me, there is the gatekeeper, who observes it well: go and get it from him." So they went off and asked the gatekeeper.

Now it so happened that one day, at the time for closing the city gate, he cried aloud three times. And a certain poor man, who had gone into the woodland a-gathering sticks and leaves with his youngest sister, hearing the sound came running up with her. Says the door keeper—"What! don't you know that the king is in the city? Don't you know that the gate of this town is shut betimes? Is that why you go out into the woods, making love?" Said the other, "No, master, it is not my wife, but my sister." Then the porter thought, "How unseemly to address a sister as a wife! And I keep the rules of the Kurus; surely I must have broken them now!" This he told the messengers, adding, "In this way I have my doubts whether I really keep the Kuru righteousness, and so I cannot give it to you." But they said, "You said it because you thought so; [380] this does not break your virtue. If you feel remorse on so slight a cause, how could you ever tell a lie with intent?" And so they took down those virtues from him too, and wrote them on their golden plate.

Then he said, "But though this virtue does not bless me, there is a courtesan who keeps it well; go and ask her." And so they did. She refused as the others had done, for the following reason. Sakka, king of the gods, designed to try her goodness; so putting on the shape of a youth, he gave her a thousand pieces, saying, "I will come by and bye." Then he returned to heaven, and did not visit her for three years. And she, for honour's sake, for three years took not so much as a piece of betel from another man. By degrees she got poor; and then she thought—"The man who gave me a thousand pieces has not come these three years; and now I have grown poor. I cannot keep body and soul together. Now I must go tell the Chief Justices, and get my wage as before." So to the court she came, and said, "There was a man three years ago gave me a thousand pieces, and never came back; whether he be dead I know not. I cannot keep body and soul together; what am I to do, my lord?" Said he, "If he does not come for three years, what can you do? Earn your wage as before." As soon as she left the court, after this award, there came a man who offered her a thousand. As she held out her hands to take it, Sakka showed himself. Said she, "Here is the man who gave me a thousand pieces three years ago: I must not take your money;" and she drew back her hand. Then Sakka caused his own proper shape to be seen, and hovered in the air, shining like the sun fresh risen, and gathered all the city together. Sakka, in the midst of the crowd, [381] said, "To test her goodness I gave her a thousand pieces three years ago. Be like her, and like her keep your honour;" and with this monition, he filled her dwelling with jewels of seven kinds, and saying, "Henceforth be vigilant," he comforted her, and went away to heaven. So for this cause she refused, saying, "Because before I had earned one wage I held out my hand for another, therefore my virtue is not perfect, and so I cannot give it to you." To this the messengers replied, "Merely to hold out the hand is not a breach of virtue: that virtue of yours is the highest perfection!" And from her, as from the rest, they received the rules of virtue, and wrote them on their golden plate. They took it with them to Dantapura, and told the king how they had fared.

Then their king practised the Kuru precepts, and fulfilled the Five Virtues. And then in all the realm of Kāliṅga the rain fell; the three fears were allayed; the land became prosperous and fertile. The Bodhisatta all his life long gave alms and did good, and then with his subjects went to fill the heavens.

When the Teacher had ended this discourse, he declared the Truths, and explained the Birth-tale. At the conclusion of the Truths, some entered the First Path, some the Second, some entered the Third, and some became saints. And the Birth-tale is thus explained:

"Uppalavaṇṇā was the courtesan,
Puṇṇa the porter, and the driver was
Kuccāna; Kolita, the measurer;
The rich man, Sāriputta; he who drove
The chariot, Anuruddha; and the priest
Was Kassapa the Elder; he that was
The Viceroy, now is Nandapaṇḍita;
Rāhula's mother was the queen-consort,
The Queen-mother was Māyā; and the King
Was Bodhisatta.—Thus the Birth is clear."

No. 277.

ROMAKA-JĀTAKA.

[382] "*Here in the hills*," *etc.*—This story was told by the Master when at the Bamboo-grove, about attempted murder. The circumstances explain themselves.

Once on a time, when Brahmadatta was king of Benares, the Bodhisatta became a Pigeon, and with a large flock of pigeons he lived amidst the woodland in a cave of the hills. There was an ascetic, a virtuous man, who had built him a hut near a frontier village not far from the place where the pigeons were, and there in a cave of the hills he lived. Him the Bodhisatta visited from time to time, and heard from him things worth hearing.

After living there a long time, the ascetic went away; and there came a sham ascetic, and lived there. The Bodhisatta, attended by his flock of pigeons, visited him and greeted him respectfully; they spent the day in hopping about the hermit's abode, and picking up food before the cave, and returned home in the evening. There the sham ascetic lived for more than fifty years.

One day the villagers gave him some pigeon's flesh which they had cooked. He was taken with the flavour, and asked what it was. "Pigeon," said they. Thought he, "There come flocks of pigeons to my hermitage; I must kill some of them to eat."

So he got rice and ghee, milk and cummin and pepper, and put it by all ready; in a corner of his robe he hid a staff, and sat down at the hut door watching for the pigeons' coming.

The Bodhisatta came, with his flock, and spied out what wicked thing this sham ascetic would be at. "Yon wicked ascetic sitting there goes under false pretences! Perhaps he has been feeding on some of our kind; I'll find him out!"

So he alighted to leeward, and scented him. [383] "Yes," said he, "the man wants to kill us and eat us; we must not go near him;" and away he flew with his flock. On seeing that he kept aloof, the hermit thought, "I will speak words of honey to him, and make friends, and then kill and eat him!" and he uttered the two first stanzas:

"Here in the hills, for one and fifty years,
O feathered fowl! the birds would visit me,
Nothing suspecting, knowing nought of fears,
In sweet security!

"These very children of the eggs now seem
To fly suspicious to another hill.
Have they forgotten all their old esteem?
Are they the same birds still?"

[384] Then the Bodhisatta stept back and repeated the third:

"We are no fools, and we know you;
We are the same, and you are too:
You have designs against our weal,
So, heretic, this fear we feel."

"They have found me out!" thought the false ascetic. He threw his staff at the bird, but missed him. "Get away!" said he—"I've missed you!"

"You have missed us," said the Bodhisatta, "but you shall not miss the four hells! If you stay here, I'll call the villagers and make them catch you for a thief. Run off, quick!" Thus he threatened the man, and flew away. The hermit could live there no longer.

The Teacher having ended this discourse, identified the Birth: "At that time Devadatta was the ascetic; the first ascetic, the good one, was Sāriputta; and the chief of the Pigeons was I myself."

No. 278.[1]

MAHISA-JĀTAKA.

[385] "*Why do you patiently,*" *etc.* This story the Master told at Jetavana, about a certain impertinent monkey. At Sāvatthi, we are told, was a tame monkey in a certain family; and it ran into the elephant's stable, and perching on the back of a virtuous elephant, voided excrement, and began to walk up and down. The elephant, being both virtuous and patient, did nothing. But one day in this elephant's place stood a wicked young one. The monkey thought it was the same, and climbed upon its back. The elephant seized him in his trunk, and dashing him to the ground, trod him to pieces. This became known in the meeting of the Brotherhood; and one day they all began to talk about it. "Brother, have you heard how the impertinent monkey mistook a bad elephant for a good one, and climbed on his back, and how he lost his life for it?" In came the Master, and asked, "Brethren, what are you talking of as you sit here?" and when they told him, "This is not the first time," said he, "that this impertinent monkey behaved so; he did the same before:" and he told them an old-world tale.

Once on a time, when Brahmadatta was king of Benares, the Bodhisatta was born in the Himalaya region as a Buffalo. He grew up strong and big, and ranged the hills and mountains, peaks and caves, tortuous woods a many.

Once, as he went, he saw a pleasant tree, and took his food, standing under it.

[1] *Jātaka Mālā*, no. 33 (*Mahisa*); *Cariyā-Piṭaka*, II. 5.

Then an impertinent monkey came down out of the tree, and getting on his back, voided excrement; then he took hold of one of the Buffalo's horns, and swung down from it by his tail, disporting himself. The Bodhisatta, being full of patience, kindliness, and mercy, took no notice at all of his misconduct. This the monkey did again and again.

But one day, the spirit that belonged to that tree, standing upon the tree-trunk, asked him, saying, [386] "My lord Buffalo, why do you put up with the rudeness of this bad Monkey? Put a stop to him!" and enlarging upon this theme he repeated the first two verses as follows:

"Why do you patiently endure each freak
This mischievous and selfish ape may wreak?

"Crush underfoot, transfix him with your horn!
Stop him or even children will show scorn."

The Bodhisatta, on hearing this, replied, "If, Tree-sprite, I cannot endure this monkey's ill-treatment without abusing his birth, lineage, and powers, how can my wish ever come to fulfilment? But the monkey will do the same to any other, thinking him to be like me. And if he does it to any fierce Buffalos, they will destroy him indeed. When some other has killed him, I shall be delivered both from pain and from bloodguiltiness." And saying this he repeated the third verse:

"If he treats others as he now treats me,
They will destroy him; then I shall be free."

A few days after, the Bodhisatta went elsewhither, and another Buffalo, a savage beast, went and stood in his place. The wicked Monkey, [387] thinking it to be the old one, climbed upon his back and did as before. The Buffalo shook him off upon the ground, and drove his horn into the Monkey's heart, and trampled him to mincemeat under his hoofs.

When the Master had ended this teaching, he declared the Truths, and identified the Birth: "At that time the bad buffalo was he who now is the bad elephant, the bad monkey was the same, but the virtuous noble Buffalo was I myself."

No. 279.

SATAPATTA-JĀTAKA.

"*As the youth upon his way*," *etc.* This story the Master told in Jetavana, about Paṇḍuka and Lohita. Of the Six Heretics, two—Mettiya and Bhummaja—lived hard by Rājagaha; two, Assaji and Punabbasu, near Kīṭāgiri, and at Jetavana near Sāvatthi the two others, Paṇḍuka and Lohita. They questioned matters laid down in the doctrine; whoever were their friends and intimates, they would encourage, saying, "You are no worse than these, brother, in birth, lineage, or character; if you give up your opinions, they will have much the better of you," and by saying this kind of thing they prevented their giving up their opinions, and thus strifes and quarrels and contentions arose. The Brethren told this to the Blessed One. The Blessed One assembled the Brethren for that cause, to make explanation; and causing Paṇḍuka and Lohita to be summoned, addressed them: "Is it true, Brethren, that you really yourselves question certain matters, and prevent people from giving up their opinions?" "Yes," they replied. "Then," said he, "your behaviour is like that of the Man and the Crane;" and he told them an old-world tale.

Once on a time, when Brahmadatta was reigning in Benares, the Bodhisatta was born to a certain family in a Kāsi village. When he grew up, instead of earning a livelihood by farming or trade, [388] he gathered five hundred robbers, and became their chief, and lived by highway robbery and housebreaking.

Now it so happened that a landowner had given a thousand pieces of money to some one, and died before receiving it back again. Some time after, his wife lay on her deathbed, and addressing her son, said,

"Son, your father gave a thousand pieces of money to a man, and died without getting it back; if I die too, he will not give it to you. Go, while I yet live, get him to fetch it and give it back."

So the son went, and got the money.

The mother died; but she loved her son so much, that she suddenly reappeared[1] as a jackal on the road by which he was coming. At that time, the robber chief with his band lay by the road in wait to plunder travellers. And when her son had got to the entrance of the wood, the Jackal returned again and again, and sought to stay him; saying, "My son, don't enter the wood! there are robbers there, who will slay thee and take thy money!"

[1] The word implies a creature not born in the natural way, but taking shape without the need of parents.

But the man understood not what she meant. "Ill luck!" said he, "here's a jackal trying to stop my way!" he said; and he drove her off with sticks and clods, and into the wood he went.

And a crane flew towards the robbers, crying out—"Here's a man with a thousand pieces in his hand! Kill him, and take them!" The young fellow did not know what it was doing, so he thought, "Good luck! here's a lucky bird! now there is a good omen for me!" He saluted respectfully, crying, "Give voice, give voice, my lord!"

The Bodhisatta, who knew the meaning of all sounds, observed what these two did, and thought: "You jackal must be the man's mother; so she tries to stop him, and tell him that he will be killed and robbed; but the crane must be some adversary, and that is why it says 'Kill him, and take the money;' and the man does not know what is happening, [389] and drives off his mother, who wishes his welfare, while the crane, who wishes him ill, he worships, under the belief that it is a well-wisher. The man is a fool."

(Now the Bodhisattas, even though they are great beings, sometimes take the goods of others by being born as wicked men; this they say comes from a fault in the horoscope.)

So the young man went on, and by and bye fell in with the robbers. The Bodhisatta caught him, and "Where do you live?" said he.

"In Benares."

"Where have you been?"

"There was a thousand pieces due to me in a certain village; and that is where I have been."

"Did you get it?"

"Yes, I did."

"Who sent you?"

"Master, my father is dead, and my mother is ill; it was she sent me, because she thought I should not get it if she were dead."

"And do you know what has happened to your mother now?"

"No, master."

"She died after you left; and so much did she love you, that she at once became a jackal, and kept trying to stop you for fear you should get killed. She it was that you scared away. But the crane was an enemy, who came and told us to kill you, and take your money. You are such a fool that you thought your mother was an illwisher, when she wished you well, and thought the crane was a wellwisher when it wished ill to you. He did you no good, but your mother was very good to you. Keep your money, and be off!" And he let him go.

When the Master had finished this discourse, he repeated the following stanzas:

"As the youth upon his way
 Thought the jackal of the wood
Was a foe, his path to stay,
 While she tried to do him good:
That false crane his true friend deeming
Which to ruin him was scheming:

"Such another, who is here,
 Has his friends misunderstood;
They can never win his ear
 Who advise him for his good.

[390] "He believes when others praise—
 Awful terrors prophesying:
As the youth of olden days
 Loved the crane above him flying[1]."

When the Master had enlarged upon this theme, he identified the Birth: "At that time the robber chief was I myself."

No. 280.

PUṬA-DŪSAKA-JĀTAKA.

"*No doubt the king,*" *etc.*—This story the Master told in Jetavana, about one who destroyed pottles. At Sāvatthi, we learn, a certain courtier invited the Buddha and his company, and made them sit in his park. [391] As he was distributing to them, during the meal, he said, "Let those who wish to walk about the park, do so." The Brothers walked about the park. At that time the gardener climbed up a tree which had leaves upon it, and said, taking hold of some of the large leaves, "This will do for flowers, this one for fruit," and making them into pottles he dropt them to the foot of the tree. His little son destroyed each as soon as it fell. The Brothers told this to the Master. "Brothers," said the Master, "this is not the first time that this lad has destroyed pottles: he did it before." And he told them an old-world tale.

---

[1] The scholiast adds the following lines:

The friend who robs another without ceasing;
 He that protests, protests incessantly;
The friend who flatters for the sake of pleasing;
 The boon companion in debauchery;—
These four the wise as enemies should fear,
And keep aloof, if there be danger near.

Once upon a time, when Brahmadatta was king of Benares, the Bodhisatta was born in a certain family of Benares. When he grew up, and was living in the world as a householder, it happened that for some reason he went into a park, where a number of monkeys lived. The gardener was throwing down his pottles as we have described, and the chief of the monkeys was destroying them as they fell. The Bodhisatta, addressing him, said, "As the gardener drops his pottles, the monkey thinks he is trying to please him by tearing them up[1]," and repeated the first stanza:—

"No doubt the king of beasts is clever
In pottle-making; he would never
Destroy what's made with so much pother,
Unless he meant to make another."

On hearing this the Monkey repeated the second stanza:—

"Neither my father nor my mother
Nor I myself could make another.
What others make, we tear to pieces:
The proper way of monkeys, this is!"

[392] And the Bodhisatta responded with the third:—

"If this is proper monkey nature,
What's the improper way of such a creature!
Be off—it does not matter whether
You're proper or improper—both together!"

and with these words of blame he departed.

When the Master had ended this discourse, he identified the Birth: "At that time the monkey was the boy who has been destroying the pottles; but the wise man was I myself."

No. 281.

ABBHANTARA-JĀTAKA.

"*There grows a tree,*" *etc.*—This story the Master told in Jetavana, about the Elder Sāriputta giving mango juice to the Sister Bimbādevī. When the Supreme Buddha inaugurated the universal reign of religion, whilst living in a room at Vesāli, the chief wife of the Gotama with five hundred of the Sākiya clan asked for initiation, and received initiation and full orders. Afterwards the five

[1] Should we read, "... Kātukāmo ti maññe" ti?

hundred Sisters became saints on hearing the preaching of Nandaka. But when the Master was living near Sāvatthi, the mother of Rāhula thought to herself, "My husband on embracing the religious life has become omniscient; my son too has become a religious, and lives with him. What am I to do in the midst of the house? I will enter on this life, and go to Sāvatthi, and I will live looking upon the Supreme Buddha and my son continually." So she betook herself to a nunnery, and entered the order, and went and lived in a cell at Sāvatthi, in company of her teachers and preceptors, beholding the Master and her beloved son. The novice Rāhula came and saw his mother.

One day, the Sister was afflicted with flatulence; [393] and when her son came to see her, she could not get to see him, but some others came and told him she was ill. Then he went in, and asked his mother, "What ought you to take?" "Son," said she, "at home this pain used to be cured by mango juice flavoured with sugar; but now we live by begging, and where can we get it?" Said the novice, "I'll get it for you," and departed. Now the preceptor of his reverence Rāhula was the Captain of the Faith, his teacher was the great Moggallāna, his uncle was the Elder Ānanda, and his father was the Supreme Buddha: thus he had great luck. However, he went to no other save only to his preceptor; and after greeting him, stood before him with a sad look. "Why do you seem sad, Rāhula?" asked the Elder. "Sir," he replied, "my mother is ill with flatulence." "What must she take?" "Mango juice and sugar does her good." "All right, I'll get some; don't trouble about it." So next day he took the lad to Sāvatthi, and seating him in a waiting-room, went up to the palace. The king of Kosala bade the Elder be seated. At that very moment the gardener brought a basket of sweet mangoes ripe for food. The king removed the skin, sprinkled sugar, crushed them up himself, and filled the Elder's bowl for him. The Elder returned to the place of waiting and gave them to the novice, bidding him give them to his mother; and so he did. No sooner had the Sister eaten, than her pain was cured. The king also sent messengers, saying, "The Elder did not sit here to eat the mango juice. Go and find out whether he gave it to any one." The messenger went along with the elder, and found out, and then returned to tell the king. Thought the king: "If the Master should return to a worldly life, he would be an universal monarch; the novice Rāhula would be his treasure the Crown Prince[1], the holy Sister would be his treasure the Empress, and all the universe would belong to them. I must go and attend upon them. Now they are living close by there is no time to be lost." So from that day he continually gave mango syrup to the Sister.

It became known among the Brothers how the Elder gave mango syrup to the holy Sister. [394] And one day they fell a-talking in the Hall of Truth: "Friend, I hear that the Elder Sāriputta comforted Sister Bimbādevī with mango syrup." The Master came in and asked, "What are you talking about now?" When they told him—"This is not the first time, Brothers, that Rāhula's mother was comforted with mango syrup by the Elder; the same happened before;" and he told them an old-world tale.

Once upon a time, when Brahmadatta was reigning in Benares, the Bodhisatta was born in a brahmin family living in a village of Kāsi. When he grew up, he was educated at Takkasilā, settled down into family life, and on the death of his parents embraced the religious life. After that he remained in the region of Himalaya, cultivating the Faculties and the Attainments. A body of sages gathered round him, and he became their teacher.

[1] Two of the seven *ratanas*, or Treasures of the Empire of an universal monarch.

At the end of a long time time he came down from the hills to get salt and seasoning, and in the course of his wanderings arrived at Benares, where he took up his abode in a park. And at the glory of the virtue of this company of holy men the palace of Sakka shook. Sakka reflected, and perceived what it was. Thought he, "I will do an injury to their dwelling; then their stay will be disturbed; they will be too much distressed to have tranquillity of mind. Then I shall be comfortable again." As he bethought him how to do it, he hit upon a plan. "I will enter the chamber of the chief queen, just at the middle watch of the night, and hovering in the air, I will say—'Lady, if you eat a midmost mango[1], you will conceive a son[2], who shall become a universal monarch.' She will tell the king, and he will send to the orchard for a mango fruit: I will cause all the fruit to disappear. They will tell the king that there is none, and when he asks who eats it, they will say 'The ascetics'." So just in the middle watch, he appeared in the queen's chamber, and hovering in the air, revealed his godhead, and conversing with her, repeated the first two stanzas:—[395]

"There grows a tree, with fruit divine thereon;
Men clepe it Middlemost: and if one be
With child, and eat of it, she shall anon
Bear one to hold the whole wide earth in fee.

"Lady, you are a mighty Queen indeed;
The King, your husband, holds you lief and dear.
Bid him procure the mango for your need,
And he the Midmost fruit will bring you here."

These stanzas did Sakka recite to the queen; and then bidding her be careful, and make no delay, but tell the matter to the king herself, he encouraged her, and went back to his own place.

Next day, the queen lay down, as though ill, giving instructions to her maidens. The king sat upon his throne, under the white umbrella, and looked on at the dancing. Not seeing his queen, he asked a handmaid where she was.

"The queen is sick," replied the girl.

So the king went to see her; and sitting by her side, stroked her back, and asked, "What is the matter, lady?"

"Nothing," said she, "but that I have a craving for something."

"What is it you want, lady?" he asked again.

"A middle mango, my lord."

"Where is there such a thing as a middle mango?"

[1] The phrase is meant to be enigmatical. It is explained below.

[2] The idea of conception by eating of fruit and in other abnormal ways is fully discussed in *The Legend of Perseus*, E. S. Hartland, vol. i. chaps. 4—6.

"I don't know what a middle mango is; but I know that I shall die if I don't get one."

"All right, we will get you one; don't trouble about it."

So the king consoled her, and went away. He took his seat upon the royal divan, and sent for his courtiers. [396] "My queen has a great craving for a *middle mango.* What is to be done?" said he.

Some one told him, "A middle mango is one which grows between two others. Send to your park, and find a mango growing between two others; pluck its fruit and let us give it to the queen." So the king sent men to do after this manner.

But Sakka by his power made all the fruit disappear, as though it had been eaten. The men who came for the mangoes searched the whole park through, and not a mango could they find; so back they went to the king, and told him that mangoes there were none.

"Who is it eats the mangoes?" asked the king.

"The ascetics, my lord."

"Give the ascetics a drubbing, and bundle them out of the park!" he commanded. The people heard and obeyed: Sakka's wish was fulfilled. The queen lay on and on, longing for the mango.

The king could not think what to do. He gathered his courtiers and his brahmins, and asked them, "Do you know what a *middle mango* is?"

Said the brahmins: "My lord, a middle mango is the portion of the gods. It grows in Himalaya, in the Golden Cave. So we have heard by immemorial tradition."

"Well, who can go and get it?"

"A human being cannot go; we must send a young parrot."

At that time there was a fine young parrot in the king's family, as big as the nave of the wheel in the princes' carriage, strong, clever, and full of sharp devices. This parrot the king sent for, and thus addressed him,

"Dear parrot, I have done a great deal for you: you live in a golden cage; you have sweet grain to eat on a golden dish; you have sugared water to drink. There's something I want you to do for me."

"Speak on, my lord," said the parrot.

"Son, my queen has a craving for a *middle mango;* this mango grows in Himalaya, in the Golden Mountain; it is the gods' portion, [397] no human being can go thither. You must bring the fruit back from thence."

"Very good, my king, I will," said the parrot. Then the king gave him sweetened grain to eat, on a golden plate, and sugar-water to drink; and anointed him beneath the wings with oil an hundred times refined; then he took him in both hands, and standing at a window, let him fly away.

The parrot, on the king's errand, flew along in the air, beyond the ways of men, till he came to some parrots which dwelt in the first hill-region of Himalaya. "Where is the middle mango?" he asked them; "tell me the place."

"We know not," said they, "but the parrots in the second range of hills will know."

The parrot listened, and flew away to the second range. After that he went on to the third, fourth, fifth, and sixth. There too the parrots said, "We do not know, but those in the seventh range will know." So he went on there, and asked where the middle mango tree grew.

"In such and such a place, on the Golden Hill," they said.

"I have come for the fruit of it," said he, "guide me thither, and procure the fruit for me."

"That is the portion of the king Vessavaṇa. It is impossible to get near it. The whole tree from the roots upwards is encircled with seven iron nets; it is guarded by thousands of millions of Kumbhaṇḍa goblins; if they see any one, he's done for. The place is like the fire of the dissolution and the fire of hell. Do not ask such a thing!"

"If you will not go with me, then describe the place to me," said he.

So they told him to go by such and such a way. He listened carefully to their instructions. He did not show himself by day; but at dead of night, when the goblins were asleep, he approached the tree, and began softly to climb on one of its roots, when clink! went the iron net [398]—the goblins awoke—saw the parrot, and seized him, crying, "Thief!" Then they discussed what was to be done with him.

Says one, "I'll throw him into my mouth, and swallow him!"

Says another, "I'll crush him and knead him in my hands and scatter him in bits!"

Says a third, "I'll split him in two, and cook him on the coals and eat him!"

The parrot heard them deliberating. Without any fear he addressed them, "I say, Goblins, whose men are you?"

"We belong to king Vessavaṇa."

"Well, you have one king for your master, and I have another for mine. The king of Benares sent me here to fetch a fruit of the middle mango tree. Then and there I gave my life to my king, and here I am. He who loses his life for parents or master is born at once in heaven. Therefore I shall pass at once from this animal form to the world of the gods!" and he repeated the third stanza:

"Whatever be the place which they attain
Who, by heroic self-forgetfulness,
Strive with all zeal a master's end to gain—
To that same place I soon shall win access."

After this fashion did he discourse, repeating this stanza. The goblins listened, and were pleased in their heart. "This is a righteous creature," said they, "we must not kill him—let him go!" So they let him go, and said, "I say, Parrot, you're free! Go unharmed out of our hands!" [399]

"Do not let me return empty-handed," said the parrot: "give me a fruit off the tree!"

"Parrot," they said, "it is not our business to give you fruit off this tree. All the fruit on this tree is marked. If there is one fruit wrong we shall lose our lives. If Vessavaṇa is angry and looks but once, a thousand goblins are broken up and scattered like parched peas hopping about on a hot plate. So we cannot give you any. But we will tell you a place where you can get some."

"I care not who gives it," said the parrot, "but the fruit I must have. Tell me where I may get it."

"In one of the tortuous paths of the Golden Mountain lives an ascetic, by name Jotirasa, who watches the sacred fire in a leaf-thatched hut, called Kañcana-patti or Goldleaf, a favourite of Vessavaṇa; and Vessavaṇa sends him constantly four fruits from the tree; go to him."

The parrot took his leave, and came to the ascetic; he gave him greeting, and sat down on one side. The ascetic asked him,

"Where have you come from?" "From the king of Benares." "Why are you come?"

"Master, our Queen has a great craving for the fruit of the middle mango, and that is why I am come. Howbeit the goblins would not give me any themselves, but sent me to you."

"Sit down, then, and you shall have one," said the ascetic. Then came the four which Vessavaṇa used to send. The ascetic ate two of them, gave the parrot one to eat, and when this was eaten he hung the fourth by a string, and made it fast around the parrot's neck, and let him go—"Off with you, now!" said he. The parrot flew back and gave it to the Queen. She ate it, and satisfied her craving, but still all the same she had no son.

---

[400] When the Master had ended this discourse, he identified the Birth in these words: "At that time Rāhula's mother was the Queen, Ānanda was the parrot, Sāriputta was the ascetic who gave the mango fruit, but the ascetic who lived in the park was I myself."

No. 282.

SEYYA-JĀTAKA.

"*'Tis best that you should know*," *etc.*—This tale the Master told at Jetavana, about a courtier of the king of Kosala. This man was very useful to the king, we are told, and did everything that had to be done. Because he was very useful, the king did him great honour. The others were jealous, and concocted a slander, and calumniated him. The king believed their saying, and without enquiring into his guilt, bound him in chains, though virtuous and innocent, and cast him into prison. There he dwelt all alone; but by reason of his virtue, he had peace of mind, and with mind at peace he understood the conditions of existence, and attained the fruition of the First Path. By and bye the king found that he was guiltless, and broke his chains and gave him honour more than before. The man wished to pay his respects to the Master; and taking flowers and perfumes, he went to the monastery, and did reverence to the Buddha, and sat respectfully aside. The Master talked graciously with him. "We have heard that ill fortune befel you," said he. "Yes, sir, but I made my ill fortune into good; and as I sat in prison, I produced the fruition of the First Path." "Good friend," said the Master, "you are not the only one who has turned evil into good; for wise men in the olden time turned evil into good as you did." And he told an old-world tale.

Once on a time, when Brahmadatta was king of Benares, the Bodhisatta was born as the son of his Queen Consort. He grew up and was educated at Takkasilā; and on his father's death he became king, and kept the ten royal rules: he gave alms, practised virtue, [401] and observed the sacred day.

Now one of his courtiers intrigued among the king's wives. The servants noticed it, and told the king that so and so was carrying on an intrigue. The king found out the very truth of the matter, and sent for him. "Never show yourself before me again," said he, and banished him. The man went off to the court of a neighbouring king, and then all happened as described above in the Mahāsīlava Birth[1]. Here too this king thrice tested him, and believing the word of the courtier came with a great army before Benares with intent to take it. When this was known to the chief warriors of the king of Benares, five hundred in number, they said to the king,

"Such and such a king has come here, wasting the country, with intent to take Benares—here, let us go and capture him!"

"I want no kingdom that must be kept by doing harm," said the king. "Do nothing at all."

[1] No. 51 (vol. i. p. 129 of this translation).

The marauding king surrounded the city. Again the courtiers approached the king, and said,

"My lord, be advised—let us capture him!"

"Nothing can be done," said the king. "Open the city gates." Then, surrounded by his court, he sate down in state upon the great dais.

The marauder entered the town, felling the men at the four gates and ascended the terrace. There he took prisoner the king with all his court, threw chains upon them and cast them into prison. The king, as he sat in prison, pitied the marauder, and an ecstasy of pity was stirred in him. By reason of this pity, the other king felt great torment in his body; he burnt all through as though with a twofold flame; and smitten with great pain, he asked what the matter was.

They replied, "You have cast a righteous king into prison, that is why this is come upon you."

He went and craved pardon of the Bodhisatta, and restored his kingdom, saying, "Your kingdom be your own. [402] Henceforward leave your enemies for me to deal with." He punished the evil counsellor, and returned to his own city.

The Bodhisatta sat in state upon his high dais, in festal array, with his court around him; and addressing them repeated the first two stanzas:

"'Tis best that you should know, the better part
Is evermore the better thing to do.
By treating one with kindliness of heart,
I saved an hundred men from death their due.

"Therefore to all the world I bid you show
The grace of kindliness and friendship dear;
And then alone to heaven you shall not go.
O people of the Kāsi country, hear!"

Thus the great Being praised virtue in the way of pitying the great multitude; and leaving the white umbrella in the great city of Benares, twelve leagues in extent, retired to Himalaya, and embraced the religious life.

[403] The Master, in his perfect wisdom, repeated the third stanza:

"These are the words that I, king Kaṁsa, said,
I the great ruler of Benares town.
I laid my bow, I laid my quiver down,
And my self-mastery I perfected."

When the Master had ended this discourse, he identified the Birth: "At that time Ānanda was the marauding king, but the king of Benares was I myself."

No. 283.

VAḌḌHAKI-SŪKARA-JĀTAKA[1].

"*The best, the best you always,*" *etc.*—This story the Master told in Jetavana about the Elder Dhanuggahatissa. Mahākosala, the father of king Pasenadi, when he married his daughter, the Lady Kosalā, to king Bimbisāra, gave a village of Kāsi, producing a revenue of a hundred thousand, for bath and perfume money. When Ajātasattu murdered the king his father, the lady Kosalā died of grief. Then thought king Pasenadi, "Ajātasattu has killed his father, my sister has died from sympathy with her husband's misfortune; I will not give the Kāsi town to the parricide." So he refused to give it to Ajātasattu. About this village there was war betwixt these two from time to time. Ajātasattu was fierce and strong, and Pasenadi was a very old man, so he was beaten again and again, and the people of Mahākosala were generally conquered. Then the king asked his courtiers, "We are constantly being beaten; what is to be done?" "My lord," said they, "the reverend fathers are skilled in incantations. We must hear the word of the Brothers who dwell in the Jetavana monastery." Then the king despatched couriers, bidding them listen to the converse of the Brothers at a suitable time. Now at the time there were two old Elders living in a leaf-hut close to the monastery, whose names were Elder Utta and Elder Dhanuggahatissa. [404] Dhanuggahatissa had slept through the first and second watch of the night; and awaking in the last watch, he broke some sticks, lit a fire, and sitting down said, "Utta, my friend!" "What is it, friend Tissa?" "Are you not asleep?" "Now we are awake, what's to do?" "Get up, now, and sit by me." So he did, and began to talk to him. "That stupid, pot-bellied Kosala never has a jar full of boiled rice without letting it spoil; how to plan a war he knows not a bit. He is always being beaten and forced to pay." "But what should he do?" Now just then the couriers stood listening to their talk. The Elder Dhanuggahatissa discussed the nature of war. "War, Sir," said he, "consists of three kinds: the lotus army, the wheel army, and the waggon army[2]. If those who wish to capture Ajātasattu will post garrisons in two hill-forts right away in the hills, and pretend that they are weak, and watch till they get him among the hills, and bar his passage, leap out from the two forts and take him in front and in the rear, and shout aloud, they will quickly have him like a landed fish, like a frog in the fist; and so they will be able to secure him." All this the couriers told their king. The king caused the drum to be beaten for the attack, arranged his army waggon-wise, took Ajātasattu alive; his daughter, Princess Vajirā he gave in marriage to his sister's son, and dismissed her with the Kāsi village for her bath-money.

This event became known among the Brotherhood. One day, they were all talking about it in the Hall of Truth; "Friend, I hear that the king of Kosala conquered Ajātasattu through the instructions of Dhanuggahatissa." The Master

[1] See Morris, *Folk-lore Journal*, iv. 48.

[2] These are technical terms in Sanskrit also (*padmavyūho*, *çakaṭa*°, *cakra*°); see Manu 7. 188, 7. 187, and B. R. dict. *s.v.* The 'wheel' explains itself: the 'waggon' was a wedge-shaped phalanx; the 'lotus,' as noted by Bühler (trans. of Manu in *S. B. E.* page 246), is "equally extended on all sides and perfectly circular, the centre being occupied by the king."

came in; "What do you sit here talking about now, Brothers?" asked he. They told him. He said, "This is not the first time that Dhanuggahatissa was clever in discussing war": and he told them an old-world tale.

---

[405] Once upon a time, when Brahmadatta was reigning in Benares, the Bodhisatta came to life as a tree-spirit. At that time there were some carpenters settled in a village near Benares. One of them, on going into the forest to get wood, found a young boar fallen in a pit, which he took home and kept. He grew big, with curved tusks, and was a well-mannered creature. Because the carpenter kept him, he went by the name of Carpenter's Boar. When the carpenter was chopping up a tree, the boar used to turn the tree over with his snout, and with his teeth fetch hatchet and adze, chisel and mallet, and pull along the measuring line by the end. The carpenter was afraid somebody might eat him up; so he took him and let him go in the forest. The Boar ran into the forest, looking for a safe and pleasant place to live in; and at last he espied a great cave up in a mountain side, with plenty of bulbs, and roots, and fruits, a pleasant living-place. Some hundreds of other boars saw him and approached him.

Said he to them, "You are just what I am looking for, and here I have found you. This seems a nice place; and here I mean to live now with you."

"A nice place it certainly is," said they, "but dangerous."

"Ah," said he, "as soon as I saw you, I wondered how it was that those who dwell in so plentiful a place could be so meagre in flesh and blood. What is it you are afraid of?"

"There is a tiger comes in the morning, and every one he sees he seizes and carries off."

"Does this always happen, or only now and then?"

"Always."

"How many tigers are there?"

"Only one."

"What—one alone too many for all of you!"

"Yes, Sir."

"I'll catch him, if you only do what I tell you. Where does this tiger live?"

"On that hill yonder."

So at night he drilled the Boars and prepared them for war; explaining to them the science. [406] "War is of three kinds—the lotus army, the wheel army, and the waggon army:" and he arranged them after the lotus pattern. He knew the place of vantage; so, says he, "Here we must set our battle." The mothers and their suckling brood he placed in the middle; around these he put the sows that had no young; around these, the little boars; around these, those which were rather young; around these, all whose tusks were grown; around these, the boars fit for battle, strong and powerful, by tens and by twenties; thus he placed them in serried ranks. Before his own position he had a round hole dug; behind it, a pit getting gradually deeper and deeper, shaped like a winnowing basket[1]. As he moved about amongst them, followed by sixty or seventy Boars, bidding them be of good courage, the dawn broke.

The Tiger awoke. "Time now!" thought he. He trotted up till he caught sight of them; then stopped still upon the plateau, glaring at the crowd of Boars. "Glare back!" cried the Carpenter's Boar, with a signal to the rest. They all glared. The Tiger opened his mouth, and drew a long breath: the Boars all did the same. The Tiger relieved himself: so did the Boars. Thus whatever the Tiger did, the Boars did after him.

"Why, what's this!" the Tiger wondered. "They used to take to their heels as soon as they saw me—indeed, they were too much frightened even to run. Now so far from running, they actually stand up against me! Whatever I do, they mimic. There's a fellow yonder on a commanding position: he it is who has organised the rabble. Well, I don't see how to get the better of them." And he turned away and went back to his lair.

Now there was a sham hermit, who used to get a share of the Tiger's prey. This time the Tiger returned empty-handed. Noticing this, the hermit repeated the following stanza. [407]

> "The best, the best you always brought before
> When you went hunting after the wild boar.
> Now empty-handed you consume with grief,
> To-day where is the strength you had of yore?"

At this address, the Tiger repeated another stanza:

> "Once they would hurry-scurry all about
> To find their holes, a panic-stricken rout.
> But now they grunt in serried ranks compact:
> Invincible, they stand and face me out."

"Oh, don't be afraid of them!" urged the hermit. "One roar and one leap will frighten them out of their wits, and send them pell-mell." The Tiger yielded to this insistence. Plucking up his courage, he went back and stood upon the plateau.

Carpenter's Boar stood between the two pits. "See Master! here's the scoundrel again!" cried the Boars. "Oh, don't be afraid," said he, "we have him now."

[1] The winnowing basket has low walls on three sides, two of them sloping towards the open end. See a picture in Grierson, *Bihar Peasant Life*, 118.

With a roar the Tiger leapt upon Carpenter's Boar. At the very instant he sprang, [408] the Boar dodged and dropped straight into the round hole. The Tiger could not stop, but tumbled over and over and fell all of a heap in the jaws of the other pit, where it got very narrow. Up jumps the Boar out of his hole, and quick as lightning ran his tusk into the Tiger's thighs, tore him about the kidneys, buried his fangs in the creature's sweet flesh, and wounded his head. Then he tosses him out of the pit, crying aloud—"Here's your enemy for you!" They who came first had tiger to eat; but they who came after went about sniffing at the others' mouths, and asking what tiger's flesh tasted like!

But the Boars were still uneasy. "What's the matter now?" asked our Hog, who had noticed their movements.

"Master," said they, "it's all very well to kill one tiger, but the sham hermit can bring ten tigers more!"

"Who is he?"

"A wicked ascetic."

"The tiger I have killed; do you suppose a man can hurt me? Come along, and we'll get hold of him." So they all set forth.

Now the man had been wondering why the Tiger was so long in coming. Could the Boars have caught him? he thought. At last he started to meet him on the way; and as he went, there came the Boars! He snatched up his belongings, and off he ran. The Boars tore after him. He threw away his encumbrances, and with all speed climbed up a fig-tree.

"Now, Master, it's all up!" cried the herd. "The man has climbed a tree!"

"What tree?" their leader asked.

They replied, "A fig-tree."

"Oh, very well," said the leader. "The sows must bring water, the young ones dig about the tree, the tuskers tear at the roots, and the rest surround it and watch." They did their several tasks as he bade them; he meanwhile charged full at a great thick root, [409]—'twas like an axe-blow; and with this one blow he felled the tree to the ground. The Boars who were waiting for the man, knocked him down, tore him to pieces, gnawed the bones clean in a moment!

Now they perched Carpenter's Boar on the tree-trunk. They filled the dead man's shell with water, and sprinkled the Boar to consecrate him for their king; a young sow they consecrated to be his Consort.

This, the saying goes, is the origin of the custom still observed. When people make a king now-a-days, he is placed on a fine chair of fig-wood, and sprinkled out of three shells.

A sprite that dwelt in that forest beheld this marvel. Appearing before the Boars in a cleft of his tree-trunk, he repeated the third stanza:—

"Honour to all the tribes assembled be!
A wondrous union I myself did see!
How tuskers once a tiger overcame
By federal strength and tusked unity!"

After this discourse the Master identified the Birth: "Dhanuggaha the Elder was the Carpenter's Boar, and I was the tree-sprite."

No. 284.

SIRI-JĀTAKA.

"*Whatever riches they who strive*," *etc.*—This story the Master told about a brahmin who stole good luck. [410] The circumstances of this birth-tale are given above in the Khadiraṅga Birth[1]. As before, the heretical spirit that lived in the gate tower of Anāthapiṇḍika's house, doing penance, brought four and fifty crores of gold and filled the store-rooms, and became a friend of the great man. He led her before the Master. The Master discoursed to her. She heard, and entered on the stream of conversion. Thenceforward the great man's honour was great as before. Now there was living in Sāvatthi a brahmin, versed in lucky marks, who thought on this wise. "Anāthapiṇḍika was poor, and then became famous. What if I make as though I went to see him, and steal his luck?" So to the house he went, and was welcomed hospitably. After exchanging civilities, the host asked why he had come. The brahmin was looking about to see where the man's luck lay. Now Anāthapiṇḍika had a white cock, white as a scoured shell, which he kept in a golden cage, and in the comb of this cock lay the great man's luck. The brahmin looked about and spied where the luck lay. "Noble sir," said he, "I teach magic charms to five hundred young fellows. We are plagued by a cock that crows at the wrong time. Your cock crows at the right time. For him I have come; will you give him to me?" "Yes," said the other: and at the instant the word was uttered, the luck left the cockscomb, and settled in a jewel put away in the pillow. The brahmin observed that the luck had gone into this jewel, and asked for it too. As soon as the owner agreed to give it, the luck left the jewel, and settled in a club for self-defence which lay upon the pillow. The brahmin saw it and asked again. "Take it, and take your leave," said the owner; and in an instant the luck left the club, and settled on the head of the owner's chief wife, who was named the Lady Puññalakkhaṇā. The thievish brahmin thought, when he saw this, "This is an inalienable article which I cannot ask for." Then he told the great man, "Noble sir," said he, "I came to your house to steal your luck. The luck was in the comb of your

[1] No. 40, vol. i. page 100.

cock. But when you gave me the cock, the luck passed into this jewel; when you gave me the jewel it passed into your stick; when you gave the stick to me, it went out of it [411] and passed into the head of the Lady Puññalakkhaṇā. Surely this is inalienable, I can never get it. It is impossible to steal your luck —keep it, then!" and rising from his seat, he departed. Anāthapiṇḍika determined to tell the Master; so he came to the monastery, and after respectfully greeting him, sat on one side, and told the Buddha all about it. The Master listened, and said, "Goodman, now-a-days the luck of one man does not go to another. But formerly the luck belonging to those of small wit went to the wise;" and he told him an old-world tale.

Once on a time, when Brahmadatta reigned in Benares, the Bodhisatta was born into a Brahmin family in the realm of Kāsi. On growing up, he was educated at Takkasilā, and lived among his family; but when his parents died, much distressed he retired to the life of a recluse in Himalaya, and there he cultivated the Faculties and the Attainments.

A long time passed, and he came down to inhabited parts for salt and savouring, and took up his quarters in the gardens of the king of Benares. Next day, on his begging rounds, he came to the door of an elephant-trainer. This man took a fancy to his ways and manners, fed him, and gave him lodging in his own grounds, waiting upon him continually.

Now it happened just then that a man whose business it was to gather firewood failed to get back to town from the woods in time. He lay down for the night in a temple, placing a bundle of sticks under his head for a pillow. At this temple there were a number of cocks quite free, which had perched close by on a tree. Towards morning, one of them, who was roosting high, let fall a dropping on the back of a bird below. "Who dropt that on me?" cried this one. "I did," cried the first. "And why?" "Didn't think," said the other; and then did it again. Hereupon they both began to abuse each other, crying—"What power have you? what power have *you?*" At last the lower one said, "Anybody who kills me, and eats my flesh roasted on the coals, [412] gets a thousand pieces of money in the morning!" And the one above answered—"Pooh, pooh, don't boast about a little thing like that! Anybody who eats my fleshy parts will become king; if he eats my outside, he'll become commander-in-chief or chief queen, according as he's man or woman; if he eats the flesh by my bones, he'll get the post of royal Treasurer, if he be a householder; or, if a holy man, will become the king's favourite!"

The stick-picker heard all this, and pondered. "Now if I become king, there'll be no need of a thousand pieces of money." Quietly he climbed the tree, caught the topmost cock and killed him: he fastened him in a fold of his dress, saying to himself—"Now I'll be king!" As soon as the gates were opened, in he walked. He plucked the fowl, and cleaned it, and gave it to his wife, bidding her make the meat nice for eating. She got ready the meat with some rice, and set it before him, bidding her lord eat.

"Goodwife," said he, "there's great virtue in this meat. By eating it I shall become king, and you my queen!" So they took the meat and rice down to the Ganges bank, intending to bathe before eating it. Then, putting meat and rice down upon the bank, in they went to bathe.

Just then a breeze stirred up the water, which washed away the meat. Down the river it floated, till it came in sight of an elephant-trainer, a great personage, who was giving his elephants a bath lower down. "What have we here?" said he, and picked it up. "It's fowl and rice, my lord," was the reply. He bade wrap it up, and seal it, and sent it home to his wife, with a message to open it for him when he returned.

The stick-picker also ran off, with his belly puffed out with sand and water which he had swallowed.

Now a certain ascetic, who had divine vision, the favourite chaplain of the elephant-trainer, was thinking to himself, "My patron friend does not leave his post with the elephants. When will he attain promotion?" As he thus pondered, he saw this man by his divine insight, and perceived what was a-doing. He went on before, and sat in the patron's house.

When the master returned, [413] he greeted him respectfully and sat down on one side. Then, sending for the parcel, he ordered food and water to be brought for the ascetic. The ascetic did not accept the food which was offered him; but said, "I will divide this food." The master gave him leave. Then separating the meat into portions, he gave to the elephant-trainer the fleshy parts, the outside to his wife, and took the flesh about the bones for his own share. After the meal was over, he said, "On the third day from this you will become king. Take care what you do!" and away he went.

On the third day a neighbouring king came and beleaguered Benares. The king told his elephant-trainer to dress in the royal robes, bidding him go mount his elephant and fight. He himself put on a disguise, and mingled with the ranks; swift came an arrow, and pierced him, so that he perished then and there. The trainer, learning that the king was dead, sent for a great quantity of money, and beat the drum, proclaiming, "Let those who want money, advance, and fight!" The warrior host in a twinkling slew the hostile king.

After the king's obsequies the courtiers deliberated who was to be made king. Said they, "While our king was yet alive, he put his royal robes upon the elephant-trainer. This very man has fought and won the kingdom. To him the kingdom shall be given!" And they consecrated him king, and his wife they made the chief queen. The Bodhisatta became his confidant.

After this discourse the Master, in his perfect wisdom, gave utterance to the two stanzas following:

"Whatever riches they who strive amain
Without the aid of luck can ever gain,
All that, by favour of the goddess Luck,
Both skilled and unskilled equally obtain.

"All the world over many meet our sight,
Not only good, but creatures different quite,
Whose lot it is fruition to possess
Of wealth in store which is not theirs by right."

[414] After this the Master added, "Good sir, these beings have no other resource but their merit won in previous births; this enables you to obtain treasures in places where there is no mine." Then he recited the following scripture[1].

"There is a treasury of all good things
Which both to gods and men their wishes brings.
Fine looks, voice, figure, form, and sovranty
With all its pomp, lies in that treasury.
Lordship and government, imperial bliss,
The crown of heaven, within that treasure is.
All human happiness, the joys of heaven,
Nirvana's self, from out that store is given.
True ties of friendship, wisdom's liberty,
Firm self-control, lies in that treasury.
Salvation, understanding, training fit
To make Pacceka Buddhas come from it.
Thus hath this merit a virtue magical;
The wise and stedfast praise it one and all."

[415] Lastly the Fowl repeated the third stanza, explaining the treasures in which lay the luck of Anāthapiṇḍika.

"A fowl, a gem, a club, a wife—
All these with lucky marks were rife.
For all these treasures, be it known,
A good and sinless man did own."

Then he identified the Birth: "Elder Ānanda was the King, and the family priest was the Very Buddha."

[1] *Khud. Pāṭha*, p. 14.

No. 285.

MAṆISŪKARA-JĀTAKA[1].

"*To hell shall go he*" *etc.*—This story the Master told at Jetavana, about the murder of Sundarī. At that time we learn that the Bodhisatta was honoured and respected. The circumstances were the same as in the Kandhaka[2]; this is an abstract of them. The brotherhood of the Blessed One had received gain and honour like five rivers pouring in a mighty flood; the heretics, finding that gain and honour came to them no longer, becoming dim like fireflies at sunrise, they collected together, and took counsel: "Ever since the priest Gotama appeared, our gain and glory has gone from us. Not a soul ever knows that we exist. Who will help us to bring reproach on Gotama, and prevent him from getting all this?" Then an idea occurred to them. "Sundarī will make us able to do it." So when one day Sundarī visited the heretics' grove, they gave her greeting, but said nothing more. She addressed them again and again, but received no answer. "Has anything annoyed the holy fathers?" she asked. "Why, sister," said they, "do not you see how the priest Gotama annoys us, depriving us of alms and honour?" "What can I do about it?" she said. "You, sister, are fair and lovely. You can bring disgrace upon Gotama, and your words will influence a great many, [416] and you can thus restore our gains and good repute." She agreed, and took her leave. After this she used to take flowers and scents and perfumes, camphor, condiments and fruits, and at evening time, when a great crowd had entered the city after hearing the Master's discourse, she would set her face towards Jetavana. If any asked where she was going, she would say, "To the Priest Gotama; I live with him in one perfumed chamber." Then she spent the night in a heretical settlement, and in the morning entered the road which led from Jetavana into the city. If any asked her where she was going, she replied, "I have been with the priest Gotama in one perfumed chamber, and he made love to me." After the lapse of some days they hired some ruffians to kill Sundarī before Gotama's chamber and throw her body into the dust-heap. And so they did. Then the heretics made a hue and cry after Sundarī, and informed the king. He asked where their suspicions pointed. They answered that she had gone the last few days to Jetavana, but what happened afterwards they did not know. He sent them to search for her. Acting on this permission, they took his own servants, and went to Jetavana, where they hunted about till they found her in the dust-heap. Calling for a litter, they brought the body into the town, and told the king that the disciples of Gotama had killed Sundarī, and thrown her in the dust-heap, in order to cloak the sin of their Master. The king bade them scour the city. All through the streets they went, crying, "Come and see what has been done by the priests of the Sakya prince!" and came back to the palace door. The king had placed the body of Sundarī upon a platform, and had it watched in the cemetery. All the populace, except the holy disciples, went about inside the town, outside the town, in the parks and in the woods, abusing the Brethren, and crying out, "Come and see what the priests of the Sakya prince have done!" The Brethren told all this to the Buddha. Said the Master, "Well, go and reprove these people in these words:

[1] Cf. Morris, *Folk-lore Journal*, iv. 58.

[2] This story is given in *Udānaṁ*, iv. 8 (p. 43). *Khandhakaṁ* seems to mean the Vinaya (Childers *s. v.*, *J. P. T. S.* 1888 *s. v.*), but I cannot find the story there.

"To hell shall go he that delights in lies,
And he who having done a thing, denies:
[417] Both these, when death has carried them away,
As men of evil deeds elsewhere shall rise[1]."

The king directed some men to find out whether Sundarī had been killed by anybody else. Now the ruffians had drunk the blood-money, and were quarrelling together. Said one to another, "You killed Sundarī with one blow, and then threw her in the dust-heap, and here you are, buying liquor with the blood-money!" "All right, all right," said the king's messengers; and they caught the ruffians and dragged them before the king. "Did you kill her?" asked the king. They said, yes, they did. "Who bade you?" "The heretics, my lord." The king had the heretics summoned. "Lift up Sundarī," said he, "and carry her round the city, crying as you go: 'This woman Sundarī wanted to bring disgrace upon the priest Gotama; we had her murdered; the guilt is not Gotama's, nor his disciples'; the guilt is ours!'" They did so. A multitude of the unconverted believed, and the heretics were kept out of mischief by receiving the punishment for murder. Thenceforward the Buddha's reputation grew greater and greater. And then one day they began to gossip in the Hall of Truth: "Friend, the heretics thought to blacken the Buddha, and they only blackened themselves: ever since, our gains and glory have increased!" The Master came in, and asked what they were talking about? They told him. "Brethren," said he, "it is impossible to make the Buddha impure. Trying to stain the Buddha, is like trying to stain a gem of the first water. In bygone ages people have wished to stain a fine jewel, and no matter how they tried, they failed to do it." And he told them an old-world tale.

Once upon a time, when Brahmadatta was king of Benares, the Bodhisatta was born into a Brahmin family. When he grew up, perceiving the suffering that arises from desire, he went away, and traversed three ranges of Himalaya, where he became a hermit, and lived in a hut of leaves.

Near his hut was a crystal cave, in which lived thirty Boars. Near the cave a Lion used to range. [418] His shadow used to be reflected in the crystal. The Boars used to see this reflection, and terror made them lean and thin-blooded. Thought they, "We see the reflection because this crystal is clear. We will make it dirty and discolour it." So they got some mud from a pool close by, and rubbed and rubbed the crystal with it. But the crystal, being constantly polished by the boars' bristles, got brighter than ever.

They did not know how to manage it; so they determined to ask the hermit how they might sully the crystal. To him therefore they came, and after respectful greeting, they sat down beside him, and gave utterance to these two verses:

"Seven summers we have been
Thirty in a crystal grot.
Now we are keen to dull the sheen—
But dull it we can not.

[1] *Dhammapada*, v. 306; *Sutta Nipāta*, v. 661.

"Though we try with all our might
To obscure its brilliancy,
Still more bright shines forth the light,
What can the reason be?"

The Bodhisatta listened. Then he repeated the third stanza:

"'Tis precious crystal, spotless, bright, and pure;
No glass—its brilliancy for ever sure.
Nothing on earth its brightness can impair.
Boars, you had best betake yourselves elsewhere."

And so they did, on hearing this answer. The Bodhisatta lost himself in rapturous ecstasy, and became destined to Brahma's world.

———

After this discourse was ended, the Master identified the Birth: "At that time, I was the hermit."

No. 286.

SĀLŪKA-JĀTAKA[1].

[419] "*Envy not what Celery eats*" *etc.*—This story the Master told in Jetavana, about the temptation springing from a fat girl. The circumstances will be explained in the Cullanāradakassapa[2] story. So the Master asked this brother whether it was true he had fallen in love. Yes, he said. "With whom?" the Master asked. "With a fat girl." "That woman, brother," said the Master, "is your bane; long ago, as now, you became food for the crowd through your desire to marry her." Then at the request of the brethren he told an old-world tale.

———

Once upon a time, when Brahmadatta reigned in Benares, the Bodhisatta was an ox named Big Redcoat, and he had a young brother called Little Redcoat. Both of them worked for a family in some village.

[1] Compare No. 30, Vol. I. p. 75, and No. 477; parallels are quoted by Benfey, *Pañcatantra* pref. pp. 228, 229. Æsop's fable of the Calf and the Ox will occur to the reader. See also Rhys Davids' note to his translation of No. 30.

[2] No. 477.

There was in this family a grown-up girl, who was asked in marriage by another family. Now in the first family a pig called Sālūka or Celery[1], was being fatted, on purpose to serve for a feast on the wedding-day; it used to sleep in a sty[2].

One day, Little Redcoat said to his brother, "Brother, we work for this family, and we help them to get their living. Yet they only give us grass and straw, while they feed yon pig with rice porridge, and let it sleep in a sty; and what can it do for them?"

"Brother," said Big Redcoat, "don't covet his porridge. They want to make a feast of him on our young lady's wedding-day, that's why they are fattening him up. Wait a few days, and you'll see him dragged out of his sty, killed, chopped into bits, and eaten up by the visitors." So saying, he composed the first two stanzas: [420]

"Envy not what Celery eats;
Deadly is the food he gets.
Be content and eat your chaff:
It means long life on your behalf.

"By and bye the guest will come,
With his gossips all and some.
All chopt up poor Celery
With his big flat snout will lie."

A few days after, the wedding guests came, and Sālūka was killed and made a meal of. Both oxen, seeing what became of him, thought their own chaff was the best.

The Master, in his perfect wisdom, repeated the third stanza by way of explanation:

"When they saw the flat-snout lie
All chopt up, poor Celery,
Said the oxen, Best by half
Surely is our humble chaff!"

When the Master had finished this discourse, he declared the Truths, and identified the Birth:—at the conclusion of the Truths, the Brother in question attained the fruition of the First Path:—"At that time, the stout girl was the same, the lovesick brother was Sālūka, Ānanda was Little Redcoat, and I was Big Redcoat myself."

[1] Lit. edible lotus root.

[2] Heṭṭhamañca, 'perhaps the platform outside the house under the eaves, a favourite resort.' Cp. Rhys Davids, *Buddhist Birth Stories*, p. 277.

No. 287.

LĀBHA-GARAHA-JĀTAKA.

"*He that hath madness," etc.*—This story the Master told at Jetavana, about a fellow-priest of the Elder Sāriputta. [421] This brother came and greeted the Elder, and sitting on one side, he asked him to tell the way in which one could get gain, and how he could get dress and the like. The Elder replied, "Friend, there are four qualities which make a man successful in getting gain. He must get rid of modesty from his heart, must resign his orders, must seem to be mad even if he is not; he must speak slander; he must behave like a dancer; he must use unkind words everywhere." Thus he explained how a man gets a great deal. The brother objected to this method, and went away. The Elder went to his Master, and told him about it. The Master said, "This is not the first time that this brother spoke in dispraise of gain; he did the same before;" and then, at the request of the Elder, he told an old-world tale.

Once upon a time, when Brahmadatta was king of Benares, the Bodhisatta was born in a Brahmin family. When he grew up to the age of sixteen years, he had already mastered the three Vedas and the eighteen accomplishments; and he became a far-famed teacher, who educated a body of five hundred young men. One young man, a youth of virtuous life, approached his teacher one day with the question, "How is it these people get gain?"

The teacher answered, "My son, there are four qualities which procure gain for those people;" and he repeated the first stanza:—

"He that hath madness, he that slanders well,
That hath an actor's tricks, ill tales doth tell,
Such is the man that wins prosperity
Where all are fools: let this your maxim be."

[422] The pupil, on hearing his master's words, expressed his disapproval of gain-getting in the two following stanzas:—

"Shame upon him that gain or glory wins
By dire destruction and by wicked sins.

"With bowl in hand a homeless life I'll lead
Rather than live in wickedness and greed."

[423] Thus did the youth praise the quality of the religious life; and straight became a hermit, and craved alms with righteousness, cultivating the Attainments, until he became destined to Brahma's world.

When the Master had ended this discourse he thus identified the Birth:—"At that time the brother who disapproved of gain was the young man, but his teacher was I myself."

No. 288.

MACCH-UDDĀNA-JĀTAKA[1].

"*Who could believe the story,*" *etc.*—This story the Master told at Jetavana about a dishonest merchant. The circumstances have been told above.

Once upon a time, when Brahmadatta was king of Benares, the Bodhisatta was born in the family of a landed proprietor.

When he grew up, he became a wealthy man. He had a young brother. Afterwards their father died. They determined to arrange some business of their father's. This took them to a village, where they were paid a thousand pieces of money. On their way back, as they waited on a river-bank for the boat, they ate a meal out of a leaf-pottle. The Bodhisatta threw what he left into the Ganges for the fishes, giving the merit to the river-spirit. The spirit accepted this with gratification, which increased her divine power, and on thinking over this increase of her power, became aware what had happened. The Bodhisatta [424] laid his upper garment upon the sand, and there he lay down and went to sleep.

Now the young brother was of a rather thievish nature. He wanted to filch the money from the Bodhisatta and keep it himself; so he packed a parcel of gravel to look like the parcel of money, and put them both away.

When they had got aboard, and were come to mid-river, the younger stumbled against the side of the boat, and dropt overboard the parcel of gravel, as he thought, but really the money.

"Brother, the money's overboard!" he cried. "What's to be done?"

"What can we do? What's gone is gone. Never mind about it," replied the other.

But the river-spirit thought how pleased she had been with the merit she had received, and how her divine power had been increased, and resolved to take care of his property. So by her power she made a big-mouthed fish swallow the parcel, and took care of it herself.

When the thief got home, he chuckled over the trick he had served his brother, and undid the remaining parcel. There was nothing but gravel to be seen! His heart dried up; he fell on his bed, and clutched the bedstead.

[1] *Folk-lore Journal*, iii. 364.

Now some fishermen just then cast their nets for a draught. By power of the river-spirit, this fish fell into the net. The fishers took it to town to sell. People asked what the price was.

"A thousand pieces and seven annas," said the fishermen.

Everybody made fun of them. "We have seen a fish offered for a thousand pieces!" they laughed.

The fishers brought their fish to the Bodhisatta's door, and asked him to buy it.

"What's the price?" he asked.

"You may have it for seven annas," they said.

"What did you ask other people for it?"

"From other people we asked a thousand rupees and seven annas; but you may have it for seven annas," they said.

He paid seven annas for it, and sent it to his wife. She cut it open, and there was the parcel of money! [425] She called the Bodhisatta. He gave a look, and recognising his mark, knew it for his own. Thought he, "These fishers asked other people the price of a thousand rupees and seven annas, but because the thousand rupees were mine, they let me have it for seven annas only! If a man does not understand the meaning of this, nothing will ever make him believe:" and then he repeated the first stanza:—

"Who could believe the story, were he told,
That fishes for a thousand should be sold?
They're seven pence to me: how I could wish
To buy a whole string of this kind of fish!"

When he had said this, he wondered how it was that he had recovered his money. At the moment the river-spirit hovered invisibly in the air, and declared—

"I am the Spirit of the Ganges. You gave the remains of your meal to the fishes, and let me have the merit. Therefore I have taken care of your property;" and she repeated a stanza:—

"You fed the fish, and gave a gift to me.
This I remember, and your piety."

[426] Then the spirit told about the mean trick which the younger brother had played. Then she added, "There he lies, with his heart dried up within him. There is no prosperity for the cheat. But I have brought you your own, and I warn you not to lose it. Don't give it to your young thief of a brother, but keep it all yourself." Then she repeated the third stanza:—

"There's no good fortune for the wicked heart,
And in the sprites' respect he has no part;
Who cheats his brother of paternal wealth
And works out evil deeds by craft and stealth."

Thus spoke the spirit, not wishing that the treacherous villain should receive the money. But the Bodhisatta said, "That is impossible," and all the same sent the brother five hundred.

After this discourse, the Master declared the Truths:—at the conclusion of which the merchant entered upon the fruition of the first path:—and identified the Birth:—"At that time the younger brother was the dishonest merchant, but the elder was I myself."

No. 289.

NĀNA-CCHANDA-JĀTAKA.

"*We live in one house*," *etc.*—This story the Master told in Jetavana, about the venerable Ānanda's taking a valuable article. The circumstances will be explained in the Juṇha Birth, in the Eleventh Book[1].

---

[427] Now once upon a time, when Brahmadatta was reigning in Benares, the Bodhisatta was born as the son of his Queen Consort. He grew up, and was educated at Takkasilā; and became king on his father's death. There was a family priest of his father's who had been removed from his post, and being very poor lived in an old house.

One night it happened that the king was walking about the city in disguise, to explore it. Some thieves, their work done, had been drinking in a wine-shop, and were carrying some more liquor home in a jar. They spied him there in the street, and crying—"Halloo, who are you?" they knocked him down, and took his upper robe; then, they picked up their jar, and off they went, scaring him the while.

The aforesaid brahmin chanced at the time to be in the street observing the constellations. He saw how the king had fallen into unfriendly hands, and called to his wife; quickly she came, asking what it was. Said he[2], "Wife, our king has got into the hands of his enemies!" "Why,

[1] No. 456.

[2] *sā* is a mistake for *so*.

your reverence," said she, "what dealings have you with the king? His brahmins will see to it." This the king heard, and, going on a little, called out to the rascals, "I'm a poor man, masters—take my robe and let me go!" As he said this again and again, they let him go out of pity. He took note of the place they lived in, and turned back again.

Said the brahmin to his wife, "Wife, our king has got away from the hands of his enemies!" The king heard this as before; and entered his palace.

When dawn came, the king summoned his brahmins, and asked them a question.

"Have you been taking observations?"

"Yes, my lord."

"Was it lucky or unlucky?"

"Lucky, my lord."

"No eclipse?"

"No, my lord, none."

Said the king, "Go and fetch me the brahmin from such and such a house," giving them directions.

So they fetched the old chaplain, and the king proceeded to question him. [428]

"Did you take observations last night, master?"

"Yes, my lord, I did."

"Was there any eclipse?"

"Yes, my lord: last night you fell into the hands of your enemies, and in a moment you got free again."

The king said, "That is the kind of man a star-gazer ought to be." He dismissed the other brahmins; he told the old one that he was pleased with him, and bade him ask a boon. The man asked leave to consult with his family, and the king allowed him.

The man summoned wife and son, daughter-in-law and maidservant, and laid the matter before them. "The king has granted me a boon; what shall I ask?"

Said the wife, "Get me a hundred milch kine."

The son, named Chatta, said, "For me, a chariot drawn by fine lily-white thoroughbreds."

Then the daughter-in-law, "For me, all manner of trinkets, earrings set with gems, and so forth!"

And the maidservant (whose name was Puṇṇā), "For me, a pestle and mortar, and a winnowing basket."

The brahmin himself wanted to have the revenue of a village as his boon. So when he returned to the king, and the king wanted to know whether his wife had been asked, the brahmin replied, "Yes, my lord king; but those who are asked are not all of one mind"; and he repeated a couple of stanzas:—

"We live in one house, O king,
But we don't all want the same thing.
My wife's wish—a hundred kine;
A prosperous village is mine;
The student's of course is a carriage and horses,
Our girl wants an earring fine.
While poor little Puṇṇā, the maid,
Wants pestle and mortar, she said!"

"All right," said the king, "they shall all have what they want"; and repeated the remaining lines:—[429]

"Give a hundred kine to the wife,
To the goodman a village for life,
And a jewelled earring to the daughter:
A carriage and pair be the student's share,
And the maid gets her pestle and mortar[1]."

Thus the king gave the brahmin what he wished, and great honour besides; and bidding him thenceforward busy himself about the king's business, he kept the brahmin in attendance upon himself.

When the Master had ended this discourse, he identified the Birth: "At that time the Brahmin was Ānanda, but the king was I myself."

No. 290.

SĪLA-VĪMAṀSA-JĀTAKA[2].

"*Virtue is lovely*," *etc.*—This story the Master told at Jetavana, about a brahmin who put his reputation to the test. The circumstances which gave rise to it, and the story itself, are both given in the Sīlavīmaṁsa Birth-tale, in the First Book. Here, as before—

When Brahmadatta was king of Benares, his chaplain resolved to test his own reputation for virtue, and on two days abstracted a coin from the

[1] I hope the indulgent reader will pardon the rime.

[2] Compare Nos. 86, 290, 305, 330, 362.

Treasurer's counter. On the third day they dragged him to the king, and accused him of theft. On the way he noticed some snake-charmers making a snake dance. The king asked him what he had done such a thing for. The brahmin replied, "To try my reputation for virtue": and went on

"Virtue is lovely—so the people deem—
Virtue in all the world is held supreme.
Behold! this deadly snake they do not slay,
'For he is good,' they say.

[430] "Here I proclaim how virtue is all-blest
And lovely in the world: whereof possest
He that is virtuous evermore is said
Perfection's path to tread.

"To kinsfolk dear, he shines among his friends;
And when his union with the body ends,
He that to practise virtue has been fain
In heaven is born again."

Having thus in three stanzas declared the beauty of virtue and discoursed to them, the Bodhisatta went on—"Great king, a great deal has been given to you by my family, my father's property, my mother's, and what I have gained myself: there is no end to it. But I took these coins from the treasury to try my own value. Now I see how worthless in this world is birth and lineage, blood and family, and how much the best is virtue. I will embrace the religious life; allow me to do so!" After many entreaties, the king at last consented. He left the world, and retired to Himalaya, where he took to the religious life, and cultivated the Faculties and the Attainments until he came to Brahma's world.

When the Master had ended this discourse, he identified the Birth: "At that time the Brahman chaplain who tried his reputation for virtue was I myself."

No. 291.

BHADRA-GHAṬA-JĀTAKA.

[431] "*A ne'er-do-well did once,*" *etc.*—This story the Master told at Jetavana, about a nephew of Anāthapiṇḍika. This person had squandered an inheritance of forty crores of gold. Then he visited his uncle, who gave him a thousand, and bade him trade with it. The man squandered this, and then came again; and

once more he was given five hundred. Having squandered this like the rest, next time his uncle gave him two coarse garments; and when he had worn these out, and once more applied, his uncle had him taken by the neck and turned out of doors. The fellow was helpless, and fell down by a side-wall and died. They dragged him outside and threw him down there. Anāthapiṇḍika went and told the Buddha what had happened to his nephew. Said the Master, "How could you expect to satisfy the man whom I long ago failed to satisfy, even when I gave him the Wishing Cup?" and at his request, he proceeded to tell him an old-world tale.

Once upon a time, when Brahmadatta was reigning in Benares, the Bodhisatta was born as a rich merchant's son; and after his father's death, took his place. In his house was buried a treasure of four hundred million. He had an only son. The Bodhisatta gave alms and did good until he died, and then he came to life again as Sakka, king of the gods. His son proceeded to make a pavilion across the road, and sat down with many friends round him, to drink. He paid a thousand pieces to runners and tumblers, singers and dancers, and passed his time in drinking, gluttony, and debauchery; he wandered about, asking only for song, music, and dancing, devoted to his boon-companions, sunk in sloth. So in a short time he squandered all his treasure of four hundred millions, [432] all his property, goods, and furniture, and got so poor and miserable that he had to go about clad in rags.

Sakka, as he meditated, became aware how poor he was. Overcome with love for his son, he gave him a Wishing Cup, with these words: "Son, take care not to break this cup. So long as you keep it, your wealth will never come to an end. So take good care of it!" and then he returned to heaven.

After that the man did nothing but drink out of it. One day, he was drunk, and threw the cup into the air, catching it as it fell. But once he missed it. Down it fell upon the earth, and smashed! Then he got poor again, and went about in rags, begging, bowl in hand, till at last he lay down by a wall, and died.

When the Master had finished this tale, he went on:—

"A ne'er-do-well did once a Bowl acquire,
A Bowl that gave him all his heart's desire.
And of this Bowl so long as he took care,
His fortunes were all fair.

"When, proud and drunken, in a careless hour,
He broke the Bowl that gave him all this power,
Naked, poor fool! in rags and tatters, he
Fell in great misery.

"Not otherwise whoso great fortune owes,
But in the enjoying it no measure knows,
Is scorched anon, even as the knave—poor soul!—
That broke his Wishing Bowl."

Repeating these stanzas in his perfect wisdom, he identified the Birth: "At that time Anāthapiṇḍika's nephew was the rascal who broke the Lucky Cup, but I myself was Sakka."

No. 292.

SUPATTA-JĀTAKA[1].

[433] "*Here, in Benares city,*" *etc.*—This story the Master told in Jetavana, about a meal of rice mixed with new ghee, with red fish to flavour it, which was given by Elder Sāriputta to Bimbādevī. The circumstances are like those given above in the Abbhantara Birth-tale[2]. Here too the holy Sister had a pain in the stomach. The excellent Rāhula told the Elder. He seated Rāhula in his waiting-room, and went to the king to get the rice, red fish and new ghee. The lad gave it to the holy sister, his mother. No sooner had she eaten than the pain subsided. The king sent messengers to make enquiries, and after that always sent her that kind of food. One day they began to talk about it in the Hall of Truth: "Friend, the Captain of the Faith satisfied the Sister with such and such food." The Master came in, and asked what they were talking about: they told him. Said he, "This is not the first time, Brother, that Sāriputta has given Rāhula's mother what she wanted; he did the same before." So saying, he told an old-world tale.

Once upon a time, when Brahmadatta was king in Benares, the Bodhisatta was born as a Crow. He grew up, and became chief of eighty thousand crows, a Crow king, by name, Supatta, or Fairwing; and his chief mate went by the name of Suphassā or Softie, his chief Captain was called Sumukho—Prettybeak. With his eighty thousand subjects, he dwelt hard by Benares.

One day he and his mate in search of food passed over the king's kitchen. The king's cook had been preparing a host of dishes, of all sorts of fish, and he had uncovered the dishes for a moment, to cool them. Queen Crow smelt the odour of the food, and longed for a bit. But that day she said nothing.

[1] *Folk-lore Journal*, 3. 360.
[2] No. 281, above.

However the next day, when King Crow proposed that they should go a-feeding, she said, "Go by yourself: there's something I want very much!"

"What is it?" asked he.

"I want some of the king's food to eat; [434] and as I can't get it, I am going to die."

The Crow sat down to think. Prettybeak approached him and asked if anything had displeased him. King Crow told him what it was. "Oh, that'll be all right," said the Captain; and added, to console them both, "you stay where you are to-day, and I'll fetch the meat."

So he gathered the Crows together, and told them the matter. "Now come, and let's get it!" said he; and off they all flew together to Benares. He posted them in companies here and there, near the kitchen to watch; and he, with eight champions, sat on the kitchen roof. While waiting for the king's food to be served, he gave his directions to these: "When the food is taken up, I'll make the man drop the dishes. Once that is done there's an end of me. So four of you must fill your mouths with the rice, and four with the fish, and feed our royal pair with them; and if they ask where I am, say I'm coming."

Well, the cook got his various dishes all ready, hung them on a balance-pole, and went off towards the king's rooms. As he passed through the court, the Crow Captain with a signal to his followers flew and settled upon the carrier's chest, struck him with extended claws, with his beak, sharp as a spear-point, pecked the end of the man's nose, and with his two feet stopped up his jaws.

The king was walking up and down upon an upper floor, when looking out of a large window he saw what the crow was doing. He hailed the carrier: "—Hullo you, down with the dishes and catch the crow!" so the man dropt the dishes and caught the crow tight.

"Come here!" cried the king.

Then the crows ate all they wanted, [435] and picked up the rest as they had been told, and carried it off. Next all the others flocked up, and ate what remained. The eight champions gave it to their king and queen to eat. The craving of Softie was appeased.

The servant who was carrying the dinner brought his crow to the king.

"O Crow!" said he, "you have shown no respect for me! you have broken my servitor's nose! you have smashed my dishes! you have recklessly thrown away your life! What made you do such things?"

Answered the Crow, "O great king! Our king lives near Benares, and I am captain of his forces. His wife (whose name is Softie) conceived a great longing, and wanted a taste of your food. Our king told me what she craved. At once I devoted my life. Now I have sent her the food;

my desire is accomplished. This is the reason why I acted as I did." And to explain the matter, he said—

"Here in Benares city, O great king,
There dwells a king of Crows that hight Fairwing;
Who was attended by a following
Of eighty thousand Crows.

"Softie, his mate, had one o'ermastering wish:
She craved a supper of the king's own fish,
Fresh caught, cooked in his kitchen,—such a dish
As to kings' tables goes.

"You now behold me as their messenger;
It was my royal master sent me here;
And for that I my monarch do revere
I wounded that man's nose."

[436] When the king heard this, he said, "We do great honour to men, and yet cannot make friends of them. Even though we make presents of such things as a whole village, we can find no one willing to give his life for us. But this creature, crow as he is, sacrifices life for his king. He is very noble, sweet-speaking, and good." He was so pleased with the crow's good qualities that he did him the honour of giving him a white umbrella. But the crow saluted the king with this, his own gift, and descanted upon the virtues of Fairwing. The king sent for him, and heard his teaching, and sent them both food of the same sort as he ate himself; and for the rest of the crows he had cooked each day a large measure of rice. He himself walked according to the monition of the Bodhisatta, and protecting all creatures, practised virtue. The admonitions of Fairwing the crow were remembered for seven hundred years.

When the Master had ended this discourse, he identified the Birth: "At that time the king was Ānanda, the Captain was Sāriputta, but Supatta was I myself."

No. 293.

KĀYA-VICCHINDA-JĀTAKA.

"*Down smitten with a direful illness,*" *etc.*—This story the Master told at Jetavana about a certain man. We learn that there lived at Sāvatthi a man tormented by jaundice, given up by the doctors as a hopeless case. His wife and son wondered who could be found to cure him. The man thought, "If I can only get rid of this disease, I will take to the religious life." Now it happened that some days after he took something that did him good, and got well. Then he went to Jetavana, and asked admission into the Order. He received the lesser and greater orders from the Master, and before long attained to saiuthood. One day after this the brethren were talking together in the Hall of Truth: "Friend, So and so had jaundice, and vowed that if he got well he would embrace the religious life; he did so, and now he has attained sainthood." The Master came in, and asked what they talked about, sitting there together. [437] They told him. Then he said: "Brothers, this is not the only man who has done so. Long ago wise men, recovering from sickness, embraced a religious life, and secured their own advantage." And he told an old-world tale.

Once upon a time, when Brahmadatta was king of Benares, the Bodhisatta was born in a Brahmin family. He grew up, and began to amass wealth: but he fell sick of the jaundice. Even the physicians could do nothing for him, and his wife and family were in despair. He resolved that if he ever got well, he would embrace the religious life; and having taken something that did him good, he did get well, whereupon he went away to Himalaya and became a religious. He cultivated the Faculties and the Attainments, and dwelt in ecstatic happiness. "All this time," thought he, "I have been without this great happiness!" and he breathed out this aspiration:

"Down smitten with a direful illness, I
In utter torment and affliction lie,
My body quickly withers, like a flower
Laid in the sun upon the dust to dry.

"The noble seems ignoble, and pure the impure seems,
He that is blind, all beautiful a sink of foulness deems.

"Shame on that sickly body, shame, I say,
Loathsome, impure, and full of foul decay!
When fools are indolent, they fail to win
New birth in heaven, and wander from the way."

[438] Thus did the Great Being describe in various ways the nature of impurity and constant disease, and being disgusted with the body and all its parts, cultivated all his life the four excellent conditions of life, till he went to Brahma's world.

When the Master had ended this discourse, he proclaimed the Truths, and identified the Birth—many were they who attained the fruition of the First Path, and so forth—"At that time I myself was the ascetic."

No. 294.

JAMBU-KHĀDAKA-JĀTAKA[1].

"*Who is it sits,*" *etc.*—This story the Master told at the Bamboo-grove, about Devadatta and Kokālika. At the time when Devadatta began to lose his gettings and his repute, Kokālika went from house to house, saying, "Elder Devadatta is born of the line of the First Great King, of the royal stock of Okkāka[2], by an uninterrupted noble descent, versed in all the scriptures, full of ecstatic sanctity, sweet of speech, a preacher of the law. Give to the Elder, help him!" In these words he praised up Devadatta. On the other hand, Devadatta praised up Kokālika, in such words as these: "Kokālika comes from a northern brahmin family; he follows the religious life; he is learned in doctrine, a preacher of the law. Give to Kokālika, help him!" So they went about, praising each other, and getting fed in different houses. One day the brothers began to talk about it in the Hall of Truth. "Friend, Devadatta and Kokālika go about praising each other for virtues which they haven't got, and so getting food." The Master came in, and asked what they were talking about as they sat there. They told him. Said he, "Brethren, this is not the first time that these men have got food by praising each other. Long ago they did the same," and he told them an old-world tale.

Once upon a time, when Brahmadatta was king of Benares, the Bodhisatta became a tree-sprite in a certain rose-apple grove. [439] A Crow perched upon a branch of his tree, and began to eat the fruit. Then came a Jackal, and looked up and spied the Crow. Thought he, "If I flatter this creature, perhaps I shall get some of the fruit to eat!" So in flattery he repeated the first stanza:

"Who is it sits in a rose-apple tree—
Sweet singer! whose voice trickles gently to me?
Like a young peacock she coos with soft grace,
And ever sits still in her place."

The Crow, in his praise, responded with the second:

"He that is noble in breeding and birth
Can praise others' breeding, knows what they are worth.
Like a young tiger thou seemest to be:
Come, eat, Sir, what I give to thee!"

With these words she shook the branch and made some fruit drop.

[1] Compare No. 295, and Æsop's fable of the Fox and the Crow.

[2] A fabulous king, the same as Ikshvāku. See reff. in *J. P. T. S.* 1888, p. 17.

Then the spirit of the tree, beholding these two eating, after flattering each other, repeated the third stanza:

> "Liars foregather, I very well know.
> Here, for example, a carrion Crow,
> And corpse-eating Jackal, with puerile clatter
> Proceed one another to flatter!"

After repeating this stanza, the tree-sprite, assuming a fearful shape, scared them both away.

When the Master had ended this discourse, he summed up the Birth-tale; "At that time the Jackal was Devadatta, the Crow was Kokālika, but the Spirit of the Tree was I myself."

No. 295.

ANTA-JĀTAKA[1].

"*Like to a bull*," *etc.*—[440] This is another story told by the Master in the same place and about the same people. The circumstances are the same as before.

Once upon a time, when Brahmadatta was king of Benares, the Bodhisatta became the spirit of a castor-oil-tree which stood in the approach to a certain village. An old ox died in a certain village; and they dragged the carcase out and threw it down in the grove of these trees by the village gate. A Jackal came and began to eat its flesh. Then came a Crow, and perched upon the tree. When she saw the Jackal, she cast about whether by flattery she could not get some of this carcase to eat. And so she repeated the first stanza:

> "Like to a bull your body seems to be,
> Like to a lion your activity.
> O king of beasts! all glory be to thee!
> Please don't forget to leave a bit for me."

[1] *Folk-Lore Journal*, 3. 363. Compare No. 294.

On hearing this the Jackal repeated the second:

"They that of gentle birth and breeding be
Know how to praise the gentle worthily,
O Crow, whose neck is like the peacock's neck,
Come down from off the tree and take a peck!"

The Tree-spirit, on seeing this, repeated the third:

"The lowest of all beasts the Jackal is,
The Crow is lowest of all birds y-wis,
The Castor-oil of trees the lowest tree:—
And now these lowest things are here all three!"

[441] When the Master had ended this discourse he identified the Birth: "At that time Devadatta was the Jackal, Kokālika was the Crow, but the Tree-spirit was I myself.

No. 296.

SAMUDDA-JĀTAKA[1].

"*Over the salt sea wave,*" *etc.*—This story the Master told at Jetavana, about Elder Upananda. This man was a great eater and drinker; there was no satisfying him even with cartloads of provisions. During the rainy season he would pass his time at two or three different settlements, leaving his shoes in one, his walking-stick in another, and his water-jar in a third, and one he lived in himself. When he visited a country monastery, and saw the brothers with their requisites all ready, he began to talk about the four classes of contented ascetics[2]; laid hold of their garments, and made them pick up rags from the dust-heap; made them take earthen bowls, and give him any bowls that he fancied and their metal bowls; then he filled a cart with them, and carried them off to Jetavana. One day people began to talk in the Hall of Truth. "Friend, Upananda of the Sakka clan, a great eater, a greedy fellow, has been preaching religion to other people, and here he comes with a cartful of priests' property!" The Master came in, and wanted to know what they were talking of as they sat there. They told him. "Brethren," said he, "Upananda has gone wrong before by talking about this contentment. But a man ought first of all to become modest in his desires, before praising the good behaviour of other people.

"Yourself first stablish in propriety,
Then teach; the wise should not self-seeking be."

[1] *Folk-Lore Journal*, 3. 328.

[2] See Childers, p. 56 *b*. The recluse who is contented with the robes presented to him, with the food, with the bedding, and he who delights in meditation.

Pointing out this verse from the Dhammapada[1], and blaming Upananda, he went on, "This is not the first time, Brethren, that Upananda has been greedy. Long ago, he thought even the water in the ocean ought to be saved." And he told an old-world tale.

Once upon a time, when Brahmadatta was king of Benares, the Bodhisatta became a Sea-spirit. Now it so happened that a Water-crow was passing over the sea. He went flying about, and trying to check the shoals of fish and flocks of birds, crying,

"Don't drink too much of the sea-water! be careful of it!" [442] On seeing him, the Sea-spirit repeated the first stanza:

"Over the salt sea wave who flies?
Who checks the shoals of fish, and tries
The monsters of the deep to stay
Lest all the sea be drunk away?"

The Water-crow heard this, and answered with the second stanza:

"A drinker never satisfied
So people call me the world wide,
To drink the sea I fain would try,
And drain the lord of rivers dry."

On hearing which the Sea-spirit repeated the third:

"The ocean ever ebbs away,
And fills again the selfsame day.
Who ever knew the sea to fail?
To drink it up can none avail!"

With these words the spirit assumed a terrible shape and frightened the Water-crow away.

When the Master had ended this discourse, he identified the Birth: "At that time, Upananda was the Water-crow, but the Spirit was I myself."

No. 297.

KĀMA-VILĀPA-JĀTAKA.

"*O bird, that fliest,*" *etc.*—This story the Master told at Jetavana, about a man who pined for his former wife. The circumstances which called it forth are[2] explained in the Puppharatta Birth-tale[3], and the tale of the past in the Indriya Birth-tale[4].

---

[1] Verse 158.
[2] Reading *kathitaṁ*.
[3] No. 147 above, vol. i. page 312.
[4] No. 423.

So the man was impaled alive. As he hung there, he looked up and saw a crow flying through the air; and, nought recking of the bitter pain, he hailed the crow, to send a message to his dear wife, repeating these verses following:

"O bird, that fliest in the sky!
O winged bird, that fliest high!
Tell my wife, with thighs so fair:
Long will seem the time to her.

"She knows not sword and spear are set:
Full wroth and angry she will fret.
That is my torment and my fear,
And not that I am hanging here.

"My lotus-mail I have put by,
And jewels in my pillow lie,
And soft Benares cloth beside.
With wealth let her be satisfied."

[444] With these lamentations, he died.

When the Master had ended this discourse, he declared the Truths, and identified the Birth (now at the conclusion of the Truths, the lovesick brother attained the fruition of the First Path): "The wife then was the wife now; but the spirit who saw this, was I myself."

No. 298.

UDUMBARA-JĀTAKA[1].

"*Ripe are the figs,*" etc.—This story the Master told at Jetavana, about a certain Brother, who had made a hermitage to live in at a certain village on the frontier. This delightful dwelling stood upon a flat rock; a little well-swept spot, with enough water to make it pleasant, a village close at hand to go your rounds in, and friendly people to give food. A Brother on his rounds arrived at this place. The Elder who lived in it did the duties of host to the new arrival, and next day took him along with him for his rounds. The people gave him food, and invited him to visit them again next day. After the new-comer had thus fared a few days, he meditated by what means he could oust the other [445] and get hold of the hermitage. Once when he had come[2] to wait upon the Elder, he asked, "Have you ever visited the Buddha, friend?" "Why no, Sir; there's

[1] *Folk-Lore Journal*, 3. 255.
[2] Reading *āgantvā* (which is surely right).

no one here to look after my hut, or I should have gone before." "Oh, I'll look after it while you are gone to visit the Buddha," said the new-comer; and so the owner went, after laying injunctions upon the villagers to take care of the holy Brother until his return. The new-comer proceeded to backbite his host, and hinted to the villagers all sorts of faults in him. The other visited his Master, and returned; but the new-comer refused him harbourage. He found a place to abide in, and next day went on his rounds in the village. But the villagers would not do their duty by him. He was much discouraged, and went back to Jetavana, where he told the Brethren all about it. They began to discuss the matter in their Hall of Truth: "Friend, Brother So-and-so has turned Brother So-and-so out of his hermitage, and taken it for himself!" The Master came in, and wanted to know what they were discussing as they sat there. They told him. Said he, "Brethren, this is not the first time that this man turned the other out of his dwelling;" and he told them an old-world tale.

Once on a time, when Brahmadatta was reigning in Benares, the Bodhisatta became a Tree-spirit in the woods. At that time during the rainy season rain used to pour down seven days on a stretch. A certain small red-faced Monkey lived in a rock-cave sheltered from the rain. One day he was sitting at the mouth of it, in the dry, quite happy. As he sat there, a big black-faced Monkey, wet through, perishing with cold, spied him. "How can I get that fellow out, and live in his hole?" he wondered. Puffing out his belly, and making as though he had eaten a good meal, he stopped in front of the other, and repeated the first stanza:

"Ripe are the figs, the banyans good,
And ready for the Monkey's food.
Come along with me and eat!
Why should you for hunger fret?"

[446] Redface believed all this, and longed to have all this fruit to eat. So he went off, and hunted here, and hunted there, but no fruit could he find. Then he came back again; and there was Blackface sitting inside his cave! He determined to outwit him; so stopping in front he repeated the second stanza:

"Happy he who honour pays
To his elders full of days;
Just as happy I feel now
After all that fruit, I vow!"

The big monkey listened, and repeated the third:

"When Greek meets Greek, then comes the tug of war;
A monkey scents a monkey's tricks afar.
Even a young one were too sharp by half;
But old birds never can be caught with chaff."

The other made off.

When the Master ended this discourse, he summed up the birth-tale: "At that time the owner of the hut was the little monkey, the interloper was the big black monkey, but the Tree-spirit was I myself."

No. 299.

KOMĀYA-PUTTA-JĀTAKA[1].

[447] "*Aforetime you were used,*" *etc.*—This story the Master told in Pubbārāma, about some Brethren who were rude and rough in their manners. These Brethren, who lived on the floor below that where the Master was, talked of what they had seen and heard, and were quarrelsome and abusive. The Master called Mahāmoggallāna to him, and bade him go startle them. The Elder rose in the air, and just touched the foundation of the house with his great toe. It shook to the furthest edge of ocean! The Brothers were frightened to death, and came and stood outside. Their rough behaviour became known among the Brethren. One day they got to talking about it in the Hall of Truth. "Friend, there are some Brethren who have retired to this house of salvation, who are rough and rude; they do not see the impermanence, sorrow and unreality of the world, nor do their duty." The Master came in, and asked what they were discussing as they sat there. They told him. "This is not the first time, Brethren," said he, "that they have been rough and rude. They were the same before." And he told them an old-world tale.

Once upon a time, when Brahmadatta reigned king in Benares, the Bodhisatta was born as a brahmin's son in a village. They named him Komāyaputta. By and bye he went out and embraced the religious life in the region of Himalaya. There were some frivolous ascetics who had made a hermitage in that region, and there they lived. But they did not take the means to induce religious ecstasy. They fetched the fruits from the woods, to eat; then they spent the time laughing and joking together. They had a monkey, rude-mannered like themselves, which gave them endless amusement by his grimaces and antics.

Long they lived in this place, till they had to go amongst men again to get salt and condiments. After they went away, the Bodhisatta lived in their dwelling-place. The monkey played his pranks for him as he had done for the others. The Bodhisatta snapt his fingers at him, and gave him a lecture, saying, "One who lives with well-trained ascetics [448]

[1] *Folk-Lore Journal*, 3. 254.

ought to behave properly, ought to be well-advised in his actions, and devoted to meditation." After that, the monkey was always virtuous and well-behaved.

After this, the Bodhisatta moved away. The other ascetics returned with their salt and condiments. But the monkey no longer played his pranks for them. "What's this, my friend?" they asked. "Why don't you make sport, as you used to do?" One of them repeated the first stanza:

"Aforetime you were used to play
Where in this hut we hermits stay.
O monkey! as a monkey do;
When you are good we love not you."

On hearing this, the Monkey repeated the second stanza:

"All perfect wisdom by the word
Of wise Komāya I have heard.
Think me not now as I was late;
Now 'tis my love to meditate."

Hereupon the anchorite repeated the third:

"If seed upon the rock you sow,
Though rain should fall, it will not grow.
You may hear perfect wisdom still;
But meditate you never will."

---

[449] When the Master had ended this discourse, he declared the Truths, and identified the Birth: "At that time these Brothers were the frivolous anchorites, but Komāyaputta was I myself."

No. 300.

VAKA-JĀTAKA[1].

[449] "*The wolf who takes,*" *etc.*—This story the Master told at Jetavana, about old friendship. The circumstances were the same in detail as in the Vinaya[1]; this is an abstract of them. The reverend Upasena, a two-years' man, visited

[1] *Mahāvagga*, i. 31. 3 foll. (trans. in *S. B. E.*, i. p. 175); *Folk-Lore Journal*, 3. 359; Morris, *Contemp. Rev.* xxix. 739.

the Master along with a first year's man who lived in the same monastery; the Master rebuked him, and he retired. Having acquired spiritual insight, and attained to sainthood, having got contentment and kindred virtues, having undertaken the Thirteen Practices of a Recluse, and taught them to his fellows, while the Blessed One was secluded for three months, he with his brethren, having accepted the blame first given for wrong speech and nonconformity, received in the second instance approval, in the words, "Henceforth, let any brothers visit me when they will, provided they follow the Thirteen Practices of a Recluse." Thus encouraged, he returned and told it to the Brethren. After that, the brothers followed these practices before coming to visit the Master; then, when he had come out from his seclusion, they would throw away their old rags and put on clean garments. As the Master with all the body of the Brethren went round to inspect the rooms, [450] he noticed these rags lying about, and asked what they were. When they told him, he said, "Brethren, the practice undertaken by these brothers is short-lived, like the wolf's holy day service"; and he told them an old-world tale.

Once upon a time, when Brahmadatta reigned king in Benares, the Bodhisatta came to life as Sakka, king of the gods. At that time a Wolf lived on a rock by the Ganges bank. The winter floods came up and surrounded the rock. There he lay upon the rock, with no food and no way of getting it. The water rose and rose, and the wolf pondered: "No food here, and no way to get it. Here I lie, with nothing to do. I may as well keep a sabbath feast." Thus resolved to keep a sabbath, as he lay he solemnly resolved to keep the religious precepts. Sakka in his meditations perceived the wolf's weak resolve. Thought he, "I'll plague that wolf"; and taking the shape of a wild goat, he stood near, and let the wolf see him.

"I'll keep Sabbath another day!" thought the Wolf, as he spied him; up he got, and leapt at the creature. But the goat jumped about so that the Wolf could not catch him. When our Wolf saw that he could not catch him, he came to a standstill, and went back, thinking to himself as he lay down again, "Well, my Sabbath is not broken after all."

Then Sakka, by his divine power, hovered above in the air; said he,

"What have such as you, all unstable, to do with keeping a Sabbath? You didn't know that I was Sakka, and wanted a meal of goat's-flesh!" and thus plaguing and rebuking him, he returned to the world of the gods.

"The wolf, who takes live creatures for his food,
And makes a meal upon their flesh and blood,
Once undertook a holy vow to pay,—
Made up his mind to keep the Sabbath day.

"When Sakka learnt what he resolved to do,
He made himself a goat to outward view.
Then the blood-bibber leaped to seize his prey,
His vow forgot, his virtue cast away.

[451] "Even so some persons in this world of ours,
That make resolves which are beyond their powers,
Swerve from their purpose, as the wolf did here
As soon as he beheld the goat appear."

When the Master had ended this discourse, he identified the Birth as follows: "At that time I myself was Sakka."

END OF THE THIRD BOOK.

INDEX OF NAMES AND PALI WORDS.

*** This Index contains all names of persons and places, real or legendary (except such as in the Stories of the Past are manifestly invented); all names of literary documents quoted in the text; and the parallels or illustrations given in the notes; but it does not include the names of previous translators of any of the stories.

Aciravatī, river 65, 251
Aesop referred to 76, 285, 299
Aggālava, shrine of 197
Ajātasattu, a king 164, 165, 168, 275
Ālavī, a place 197
Ambala tower 170
Ānanda 4, 13, 17, 18, 21, 22, 26, 28, 34, 36, 45, 52, 56, 63, 64, 65, 66, 67, 85, 89, 94, 119, 122, 124, 142, 160, 170, 178, 193, 199, 203, 215, 218, 220, 223, 268, 272, 274, 282, 286, 290, 292, 297
Ānanda, a fish 242
Anātha-piṇḍika 200, 239, 279, 280, 282, 293, 294, 295
" the younger 200
Aṅga, kingdom of 148
Anotatta, lake 63
Anuruddha 64, 87, 178, 260
Araka 43, 137
Assaji, a heretic 264
Atharva Veda referred to 101

Babrius referred to 123
Bamboo Grove (Veluvana) 26, 48, 67, 85, 106, 113, 131, 138, 140, 145, 154, 168, 172, 260, 299
Benares 1, 3, 5, 8, 10, 11, 13, 19, 21, 23, 24, 28, 32, 33, 34, 35, 36, 39, 41, 44, 46, 47, 48, 50, 51, 52, 53, 55, 57, 59, 60, 62, 64, 66, 67, 68, 69, 70, 75, 76, 79, 80, 81, 83, 84, 85, 86, 87, 88, 92, 93, 94, 96, 97, 99, 101, 103, 104, 105, 106, 111, 113, 114, 115, 117, 121, 123, 125, 126, 127, 129, 131, 138, 139, 140, 141, 143, 145, 146, 149, 152, 153, 154, 156, 157, 158, 159, 160, 162, 163, 164, 165, 166, 168, 169, 171, 172, 178, 179, 180, 182, 183, 184, 186, 187, 189, 190, 193, 194, 195, 197, 200, 203, 205, 207, 218, 219, 221, 223, 224, 227, 232, 233, 235, 238, 240, 242, 244, 245, 246, 248, 261, 262, 264, 265, 267, 268, 269, 271, 273, 274, 276, 280, 284, 285, 287, 288, 290, 292, 294, 296, 297, 298, 299, 300, 302, 304, 305, 307
Bhaddaji, Elder 229, 230, 231
Bhaddiya, city 229, 230
Bhaggava 56
Bharhut Stupa 60, 106, 152, 197, 235, 237, 248
Bharu, king, city, kingdom 119, 121
Bhummaja, a heretic 264
Bimbā, Sister 267, 268, 295
Bimbisāra, a king 164, 275
Bodhisatta 1, 2, 5, 6, 8, 10, 11, 12, 16, 17, 19, 21, 22, 23, 24, 25, 26, 27, 28, 29, 32, 33, 34, 36, 37, 38, 39, 40, 41, 43, 44, 45, 46, 47, 48, 49, 50, 52, 53, 55, 56, 57, 58, 59, 60, 62, 64, 66, 67, 68, 74, 75, 76, 79, 81, 82, 83, 84, 85, 86, 88, 90, 92, 93, 94, 96, 97, 98, 99, 101, 102, 103, 105, 106, 110, 111, 113, 114, 115, 117, 119, 121, 122, 123, 124, 125, 126, 127, 128, 129, 130, 131, 132, 133, 134, 135, 138, 139, 140, 141, 143, 144, 146, 149, 152, 153, 154, 155, 156, 157, 159, 160, 161, 162, 163, 165, 166, 167, 168, 169, 170, 171, 172, 173, 174, 175, 177, 178, 179, 180, 181, 182, 183, 186, 187, 188, 189, 190, 191, 192, 197, 200, 201, 202, 203, 205, 206, 207, 208, 209, 218, 219, 220, 221, 223, 224, 227, 228, 229, 232, 233, 236, 238, 239, 240, 241, 244, 245, 246, 247, 248, 250, 251, 253, 260, 261, 262, 263, 264, 265, 267, 268, 273, 274, 276, 280, 282, 284, 285, 287, 288, 289, 290, 293, 294, 297, 298, 299, 300, 302, 304, 305, 307

Book of the Knight de la Tour Landry referred to 92
Bower MS. referred to 100
Brahma 29, 30, 31, 37, 39, 42, 43, 45, 48, 51, 62, 92, 98, 153, 188, 193, 199, 220, 229, 247, 285, 287, 293, 298
Brahmadatta 1, 2, 3, 5, 8, 10, 11, 19, 21, 23, 28, 34, 36, 39, 41, 44, 46, 47, 48, 50, 51, 53, 55, 57, 59, 60, 64, 66, 68, 70, 75, 76, 79, 81, 85, 88, 92, 93, 94, 96, 97, 99, 101, 103, 105, 106, 111, 113, 114, 115, 117, 121, 123, 125, 126, 127, 129, 138, 140, 143, 145, 152, 154, 156, 159, 160, 162, 163, 165, 168, 171, 172, 179, 180, 182, 183, 184, 186, 187, 189, 193, 197, 200, 203, 205, 218, 221, 223, 224, 227, 232, 233, 235, 240, 245, 246, 248, 261, 262, 264, 267, 268, 273, 276, 280, 284, 285, 287, 288, 290, 292, 294, 298, 299, 300, 302, 304, 305, 307
Buddha 11, 31, 37, 51, 53, 54, 56, 57, 58, 59, 64, 77, 91, 92, 97, 101, 103, 121, 127, 130, 137, 140, 151, 153, 161, 166, 172, 178, 180, 182, 189, 199, 207, 218, 229, 230, 238, 251, 266, 267, 268, 273, 280, 282, 283, 284, 303, 304
Buddhaghosha referred to 122
Buddha Kassapa 177
Buddhas, Seven 102

Cariyā-pitaka referred to 110, 251, 262
Çatapatha-brāhmaṇa referred to 12
Ceylon 89
Ciñcā 85, 112
Cittakūṭa, Mount 74, 123
Cittalatā, a grove 133
Cittarāja, a goblin 254
Cullavagga quoted or referred to 11, 17, 26, 75, 100, 103, 110, 140, 168

Daddara, Mount 6, 46
Dakkhiṇāgiri, a place 237, 238
Daṇḍaka 23, 24, 26
Dantapura, city 252, 260
Dasaratha, a name 208
Devadatta 26, 27, 28, 42, 48, 49, 68, 85, 87, 103, 104, 106, 107, 110, 112, 113, 114, 131, 138, 139, 140, 142, 145, 154, 155, 165, 166, 167, 168, 170, 172, 178, 262, 299, 300, 301
Dhammapada (or its Commentary) referred to 3, 65, 66, 115, 123, 177, 218, 241, 251, 257, 284, 302
Dhanañjaya, a merchant 239
,, a legendary king 251, 252, 254
Dhanuggahatissa, Elder 275, 279
Divyāvadāna referred to 118, 216, 229

Gagga 12
Gandhāra 32, 152, 153
Ganges 101, 105, 111, 179, 197, 229, 230, 233, 237, 246, 281, 288, 289, 307
Ganges, the heavenly 45
Garahitapiṭṭhi Rock 130
Garuḷa xx, 10, 11
Gayāsīsa 26, 138
Gesta Romanorum referred to 92
Gotama 118, 151, 152, 172, 180, 182, 267, 283, 284
Gotamī 142
Grimm referred to 69, 207
Guttila, the musician 172, 178

Herodotus quoted 15
Herondas quoted 127
Hesiod quoted 15
Himalaya 5, 8, 24, 28, 36, 38, 39, 43, 45, 47, 50, 51, 53, 59, 63, 70, 71, 75, 92, 97, 110, 111, 119, 120, 123, 124, 129, 137, 138, 140, 159, 160, 162, 168, 179, 182, 187, 190, 191, 192, 193, 203, 235, 246, 262, 268, 270, 271, 274, 280, 284, 293, 298, 305
Hitopadesa referred to 181

Indapatta, a city 149, 251, 252
India, *saepissime*
Indian Nights' Entertainments quoted 129
Isipatana, a place near Benares 213, 244

Jains, the 182
Janapadakalyāṇī 63, 64
Janasandha, a legendary king 207, 209
Jātaka-Mālā referred to 44, 262
Jātakas referred to in the text:
Abbhantara 295
Cullanāradakassapa 285
(Daddara, not by name 75)
Gijjha 28
Indriya 79
,, 302
Juṇha 290
Kāka 221
(Kalāya-mutthi, not by name 146)
Kāliṅga-bodhi 222
Kāma 149
Khadiraṅga 279
Mahābodhi 53
Mahāsāra 17
Mahāsīlava 273
Mahā-ummagga 43, 53, 80
Mahilāmukha 67
(Nakula, not by name 246)
Naṅguṭṭha 29
(Paṇṇika, not by name 126)
Puppharatta 302
Sāketa 57
,, (not by name) 162
Sāma 34
Saṁvara 13
Sigāla 218
Sīlavīmaṁsa 292
Suruci 231
Takkāriya 123
,, 244
Tesakuṇa 1
Uddāla 47
Ummadantī 81
Ummagga, *see* Mahā-ummagga

Jātakas referred to in the text (*cont.*):
Uraga 36
,, (not by name) 246
Jātakas translated in this book:
Abbhantara 267
Ādiccupaṭṭhāna 50
Alīna-citta 13
Anabhirati 68
Anta 300
Araka 42
Ārāma-dūsa 237
Asadisa 60
Asitābhu 158
Assaka 108
Baka 161
Bandhanāgāra 97
Bhadra-ghaṭa 293
Bharu 118
Catumaṭṭa 73
Cūlanandiya 140
Culla-paduma 81
Culla-palobhana 227
Daddara 45
Dadhivāhana 69
Dhammadhaja 131
Dūbhiya-makkaṭa 48
Duddada 59
Dūta 221
Dutiya-palāyi 153
Ekapada 163
Gagga 11
Gahapati 94
Gāmaṇi-caṇḍa 207
Gaṅgeyya 104
Garahita 129
Gijjha 34
Giridanta 67
Guṇa 17
Gūtha-pāṇa 147
Guttila 172
Harita-māta 164
Indasamānagotta 28
Jambu-khādaka 299
Jarudapāna 205
Kacchapa 55
,, 123
,, 246
Kakaṇṭaka 43
Kakkara 112
Kakkaṭa 235
Kalāya-muṭṭhi 51
Kalyāṇa-dhamma 44
Kāmanīta 149
Kāmavilāpa 302
Kandagalaka 113
Kapi 187
Kāsāva 138
Kāya-vicchinda 297
Keḷisīla 98
Khandha-vatta 100
Khanti-vaṇṇana 145
Khurappa 231
Kiṁsukopama 184
Komāyaputta 305
Jātakas translated in this book (*cont.*):
Kosiya 146
Kumbhīla 145
Kuṇḍaka-kucchi-sindhava 199
Kuru-dhamma 251
Kuruṅga-miga 106
Kūṭa-vāṇija 127
Lābha-garaha 287
Lola 248
Maccha 125
Macchuddāna 288
Mahā-panāda 229
Mahā-piṅgala 165
Mahisa 262
Makkaṭa 47
Mandhātu 216
Maṇi-cora 85
Maṇi-kaṇṭha 197
Maṇi-sūkara 283
Mittāmitta 91
Mora 23
Mudu-pāṇi 224
Mūla-pariyāya 180
Nakula 36
Nānacchanda 290
Pabbatūpatthara 88
Pādañjali 183
Paduma 222
Palāyi 151
Puṇṇa-nadī 121
Puṭa-bhatta 142
Puṭa-dūsaka 266
Rādha 92
Rājovāda 1
Romaka 260
Rucira 250
Ruhaka 79
Sabba-dāṭha 168
Sādhu-sīla 96
Sāketa 162
Sakuṇagghi 40
Sālaka 186
Sālūka 285
Saṁgāma-vacara 63
Samiddhi 39
Saṁkappa 189
Samudda 301
Santhava 29
Sata-dhamma 57
Satapatta 264
Seggu 126
Seyya 273
Sigāla 4
Sīha-camma 76
Sīha-koṭṭhuka 75
Sīlānisaṁsa 77
Sīla-vīmaṁsa 292
Siri 279
Siri-kālakaṇṇi 80
Somadatta 115
Suhanu 21
Sujāta 239
Suka 203
Sūkara 7
Suṁsumāra 110

Jātakas referred to in this book (*cont.*):
Sunakha 170
Supatta 295
Susīma 31
Telovāda 182
Tila-muṭṭhi 193
Tinduka 53
Tirīṭa-vaccha 218
Ucchiṭṭha-bhatta 117
Udapāna-dūsaka 243
Udumbara 303
Ulūka 242
Upāhana 154
Upasāḷha 37
Uraga 9
Vaccha-nakha 160
Vaḍḍhaki-sūkara 275
Vaka 306
Valāhassa 89
Vālodaka 65
Vātagga-sindhava 233
Vikaṇṇaka 157
Vīṇā-thūṇa 156
Vinīlaka 26
Vīraka 103
Vīticcha 178
Vyaggha 244
Jātiyā grove 229
Jeta, prince 152
Jetavana 7, 11, 13, 17, 21, 23, 28, 29, 31, 36, 37, 40, 42, 44, 45, 47, 50, 51, 55, 59, 60, 63, 64, 65, 68, 69, 73, 75, 76, 77, 79, 88, 89, 92, 94, 96, 97, 98, 103, 104, 108, 112, 117, 118, 119, 121, 123, 125, 126, 127, 129, 138, 142, 145, 146, 147, 149, 151, 152, 153, 156, 157, 158, 160, 161, 163, 165, 170, 178, 183, 184, 186, 187, 193, 199, 200, 203, 205, 207, 216, 218, 221, 222, 223, 224, 227, 231, 233, 235, 237, 242, 244, 246, 248, 250, 251, 262, 264, 266, 267, 273, 275, 283, 285, 287, 288, 290, 292, 293, 295, 297, 298, 301, 302, 303, 306
Jumna 105

Kāliṅga, a kingdom 252, 260
Kalyāṇi, river in Ceylon 90
Kāmanīta, a brahmin 149
Kaṁsa, King 274
Kapila 63
Kāsi 11, 39, 47, 48, 50, 59, 70, 71, 92, 94, 101, 103, 108, 115, 117, 121, 143, 154, 164, 171, 179, 218, 246, 264, 268, 275, 280
Kassapa 13
,, Buddha 77, 177
,, the Elder 260
,, the tortoise clan 247
Kattika, a month 254
,, feast 254
Kekaka, a city 149, 150
Khandhakaṁ 283
Khemā 24
Khuddaka Pāṭha quoted 280
Kīṭāgiri, a place 264
Kitavāsa, King 137
Kokālika 45, 46, 75, 76, 77, 123, 124, 244, 245, 246, 299, 300, 301
Kolita, a man 260
Komāya 306
Koṇḍañña clan 247
Kosala 1, 2, 3, 4, 9, 16, 17, 51, 88, 89, 97, 118, 145, 146, 164, 200, 218, 246, 268, 273, 275
Kosalā, a princess 275
Kosiya ('owl'), name of a clan 175
Koṭi, a village 230
Kuccāna, a man 260
Kukkurovāda referred to 40
Kuru, a city 150
,, kingdom 251

Lakuṇṭaka, Elder 98, 100
Lāḷudāyi, Elder, *see* Udāyi.
Licchavi 4, 7
Lohita, a heretic 264

Magadha 38, 148
Mahākassapa 64, 197
Mahākosala, King 164, 275
Mahāmāyā 17, 34, 98
Mahānāma the Sakya 54
Mahāsoṇa 21
Mahāvagga referred to 230, 306
Mahāvana 4
Mahāvastu referred to 60, 62, 110, 112
Mallians, the 65, 160
Mallikā 2, 3
Manosilā 63
Manu quoted 275
Māra 41, 167
Mātali, charioteer of Sakka 176, 178
Mathura, carving at, identified as a Jātaka scene 90
Māyā 260
Mettiya, a heretic 264
Milinda referred to 140, 168, 172, 216
Mithilā, a town 27, 231
Moggallāna 4, 7, 26, 64, 74, 107, 119, 183, 244, 245, 246, 268, 305

Nāgadīpa, island off Ceylon 90
Nāḷāgiri, elephant 140, 168
Nāḷikera, island of 121
Nanda 63, 64, 65
,, a place 137
Nandaka's preaching 268
Nandana, a grove 133
Nandapaṇḍita, a man 260
Nātaputta 182
Nāthaputta 182, 183
Nerbudda, the 237
New Testament referred to 77
Nirvana 17, 26, 78, 91, 139, 184, 230, 282
North Indian Notes and Queries quoted 30, 72, 129, 132

Okkāka, a mythical king 299

Pacceka-buddha 57, 137, 139, 231, 282
Pāli words explained:
agatigataṁ 1
ahivātaroga 55, 206
āḷambara drum 237
ānaka drum 237
aññaṁ vyākaroti 230
asura (fallen angel) 99
caturaṅgasamannāgataṁ 134
citta-pasāda 59
dija, 'twice-born,' of birds and brahmins 162
gandhakuṭī 152
gandhapañcaṅgulikaṁ 72
gāvutaddhayojanamatte 147
heṭṭhamañca 286
-jaṁghakahāpaṇādigahanena 166
jātaveda, 'fire' 226
kākaguyha 122
kākapeyya 122, 302
kālaghasa 181
kiṁsuka tree 184
lakāra, laṅkāra 78
nakkhatta 194
nāsikavāta 206
ñatti 258
peta (ghost) 99
rajjugāhakaamacca 257
sālaka, a term of abuse 186
sāratthi 257
tinduka tree 53
titthiya 182
Panāda, a legendary king 230, 231
Pañcatantra referred to 79, 81, 83, 123, 285
Paṇḍuka, a heretic 264
Pāṇini referred to 122
Pārāsariya, a brahmin teacher 142
Pasenadi, King 11, 200, 275
Phaedrus referred to 123
Piṭakas, the Three 172, 180
Plato referred to 134
Potali, city of 108
Pubbārāma 305
Punabbasu, a heretic 264
Puṇṇa, a man 260
Puññalakkhaṇā, Lady 279, 280
Pythagoreans compared 134

Questions of Milinda referred to 140, 168, 172, 216

Raghuvaṁsa quoted 32
Rāhula 46, 48, 75, 98, 188, 268, 295
Rāhula's mother 87, 98, 260, 268, 272, 295
Rājagaha 38, 39, 138, 264
Roja the Mallian 160, 161

Sāketa, a place 162
,, a name 162
Sakka 63, 70, 87, 99, 100, 132, 133, 134, 135, 149, 150, 151, 152, 174, 175, 176, 177, 216, 217, 231, 259, 260, 269, 294, 295, 307, 308
Sakunovāda-sutta 40
Sakya clan (Sākiya, Sakka) 11, 267, 283, 301
Samiddhi 39
Saṁyutta Nikāya referred to 100
Sanchi Tope 60, Addenda p. xx
Sāriputta 4, 7, 17, 26, 27, 34, 36, 64, 74, 78, 103, 107, 110, 112, 119, 138, 142, 183, 199, 200, 203, 244, 245, 246, 260, 262, 267, 268, 272, 287, 295, 297
Satadhamma 57
Sāvatthi 9, 31, 44, 52, 55, 59, 65, 68, 91, 104, 127, 138, 142, 151, 156, 158, 163, 178, 189, 199, 205, 216, 223, 229, 233, 235, 251, 262, 264, 266, 268, 297
Senaka 54
Seneca quoted 127
Sīhasenapati 182
Simonides referred to 134
Sineru, Mount 189
Sirīsavatthu, a goblin town 89
Subhagavana Park 180
Suddhodhana 34, 98
Suhanu 22
Sujātā, a lady 239, 240, 242
Sundarī, a woman murdered by the heretics 283, 284
Susīma 32, 33, 34
Sutta Nipāta referred to 196, 284
Suttavibhaṅga referred to 197

Takkasilā 2, 27, 32, 36, 47, 50, 59, 60, 68, 96, 121, 141, 152, 153, 189, 193, 195, 196, 218, 221, 224, 241, 251, 273, 280, 290
Talmud referred to 221
Tapoda Park 39
Tathāgata 60, 140, 154, 163, 184, 251
Tevijja-Sutta referred to 127
Therīgāthā referred to 55
Tibetan Tales referred to 80, 81, 216
Tunisische Märchen referred to 129

Udāna quoted 283
Udāyi, a foolish Elder 115, 116, 183, 184
Ukkaṭṭhā, a place 180
Upananda, Elder 301, 302
Upasāḷha 37, 38
Upasena, a Brother 306
Uppalavaṇṇā, a woman 260
Utta, Elder 275
Uttarapañcāla, a city 149, 150

Vacaspati's Dictionary quoted 122
Vajirā, princess 275
Vedas, the Three 30, 32, 33, 34, 60, 68, 69, 168, 180, 181, 287
Vejayanta, Sakka's palace 152
Veḷuvana, *see* Bamboo Grove
Vesāli, a place 4, 180
Vessavana, 12, 271, 272
Videha, kingdom of 27, 28, 231
Vimāna-vatthu referred to 175, 177, 178
Vinaya mentioned 306
Visākhā, a lady 200, 239

Yama, gatekeeper of hell 167

INDEX OF MATTERS.

Accomplishments, Eighteen 60, 287
Air, passing through the, a supernatural power of ascetics 70, 71, 191, 192, 229
Alms for alms 57, 214
Alms-halls 83, 84, 252, 253
Alms, how not to give 31
Alms-pilgrimage 230, 237
Archer's garb 61
Army, its four parts 60
,, modes of drawing up 275
Ascetics, four classes of contented 301
,, Thirteen Practices of 307
Ascetic, sham 47, 139, 188, 261, 278
Astrology 16, 127, 291
Attainments, *see* Faculties and 287

Bath-money, a queen's allowance 164, 275
Being, Five Elements of 184
,, Eighteen Constituents of 184
Birth: immediate re-incarnation due to keen desire, and brought about without parents 264
Birth-fire 30
Blessings, Eleven 9, 42
Bodhisatta peculiar from his birth 228
,, tempted and sins 228, 265
Bonds, what are the real 228
Buddha, attempts to injure 85, 106, 110, 131, 140, 165, 166, 168, 172
,, imitating of 103, 113

Captain of the Faith 7, 64, 112, 138, 200, 268, 295
Carpenters, village of 14; their tools and mode of work 14
Chinese funeral custom 25
City guards 98
Clan, tortoise 247
Commander-in-chief 13
Constituents of Being, Eighteen 184
Conception by eating fruit alluded to 269
,, ceremonies done at 1
Coronation: fig-wood chair and three shells used in the ceremony 278
Cranes conceived at the sound of thunder 249
'Crane's sleep,' proverb for trickery 162

Disciples, four classes of 7
Discrepancy between verses and story 127, 155
Disease tricked by escaping through a hole in the wall 55
'Door' question, the 163
Dove's-foot nymphs 63
Drum made of a crab's claw 237

Earning a living, Twenty-one unlawful ways 57
Ecstasies, Four 172
Eighteen Accomplishments 60, 287
Eighteen Constituents of Being 184
Eight Stages of Knowledge 180
Elements of Being, Five 184
,, Four Principal 184
Elephant Festivals 32, 33, 34
,, manual 32, 33, 34
,, of State 16
,, with thorn in its foot 14
Eleven Blessings, 9, 42
Emendations suggested 1, 104, 167, 168, 174, 194, 197, 267, 290, 302, 303
Excellences, the four 29, 37, 39, 42, 43, 48, 92, 102
Existence, three stages of 56

Faculties and Attainments, the 31, 36, 38, 39, 45, 50, 62, 92, 98, 108, 120, 159, 188, 190, 199, 220, 229, 246, 268, 280, 293, 298
Fate written upon the forehead 84, 195
Festivals 32, 254
Fire lit at birth 30
,, sacred 30
Five Elements of Being 184
Five Pleasures of Sense 41
Five Precepts, *see* Precepts
Five-spray garlands 72, 177
Five Virtues 44, 251, 252, 260
Flying horse 90
Forehead, fate written upon 84, 195
Four Ecstasies 172
Four Excellences, *see* Excellences
Four Great Kings 61, 62, 217
Four Principal Elements 184
Four Supernatural Powers 216
Four Virtues, a man with 134, 145
Four worlds of misery 98, 262
Friends, which should be avoided 266

Gifts, rules about 18
Goblins 12, 89, 103, 271
Grain, measuring of 258
Grateful Beasts, new form of 35
Great Renunciation 60

Hall of Truth 9, 21, 31, 44, 46, 48, 64, 91, 112, 121, 140, 148, 154, 156, 157, 159, 164, 166, 168, 171, 182, 183, 186, 187, 193, 200, 203, 207, 216, 223, 224, 227, 240, 242, 243, 245, 268, 275, 295, 298, 299, 301, 304, 305
Headman, village 94
Heaven, by what deeds won 177 f.
,, of the Four Great Kings 217
,, Brahma's, *saepe*
Hells, the Four 98, 262
Hereditary rights 32
Heretics 31, 118, 119, 182, 264, 283
Hero's Tasks, new form of 131

Imitating the Buddha, 103, 113
Immortality won by eating a Golden Peacock 25
Inscriptions, upon golden plates 24, 255 ff.
Insight 268

Jains, the 182
Japanese variant 110
Jewel of serpent 197 ff.
Judas tree 184, 185
Judgements given 212 f.

Kalevala quoted 1
King as rain-maker 252
Kings dress like the gods 252
'King's officer' 209
Knowledge, Eight Stages of 180
Kuru righteousness 251 ff.

Life-token 111, cp. 279
Lotus army 275
Luck 44, 127, 265, 279, 282, 291
Lucky days 194
,, speech 44, 265

Magic razor-axe 70
,, milk-bowl 70
,, drum 70
,, gem 70
,, powers gained by eating certain birds 280
Marriage rule 247
Master of the Ceremonies 32
Meat-eating 182
Merit, how conferred 221, 288, 289
'Messenger' 221
Metre in the text of the Jātakas 23, 24
Mice and rats, their gnawing unlucky 127
Miracles of saints 77
Moderation 204
Music, technicalities of 172, 173, 175, 176

Naked ascetics 182, 183
Name-day 218
Northern brahmin 57, 299
Nymphs 63, 175, 177

Ordination 230, 298
Owl clan 175

Palace of Sakka 132, 269
Paths, the 9, 17, 21, 26, 31, 34, 36, 38, 39, 42, 56, 58, 65, 69, 77, 78, 80, 85, 91, 94, 95, 97, 98, 100, 110, 118, 125, 126, 130, 144, 158, 159, 163, 164, 188, 193, 196, 203, 205, 215, 218, 222, 226, 229, 230, 232, 250, 260, 268, 286, 290, 298, 303
Precepts, Five 4, 13, 25, 205
Precious Things, the Seven 216
Problems in folk-tales 207, 209
Processions 16

Rain-maker 252
Refuges, Three 4, 17, 44, 205
Release 9
Renunciation, Great 60
Riddles 122, 130, 225, 269
Robes for Buddhist priests, rules about 18
Royal Virtues, ten 1, 273
Russian unpublished variant 110

Seven Precious Things 216
Seven Treasures of Empire 268
Similes 155, 166, 191, 220, 229, 236, 284
Sin of the Bodhisatta 228, 265
Snake-charmer 186
Snakes' breath poisonous 55, 206; Breeds of snakes 101; Charms against 101; Guardians of treasure 214; Jewels in their heads 197 ff.
Sneezing, an omen 11 ff.
Spells 23, 101, 168
Spirit of hill 82; river 288, 289; sea 78, 302; tree 105, 113, 148, 211, 245, 263, 276, 278, 299, 300, 301, 304, 305; woodland 159
State elephant 16
Succession of Causes, chapter on 180
Sun, adjured 23, 24
Supernatural power 229
,, Powers, the Four 216

Tax-gatherer 13
Ten Royal Virtues 1, 273
Thirty-three Archangels 25, 62, 63, 64, 216, 217
Thirty-six, the 216
Three Refuges, *see* Refuges
Three stages of existence 56
Three Treasures 78, 102, 189
Throne of Sakka grows hot 87, 132, 174
Thunder, proverb concerning 237
,, cranes conceived at the sound of 249
Tortoise clan 247
Touch, six spheres of 184
Trance, mystic 188, 192

Treasure guarded by snakes 211
Treasurer of the faith 18, 64
Treasures of Empire, the seven 268
Truths, the 9, 17, 21, 26, 34, 36, 39, 42, 56, 58, 69, 78, 80, 85, 91, 94, 95, 97, 98, 100, 110, 118, 125, 126, 130, 144, 158, 159, 164, 188, 189, 193, 196, 203, 205, 215, 218, 222, 226, 229, 232, 243, 244, 247, 250, 260, 263, 286, 290, 298, 303, 306
Twenty-one unlawful ways of earning a living 57

Umbrella, white 274
'Uncle' = mother's brother, term of affection 210

Verses and story, discrepancy between 127, 155
Village headman 94
Virtues, Five 251, 252, 260
,, Ten 1, 273

Waggon army 275
Water, not to be defiled 15
Waxing and waning period 42
Wheel army 275
Wheel of Empire 217
Wickedness, Four Ways of 1
Winnowing basket 277
Wishing Cup 294
Wives, seven kinds of 239, 240
Women, Buddhist opinion of 226, 228, 234
Writing upon a leaf 122
,, on a golden plate 24

Yellowstone throne of Sakka 63

CAMBRIDGE: PRINTED BY J. AND C. F. CLAY, AT THE UNIVERSITY PRESS.

www.ingramcontent.com/pod-product-compliance
Lightning Source LLC
Chambersburg PA
CBHW021158230426
43667CB00006B/456
* 9 7 8 3 3 3 7 2 4 6 9 0 7 *